*E*ssentials of Organizational Behavior

Fifth Edition

Stephen P. Robbins

San Diego State University

Prentice Hall
Upper Saddle River, New Jersey 07458

Acquisitions Editor: David Shafer
Associate Editor: Lisamarie Brassini
Marketing Manager: Sandra Steiner
Editorial Assistant: Brett Moreland
Editor-in-Chief: James Boyd
Production Editor: Lynne Breitfeller
Production Coordinator: David Cotugno
Managing Editor: Carol Burgett
Manufacturing Supervisor: Arnold Vila
Manufacturing Manager: Vincent Scelta
Electronic Artist: Warren Fischbach
Production Manager: Lorraine Patsco
Senior Designer: Ann France
Design Director: Patricia Wosczyk
Interior/Cover Design: Donna Wickes
Composition: Beaumont Graphics
Illustration/Cover: Susan Le Van

 Copyright © 1997, 1994, 1992, 1988, 1984 by Prentice–Hall, Inc.
A Simon & Schuster Company
Upper Saddle River, New Jersey 07458

Library of Congress Cataloging-in-Publication Data

Robbins, Stephen P.
   Essentials of organizational behavior / Stephen P. Robbins. — 5th ed.
     p.   cm.
   Includes bibliographical references and index.
   ISBN 0-13-520305-8 (pbk.)
    1. Organizational behavior. I. Title.
   HD58.7.R6   1996
   658.3—dc20   96-21277
                                                        CIP

Prentice–Hall International (UK) Limited, London
Prentice–Hall of Australia Pty. Limited, Sydney
Prentice–Hall Canada, Inc., Toronto
Prentice–Hall Hispanoamericana, S.A., Mexico
Prentice–Hall of India Private Limited, New Delhi
Prentice–Hall of Japan, Inc., Tokyo
Simon & Schuster Asia Pte. Ltd., Singapore
Editora Prentice–Hall do Brasil, Ltda., Rio de Janeiro

Printed in the United States of America

10 9 8 7 6 5 4

With thanks to my friends in

**The Organizational Behavior
Teaching Society**

$\mathcal{C}$ ontents

PREFACE

PART I. PROLOGUE

    1. Introduction to Organizational Behavior / 1
    2. Organizational Behavior in a Global Context / 16

PART II. THE INDIVIDUAL IN THE ORGANIZATION

    3. Foundations of Individual Behavior / 30
    4. Basic Motivation Concepts / 46
    5. Motivation: From Concepts to Applications / 61
    6. Individual Decision Making / 76

PART III. GROUPS IN THE ORGANIZATION

    7. Foundations of Group Behavior / 91
    8. Understanding Work Teams / 108
    9. Communication / 123
    10. Leadership / 138
    11. Power and Politics / 154
    12. Conflict and Negotiation / 168

PART IV. THE ORGANIZATION SYSTEM

    13. Foundations of Organization Structure / 184
    14. Technology and Work Design / 203
    15. Performance Appraisal and Reward Systems / 218
    16. Organizational Culture / 236
    17. Organizational Change and Development / 252

Epilogue / 272
Endnotes / 273
Index/Glossary / 285

*P*reface

This book originated from a conversation I had with a colleague back in the early 1980s. He was frustrated by the lack of teaching-material options for his course in organizational behavior. "I don't need one of those 700-page books with all the bells and whistles," he told me. "I wish there was a short, concise OB text that gave students just the essentials." The lightbulb went on in my head. Maybe he wasn't alone. Maybe a lot of instructors would like an alternative OB text. I had already written one of those books "with all the bells and whistles." Why couldn't I take the key concepts out of that book, rewrite and massage that material, and create a unique alternative to the comprehensive OB textbook?

Fifteen years later, I can attest that my colleague was not alone. The first four editions of this book have been used by more than 100,000 students. They've been widely used in Canada, Europe, and Asia, as well as the United States. This book has also been translated into Danish and Chinese. Users of past editions tell me they've found this book to be ideally suited for use in short courses and executive programs and as a companion to experiential, skill development, case, or readings books.

But that's all in the past. You can't rest on yesterday's accomplishments. So let me highlight the changes I've made in this fifth edition.

- The entire text has been updated. I've added new examples and expanded the referencing of research findings.
- There are two new chapters in this edition. Chapter 5 ("Motivation: From Concepts to Applications") provides practical applications of motivation concepts introduced in Chapter 4. A new chapter on work teams has also been added (Chapter 8).
- The two chapters on organization structure and design from the previous edition have been condensed into a single chapter and completely rewritten (see Chapter 13).
- The chapter on individual decision making (Chapter 6) has been rewritten to emphasize the behavioral aspects of decision making.
- The discussion of group decision making has been moved from the chapter on communication to the one on group behavior (Chapter 7).
- New material has been included on TQM, reengineering, technology, empowerment, coping with "temporariness," declining employee loyalty, the Myers-Briggs Type Indicator, the Big-Five model of personality, virtual and boundaryless organizations, and 360-degree performance appraisals.

- Readers will also find that the end-of-text index is now combined with a glossary to create a single source for finding key terms, definitions, and topics.

I conclude by acknowledging those who suggested improvements for this edition. Special thanks are extended to Gail Hankins of North Carolina State University, Jane Gibson of Southeastern University, Sherry Moss of Florida International University, and Nancy Nightingale of International College for their helpful comments. And, of course, I thank the people at Prentice–Hall—especially Lisamarie Brassini, David Shafer, Jo-Ann Deluca, and Lynne Breitfeller—for overseeing the production and marketing of this book.

Stephen P. Robbins

Introduction to Organizational Behavior

Chapter 1

After reading this chapter, you should be able to:

1. Define organizational behavior (OB)

2. Identify the primary behavioral disciplines contributing to OB

3. Describe the three goals of OB

4. List the major challenges and opportunities for managers to use OB concepts

5. Explain the key elements in total quality management (TQM)

6. Discuss why work force diversity has become an important issue in management

7. Explain how managers and organizations are responding to the problem of employee ethical dilemmas

When I ask managers to describe their most frequent or troublesome problems, the answers I get tend to exhibit a common theme. The managers most often describe *people* problems. They talk about their bosses' poor communication skills, subordinates' lack of motivation, conflicts between employees in their department, overcoming employee resistance to a departmental reorganization, and similar concerns.

Because a manager's job is inherently one of working with and through other people—bosses, peers, and subordinates—good "people skills" are a valuable, even necessary asset, in solving these problems. This book has been written to help managers, and potential managers, develop these people skills.

The Field of Organizational Behavior

The study of people at work is generally referred to as the study of organizational behavior. Let's begin, then, by defining the term *organizational behavior* and briefly reviewing its origins.

Definition

Organizational behavior (OB) is the systematic study of the actions and attitudes that people exhibit within organizations. Let's look at the key parts of this definition.

Each of us regularly uses intuition, or our "gut feelings," in trying to explain phenomena. For instance, a friend catches a cold and we're quick to remind him that he "didn't take his vitamins," "doesn't dress properly," or that "it happens every year when the seasons change." We're not really sure why he caught cold, but that doesn't stop us from offering our intuitive analysis. The field of OB seeks to replace intuitive explanations with systematic study: that is, the use of scientific evidence gathered under controlled conditions and measured and interpreted in a reasonably rigorous manner to attribute cause and effect. The objective, of course, is to draw accurate conclusions. So the field of OB—its theories and conclusions—is based on a large number of systematically designed research studies.

What does OB systematically study? Actions (or behaviors) and attitudes! But not *all* actions and attitudes. Three types of behavior have proved to be important determinants of employee performance: *productivity, absenteeism,* and *turnover.* The importance of productivity is obvious. Managers clearly are concerned with the quantity and quality of output that each employee generates. But absence and turnover—particularly excessively high rates—can adversely affect this output. In terms of absence, it's hard for an employee to be productive if he or she isn't at work. In addition, high rates of employee turnover increase costs and tend to place less experienced people into jobs.

Organizational behavior is also concerned with employee *job satisfaction,* which is an attitude. Managers should be concerned with their employees' job satisfaction for three reasons. First, there may be a link between satisfaction and productivity. Second, satisfaction appears to be negatively related to absenteeism and turnover. Finally, it can be argued that managers have a humanistic responsibility to provide their employees with jobs that are challenging, intrinsically rewarding, and satisfying.

The last part of our OB definition that needs elaboration is the term *organization.* The fields of psychology and sociology are well-known disciplines that study behavior, but they do not concentrate solely on work-related issues. In contrast, OB is specifically concerned with work-related behavior—and *that* takes place in organizations. An **organization** is a formal structure of planned coordination, involving two or more people, in order to achieve a common goal. It is characterized by authority relationships and some degree of division of labor. So OB encompasses the behavior of people in such diverse organizations as manufacturing and service firms; schools; hospitals; churches; military units; charitable organizations; and local, state, and federal government agencies.

Contributing Disciplines

Organizational behavior is applied behavioral science and, as a result, is built upon contributions from several behavioral disciplines. The predominant areas are psychology, sociology, social psychology, anthropology, and political science. As we shall learn, psychology's contributions have been mainly at the individual or micro level of analysis, whereas the latter disciplines have contributed to our understanding of macro concepts—group processes and organization. Exhibit 1-1 provides an overview of the contributions made toward a distinct field of study: organizational behavior.

Psychology. **Psychology** is the science that seeks to measure, explain, and sometimes change the behavior of humans and other animals. Psychologists concern themselves with studying and attempting to understand *individual* behavior. Those who have contributed and continue to add to the knowledge of OB are learning theorists, personality theorists, counseling psychologists, and, most important, industrial and organizational psychologists.

Early industrial psychologists concerned themselves with problems of fatigue, boredom, and any other factor relevant to working conditions that could impede efficient work performance. More recently, their contributions have been expanded to include learning, perception, personality, training, leadership effectiveness, needs and motivational forces, job satisfaction, decision-making processes, performance appraisals, attitude measurement, employee-selection techniques, job design, and work stress.

Sociology. Whereas psychologists focus on the individual, sociologists study the social system in which individuals fill their roles; that is, **sociology** studies people in relation to their fellow human beings. Sociologists have made their greatest contribution to OB through their study of group behavior in organizations, particularly formal and complex organizations. Areas within OB that have received valuable input from sociologists include group dynamics, design of work teams, organizational culture, formal organization theory and structure, bureaucracy, communications, status, power, and conflict.

Social Psychology. **Social psychology** is an area within psychology, blending concepts from psychology and sociology. It focuses on the influence of people on one another. One of the major areas receiving considerable investigation by social psychologists has been *change*—how to implement it and how to reduce barriers to its acceptance. In addition, social psychologists have made significant contributions in measuring, understanding, and changing attitudes, communication patterns, the ways in which group activities can satisfy individual needs, and group decision-making processes.

Anthropology. **Anthropology** is the study of societies to learn about human beings and their activities. The work of anthropologists on cultures and environments, for instance, has helped us understand differences in fundamental values, attitudes, and behavior between people in different countries and within organizations. Much of our current understanding of organizational culture,

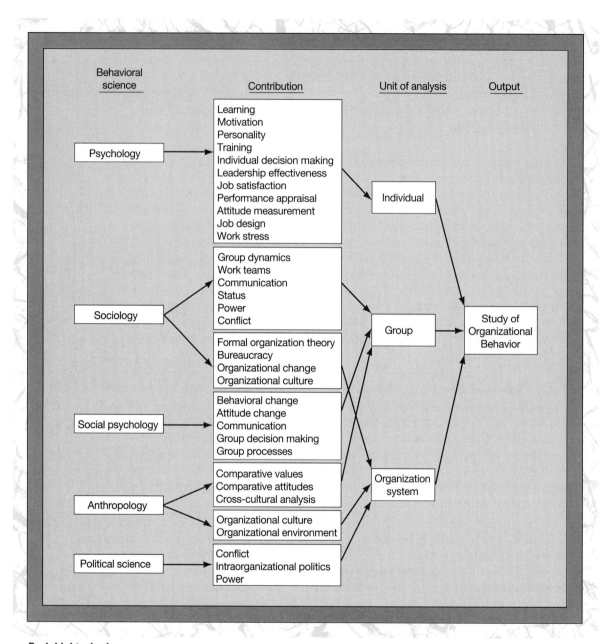

Exhibit 1-1
Toward an OB Discipline

organizational environments, and differences between national cultures is the result of the work of anthropologists or those using their methods.

Political Science.   Although frequently overlooked, the contributions of political scientists are significant to the understanding of behavior in organizations. **Political science** is the study of the behavior of individuals and groups within a political environment. Specific topics of concern to political scientists include structuring conflict, allocation of power, and how people manipulate power for individual self-interest.

Goals of Organizational Behavior

What does OB seek to do? We know it is concerned with developing people skills, but what precisely are its goals? The goals of OB are to help you to *explain, predict,* and *control* human behavior.

Explanation

When we seek answers to *why* an individual or a group of individuals did something, we are pursuing the explanation objective. It is probably the least important of the three goals, from a management perspective, because it occurs after the fact. Yet, if we are to understand a phenomenon, we must begin by trying to explain it. We can then use this understanding to determine a cause. For example, if a number of valued employees resign, we undoubtedly want to know why, in order to determine if it was something that could have been prevented. Obviously, employees quit their jobs for many reasons, but if the explanation for a high quit rate is inadequate pay or boring jobs, managers often can take actions that will correct this situation in the future.

Prediction

The goal of prediction focuses on future events. It seeks to determine what outcomes will result from a given action. A manager of a small factory who attempts to assess how employees will respond to the installation of new robotic equipment is engaging in a predictive exercise. On the basis of a knowledge of OB, the manager can predict certain behavioral responses to the change. Of course, there are various ways to implement a major change, so the manager is likely to assess employee responses to several change interventions. In this way, the manager can anticipate which approaches will generate the least degree of employee resistance and use that information in making his or her decision.

Control

The most controversial goal is using OB knowledge to control behavior. When a manager asks, for instance, "What can I do to make Dave put out more effort on his job?" that manager is concerned with control.

Why is control controversial? Most of us live in democratic societies, which are built upon the concept of personal freedom. Therefore, the idea that one person should attempt to get others to behave in a certain way, when the subjects of that control may be unaware that their behavior is being manipulated, has been viewed in some circles as unethical and repugnant. That OB offers technologies that facilitate the control of people is a fact. Whether those technologies should be used in organizations becomes an ethical question. You should be aware, however, that the control objective is frequently seen by managers as the most valuable contribution that OB makes toward their effectiveness on the job.

Challenges and Opportunities for OB: A Managerial Perspective

The ability to explain, predict, and control organizational behavior has never been more important to managers. A quick look at a few of the dramatic changes now taking place in organizations supports this claim. For instance, the typical employee is getting older; there are more and more women and nonwhites in the workplace; corporate restructuring and cost cutting are severing the bonds of loyalty that historically tied many employees to their employers; and global competition is requiring employees to become more flexible and to learn to cope with rapid change and innovation.

In short, there are a lot of challenges and opportunities today for managers to use OB concepts. In this section, we'll review some of the most critical issues confronting managers for which OB offers solutions—or at least some meaningful insights toward solutions.

Improving Quality and Productivity

Tom Rossi manages in a tough business. He runs a light-bulb plant in Mattoon, Illinois, for General Electric. His business has seen tough competition from manufacturers in the United States, Europe, Japan, and even China. To survive, he's had to cut fat, increase productivity, and improve quality. And he's succeeded. During a recent five-year period, the Mattoon plant has averaged annual cost-productivity improvements of approximately eight percent. By focusing on continuous improvement, streamlining processes, and cost cutting, GE's Mattoon plant has remained viable and profitable.

More and more managers are confronting the challenges that Tom Rossi is facing. They are having to improve their organization's productivity and the quality of the products and services they offer. Toward improving quality and productivity, they are implementing programs such as total quality management and reengineering—programs that require extensive employee involvement.

As Exhibit 1-2 describes, **total quality management (TQM)** is a philosophy of management that is driven by the constant attainment of customer satisfaction through the continuous improvement of all organizational processes.[1] TQM has implications for OB because it requires employees to rethink what they do and become more involved in workplace decisions.

1. Intense focus on the *customer*. The customer includes not only outsiders who buy the organization's products or services but also internal customers (such as shipping or accounts payable personnel) who interact with and serve others in the organization.

2. Concern for *continual improvement*. TQM is a commitment to never be satisfied. "Very good" is not good enough. Quality can always be improved.

3. Improvement in the *quality of everything* the organization does. TQM uses a broad definition of *quality*. The term applies not only to the final product but also to how the organization handles deliveries, how rapidly it responds to complaints, how politely the phones are answered, and the like.

4. Accurate *measurement*. TQM uses statistical techniques to measure every critical performance variable in the organization's operations. These performance variables are then compared against standards or benchmarks to identify problems, the problems are traced to their roots, and the causes are eliminated.

5. *Empowerment of employees*. TQM involves the people on the line in the improvement process. Teams are widely used in TQM programs as empowerment vehicles for finding and solving problems.

Exhibit 1-2
What Is Total Quality Management?

In times of rapid and dramatic change, it's sometimes necessary to approach improving quality and productivity from the perspective of "How would we do things around here if we were starting over from scratch?" That, in essence, is the approach of *reengineering*. It asks managers to reconsider how work would be done and their organization structured if they were starting over.[2] To illustrate the concept of reengineering, consider a manufacturer of rollerskates. His product is essentially a shoe with wheels beneath it. The typical rollerskate was a leather boot with shoe laces, attached to a steel platform that held four wooden wheels. If our manufacturer took a continuous improvement approach to change, he would look for small, incremental improvements that he could introduce in his product. For instance, he might consider adding hooks to the upper part of the boot for fast lacing, or changing the weight of leather used for improved comfort, or using different ball bearings to make the wheels spin more smoothly. Now most of us are familiar with in-line skates. They represent a reengineering approach to rollerskates. The goal was to come up with a skating device that could improve skating speed, mobility, and control. Rollerblades provided those goals in a completely different type of shoe. The upper was made of injected plastic, made popular in skiing. Laces were replaced by easy-close clamps. And the four wheels, set in pairs of two, were replaced by four to six in-line plastic wheels. The reengineered result, which didn't look much like the traditional rollerskate, proved universally superior. The rest, of course, is history. In-line skates have revolutionized the rollerskate business.

Our point is that today's managers understand that the success of any effort at improving quality and productivity must include their employees. These employees will not only be a major force in carrying out changes but increasingly will actively participate in planning those changes. OB offers important insights into helping managers work through these changes.

Improving People Skills

We opened this chapter by demonstrating how important people skills are to managerial effectiveness. We said that "this book has been written to help managers, and potential managers, develop these people skills."

As you proceed through this text, we'll present relevant concepts and theories that can help you explain and predict the behavior of people at work. In addition, you'll also gain insights into specific people skills that you can use on the job. For instance, you'll learn a variety of ways to motivate people, how to be a better communicator, and how to create more effective teams.

Managing Work Force Diversity

One of the most important and broad-based challenges currently facing U.S. organizations is adapting to people who are different. The term we use for describing this challenge is **work force diversity.**

Work force diversity means that organizations are becoming more heterogeneous in terms of gender, race, and ethnicity. But the term encompasses anyone who varies from the "norm." In addition to the more obvious groups—women, African-Americans, Hispanic-Americans, Asian-Americans—it also includes the physically disabled, gays and lesbians, and the elderly.

We used to take a "melting pot" approach to differences in organizations, assuming that people who were different would somehow automatically want to assimilate. But we now recognize that employees don't set aside their cultural values and lifestyle preferences when they come to work. The challenge for organizations, therefore, is to make themselves more accommodating to diverse groups of people by addressing their different lifestyles, family needs, and work styles. The melting pot assumption is being replaced by one that recognizes and values differences.

Haven't organizations always included members of diverse groups? Yes, but they were such a small percentage of the work force that no one paid much attention to them. Moreover, it was assumed that these minorities would seek to blend in and assimilate. The bulk of the pre-1980s work force were male Caucasians working full time to support a nonemployed wife and school-aged children. Now such employees are the true minority! Currently, forty-five percent of the U.S. labor force are women. Minorities and immigrants make up twenty-two percent.[3] As a case in point, Hewlett-Packard's work force is nineteen percent minorities and forty percent women. A Digital Equipment Corporation plant in Boston provides a partial preview of the future. The factory's 350 employees include men and women from forty-four countries who speak nineteen languages. When plant management issues written announcements, they are printed in English, Chinese, French, Spanish, Portuguese, Vietnamese, and Haitian Creole.

Work force diversity has important implications for management practice. Managers will need to shift their philosophy from treating everyone alike to recognizing differences and responding to those differences in ways that will ensure employee retention and greater productivity—while, at the same time, not discriminating. Diversity, if positively managed, can increase creativity and innovation in organizations as well as improve decision making by providing different perspectives on problems.[4] When diversity is not managed properly, there is potential for higher turnover, more difficult communication, and more interpersonal conflicts.

Responding to Globalization

Management is no longer constrained by national borders. Burger King is owned by a British firm, and McDonald's sells hamburgers in Moscow. Exxon, a so-called American company, receives almost seventy-five percent of its revenues from sales outside the United States. Toyota makes cars in Kentucky; General Motors makes cars in Brazil; and Ford (which owns part of Mazda) transfers executives from Detroit to Japan to help Mazda manage its operations. These examples illustrate that the world has become a global village. In turn, managers have to become capable of working with people from different cultures.

Globalization affects a manager's people skills in at least two ways. First, if you're a manager you're increasingly likely to find yourself in a foreign assignment. You'll be transferred to your employer's operating division or subsidiary in another country. Once there, you'll have to manage a work force that is likely to be very different in needs, aspirations, and attitudes from the ones you were used to back home. Second, even in your own country, you're going to find yourself working with bosses, peers, and subordinates who were born and raised in different cultures. What motivates you may not motivate them. Your style of communication may be straightforward and open, but they may find this style uncomfortable and threatening. To work effectively with these people, you'll need to understand their culture, how it has shaped them, and how to adapt your management style to their differences. In the next chapter, we'll provide some frameworks for understanding differences among national cultures. Further, as we discuss OB concepts throughout this book, we'll focus on how cultural differences might require managers to modify their practices.

Empowering People

If you pick up any popular business periodical nowadays, you'll read about the reshaping of the relationship between managers and those they're supposedly responsible for managing. You'll find managers being called coaches, advisers, sponsors, or facilitators. In many organizations, employees are now called associates. And there's a blurring between the roles of managers and workers.[5] Decision making is being pushed down to the operating level, where workers are being given the freedom to make choices about schedules and procedures and to solve work-related problems. In the 1980s, managers were encouraged to get their employees to *participate* in work-related decisions. Now, managers are going considerably further by allowing employees full control of their work. Self-managed teams, where workers operate largely without bosses, have become the rage of the 1990s.

What's going on? What's going on is that managers are *empowering employees*. They are putting employees in charge of what they do. And in so doing, managers are having to learn how to give up control, and employees are having to learn how to take responsibility for their work and make appropriate decisions. In later chapters, we'll show how empowerment is changing leadership styles, power relationships, the way work is designed, and the way organizations are structured.

Stimulating Innovation and Change

Whatever happened to W. T. Grant, Gimbel's, and Eastern Airlines? All these giants went bust! Why have other giants, such as General Motors, Sears, Westinghouse, Boeing, and AT&T, implemented huge cost-cutting programs and eliminated thousands of jobs? To *avoid* going bust!

Today's successful organizations must foster innovation and master the art of change or they'll become candidates for extinction. Victory will go to those organizations that maintain their flexibility, continually improve their quality, and beat their competition to the marketplace with a constant stream of innovative products and services. Domino's single-handedly brought on the demise of thousands of small pizza parlors whose managers thought they could continue doing what they had been doing for years. Fox Television has successfully stolen a major portion of the under-25 viewing audience from their much larger network rivals through innovative programming including *The Simpsons, Beverly Hills 90210,* and *Melrose Place.*

An organization's employees can be the impetus for innovation and change or they can be a major stumbling block. The challenge for managers is to stimulate employee creativity and tolerance for change. The field of OB provides a wealth of ideas and techniques to aid in realizing these goals.

Coping with "Temporariness"

Managers have always been concerned with change. What's different nowadays is the length of time between change implementations. In the past, managers needed to introduce major change programs once or twice a decade. Today, change is an ongoing activity for most managers. The concept of continuous improvement, for instance, implies constant change.

Managing in the past could be characterized by long periods of stability, interrupted occasionally by short periods of change. Managing today would be more accurately described as long periods of ongoing change, interrupted occasionally by short periods of stability! The world that most managers and employees face today is one of permanent "temporariness." The actual jobs that workers perform are in a permanent state of flux. So workers need to continually update their knowledge and skills to perform new job requirements. For example, production employees at companies such as Caterpillar, Chrysler, and Reynolds Metals now need to know how to operate computerized production equipment. That was not part of their job description fifteen years ago. Work groups are also increasingly in a state of flux. In the past, employees were assigned to a specific work group, and that assignment was relatively permanent. There was a considerable amount of security in working with the same people day in and day out. That predictability has been replaced by temporary work groups, teams that include members from different departments and whose members change all the time, and the increased use of employee rotation to fill constantly changing work assignments. Finally, organizations themselves are in a state of flux. They continually reorganize their various divisions, sell off poorly performing businesses, downsize operations, and replace permanent employees with temporaries.

Today's managers and employees must learn to cope with temporariness. They have to learn to live with flexibility, spontaneity, and unpredictability. The study of OB can provide important insights into a work world of continual change, how to overcome resistance to change, and how best to create an organizational culture that thrives on change.

Declining Employee Loyalty

Corporate employees used to believe that their employers would reward their loyalty and good work with job security, generous benefits, and pay increases. But beginning in the mid-1980s, in response to global competition, unfriendly takeovers, leveraged buyouts, and the like, corporations began to discard traditional policies on job security, seniority, and compensation. They sought to become "lean and mean" by closing factories, moving operations to lower-cost countries, selling off or closing down less-profitable businesses, eliminating entire levels of management, and replacing permanent employees with temporaries. Importantly, this is not just a North American phenomenon. European companies are doing the same. For instance, Barclays, the big British bank, recently cut staff levels by twenty percent. And some German firms have trimmed their work force and management ranks: Siemens, the electronic engineering conglomerate, shed more than 3,000 jobs in 1993 alone; steelmaker Krupp-Hoesch cut its management hierarchy from five to three levels; and Mercedes-Benz trimmed its number of levels from seven to five.

These changes have resulted in a sharp decline in employee loyalty. In a 1993 survey of workers, for instance, more than seventy-seven percent said that there is less loyalty between companies and employees than in 1988.[6] Employees perceive that their employers are less committed to them, and, as a result, employees respond by being less committed to their companies (see Exhibit 1-3).

An important OB challenge will be for managers to devise ways to motivate workers who feel less committed to their employers, while maintaining their organizations' global competitiveness.

Motivating the Bi-Modal Work Force

As recently as twenty years ago, plenty of unskilled jobs in the steel, automobile, rubber, and similar manufacturing industries paid solid middle-class wages. A young man in Pittsburgh, for example, could graduate from high school and immediately get a relatively high-paying and secure job in a local steel plant. That job would allow him to buy a home, finance a car or two, support a family, and enjoy other lifestyle choices that come with a middle-class income. But that's ancient history. A good portion of those manufacturing jobs in developed industrialized countries are gone—either replaced by automated equipment,

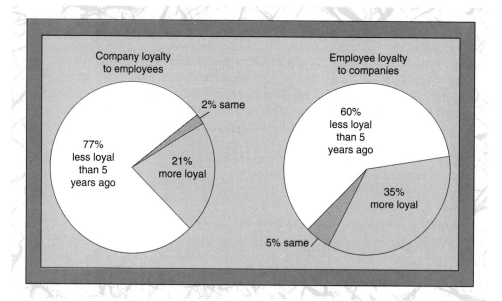

Exhibit 1-3

Changing Views of Loyalty, 1993 vs. 1988

Source: B. S. Moskal, "Company Loyalty Dies, A Victim of Neglect." *Industry Week.* March 1, 1993, p. 12

reconstituted into a job requiring considerably higher technical skills, or taken by workers in other countries who will do this same work for a fraction of the wages. What's left can best be described as a *bi-modal work force,* in which employees tend to perform either low-skilled service jobs for near-minimum wage or high-skilled jobs that provide the means to maintain a middle-class or upper-class lifestyle.

Exhibit 1-4 illustrates this bi-modal phenomenon. It has been created by the massive decline of blue-collar manufacturing jobs that pay $25,000 to $40,000 a year in current dollars.

Most organizations' employee practices were designed to keep and motivate well-paid manufacturing employees and high-paid skilled workers. They don't, however, seem to be working very well with the low-skilled, low-paid service workers in the left curve of Exhibit 1-4.

At wages of $4.75 to $8.00 an hour, today's low-skilled workers can't come close to moving into the middle class. Moreover, their promotion opportunities are limited. This situation leads to a major challenge for managers: How do you motivate individuals who are making very low wages and have little opportunity to significantly increase their pay either in their current jobs or through promotions? Can effective leadership fill the void? Can these employees' jobs be redesigned to make them more challenging? Should managers target these jobs for elimination? Until twenty years ago, managers didn't have to concern themselves with such questions.

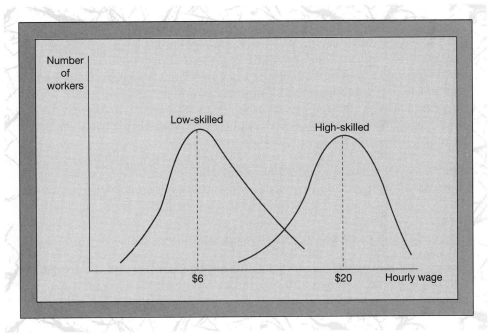

Exhibit 1-4
The Bi-Modal Work Force

Improving Ethical Behavior

In an organizational world characterized by cutbacks, expectations of increasing worker productivity, and tough competition in the marketplace, it's not altogether surprising that many employees feel pressured to cut corners, break rules, and engage in other forms of questionable practices.

Members of organizations are increasingly finding themselves facing **ethical dilemmas,** situations in which they are required to define right and wrong conduct. For example, should they "blow the whistle" if they uncover illegal activities taking place in their company? Should they follow orders with which they don't personally agree? Do they give an inflated performance evaluation to an employee whom they like, knowing that such an evaluation could save that employee's job? Do they allow themselves to "play politics" in the organization if it will help their career advancement?

What constitutes good ethical behavior has never been clearly defined. And, in recent years, the line differentiating right from wrong has become even more blurred. Employees see people all around them engaging in unethical practices— elected officials are indicted for padding their expense accounts or taking bribes; high-powered lawyers, who know the rules, are found to be avoiding payment of Social Security taxes for their household help; successful executives use insider information for personal financial gain; employees in other companies participate in massive cover-ups of defective military weapons. They hear these people, when caught, giving excuses such as "everyone does it," or "you have to seize every advantage nowadays," or "I never thought I'd get caught."

Managers and their organizations are responding to this problem from a number of directions. They're writing and distributing codes of ethics to guide employees through ethical dilemmas. They're offering seminars, workshops, and similar training programs to try to improve ethical behaviors. They're providing in-house advisers who can be contacted, in many cases anonymously, for assistance in dealing with ethical issues. And they're creating protection mechanisms for employees who reveal internal unethical practices.

Today's manager needs to create an ethically healthy climate for his or her employees, where they can do their work productively and confront a minimal degree of ambiguity regarding what constitutes right and wrong behaviors.

The Plan of This Book

How is this book going to help you better explain, predict, and control behavior? Our approach uses a building-block process. As pictured in Exhibit 1-5, there are three levels of analysis in OB. As we move from the individual level to the organization system level, we increase in an additive fashion our understanding of behavior in organizations.

Chapters 3 through 6 deal with the individual in the organization. We begin by looking at the foundations of individual behavior—attitudes, personality, perception, and learning. Then we move to motivation issues and the topic of individual decision making.

The behavior of people in groups is something more than the sum total of each individual acting in his or her own way. People's behavior in groups is different from their behavior when they are alone. Chapters 7 through 12 address group behavior. We introduce a group behavior model, discuss ways to make teams more effective, consider communication issues and group decision making, and then investigate the important topics of leadership, power, politics, and conflict and negotiation.

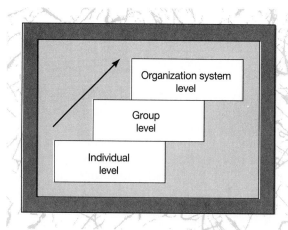

Exhibit 1-5
Levels of OB Analysis

Organizational behavior reaches its highest level of sophistication when we add the formal organization system to our knowledge of individual and group behavior. Just as groups are more than the sum of their individual members, organizations are not necessarily merely the summation of the behavior of a number of groups. In Chapters 13 through 17, we discuss how an organization's structure, technology, and work design affect behavior, the effect that an organization's formal performance appraisal and reward system has on people, how each organization has its own culture that acts to shape the behavior of its members, and the various organizational change and development techniques that managers can use to affect behavior for the organization's benefit.

Before we begin our analysis of individual behavior, however, we must discuss the importance of putting organizational behavior in a global context. Organizational behavior is different in different countries. What motivates employees in the United States doesn't necessarily motivate workers in Mexico or Denmark. The next chapter explores this theme.

Organizational Behavior in a Global Context

Chapter 2

After reading this chapter, you should be able to:

1. Define a multinational corporation

2. Describe the effects of regional cooperative arrangements on managing global enterprises

3. Contrast *parochialism* and *ethnocentrism*

4. Identify the six cultural dimensions in the Kluckhohn-Strodtbeck framework

5. Explain the four dimensions of national culture in Hofstede's framework

6. Characterize the United States on Hofstede's dimensions

The French are different from the British. Arabs are different from Canadians. Germans are different from Australians. Israelis are different from Americans. In a global economy, managers need to understand cultural differences and adjust their organizations and management style accordingly.

Take the case of National Semiconductor, Israel.[1] This manufacturing company is a subsidiary of California-based National Semiconductor. Managers at this subsidiary have had to modify their operation to reflect the fact that what works in California will not necessarily work in Israel.

Studies contrasting U.S. and Israeli workers indicate a number of differences. The following highlights some of those differences.

U.S. Workers	Israeli Workers
Work alone	Work as part of a group
Have high mobility	Have low mobility
Solve problems systematically, according to the book	Improvise, solve problems creatively
Require privacy	Identify with group, do not require privacy
Believe individual is responsible	Believe group is responsible
Avoid conflict	Tend toward conflict
Are formal	Are informal and open
Accept authority	Question authority
Have hierarchical leadership	Have natural leadership
Are cautious, avoid risks	Take risks

Practices that work in California with U.S. workers are not likely to be effective with Israeli workers. American culture, with its foundation in the Protestant ethos of Western societies, places the individual in the center. Even where work groups are used in the United States, American employees expect at least part of their performance appraisal to be based on their individual contribution to the group. In contrast, Israeli culture is influenced by both Eastern Europe and Islam. In Israeli culture, the emphasis is on the group. Individuals act primarily within, and as part of, a group.

The management at National Semiconductor, Israel, has had to modify its parent's U.S. practices in order to reflect Israeli preferences for openness, indistinct lines of authority, group decision making, and a minimum amount of rules and regulations. For instance, the Israeli subsidiary is designed around autonomous teams. To facilitate this design, management has created information channels within the organization that provide teams with the most current and complete information possible. In addition, the decision process allows everyone to be involved in any decision that affects them.

The National Semiconductor example illustrates the need for managers to adjust their style to reflect national differences. In this chapter, we'll provide a framework for assessing national differences and then show you what changes, if any, you might need to make when managing in a different country or managing people from a different culture than your own.

Welcome to the Global Village

Respected observers of world affairs have been arguing for more than a decade that our world has become a global village. Transportation and communication capabilities—for example, supersonic jets, international telephone and computer networks, and worldwide news broadcasts via satellite—make it easier to talk with or visit people on other continents than it was for people a century ago to do the same with friends in a neighboring village. Distance and national borders are rapidly disappearing as a major barrier to business transactions. With the advent of the global village, identifying the "home country" of a company and its product has become increasingly difficult. For instance, Honda is supposedly a Japanese firm, but it builds its Accords in Ohio. Ford, which has its headquarters in Detroit, builds its Mercury Tracers in Mexico. "All-American" firms such as IBM, Mobil, Citicorp, Motorola, Gillette, and Coca-Cola get more than half of their revenues from operations outside the United States; other "All-American" firms such as CBS Records, General Tire, and Pillsbury are actually foreign-owned. The reality of the global village can be demonstrated by looking at the growing impact of multinational corporations and the rise of regional cooperative arrangements between countries.

Multinational Corporations

Most of the firms currently listed in the *Fortune 500* are **multinational corporations** —companies that maintain significant operations in two or more countries simultaneously.

Although international businesses have been around for centuries, multinationals are a relatively recent phenomenon. They are a natural outcome of the global economy. Multinationals use their worldwide operations to develop global strategies. Rather than confining themselves to their domestic borders, they scan the world for competitive advantages. The result? Manufacturing, assembly, sales, and other functions are being strategically located to give firms advantages in the marketplace. A photocopying machine, for instance, might be designed in Toronto, have its microprocessing chips made in Taiwan and its physical case manufactured in Japan, be assembled in South Korea, and then be sold out of warehouses located in Melbourne, London, and Los Angeles.

How big are multinationals? In a list in which nations are ranked by gross domestic product (GDP) and industrial firms by total sales, 37 of the first 100 names on the list would not be nations; they would be industrial corporations. Exxon's sales, as a case in point, exceed the GDPs of such countries as Indonesia, Nigeria, Argentina, and Denmark.

Managers of multinationals confront a wealth of challenges. They face diverse political systems, laws, and customs. But these differences create both problems and opportunities. It's obviously more difficult to manage an operation that spans 15,000 miles and whose employees speak five languages than one located under a single roof where a common language is spoken. Differences create opportunities, and that has been the primary motivation for corporations to expand their worldwide operations.

Regional Cooperative Arrangements

National boundaries are also being blurred by the creation of regional cooperative arrangements. The most notable of these, so far, are the European Union, made up of fifteen Western European countries, and NAFTA, which reduces trade barriers between the United States, Mexico, and Canada. The reunification of Germany and the fall of communism also appear to be setting the stage for cooperative agreements among Eastern European countries.

The European Union. The year 1993 marked the creation of a United States of Europe. There are 335 million people in the fifteen nations making up the **European Union**—France, Denmark, Belgium, Greece, Ireland, Italy, Luxembourg, the Netherlands, Portugal, Spain, the United Kingdom, Austria, Finland, Sweden, and Germany. Before 1993, these countries individually had border controls, border taxes, border subsidies, nationalistic policies, and protected industries. Now they are a single market. National barriers to travel, employment, investment, and trade have been replaced by a free flow of money, workers, goods, and services. A driver hauling cargo from Amsterdam to Lisbon is now able to clear four border crossings and five countries merely by showing a single piece of paper. In 1992, that same driver needed two pounds of documents.

The primary motivation for these fifteen nations to unite was the desire to strengthen their position against the industrial might of the United States and Japan. When they were separate countries creating barriers against one another, their industries were unable to develop the economies of scale enjoyed by the United States and Japan. The new European Union, however, allows European firms to tap into a single market that is larger than either the domestic market of the United States or that of Japan. This reduction in trade barriers also encourages non-Western European companies to invest in these countries to take advantage of new opportunities. Finally, European multinationals have new clout in attacking American, Japanese, and other worldwide markets.

NAFTA. The United States and Canada established a free-trade agreement in the early 1990s. This agreement phased out tariffs on most goods traded between the two countries. The **North American Free Trade Agreement (NAFTA),** which took effect on January 1, 1994, added Mexico to create the world's largest and richest trading market, with about 370 million people and $6.5 trillion worth of goods and services annually.

Before NAFTA was established, Mexican tariffs, which averaged about 250 percent of comparable U.S. duties, restricted U.S. exports to Mexico. NAFTA immediately eliminated tariffs on more than half of the approximately 9,000 goods traded between the United States and Mexico and provided for phasing out of the others over varying periods of as long as fifteen years.

NAFTA underscores the economic interdependence of the United States, Mexico, and Canada. Although the three countries have separate political systems and cultural histories, their geographical proximity encouraged an economic partnership to better compete in the global marketplace.

The New Eastern Europe. The Cold War is over, communism is rapidly disappearing, and capitalism is spreading throughout the world. In the last several years, Germany has been reunited, countries such as Poland and Romania have introduced democratic governments, and the former Soviet Union has become a set of independent states trying to implement market-based reforms.

In terms of the changing global environment, the spread of capitalism makes the world a smaller place. Business has new markets to conquer. In addition, well-trained and reliable workers in countries such as Hungary and Slovakia provide a rich source of low-cost labor. The implementation of free markets in

Eastern Europe further underscores the growing interdependence among countries and the potential for goods, labor, and capital to easily move across national borders.

*f*acing the International Challenge

A global economy presents challenges to managers that they never had to confront when their operations were confined within national borders. They face different legal and political systems. They confront different economic climates and tax policies. But they also must deal with varying *national cultures*—the primary values and practices that characterize particular countries—many of which are nothing like those in which they have spent their entire lives.

If this were an economics text, we would carefully dissect the economic implications for managers in a global economy. But this book is about organizational behavior and understanding people at work. Therefore, let's look at why managers, especially those born and raised in the United States, often find managing people in foreign lands so difficult.

American Biases

Americans have been singled out as suffering particularly from **parochialism;** that is, they view the world solely through their own eyes and perspective. People with a parochial perspective do not recognize that other people have different ways of living and working. We see this phenomenon most explicitly in Americans' knowledge of foreign languages. It is not uncommon for Europeans to speak three or four languages, but Americans are almost entirely monolingual. The reasons probably reflect the huge domestic market in the United States, the geographical separation of the United States from Europe and Asia, and the reality that English has become the international business language in many parts of the world.

Americans have also been frequently criticized for holding **ethnocentric views.** They believe that their cultural values and customs are superior to all others. This belief may offer another explanation for why Americans don't learn foreign languages. Many think their language is superior and that it's the rest of the world's responsibility to learn English.

There is no shortage of stories illustrating the problems created when American managers failed to understand cultural differences. Consider the following examples.[2]

An American manager transferred to Saudi Arabia successfully obtained a million dollar contract from a Saudi manufacturer. The manufacturer's representative had arrived at the meeting several hours late, but the American executive considered it unimportant. The American was certainly surprised and frustrated to learn later that the Saudi had no intention of honoring the contract. He had signed it only to be polite after showing up late for the appointment.

An American executive operating in Peru was viewed by Peruvian managers as cold and unworthy of trust because, in face-to-face discussions, the American kept backing up. He did not understand that in Peru, the custom is to stand quite close to the person with whom you are speaking.

An American manager in Japan offended a high-ranking Japanese executive by failing to give him the respect his position deserved. The American was introduced to the Japanese executive in the latter's office. The American assumed that the executive was a low-level manager and paid him little attention because of the small and sparsely furnished office he occupied. The American didn't realize that top Japanese executives do not flaunt status symbols as do their American counterparts.

U.S. parochialism and ethnocentrism may not have been debilitating in the post–World War II period, when the United States accounted for seventy-five percent of the world's gross domestic product (GDP). But it is a "life-threatening disease" today, when U.S. firms produce only about twenty-two percent of the world's GDP. The point is that the world is not dominated by U.S. economic power any more, and unless U.S. managers conquer their parochialism and ethnocentrism, they will not be able to take full advantage of the new global opportunities.

Foreigners in America

Don't assume that Americans are alone in blundering on foreign soil. Cultural ignorance goes two ways. Foreign owners now control more than twelve percent of all American manufacturing assets and employ over three million American workers. In one recent year alone, foreign investors acquired nearly four hundred American businesses, worth a total of $60 billion. But these foreign owners are facing the same challenges and making many of the same mistakes that American executives have long made overseas.

Americans, for instance, are used to stability. When new owners with different management styles take over a U.S. company, American workers often feel threatened by high uncertainty, yet their feelings are often ignored by foreign managers. Some foreign owners, especially those from relatively homogeneous cultures, have the outmoded, stereotypical attitudes toward women and minorities that build ill-will. Many American employees complain that they feel left out of the established personal networks in traditional European and Asian corporations that acquire American firms. Japanese managers, as a case in point, work ten to twelve hours a day and then socialize until midnight. A lot of important business is done at these social gatherings, but American managers are excluded, and this exclusion creates feelings of hurt and distrust. The Japanese way of dealing with people also confounds Americans. Communication, for example, is often difficult. Americans are relatively more direct—they tend to say exactly what they mean. The Japanese use a subtle style and see this directness as rude and abrasive. The Japanese emphasis on group consensus is another practice that doesn't fit well in the United States. Americans, used to making decisions fast, get frustrated by what they interpret as unnecessary delays.[3]

The Relevant Question:
Are National Cultures Becoming More Homogeneous?

It can be argued that the creation of a true global village is making the concern over cultural differences irrelevant. Today, when Cable News Network is watched in more than 140 countries, Levi's are as popular in Moscow as in Dallas, and a significant portion of students in American graduate business programs are foreigners who expect to return to their homelands to practice management, it may be naive to think that cultural differences are very important. If they are, they are so only in the near term. In the long run, the global village will become a single homogeneous culture—that is, a world melting pot in which cross-cultural differences will all but disappear.

Is this argument correct? Are national cultures becoming more homogeneous? At one level, they are.[4] Research demonstrates that organizational strategies, structures, and technologies are becoming more alike, but there still are differences among people within organizations in different cultures.[5] In other words, national culture continues to be a powerful force in explaining a large proportion of organizational behavior. In further support of this viewpoint, research comparing employees in forty countries concluded that national culture explained approximately fifty percent of the differences in these employees' attitudes and behavior.[6]

If nations were becoming more homogeneous, we could take a culture-free approach to organizational behavior. But such an approach does not appear to be justified at present, for the following reasons: (1) There are differences in OB across national cultures. (2) These differences explain a large proportion of the variability in attitudes and behaviors. (3) For now at least, and probably for years to come, these differences are not decreasing at any significant rate. On the last point we might speculate that, despite the tremendous increase in cross-cultural communication, there continue to be unique country-specific traditions and customs that shape the attitudes and behaviors of the people in those countries.

Assessing Differences among Countries

American children are taught early the values of individuality and uniqueness. In contrast, Japanese children are indoctrinated to be "team players," to work within the group, and to conform. A significant part of an American student's education is to learn to think, analyze, and question. Their Japanese counterparts are rewarded for recounting facts. These different socialization practices reflect different cultures and, not surprisingly, result in different types of employees. The average U.S. worker is more competitive and self-focused than the Japanese worker. Predictions of employee behavior, based on samples of U.S. workers, are likely to be off-target when they are applied to a population of employees—such as the Japanese—who prefer and perform better in standardized tasks, as part of a work team, with group-based decisions and rewards.

It's relatively easy to learn about the Japanese culture. Dozens of books and hundreds of articles have been written on the subject. But how do you gain an understanding of Venezuela's or Denmark's national culture? A popular notion is to talk with people from those countries. Evidence suggests, however, that this method rarely works because people born and raised in a country are preprogrammed in the ways of its culture by the time they're adults. They understand how things are done and can work comfortably within their country's unwritten norms, but they *can't* explain their culture to someone else. It is pervasive, but it is hidden. Most people are unaware of just how their culture has shaped them. Culture is like water to fish. It's there all the time, but the fish are oblivious to it. So one of the frustrations of moving into a different culture is that the "natives" are often the least capable of explaining its unique characteristics to an outsider.

Although foreign cultures are difficult to fathom from what the natives tell you, there is an expanding body of research that can tell us how cultures vary and key differences between, say, the United States and Italy. Let's look at the two best known research frameworks.

The Kluckhohn-Strodtbeck Framework

One of the most widely referenced approaches for analyzing variations among cultures is the Kluckhohn-Strodtbeck framework.[7] It identifies six basic cultural dimensions: relationship to the environment, time orientation, nature of people, activity orientation, focus of responsibility, and conception of space.

Relationship to the Environment. Are people *subjugated* to their environment, in *harmony* with it, or able to *dominate* it? In many Middle Eastern countries, people see life as essentially preordained. When things happen, they tend to see it as "God's will." In contrast, Americans and Canadians believe that they can control nature. They're willing to spend billions of dollars each year on cancer research, for instance, because they think that cancer's cause can be identified, a cure can be found, and the disease can eventually be eradicated.

In between these two extreme positions is a more moderate view. This one seeks harmony with nature. In many Far Eastern countries, the way to deal with the environment is to work with it.

You should expect these different perspectives toward the environment to influence organizational practices. Take the setting of goals as an example. In a subjugation society, goal setting is not likely to be very popular. Why set goals if you believe people can't do much toward achieving them? In a harmony society, goals are likely to be used, but deviations are expected and penalties for failing to reach the goals are likely to be minimal. In a domination society, goals are widely applied. People are expected to achieve their goals, and the penalties for failure tend to be quite high.

Time Orientation. Does the culture focus on the *past, present,* or *future*? Societies differ on the value placed on time. For instance, Western cultures perceive time as a scarce resource. "Time is money" and must be used efficiently. Americans focus on the present and the near future. You see evidence of this attitude in the short-term orientation in performance appraisals. In the typical North American organization, people are evaluated every six months or a year. The Japanese, in contrast, take a longer-term view as is reflected in their performance appraisals; Japanese workers are often given ten years or more to prove their worth. Some cultures have still another approach to time: They focus on the past. Italians, for instance, follow traditions and seek to preserve historical practices.

Knowledge of a culture's time orientation can provide insights into the importance of deadlines, whether long-term planning is widely practiced, the length of job assignments, or what constitutes lateness. It can explain, for example, the fascination Americans have with making and keeping appointments.

Nature of People.   Does a culture view people as *good, evil,* or some *mix* of these two? In many Third World countries, people see themselves as basically honest and trustworthy. North Korea, on the other hand, takes a rather evil view of human nature. North Americans tend to be somewhere in between. They see people as basically good but stay on guard so as not to be taken advantage of.

You can readily see how a culture's view on the nature of people might influence the dominant leadership style of managers in a given society. A more autocratic style is likely to rule in countries that focus on the evil aspects of people. Participation or even a laissez-faire style should appeal to countries that emphasize trusting values. In mixed cultures, leadership is likely to emphasize participation but provide close controls that can quickly identify deviations.

Activity Orientation.   Some cultures emphasize *doing,* or action. They stress accomplishments. Some cultures emphasize *being,* or living for the moment. These cultures stress experiencing life and seeking immediate gratification of desires. Still other cultures focus on *controlling,* where people restrain their desires by detaching themselves from objects.

North Americans live in doing-oriented societies. They work hard and expect to be rewarded with promotions, raises, and other forms of recognition for their accomplishments. Mexico, in contrast, is being-oriented. The pace is slower and people value enjoying the moment. The French represent a controlling orientation. The emphasis is on rationality and logic.

An understanding of a culture's activity orientation can give you insights into how people approach work and leisure, how they make decisions, or the criteria they use for allocating rewards. For instance, in cultures with a dominant being orientation, decisions are likely to be emotional. In contrast, doing cultures are likely to emphasize pragmatism; and controlling cultures, rationality in decision making is emphasized.

Focus of Responsibility.   Cultures can be classified according to where responsibility lies for the welfare of others. Americans, for instance, are highly *individualistic.* They use personal characteristics and achievements to define themselves. They believe that a person's responsibility is to take care of himself or herself. Countries such as Malaysia and Israel focus more on the *group.* In an Israeli kibbutz, for example, people share chores and rewards. Emphasis is on group harmony, unity, and loyalty. The British and French follow another orientation by relying on *hierarchical* relationships. Groups in these countries are hierarchically ranked, and a group's position remains essentially stable over time. Hierarchical societies tend to be aristocratic.

This dimension of culture has implications for the design of jobs, approaches to decision making, communication patterns, reward systems, and selection practices in organizations. For instance, selection in individualistic societies emphasizes personal accomplishments. In group societies, working well with others is likely to be of primary importance. In hierarchical societies, selection decisions are made on the basis of a candidate's social ranking.

VALUE DIMENSION	VARIATIONS*		
Relationship to the environment	Domination	Harmony	Subjugation
Time orientation	Past	Present	Future
Nature of people	Good	Mixed	Evil
Activity orientation	Being	Controlling	Doing
Focus of responsibility	Individualistic	Group	Hierarchical
Conception of space	Private	Mixed	Public

*The jagged line indicates where the United States tends to fall along these dimensions.

Exhibit 2-1

Variations in Kluckhohn-Strodtbeck's Value Dimensions

Conception of Space. The final dimension in the Kluckhohn-Strodtbeck framework is related to ownership of space. Some cultures are very open and conduct business in *public*. At the other extreme are cultures that place a great deal of emphasis on keeping things *private*. Many societies *mix* the two and fall somewhere in between.

Japanese organizations reflect the public nature of their society. There are, for instance, few private offices. Managers and operative employees work in the same room, and no partitions separate the desks. North American firms also reflect their cultural values. They use offices and privacy to reflect status. Important meetings are held behind closed doors. Space is frequently given over for the exclusive use of specific individuals. In societies that have a mixed orientation, there is a blend of the private and public. For instance, there might be a large office where walls are only five or six feet high, thus creating "limited privacy." These differences in the conception of space have obvious implications for organizational concerns such as job design and communication.

Summary. Exhibit 2-1 summarizes the six cultural dimensions in the Kluckhohn-Strodtbeck framework and the possible variations for each.

The Hofstede Framework

A more comprehensive analysis of cultural diversity has been done by Geert Hofstede.[8] In contrast to most of the earlier organizational studies, which either included a limited number of countries or analyzed different companies in different countries, Hofstede's analysis surveyed more than 116,000 employees in forty countries who all worked for a single multinational corporation. This data base eliminated any differences that might be attributable to varying practices and policies in different companies. So any variations that he found between countries could reliably be attributed to national culture.

What did Hofstede find? His huge data base confirmed that national culture had a major impact on employees' work-related values and attitudes. In fact, it explained more of the differences than did age, sex, profession, or position in the organization. More important, Hofstede found that managers and employees vary on four dimensions of national culture: (1) individualism versus collectivism; (2) power distance; (3) uncertainty avoidance; and (4) masculinity versus femininity.

Individualism versus Collectivism. **Individualism** refers to a loosely knit social framework in which people are supposed to look after their own interests and those of their immediate family. An individualistic society allows individuals a large amount of freedom. **Collectivism,** in contrast, is characterized by a tight social framework in which people expect others in their group (such as an organization) to look after them and protect them when they are in trouble. In exchange, they feel that they owe absolute loyalty to the group.

Hofstede found that the degree of individualism in a country is closely related to that country's wealth. Rich countries such as the United States, Great Britain, and the Netherlands are very individualistic. Poor countries such as Colombia and Pakistan are very collectivistic.

Power Distance.   People naturally vary in terms of physical and intellectual abilities. This variation, in turn, creates differences in wealth and power. How does a society deal with these inequalities? Hofstede used the term **power distance** as a measure of the extent to which a society accepts the fact that power in institutions and organizations is distributed unequally. A high power distance society accepts wide differences in power in organizations. Employees show a great deal of respect for those in authority. Titles, rank, and status carry a lot of weight. When negotiating in high power distance countries, companies find that it helps to send representatives with titles at least as high as those with whom they're bargaining. Countries high in power distance include the Philippines, Venezuela, and India. In contrast, a low power distance society plays down inequalities as much as possible. Superiors still have authority, but employees are not fearful or in awe of the boss. Denmark, Israel, and Austria are examples of countries with low power distance scores.

Uncertainty Avoidance.   We live in a world of uncertainty. The future is largely unknown and always will be. Societies respond to this uncertainty in different ways. Some socialize their members into accepting it with equanimity. People in such societies are more or less comfortable with risks. They're also relatively tolerant of behavior and opinions that differ from their own because they don't feel threatened by them. Hofstede describes such societies as having low **uncertainty avoidance.** That is, people feel relatively secure. Countries that fall into this category include Singapore, Switzerland, and Denmark.

A society high in uncertainty avoidance is characterized by a high level of anxiety among its people, which manifests itself in nervousness, stress, and aggressiveness. Because people feel threatened by uncertainty and ambiguity in these societies, mechanisms are created to provide security and reduce risk. Their organizations are likely to have formal rules, there will be little tolerance for deviant ideas and behaviors, and members will strive to believe in absolute truths. Not surprisingly, in organizations in countries with high uncertainty avoidance, employees demonstrate relatively low job mobility, and lifetime employment is a widely practiced policy. Countries in this category include Japan, Portugal, and Greece.

Masculinity versus Femininity. The fourth dimension, like individualism and collectivism, represents a dichotomy. Hofstede called it **masculinity** versus **femininity.** Though his choice of terms is unfortunate (as you'll see, he gives them a strong sexist connotation), to maintain the integrity of his work we'll use his labels.

According to Hofstede, some societies allow both men and women to take many different roles. Others insist that people behave according to rigid sex roles. When societies make a sharp division between male and female activities, Hofstede claims "the distribution is always such that men take more assertive and dominant roles and women the more service-oriented and caring roles."[9] Under the category masculinity he puts societies that emphasize assertiveness and the acquisition of money and material things, while deemphasizing caring for others. In contrast, under the category femininity he puts societies that emphasize relationships, concern for others, and the overall quality of life. Where femininity dominates, members put human relationships before money and are concerned with the quality of life, preserving the environment, and helping others.

Hofstede found Japan to be the most masculine country. In Japan, almost all women are expected to stay home and take care of children. At the other extreme, he found the Nordic countries and the Netherlands to be the most feminine. There it's common to see men staying home as househusbands while their wives work, and working men are offered paternity leave to take care of newborn children.

The United States and Other Countries on Hofstede's Dimensions. Comparing the forty countries on the four dimensions, Hofstede found U.S. culture to rank as follows:

- Individualism/collectivism: Highest of all countries on individualism
- Power distance: Below average
- Uncertainty avoidance: Well below average
- Masculinity/femininity: Well above average on masculinity

The results are not inconsistent with the world image of the United States. The below-average score on power distance aligns with what one might expect from a representative type of government with democratic ideals. In this category, the United States would rate below nations with a small ruling class and a large, powerless set of subjects and above those nations with very strong commitments to egalitarian values. The well-below-average ranking on uncertainty avoidance is also consistent with a representative type of government having democratic ideals.

Americans perceive themselves as being relatively free from threats of uncertainty. The individualistic ethic is one of the most frequently used stereotypes to describe Americans, and, on the basis of Hofstede's research, the stereotype seems well-founded. The United States was ranked as the single most individualistic country in his entire set. Finally, the well-above-average score on masculinity is no surprise. Capitalism—which values aggressiveness and materialism—is consistent with Hofstede's masculine characteristics.

We haven't the space to review the results Hofstede obtained for each of the forty countries, although a dozen examples are presented in Exhibit 2-2. Since our concern is essentially with identifying similarities and differences among cultures, let's briefly identify those countries that are most like and least like the United States on the four dimensions.

The United States is strongly individualistic but low on power distance. This same pattern was exhibited by Great Britain, Australia, Canada, the Netherlands, and New Zealand. Those least similar to the United States on these dimensions were Venezuela, Colombia, Pakistan, Singapore, and the Philippines.

The United States scored low on uncertainty avoidance and high on masculinity. The same pattern was shown by Ireland, Great Britain, the Philippines, Canada, New Zealand, Australia, India, and South Africa. Those least similar to the United States on these dimensions were Chile, Portugal, and the former Yugoslavia republic of Macedonia.

Exhibit 2-2

Examples of Hofstede's Cultural Dimensions

Country	Individualism/ Collectivism	Power Distance	Uncertainty Avoidance	Masculinity/ Femininity*
Australia	Individual	Small	Moderate	Strong masculinity
Canada	Individual	Moderate	Low	Moderate masculinity
England	Individual	Small	Moderate	Strong masculinity
France	Individual	Large	High	Weak masculinity
Greece	Collective	Large	High	Moderate masculinity
Italy	Individual	Moderate	High	Strong masculinity
Japan	Collective	Moderate	High	Strong masculinity
Mexico	Collective	Large	High	Strong masculinity
Singapore	Collective	Large	Low	Moderate masculinity
Sweden	Individual	Small	Low	Weak masculinity
United States	Individual	Small	Low	Strong masculinity
Venezuela	Collective	Large	High	Strong masculinity

Source: Based on G. Hofstede, *Cultures and Organizations: Software of the Mind* (London: McGraw-Hill, 1991), pp. 23–138.

*A weak masculinity score is equivalent to high femininity, and a strong masculinity score is equivalent to low femininity.

Keeping OB in a Global Context

Most of the concepts that currently make up the body of knowledge we call *organizational behavior* have been developed by Americans, using American subjects, within domestic contexts. A comprehensive study, for instance, of more than 11,000 articles published in twenty-four management and organizational behavior journals over a ten-year period revealed that approximately eighty percent of the studies were of the United States and had been conducted by Americans.[10] What this means is that not all the concepts you'll read about in future chapters may be universally applicable to managing people around the world.

As you review concepts in this book, ask yourself: *Is this concept culture-bound?* If it was developed and tested in the United States, for instance, do you think it is generalizable to Mexico, or France, or India? If not, *why*?

The more a country's culture deviates from that of the United States—as depicted by the jagged line in Exhibit 2-1 or the ratings of the United States on Hofstede's four cultural dimensions—the more you need to consider how cultural differences might modify the application of OB concepts.

mplications for Managers

The findings and conclusions presented in this book are, for the most part, based on research studies conducted in the United States. As long as managers are concerned with trying to understand the behavior of employees born and raised in the United States or in countries with similar cultural values, such as Canada, Great Britain, or Australia, they should find it unnecessary to consider national culture as a confounding variable. It's not that national culture doesn't affect these employees; it's just that the concepts we discuss in this text already reflect this influence.

An understanding of differences between cultures should be particularly valuable for managers who were born and raised in non-Anglo-American countries, those who plan on living and working in another country, or those who manage people whose cultural backgrounds are different from their own. As a manager, if you fall into one of those groups, how should you use the information provided in this chapter? First, determine from what country the person comes whose behavior you are trying to understand. Second, evaluate the country of that person's origin using one or both of the cultural differences frameworks presented in this chapter. Third, compare the national culture in question against the data for the United States and identify relevant differences. This process is necessary because this text's frame of reference is essentially the United States. Finally, modify the application of concepts to reflect any differences.

Chapter 3

Foundations of Individual Behavior

After reading this chapter, you should be able to:

1. Describe the relationship between satisfaction and productivity

2. Explain the theory of cognitive dissonance

3. Summarize the relationship between attitudes and behavior

4. Identify the "Big Five" personality variables and their relationship to behavior in organizations

5. Describe the impact of job typology on the personality–job performance relationship

6. Explain how two people can see the same thing and interpret it differently

7. Summarize attribution theory

8. Outline the learning process

An understanding of individual behavior begins with a review of the major psychological contributions to OB. These contributions are subdivided into the following four concepts: attitudes, personality, perception, and learning.

Attitudes

Attitudes are evaluative statements—either favorable or unfavorable—concerning objects, people, or events. They reflect how one feels about something. When I say "I like my job," I'm expressing my attitude about work.

A person can have thousands of attitudes, but OB focuses on a very limited number of job-related attitudes. These include job satisfaction, job involvement (the degree to which a person identifies with his or her job and actively participates in it), and organizational commitment (an indicator of loyalty to, and identification with, the organization). Without question, however, job satisfaction has received the bulk of attention.

Job Satisfaction

Job satisfaction refers to an individual's general attitude toward his or her job. A person with a high level of job satisfaction holds positive attitudes toward the job; a person who is dissatisfied with his or her job holds negative attitudes about the job. When people speak of employee attitudes, more often than not they mean job satisfaction. In fact, the two terms are frequently used interchangeably.

What Determines Job Satisfaction? What work-related variables determine job satisfaction? The evidence indicates that the more important factors conducive to job satisfaction are mentally challenging work, equitable rewards, supportive working conditions, and supportive colleagues.[1]

Employees tend to prefer jobs that give them opportunities to use their skills and abilities and offer a variety of tasks, freedom, and feedback on how well they're doing. These characteristics make work mentally challenging. Jobs that have too little challenge create boredom, but too much challenge creates frustration and feelings of failure. Under conditions of moderate challenge, most employees will experience pleasure and satisfaction.

Employees want pay systems and promotion policies that they perceive as being just, unambiguous, and in line with their expectations. When pay is seen as fair, based on job demands, individual skill level, and community pay standards, satisfaction is likely to result. Similarly, individuals who perceive that promotion decisions are made in a fair and just manner are likely to experience satisfaction from their jobs.

Employees are concerned with their work environment for both personal comfort and facilitating doing a good job. They prefer physical surroundings that are safe, comfortable, clean, and with a minimum degree of distractions.

Finally, people get more out of work than merely money or tangible achievements. For most employees, work also fills the need for social interaction. Not surprisingly, therefore, having friendly and supportive co-workers leads to increased job satisfaction.

Satisfaction and Productivity. Few topics have attracted as much interest among students of organizational behavior as the satisfaction-productivity relationship.[2] The question typically posed is: Are satisfied workers more productive than dissatisfied workers?

The early views on the satisfaction-productivity relationship can be essentially summarized in the statement "a happy worker is a productive worker." Much of the paternalism shown by managers in the 1930s, 1940s, and 1950s—by forming company bowling teams and credit unions, holding company picnics, and training supervisors to be sensitive to the concerns of employees—was initiated with the intent to try to make workers happy. But belief in the happy worker thesis was based more on wishful thinking than on hard evidence.

A more careful analysis indicates that if satisfaction does have a positive effect on productivity, that effect is fairly small. The introduction of moderating variables, however, has improved the relationship. For instance, the relationship is stronger when employee's behavior is not constrained or controlled by outside factors. An employee's productivity on machine-paced jobs, for example, is going to be much more influenced by the speed of the machine than by his or her level of satisfaction.

Currently, on the basis of a comprehensive review of the evidence, it appears that productivity is more likely to lead to satisfaction rather than the other way around. If you do a good job, you intrinsically feel good about it. In addition, if we assume that the organization rewards productivity, your higher productivity should increase verbal recognition, your pay level, and probabilities for promotion. These rewards, in turn, will increase your level of satisfaction with the job.

People Seek to Reduce Dissonance

One of the most relevant findings pertaining to attitudes is the fact that individuals seek consistency. **Cognitive dissonance** occurs when there are inconsistencies between two or more of a person's attitudes or between a person's behavior and attitudes. The theory of cognitive dissonance suggests that people seek to minimize dissonance and the discomfort it causes.[3]

Of course, no individual can avoid dissonance completely. You know that "honesty is the best policy" but say nothing when a store clerk gives you back too much change. Or you tell your children to brush after every meal, but *you* don't. So how do people cope? A person's desire to reduce dissonance is determined by the importance of the elements creating the dissonance, the degree of influence the individual believes he or she has over the elements, and the rewards that may be involved in dissonance.

If the elements creating the dissonance are relatively unimportant, the pressure to correct this imbalance will be low. But, say a corporate manager—Mrs. Smith, who has a husband and several children—believes strongly that no company should pollute the air or water. Unfortunately, because of the requirements of her job, Mrs. Smith is placed in the position of having to make decisions that would trade off her company's profitability against her attitudes on pollution. She knows that dumping the company's sewage into the local river (we shall assume the practice is legal) is in the best economic interest of her firm. What will she do? Clearly, Mrs. Smith is experiencing a high degree of cognitive dissonance. Because of the importance of the elements in this example, we cannot expect Mrs. Smith to ignore the inconsistency. Besides quitting her job, there are several paths that she can follow to deal with her dilemma. She can reduce dissonance either by changing her behavior (stop polluting the river) or by concluding that the dissonant behavior is not so important after all ("I've got to make a living and, in my role as a corporate decision maker, I often have to place the good of my company above that of the environment or society"). A third alternative would be for Mrs.

Smith to change her attitude ("There is nothing wrong in polluting the river"). Still another choice would be to seek out more consonant elements to outweigh the dissonant ones ("The benefits to society from manufacturing our products more than offset the cost to society of the resulting water pollution").

The degree of influence that individuals believe they have over the elements will have an impact on how they will react to the dissonance. If they perceive the dissonance to be an uncontrollable result—something about which they have no choice—they are not likely to be receptive to attitude change. If, for example, the dissonance-producing behavior was required as a result of the boss's directive, the pressure to reduce dissonance would be less than if the behavior was performed voluntarily. Although dissonance exists, it can be rationalized and justified.

Rewards also influence the degree to which individuals are motivated to reduce dissonance. The tension inherent in high dissonance may be reduced when accompanied by a high reward. The reward acts to reduce dissonance by increasing the consistency side of the individual's balance sheet. Because people in organizations are given some form of reward or remuneration for their services, employees often can deal with greater dissonance on their jobs than off their jobs.

These moderating factors suggest that just because individuals experience dissonance, they will not necessarily move directly toward consistency, that is, toward reduction of this dissonance. If the issues underlying the dissonance are of minimal importance, if an individual perceives that the dissonance is externally imposed and is substantially uncontrollable, or if rewards are significant enough to offset the dissonance, the individual will not be under great tension to reduce the dissonance.

What are the organizational implications of the theory of cognitive dissonance? It can help to predict the propensity to engage in both attitude and behavioral change. For example, if individuals are required by the demands of their job to say or do things that contradict their personal attitude, they will tend to modify their attitude in order to make it compatible with the cognition of what they must say or do. In addition, the greater the dissonance—after it has been moderated by importance, choice, and reward factors—the greater the pressures to reduce the dissonance.

The Attitude-Behavior Relationship

The early research on the relationship between attitudes and behavior assumed them to be causally related; that is, the attitudes people hold determine what they do. Common sense, too, suggests a relationship. Isn't it logical that people watch television programs they like or that employees try to avoid assignments they find distasteful?

In the late 1960s, however, this assumed relationship between attitudes and behavior (A-B) was challenged by a review of the research.[4] On the basis of an evaluation of a number of studies that investigated the A-B relationship, the reviewer concluded that attitudes were unrelated to behavior or, at best, only slightly related. More recent research has demonstrated that there is indeed a measurable relationship if moderating contingency variables are taken into consideration.

One thing that improves our chances of finding significant A-B relationships is the use of both specific attitudes and specific behaviors. It is one thing to talk about a person's attitude toward "being socially responsible" and another to speak of her attitude toward "donating $25 to the National Multiple Sclerosis Society." The more specific the attitude we are measuring and the more specific we are in identifying a related behavior, the greater the probability that we can show a relationship between A and B.

Another moderator is social constraints on behavior. Discrepancies between attitudes and behavior may occur because the social pressures on the individual to behave in a certain way hold exceptional power. Group pressures, for instance, may explain why an employee who holds strong anti-union attitudes attends pro-union organizing meetings.

Of course, A and B may be at odds for other reasons. Individuals can and do hold contradictory attitudes at a given time, though, as we have noted, there are pressures toward consistency. In addition, other things besides attitudes influence behavior. But it is fair to say that, in spite of some attacks, most A-B studies yield positive results—in other words, attitudes *do* influence behavior.

Personality

Some people are quiet and passive; others are loud and aggressive. When we describe people in terms of characteristics such as quiet, passive, loud, aggressive, ambitious, loyal, or sociable, we are categorizing them in terms of personality traits. An individual's **personality,** therefore, is the combination of psychological traits we use to classify that person.

1.	Reserved	vs.	Outgoing
2.	Low intelligence	vs.	High intelligence
3.	Affected by feelings	vs.	Emotionally stable
4.	Submissive	vs.	Dominant
5.	Serious	vs.	Happy-go-lucky
6.	Expedient	vs.	Conscientious
7.	Timid	vs.	Venturesome
8.	Tough-minded	vs.	Sensitive
9.	Trusting	vs.	Suspicious
10.	Practical	vs.	Imaginative
11.	Forthright	vs.	Shrewd
12.	Self-assured	vs.	Apprehensive
13.	Conservative	vs.	Experimenting
14.	Group-dependent	vs.	Self-sufficient
15.	Uncontrolled	vs.	Controlled
16.	Relaxed	vs.	Tense

Exhibit 3-1
Sixteen Primary Personality Traits

Psychologists have studied personality traits extensively, resulting in the identification of sixteen primary personality traits.[5] They are shown in Exhibit 3-1. Notice that each trait is bipolar; that is, each has two extremes (e.g., reserved versus outgoing). These sixteen traits have been found to be generally steady and constant sources of behavior, allowing prediction of an individual's behavior in specific situations by weighing the characteristics for their situational relevance. Unfortunately, the relevance of these traits for understanding behavior in organizations is far from clear.

The Myers-Briggs Type Indicator

One of the most widely used personality frameworks is called the **Myers-Briggs Type Indicator (MBTI)**.[6] It is essentially a 100-question personality test that asks people how they usually feel or act in particular situations.

On the basis of the answers individuals give to the test, they are classified as extroverted or introverted (E or I), sensing or intuitive (S or N), thinking or feeling (T or F), and perceiving or judging (P or J). These classifications are then combined into sixteen personality types. (These are different from the sixteen primary traits in Exhibit 3-1.) To illustrate, let's take several examples. INTJs are visionaries. They usually have original minds and great drive for their own ideas and purposes. They're characterized as skeptical, critical, independent, determined, and often stubborn. ESTJs are organizers. They're practical, realistic, matter-of-fact, with a natural head for business or mechanics. They like to organize and run activities. The ENTP type is a conceptualizer. He or she is quick, ingenious, and good at many things. This person tends to be resourceful in solving challenging problems but may neglect routine assignments. A recent book that profiled thirteen contemporary businesspeople who created super-successful firms such as Apple Computer, Federal Express, Honda Motors, Microsoft, Price Club, and Sony found that all thirteen are intuitive thinkers (NTs).[7] This finding is particularly interesting because intuitive thinkers represent only about five percent of the population.

More than two million people a year take the MBTI in the United States alone. Organizations using the MBTI include Apple Computer, AT&T, Citicorp, Exxon, GE, 3M Co., plus many hospitals, educational institutions, and even the U.S. Armed Forces. There is no hard evidence that the MBTI is a valid measure of personality. But lack of such evidence this doesn't seem to deter organizations from using it.

The Big-Five Model

Whereas the MBTI lacks valid supporting evidence, that can't be said for the five-factor model of personality—more typically called the "Big Five."[8]

In recent years, an impressive body of research supports that five basic personality dimensions underlie all others. The Big Five factors are:

Extroversion: Sociable, talkative, assertive
Agreeableness: Good-natured, cooperative, and trusting

Conscientiousness: Responsible, dependable, persistent, and achievement-oriented

Emotional stability: Calm, enthusiastic, secure (positive) to tense, nervous, depressed, and insecure (negative)

Openness to experience: Imaginative, artistically sensitive, and intellectual

In addition to providing a unifying personality framework, research on the Big Five also has found important relationships between these personality dimensions and job performance.[9] Five categories of occupations were looked at: professionals (including engineers, architects, accountants, attorneys), police, managers, sales, and semiskilled and skilled employees. Job performance was defined in terms of performance ratings, training proficiency (performance during training programs), and personnel data such as salary level. The results showed that conscientiousness predicted job performance for all five occupational groups. For the other personality dimensions, predictability depended on both the performance criterion and occupational group. For instance, extroversion predicted performance in managerial and sales positions. This result makes sense because these occupations involve high social interaction. Similarly, openness to experience was found to be important in predicting training proficiency; which, too, seems logical. What wasn't so clear was why emotional stability wasn't related to job performance. Intuitively, it would seem that people who are calm and secure would do better on almost all jobs than people who were anxious and insecure. The researchers suggested that the answer might be that only people who score fairly high on emotional stability retain their jobs. If that is true, then the range among those people studied, all of whom were employed, would tend to be quite small.

Other Key Personality Attributes

Five additional personality attributes have been identified that appear to have more direct relevance for explaining and predicting behavior in organizations. They are locus of control, authoritarianism, Machiavellianism, self-monitoring, and risk propensity.

Some people believe they are masters of their own fate. Other people see themselves as pawns of fate, believing that what happens to them is due to luck or chance. **Locus of control** in the first case is internal; these people believe they control their destiny. Those who see their life as being controlled by outsiders are externals. The evidence shows that employees who rate high in externality are less satisfied with their jobs, more alienated from the work setting, and less involved in their jobs than are internals. A manager might also expect to find that externals blame a poor performance evaluation on their boss's prejudice, their co-workers, or other events outside their control. Internals would probably explain the same evaluation in terms of their own actions.

Authoritarianism is the belief that there should be status and power differences among people in organizations. The extremely high authoritarian personality is intellectually rigid, judgmental of others, deferential to those above and exploitive of those below, distrustful, and resistant to change. Of course, few people are extreme authoritarians, so conclusions must be guarded. It seems reasonable to postulate, however, that possessing a high authoritarian personality would be related negatively to performance where the job demands sensitivity to the feelings of others, tact, and the ability to adapt to complex and changing situations. On the other hand, where jobs are highly structured and success depends on close conformity to rules and regulations, the high authoritarian employee should perform quite well.

Closely related to authoritarianism is **Machiavellianism** (Mach), named after Niccolo Machiavelli, who wrote in the sixteenth century on how to gain and use power. An individual exhibiting strong Machiavellian tendencies is Hpragmatic, maintains emotional distance, and believes that ends can justify means. "If it works, use it" is consistent with a high Mach perspective. Do high Machs make good employees? That answer depends on the type of job and whether you consider ethical implications in evaluating performance. In jobs that require bargaining skills (such as labor negotiator) or where there are substantial rewards for winning (as in commissioned sales), high Machs will be productive. But if the ends can't justify the means or if there are no absolute standards of performance, our ability to predict a high Mach's performance will be severely curtailed.

Did you ever notice that some people are much better than others at adjusting their behavior to changing situations? This is because they score high in **self-monitoring.** High self-monitors are sensitive to external cues and can behave differently in different situations. They're chameleons—able to change to fit the situation and to hide their true selves. On the other hand, low self-monitors are consistent. They display their true dispositions and attitudes in every situation. The evidence suggests that high self-monitors tend to pay closer attention to the behavior of others and are more capable of conforming than low self-monitors. High self-monitors also tend to be better at playing organizational politics because they're sensitive to cues and can put on different "faces" for different audiences.

People differ in their willingness to take chances. Individuals with a high **risk propensity** make more rapid decisions and use less information in making their choices than individuals with low risk propensity. Managers might use this information to align employee risk-taking propensity with specific job demands. For instance, a high risk-taking propensity may lead to more effective performance for a stock trader in a brokerage firm. This type of job demands rapid decision making. On the other hand, this personality characteristic might prove a major obstacle to an accountant who performs auditing activities. This latter job might be better filled by someone with a low risk-taking propensity.

Matching Personalities and Jobs

Obviously, individual personalities differ. So, too, do jobs. Following this logic, efforts have been made to match the proper personalities with the proper jobs. The most researched personality job-fit theory is the *six-personality-types model.* This model states that an employee's satisfaction with and propensity to leave his or

Exhibit 3-2

Holland's Typology of Personality and Sample Occupations

Type	Personality Characteristics	Sample Occupations
Realistic: Prefers physical activities that require skill, strength, and coordination	Shy, genuine, persistent, stable, conforming, practical	Mechanic, drill press operator, assemblyline worker, farmer
Investigative: Prefers activities involving thinking, organizing, and understanding	Analytical, original, curious, independent	Biologist, economist, mathematician, news reporter
Social: Prefers activities that involve helping and developing others	Sociable, friendly, cooperative, understanding	Social worker, teacher, counselor, clinical psychologist
Conventional: Prefers rule-regulated, orderly, and unambiguous activities	Conforming, efficient, practical, unimaginative, inflexible	Accountant, corporate manager, bank teller, file clerk
Enterprising: Prefers verbal activities where there are opportunities to influence others and attain power	Self-confident, ambitious, energetic, domineering business manager	Lawyer, real estate agent, public relations specialist, small
Artistic: Prefers ambiguous and unsystematic activities that allow creative expression	Imaginative, disorderly, idealistic, emotional, impractical	Painter, musician, writer, interior decorator

Source: Based on J. L. Holland, *Making Vocational Choices: A Theory of Vocational Personalities and Work Environments,* 2nd ed. (Englewood Cliffs, NJ: Prentice Hall, 1985).

her job depend on the degree to which the individual's personality matches his or her occupational environment.[10] Six major personality types have been identified. They are listed in Exhibit 3-2, along with their compatible occupations.

A Vocational Preference Inventory questionnaire has been developed that contains 160 occupational titles. Respondents indicate which of these occupations they like or dislike, and their answers are used to form personality profiles. Utilizing this procedure, research strongly supports the hexagonal diagram in Exhibit 3-3. This figure shows that the closer two fields or orientations are in the hexagon, the more compatible they are. Adjacent categories are quite similar, while those diagonally opposite are highly dissimilar.

What does all this mean? The theory argues that satisfaction is highest and turnover lowest where personality and occupation are in agreement. Social individuals should be in social jobs, conventional people in conventional jobs, and so forth. A realistic person in a realistic job is in a more congruent situation than a realistic person in an investigative job. A realistic person in a social job is in the most incongruent situation possible. The key points of this model are that (1) there do appear to be intrinsic personality differences among individuals; (2) there are different types of jobs; and (3) people in job environments congruent with their personality type should be more satisfied and less likely to resign voluntarily than people in incongruent jobs.

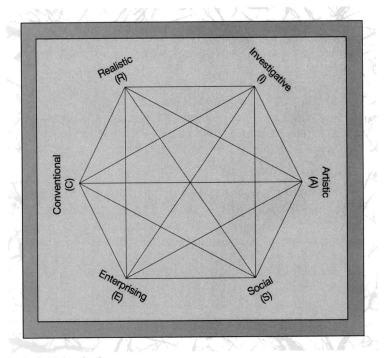

Exhibit 3-3

Hexagonal Diagram of the Relationship among Occupational
Personality Types

Source: From John L. Holland, *Making Vocational Choices: A Theory of Vocational
Personalities and Work Environments,* 2nd ed. (Englewood Cliffs, NJ: Prentice Hall,
1985), p. 23. Used by permission. [This model originally appeared in J. L. Holland
et al., "An Empirical Occupational Classification Derived from a Theory of
Personality and Intended for Practice and Research," ACT Research Report No.
29 (Iowa City): The American College Testing Program, 1969.]

*P*erception

Perception is a process by which individuals organize and interpret their sensory
impressions in order to give meaning to their environment. Research on perception consistently demonstrates that different individuals may look at the same
thing yet perceive it differently. The fact is that none of us sees reality. What we do
is interpret what we see and call it reality.

Factors Influencing Perception

How do we explain the fact that people perceive the same thing differently? A
number of factors operate to shape and sometimes distort perception. These factors can reside in the *perceiver,* in the object or *target* being perceived, or in the context of the *situation* in which the perception is made.

When an individual looks at a target and attempts to interpret what he or she
sees, that interpretation is heavily influenced by personal characteristics of the

individual perceiver. Personal characteristics affecting perception include attitudes, personality, motives, interests, past experiences, and expectations.

Characteristics of the target being observed can affect what is perceived. Loud people are more likely to be noticed in a group than quiet ones. So, too, are extremely attractive or unattractive individuals. Because targets are not looked at in isolation, the relationship of a target to its background influences perception, as does our tendency to group close things and similar things together.

The context in which we see objects or events is also important. The time at which an object or event is seen can influence attention, as can location, light, heat, or any number of situational factors.

Attribution Theory

Much of the research on perception is directed at inanimate objects. But OB is concerned with human beings, so our discussion of perception should focus on person perception.

Our perceptions of people differ from our perceptions of inanimate objects such as desks, machines, or buildings because we make inferences about the actions of people that we don't make about inanimate objects. Nonliving objects are subject to the laws of nature, but they have no beliefs, motives, or intentions. People do. The result is that when we observe people, we attempt to develop explanations of why they behave in certain ways. Our perception and judgment of a person's actions, therefore, will be significantly influenced by the assumptions we make about the person's internal state.

Attribution theory has been proposed to develop explanations of how we judge people differently depending on what meaning we attribute to a given behavior.[11] Basically, the theory suggests that when we observe an individual's behavior, we attempt to determine whether it was internally or externally caused. That determination, however, depends on three factors: (1) distinctiveness, (2) consensus, and (3) consistency. First, let's clarify the differences between internal and external causation, then elaborate on each of the three determining factors.

Internally caused behaviors are those that are believed to be under the personal control of the individual. Externally caused behavior results from outside causes; that is, the person is seen as forced into the behavior by the situation. If one of your employees was late for work, you might attribute his lateness to his partying into the wee hours of the morning and then oversleeping. This would be an internal interpretation. But if you attributed his arriving late to a major automobile accident that tied up traffic on the road he regularly uses, then you would be making an external attribution. As observers, we have a tendency to assume that others' behavior is internally controlled, while we tend to exaggerate the degree to which our own behavior is externally determined. But this is a broad generalization. There still exists a considerable amount of deviation in attribution, depending on how we interpret the distinctiveness, consensus, and consistency of the actions.

Distinctiveness refers to whether an individual displays different behaviors in different situations. Is the employee who arrives late today also the source of complaints by co-workers for being a "goof-off"? What we want to know is whether this behavior is unusual. If it is, the observer is likely to give the behavior an external attribution. If this action is not unique, it will probably be judged as internal.

If everyone who is faced with a similar situation responds in the same way, we can say the behavior shows *consensus*. Our tardy employee's behavior would meet this criterion if all employees who took the same route to work were also late. From an attribution perspective, if consensus is high you would be expected to give an external attribution to the employee's tardiness; whereas if other employees who took the same route made it to work on time, your conclusion for causation would be internal.

Finally, an observer looks for *consistency* in a person's actions. Does the person respond the same way over time? Coming in ten minutes late for work is not perceived in the same way if for one employee it represents an unusual case (she hasn't been late for several months), while for another it is part of a routine pattern (she is regularly late two or three times a week). The more consistent the behavior, the more the observer is inclined to attribute it to internal causes.

The preceding explains what you have seen operating for years. All similar behaviors are not perceived similarly. We look at actions and judge them within their situational context. If you have a reputation as a good student yet fail one test in a course, the instructor is likely to disregard the poor exam. Why? He or she will attribute the cause of this unusual performance to external conditions. It may not be your fault! But the teacher is not likely to ignore the low test score of a student who has a consistent record of being a poor performer. Similarly, if everyone in class failed the test, the instructor might attribute the outcome to external causes rather than to causes under the students' own control. (He or she might conclude that the questions were poorly written, the room was too warm, or that the students didn't have the necessary prerequisites.)

Shortcuts to Judging Others

Making judgments about others is done all the time by people in organizations. For example, managers regularly evaluate the performance of their employees, and operatives assess whether their co-workers are putting forth their full effort. But making judgments about others is difficult. To make the task easier, individuals take shortcuts. Some of these shortcuts are valuable—they allow us to make accurate perceptions rapidly and provide valid data for making predictions. However, they can also result in significant distortions.

Individuals cannot assimilate all they observe, so they engage in **selectivity.** They take in bits and pieces. But these bits and pieces are not chosen randomly; rather, they are selectively chosen depending on the interests, background, experience, and attitudes of the observer. Selective perception allows us to "speed read" others, but not without the risk of drawing an inaccurate picture.

It is easy to judge others if we assume they are similar to us. **Assumed similarity,** or the "like me" effect, results in an individual's perception of others being influenced more by what the observer is like than by what the person being observed is like. If you want challenge and responsibility in your job, you may assume that others want the same. People who assume that others are like them will be right some of the time, but only in those cases when they judge someone who actually is like them. The rest of the time, they'll be wrong.

When we judge someone on the basis of our perception of the group to which he or she belongs, we are using the shortcut called **stereotyping.** "Married people are more stable employees than singles" or "union people expect something for nothing" are examples of stereotypes. To the degree that a stereotype is a factual generalization, it helps in making accurate judgments. But many stereotypes have no foundation in fact. In these latter cases, stereotypes distort judgments.

When we draw a general impression about an individual on the basis of a single characteristic such as intelligence, sociability, or appearance, a **halo effect** is operating. It is not unusual for the halo effect to occur during selection interviews. A sloppily dressed candidate for a marketing research position may be perceived by an interviewer as an irresponsible person with an unprofessional attitude and marginal abilities, when in fact the candidate may be highly responsible, professional, and competent. What has happened is that a single trait—appearance—has overridden other characteristics in the interviewer's general perception about the individual.

*L*earning

The final concept introduced in this chapter is learning. It is included for the obvious reason that almost all complex human behavior is learned. If we want to explain, predict, or control behavior, we need to understand how people learn.

The psychologist's definition of learning is considerably broader than the layperson's view that "it's what we did when we went to school." In actuality, each of us is continuously "going to school." Learning is going on all the time. A more accurate definition of **learning,** therefore, is any relatively permanent change in behavior that occurs as a result of experience.

How do we learn? Exhibit 3-4 summarizes the learning process. First, learning helps us adapt to, and master, our environment. By changing our

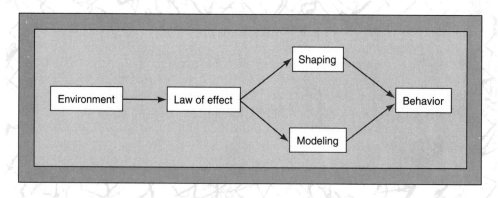

Exhibit 3-4
The Learning Process

behavior to accommodate changing conditions, we become responsible citizens and productive employees. But learning is built upon the **law of effect,** which says that behavior is a function of its consequences.[12] Behavior that is followed by a favorable consequence tends to be repeated; behavior followed by an unfavorable consequence tends not to be repeated. *Consequence,* in this terminology, refers to anything a person considers rewarding (i.e., money, praise, promotions, a smile). If your boss compliments you on your sales approach, you're likely to repeat that behavior. Conversely, if you're reprimanded for your sales approach, you're less likely to repeat it. But the keys to the learning process are the two theories, or explanations, of how we learn. One is *shaping* and the other is *modeling.*

When learning takes place in graduated steps, it is shaped. Managers shape employee behavior by systematically reinforcing, through rewards, each successive step that moves the employee closer to the desired behavior. Much of our learning has been done by shaping. When we speak of "learning by mistakes," we are referring to shaping. We try, we fail, and we try again. Through such series of trial and error, most of us have mastered such skills as riding a bicycle, performing basic mathematical computations, taking classroom notes, and answering multiple-choice tests.

In addition to shaping, much of what we have learned is the result of observing others and modeling our behavior after them. Whereas the trial-and-error learning process is usually slow, modeling can produce complex behavioral changes quite rapidly. For instance, most of us, at one time or another, when having trouble in school or in a particular class, look around to find someone who seems to have the system down pat. Then we observe that person to see what he or she is doing that is different from our approach. If we find some differences, we then incorporate them into our behavior repertoire. If our performance improves (a favorable consequence), we're likely to make a permanent change in our behavior to reflect what we've seen work for others. The process is the same at work as it is in school. A new employee who wants to be successful on her job is likely to look for someone in the organization who is well respected and successful and then try to imitate that person's behavior.

 mplications for Managers

This chapter introduced several psychological concepts. Let's now put them together and demonstrate their importance for the manager who is trying to understand organizational behavior.

Exhibit 3-5 summarizes our discussion of individual behavior. In very simplified terms, we can say that an individual enters an organization with a relatively entrenched set of attitudes and a substantially established personality. Although they are not permanently fixed, an employee's attitudes and personality are essentially "givens" at the time he or she enters an organization. How employees interpret their work environment (perception) will influence their level of motivation (the topic of our next two chapters), what they learn on the job, and, eventually, their individual work behavior. We've also added *ability* to our model to acknowledge that an individual's behavior is influenced

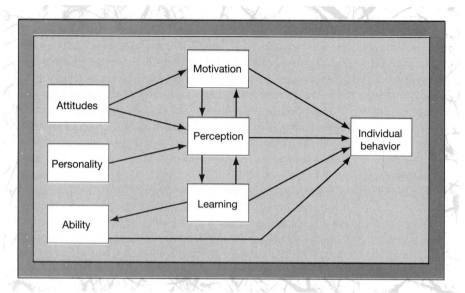

Exhibit 3-5
Key Variables Affecting Individual Behavior

by the talents and skills that person holds when he or she joins the organization. Learning, of course, will alter this variable over time.

Attitudes

Managers should be interested in their employees' attitudes because attitudes influence behavior. Satisfied employees, for instance, have lower rates of turnover and absenteeism than dissatisfied employees. Given that managers want to keep resignations and absences down—especially among their more productive employees—they will want to do those things that will generate positive job attitudes.

The findings about the satisfaction-productivity relationship have important implications for managers. They suggest that the goal of making employees happy on the assumption that doing so will lead to high productivity is probably misdirected. Managers would get better results by directing their attention primarily to what will help employees become more productive. Successful job performance should then lead to feelings of accomplishment, increased pay, promotions, and other rewards—all desirable outcomes—which then lead to satisfaction with the job.

Managers should also be aware that employees will try to reduce cognitive dissonance. More important, dissonance can be managed. If employees are required to engage in activities that appear inconsistent to them or that are at odds with their attitudes, the pressures to reduce the resulting dissonance are lessened when the employee perceives the dissonance as externally imposed and beyond his or her control or if the rewards are significant enough to offset the dissonance.

Personality

The major value of a manager's understanding personality differences probably lies in selection. You are likely to have higher-performing and more-satisfied employees if consideration is given to matching personality types with compatible jobs. In addition, there may be other benefits. For instance, managers can expect that individuals with an external locus of control may be less satisfied with their jobs than internals and also that they may be less willing to accept responsibility for their actions.

Perception

Managers need to recognize that their employees react to perceptions, not to reality. So whether a manager's appraisal of an employee is *actually* objective and unbiased or whether the organization's wage levels are *actually* among the highest in the industry is less relevant than what employees perceive. Individuals who perceive appraisals as biased or wage levels as low will behave as if those conditions actually exist. Employees naturally organize and interpret what they see; inherent in this process is the potential for perceptual distortion.

The message to managers should be clear: They need to pay close attention to how employees perceive both their jobs and management practices. Remember, the competent employee who quits for an invalid reason is just as "gone" as one who quits for a valid reason.

Learning

The issue isn't whether employees continually learn on the job or not. They do! The only issue is whether managers are going to let employee learning occur randomly or whether they are going to manage learning—through the rewards they allocate and the examples they set. If marginal employees are rewarded with pay raises and promotions, they will have little reason to change their behavior. If managers want behavior A, but reward behavior B, it shouldn't surprise them to find employees learning to engage in behavior B. Similarly, managers should expect that employees will look to them as models. Managers who are constantly late to work, or take two hours for lunch, or help themselves to company office supplies for personal use, should expect employees to read the message they're sending and model their behavior accordingly.

Basic Motivation Concepts

Chapter 4

After reading this chapter, you should be able to:

1. Outline the basic motivation process

2. Describe Maslow's hierarchy of needs theory

3. Contrast Theory X and Theory Y

4. Differentiate motivators from hygiene factors

5. List the characteristics that high achievers prefer in a job

6. Summarize the types of goals that increase performance

7. Contrast reinforcement and goal-setting theories

8. Explain equity theory

9. Clarify the key relationships in expectancy theory

Referring to their son or daughter, parents have said it for so many years that it has achieved the status of a cliché: "He/she has the ability but just won't apply him/herself." Few of us work to, or even near, our potential, and most of us will admit to that. Einstein underscored his belief in the importance of hard work for achieving success when he said that "genius is ten percent inspiration and ninety percent perspiration." The fact is that some people work harder or exert more effort than others. The result is that individuals of lesser ability can, and do, outperform their more gifted counterparts. For this reason, an individual's performance at work or otherwise depends not only on ability but on motivation as well. This chapter considers various

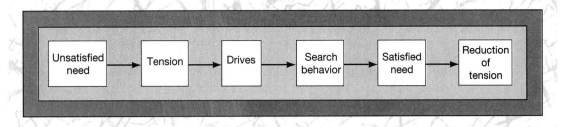

Exhibit 4-1
Basic Motivation Process

explanations of why some people exert more effort on their jobs than others. In the next chapter, we'll build on these explanations to describe a variety of applied motivation techniques.

What Is Motivation?

We might define motivation in terms of some outward behavior. People who are motivated exert a greater effort to perform than those who are not motivated. But such a definition is relative and tells us little. A more descriptive but less substantive definition would say that **motivation** is the willingness to do something and is conditioned by this action's ability to satisfy some need for the individual. A **need,** in our terminology, means a physiological or psychological deficiency that makes certain outcomes appear attractive. This motivation process can be seen in Exhibit 4-1.

An unsatisfied need creates tension, which stimulates drives within the individual. These drives generate a search to find particular goals that, if attained, will satisfy the need and lead to the reduction of tension.

Motivated employees are in a state of tension. In order to relieve this tension, they engage in activity. The greater the tension, the more activity will be needed to bring about relief. Therefore, when we see employees working hard at some activity, we can conclude they are driven by a desire to achieve some goal they value.

Early Theories of Motivation

The decade of the 1950s was a fruitful period in the development of motivation concepts. Three specific theories were formulated during this period, which, though now heavily attacked and their validity called into question, are probably still the best-known explanations for employee motivation: the hierarchy of needs theory, Theory X and Theory Y, and the motivation-hygiene theory. We have since developed more valid explanations of motivation, but you should know these early theories for at least two reasons: (1) They represent a foundation from which contemporary theories have grown, and (2) practicing managers regularly use these theories and their terminologies in explaining employee motivation.

Hierarchy of Needs Theory

It's probably safe to say that the best-known approach to motivation is Abraham Maslow's **hierarchy of needs theory.**[1] He hypothesized that within every human being there exists a hierarchy of five needs. These are:

1. *Physiological needs:* Include hunger, thirst, shelter, sex, and other bodily needs
2. *Safety needs:* Include security and protection from physical and emotional harm
3. *Social needs:* Include affection, a sense of belonging, acceptance, and friendship
4. *Esteem needs:* Include internal factors such as self-respect, autonomy, and achievement and external factors such as status, recognition, and attention
5. *Self-actualization need:* The drive to become what one is capable of becoming; includes growth, achieving one's potential, and self-fulfillment

As each of these needs becomes substantially satisfied, the next need becomes dominant. In terms of Exhibit 4-2, the individual moves up the hierarchy. From the standpoint of motivation, Maslow's theory would say that, although no need is ever fully gratified, a substantially satisfied need no longer motivates.

Maslow separated the five needs into higher and lower orders. Physiological and safety needs were described as lower order; social, esteem, and self-actualization were categorized as higher-order needs. The two orders were differentiated on the premise that higher-order needs are satisfied internally, whereas lower-order needs are predominantly satisfied externally (by such things as wages, union contracts, and tenure). In fact, the natural conclusion to be drawn from Maslow's classification is that, in times of economic plenty, almost all permanently employed workers will have their lower-order needs substantially met.

Maslow's need theory has received wide recognition, particularly among practicing managers. This acceptance can be attributed to the logic and ease with which the theory is intuitively understood. Unfortunately, however, research does not generally validate the theory. For instance, little support is found for the prediction that need structures are organized along the dimensions proposed by Maslow or the prediction that the substantial satisfaction of a given need leads to the activation of the next higher need. So, although the need hierarchy is well known and undoubtedly used by many managers as a guide toward motivating their employees, little substantive evidence exists to indicate that following the theory will lead to a more motivated work force.

Theory X and Theory Y

Douglas McGregor proposed two distinct views of human beings: one basically negative, labeled **Theory X,** and the other basically positive, labeled **Theory Y.**[2] After viewing the way managers dealt with employees, McGregor concluded that a manager's view of the nature of human beings is based on a certain grouping of

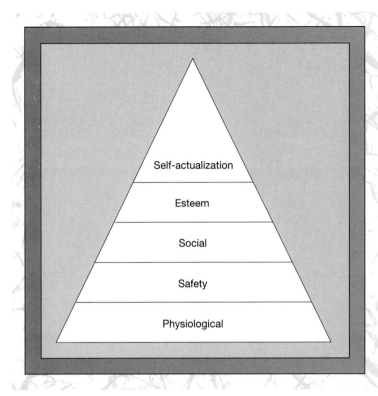

Exhibit 4-2
Maslow's Hierarchy of Needs

(The triangle, from top to bottom, is labeled: Self-actualization, Esteem, Social, Safety, Physiological)

assumptions and that he or she tends to mold his or her behavior toward subordinates according to those assumptions.

Under Theory X, four assumptions are held by the manager:

1. Employees inherently dislike work and, whenever possible, will attempt to avoid it.
2. Since employees dislike work, they must be coerced, controlled, or threatened with punishment to achieve desired goals.
3. Employees will shirk responsibilities and seek formal direction whenever possible.
4. Most workers place security above all other factors associated with work and will display little ambition.

Under Theory Y, four contrasting assumptions are held by the manager:

1. Employees can view work as being as natural as rest or play.
2. A person who is committed to the objectives will exercise self-direction and self-control.

3. The average person can learn to accept, even seek, responsibility.
4. Creativity—that is, the ability to make good decisions—is widely dispersed throughout the population and not necessarily the sole province of those in management.

What are the motivational implications if you accept McGregor's analysis? The answer is best expressed in the framework presented by Maslow. Theory X assumes that lower-order needs dominate individuals. Theory Y assumes that higher-order needs dominate individuals. McGregor, himself, held to the belief that Theory Y assumptions were more valid than Theory X. Therefore, he proposed ideas such as participation in decision making, responsible and challenging jobs, and good group relations as approaches that would maximize an employee's job motivation.

Unfortunately, there is no evidence to confirm that either set of assumptions is valid or that accepting Theory Y assumptions and altering one's actions accordingly will increase workers' motivation. As will become evident later, either Theory X or Theory Y assumptions may be appropriate in a particular situation.

Motivation-Hygiene Theory

The **motivation-hygiene theory** was proposed by psychologist Frederick Herzberg.[3] In the belief that an individual's relation to work is basic and that one's attitude toward work can very well determine success or failure, Herzberg investigated the question, "What do people want from their jobs?" He asked people to describe, in detail, situations in which they felt exceptionally good or bad about their jobs. These responses were tabulated and categorized. Factors affecting job attitudes, as reported in twelve investigations conducted by Herzberg, are illustrated in Exhibit 4-3.

From the categorized responses, Herzberg concluded that the replies people gave when they felt good about their jobs were significantly different from the replies given when they felt bad. As seen in Exhibit 4-3, certain characteristics tend to be consistently related to job satisfaction and others to job dissatisfaction. Intrinsic factors, such as achievement, recognition, the work itself, responsibility, and advancement seem to be related to job satisfaction. Respondents who felt good about their work tended to attribute these factors to themselves. On the other hand, dissatisfied respondents tended to cite extrinsic factors, such as company policy and administration, supervision, interpersonal relations, and working conditions.

The data suggest, said Herzberg, that the opposite of satisfaction is not dissatisfaction, as was traditionally believed. Removing dissatisfying characteristics from a job does not necessarily make the job satisfying. Herzberg proposed that his findings indicated the existence of a dual continuum: The opposite of "Satisfaction" is "No Satisfaction," and the opposite of "Dissatisfaction" is "No Dissatisfaction."

According to Herzberg, the factors leading to job satisfaction are separate and distinct from those that lead to job dissatisfaction. Therefore, managers who seek to eliminate factors that can create job dissatisfaction may bring about peace but not necessarily motivation. They will be placating their work force

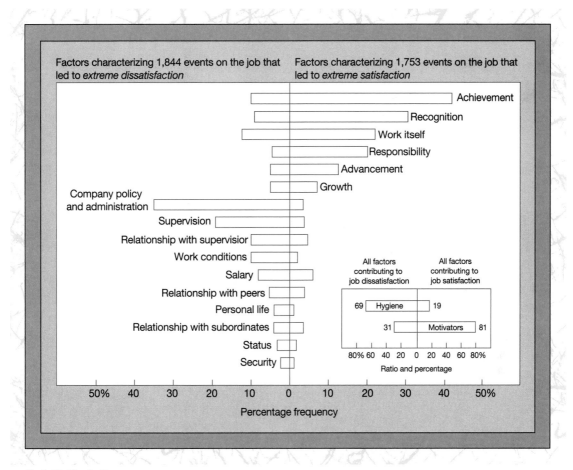

Exhibit 4-3

Comparison of Satisfiers and Dissatisfiers

Source: F. Herzberg, "One More Time, How Do You Motivate Employees?" *Harvard Business Review,* January–February 1968, p. 57. With permission. Copyright © 1968 by the President and Fellows of Harvard College; all rights reserved.

rather than motivating them. As a result, such characteristics as company policy and administration, supervision, interpersonal relations, working conditions, and salary were characterized by Herzberg as **hygiene factors.** When they're adequate, people will not be dissatisfied; neither will they be satisfied. If we want to motivate people on their jobs, Herzberg suggested emphasizing achievement, recognition, the work itself, responsibility, and growth. These are the characteristics that people find intrinsically rewarding.

The motivation-hygiene theory is not without detractors. The criticisms of the theory include the following:

1. The procedure that Herzberg used is limited by its methodology. When things are going well, people tend to take credit themselves. Contrarily, they blame failure on the extrinsic environment.

2. The reliability of Herzberg's methodology is questioned. Raters have to make interpretations, so they may contaminate the findings by interpreting one response in one manner while treating a similar response differently.

3. No overall measure of satisfaction was utilized. A person may dislike part of his or her job yet still think the job is acceptable.

4. The theory is inconsistent with previous research. The motivation-hygiene theory ignores situational variables.

5. Herzberg assumed a relationship between satisfaction and productivity, but the research methodology he used looked only at satisfaction not at productivity. To make such research relevant, one must assume a strong relationship between satisfaction and productivity.

Regardless of criticisms, Herzberg's theory has been widely popularized, and few managers are unfamiliar with his recommendations. As a case in point, much of the initial enthusiasm for vertically expanding jobs to allow workers greater responsibility in planning and controlling their work (which we discuss in Chapter 14) can probably be attributed largely to Herzberg's findings and recommendations.

Contemporary Theories of Motivation

The previous theories are well known but, unfortunately, have not held up well under close examination. All is not lost, however. There are contemporary theories that have a reasonable degree of valid supporting documentation. The following theories represent the current state of the art in explaining employee motivation.

Three-Needs Theory

David McClelland and others have proposed three major relevant motives or needs in the workplace:[4]

1. The **need for achievement (nAch):** The drive to excel, to achieve in relation to a set of standards, to strive to succeed

2. The **need for power (nPow):** The need to make others behave in a way they would not have behaved otherwise

3. The **need for affiliation (nAff):** The desire for friendly and close interpersonal relationships

Some people have a compelling drive to succeed, but they are striving for personal achievement rather than the rewards of success. They have a desire to do something better or more efficiently than it has been done before. This drive is the need for achievement. From research into the need for achievement, McClelland found that high achievers differentiate themselves from others by their desire to do things better. They seek situations in which they can attain personal responsibility for finding solutions to problems, receive rapid and unambiguous feedback on their performance, and set moderately challenging goals. They prefer working at a challenging problem and accepting the personal responsibility for success or failure rather than leaving the outcome to chance or the actions of others.

High achievers perform best when they perceive their probability of success as being 0.5, that is, when they estimate that they have a 50–50 chance of success. They dislike gambling with high odds (high probability of failure) because success in such a situation would be more a matter of luck than of ability, and they get no achievement satisfaction from happenstance success. Similarly, they dislike low odds (high probability of success) because then there is no challenge to their skills. They like to set realistic but difficult goals that require stretching themselves a little. When there is an approximately equal chance of success or failure, there is the optimum opportunity to experience feelings of accomplishment and satisfaction from their efforts.

The need for power is the desire to have an impact, to be influential, and to control others. Individuals high in *nPow* enjoy being in charge, strive for influence over others, prefer competitive and status-oriented situations, and tend to be more concerned with gaining prestige and influence over others than with effective performance.

The third need isolated by McClelland is affiliation. This need has received the least attention of researchers. Affiliation can be likened to Dale Carnegie's goals—the desire to be liked and accepted by others. Individuals with a high *nAff* strive for friendship, prefer cooperative situations rather than competitive ones, and desire relationships involving a high degree of mutual understanding.

How do you find out if someone is, for instance, a high achiever? All three motives are typically measured through a projective test in which subjects respond to a set of pictures. Each picture is briefly shown to the subject and then he or she writes a story based on the picture. For example, the picture may show a man sitting at a desk. He is looking pensively at a photograph of a woman and two children that sits at the corner of the desk. The subject will then be asked to write a story describing what is going on, what preceded this situation, what will happen in the future, and the like. The stories become, in effect, projective tests that measure unconscious motives. Each story is scored, and the subject is rated on each of the three motives.

An extensive amount of research indicates that some reasonably well-supported predictions can be made on the basis of the relationship between achievement need and job performance. Though less research has been done on power and affiliation needs, there are consistent findings in those areas too. First, individuals with a high need to achieve prefer job situations with personal responsibility, feedback, and an intermediate degree of risk. When these characteristics are prevalent, high achievers will be strongly motivated. The evidence consistently demonstrates, for instance, that high achievers are successful in entrepreneurial activities such as running their own business, managing a self-contained unit within a large organization, and many sales positions. Second, a high need to achieve does not necessarily lead to being a good manager, especially in large organizations. High *nAch* salespeople do not necessarily make good sales managers, and the good manager in a large organization does not typically have a high need to achieve. Third, the needs for affiliation and power tend to be closely related to managerial success. The best managers are high in the need for power and low in their need for affiliation. Last, employees have been successfully trained to stimulate their achievement need. If the job calls for a high achiever, management can select a person with a high *nAch* or develop its own candidate through achievement training.

Goal-Setting Theory

Considerable evidence supports **goal-setting theory.** This theory states that intentions—expressed as goals—can be a major source of work motivation. We can say, with a considerable degree of confidence, that specific goals lead to increased performance and that difficult goals, when accepted, result in higher performance than easy goals.[5]

Specific, difficult-to-achieve goals produce a higher level of output than a generalized goal of "do your best." The specificity of the goal itself acts as an internal stimulus. For instance, when a trucker commits to making eighteen round-trip hauls between Baltimore and Washington, D.C., each week, this intention gives him a specific objective to reach for. We can say that, all things being equal, the trucker with a specific goal will outperform his counterpart who operates either with no goals or with the generalized goal of "do your best."

If factors such as ability and acceptance of the goals are held constant, we can also state that the more difficult the goals, the higher the level of performance. However, it's logical to assume that easier goals are more likely to be accepted. But once an employee accepts a hard task, he or she will exert a high level of effort until the goal is achieved, lowered, or abandoned.

If employees have the opportunity to participate in the setting of their own goals, will they try harder? The evidence is mixed regarding the superiority of participation over assigned goals. In some cases, goals that have been set participatively have elicited superior performance; in other cases, individuals have performed best when assigned goals by their boss. A major advantage of participation may be in increasing acceptance of the goal itself as a desirable one to work toward. As we noted earlier, resistance is greatest when goals are difficult. People who participate in goal setting are more likely to accept even a difficult goal than one that is arbitrarily assigned to them, because individuals are more committed to choices in which they have a voice. Thus, although participative goals may have no superiority over assigned goals when acceptance is taken as a given, participation does increase the probability that more difficult goals will be agreed to and acted upon.

Studies testing goal-setting theory have demonstrated the superiority of specific and challenging goals as motivating forces. Although we can't conclude that having employees participate in the goal-setting process is *always* desirable, participation is probably preferable to assignment when you expect resistance to difficult challenges. As an overall conclusion, therefore, we have significant evidence that intentions—as articulated in terms of goals—are a potent motivating force.

The observant reader may have noted what appears to be a contradiction between the findings on achievement motivation and goal setting. Is it a contradiction that achievement motivation is stimulated by moderately challenging goals, while goal-setting theory says motivation is maximized by difficult goals? The answer is No, for two reasons. First, goal-setting theory deals with people in general. The conclusions on achievement motivation are based only on people who have a high *nAch,* and probably less than ten to twenty percent of North Americans are naturally high achievers. So difficult goals are still recommended for the majority of workers. Second, goal setting's conclusions apply to those who accept, and are committed to, the goals. Difficult goals will lead to higher performance only if they are accepted.

Reinforcement Theory

A counterpoint to goal-setting theory is reinforcement theory. The former is a cognitive approach, proposing that an individual's purposes direct his or her actions. In **reinforcement theory** we have a behavioristic approach, which argues that reinforcement conditions behavior. The two theories are clearly at odds philosophically. Reinforcement theorists see behavior as environmentally caused; internal cognitive events are not matters for concern. What controls behavior are reinforcers—any consequences that, when immediately following a response, increase the probability that the behavior will be repeated.

Reinforcement theory ignores the inner state of the individual and concentrates solely on what happens to a person when he or she takes some action. Because it does not concern itself with what initiates behavior, it is not, strictly speaking, a theory of motivation. But it does provide a powerful means of analysis of what controls behavior, and it is for that reason that it is typically considered in discussions of motivation.

The last chapter introduced the law of effect (behavior is a function of its consequences) and showed that reinforcers (consequences) condition behavior and help explain how people learn. The law of effect and the concept of reinforcement also help explain motivation. A large amount of research indicates that people will exert more effort on tasks that are reinforced than on tasks that are not.[6] Reinforcement *is* undoubtedly an important influence on work behavior. What people do on their jobs and the amount of effort they allocate to various tasks are affected by the consequences of their behavior. But reinforcement is not the single explanation for differences in employee motivation. Goals, for instance, have an impact on motivation; so, too, do levels of achievement motivation, inequities in rewards, and expectations.

Equity Theory

Employees don't work in a vacuum. They make comparisons. If someone offered you $40,000 a year for your first job upon graduation from college, you'd probably grab at the offer and report to work enthused and certainly satisfied with your pay. How would you react, however, if you found out a month or so into the job that a co-worker—another recent graduate, your age, with comparable grades from a comparable college—was getting $45,000 a year? You'd probably be upset! Even though, in absolute terms, $40,000 is a lot of money for a new graduate to make (and you know it!), that suddenly isn't the issue. The issue now centers around relative rewards and what you believe is fair. There is enough evidence for us to conclude that employees compare their own job inputs and outcomes with those of others and that inequities can influence the degree of effort that employees exert.[7]

Equity theory says that employees weigh what they put into a job situation (input) against what they get from it (outcome) and then compare their input-outcome ratio with the input-outcome ratio of relevant others. If they perceive their ratio to be equal to that of the relevant others with whom they compare themselves, a state of equity is said to exist. They feel that their situation is fair, that justice prevails. If the ratios are unequal, inequity exists; that is, the employees tend to view themselves as underrewarded or overrewarded. When inequities occur, employees will attempt to correct them.

The referent that employees choose to compare themselves against is an important variable in equity theory. The three referent categories have been classified as "other," "system," and "self." The "other" category includes other individuals with similar jobs in the same organization and also includes friends, neighbors, or professional associates. On the basis of information that employees receive through word of mouth, newspapers, and magazines, on such issues as executive salaries or a recent union contract, employees can compare their pay with that of others.

The "system" category considers organizational pay policies and procedures as well as the administration of this system. It considers organizationwide pay policies, both implied and explicit. Precedents set by the organization in terms of allocation of pay would be a major determinant in this category.

The "self" category refers to input-outcome ratios that are unique to the individual. This category is influenced by such criteria as past jobs or family commitments.

The choice of a particular set of referents is related to the information available about referents as well as to their perceived relevance. Equity theory purports that, when employees envision an inequity, they may make one or more of five choices:

1. Distort either their own or others' inputs or outcomes
2. Behave in some way so as to induce others to change their inputs or outcomes
3. Behave in some way so as to change their own inputs or outcomes
4. Choose a different comparison referent
5. Quit their job

Equity theory recognizes that individuals are concerned not only with the absolute amount of rewards they receive for their efforts but also with the relationship of that amount to what others receive. Inputs, such as effort, experience, education, and competence, are compared with outcomes such as salary levels, raises, recognition, and other factors. When people perceive an imbalance in their input-outcome ratio relative to others, tension is created. This tension provides the basis for motivation, as people strive for what they perceive as equity and fairness.

Specifically, the theory establishes four propositions relating to inequitable pay:

1. *Given payment by time, overrewarded employees will produce more than equitably paid employees.* Hourly and salaried employees will generate a high quantity or quality of production in order to increase the input side of the ratio and bring about equity.

2. *Given payment by quantity of production, overrewarded employees will produce fewer but higher-quality units than equitably paid employees.* Individuals paid on a piece-rate basis will increase their effort to achieve equity, which can result in greater quality or quantity. Increases in quantity, however, will only increase inequity, since every unit produced results in further overpayment. Therefore, effort is directed toward increasing quality rather than quantity.

3. *Given payment by time, underrewarded employees will produce less or a poorer quality of output.* Effort will be decreased, and the result will be lower productivity or poorer quality of output than that produced by equitably paid employees.

4. *Given payment by quantity of production, underrewarded employees will produce a large number of low-quality units in comparison with equitably paid employees.* Employees on piece-rate pay plans can bring about equity because trading off quality of output for quantity will result in an increase in rewards with little or no increase in contributions.

A review of the recent research tends to consistently confirm the equity thesis: Employee motivation is influenced significantly by relative rewards as well as by absolute rewards. When employees perceive inequity, they will act to correct the situation. The result might be lower or higher productivity, improved or reduced quality of output, increased absenteeism, or voluntary resignation.

The preceding does not mean that equity theory is without problems. The theory leaves some key issues unclear. For instance, how do employees select who is included in the "other" referent category? How do they define inputs and outcomes? How do they combine and weigh their inputs and outcomes to arrive at totals? When and how do the factors change over time? Regardless of these problems, equity theory has an impressive amount of research support and offers us some important insights into employee motivation.

Expectancy Theory

The most comprehensive explanation of motivation is expectancy theory.[8] Though it, too, has its critics, most of the research evidence supports the theory. Essentially, **expectancy theory** argues that the strength of a tendency to act in a certain way depends on the strength of an expectation that the act will be followed by a given outcome and on the attractiveness of that outcome to the individual. Therefore, it includes these three variables:

1. *Attractiveness:* The importance the individual places on the potential outcome or reward that can be achieved on the job. This variable considers the unsatisfied needs of the individual.

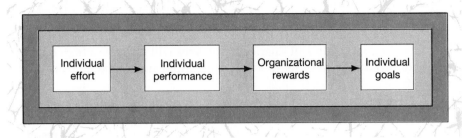

Exhibit 4-4
Simplified Expectancy Model

2. *Performance-reward linkage:* The degree to which the individual believes that performing at a particular level will lead to the attainment of a desired outcome.

3. *Effort-performance linkage:* The probability perceived by the individual that exerting a given amount of effort will lead to performance.

Although this theory may sound pretty complex, it really isn't that difficult to visualize. Whether one has the desire to produce at any given time depends on one's particular goals and one's perception of the relative worth of performance as a path to the attainment of those goals.

Exhibit 4-4 is a considerable simplification of expectancy theory but expresses its major contentions. The strength of a person's motivation to perform (effort) depends on how strongly she believes she can achieve what she attempts. If she achieves this goal (performance), will she be adequately rewarded and, if she is rewarded by the organization, will the reward satisfy her individual goals? Let us consider the four steps inherent in the theory.

First, what perceived outcomes does the job offer the employee? Outcomes may be positive: pay, security, companionship, trust, fringe benefits, a chance to use talent or skills, congenial relationships. On the other hand, employees may view the outcomes as negative: fatigue, boredom, frustration, anxiety, harsh supervision, threat of dismissal. Importantly, reality is not relevant here; the critical issue is what the individual employee *perceives* the outcome to be, regardless of whether her perceptions are accurate.

Second, how attractive do employees consider these outcomes? Are they valued positively, negatively, or neutrally? This is obviously an internal issue to the individual and considers personal attitudes, personality, and needs. The individual who finds a particular outcome attractive—that is, positively valued—will prefer attaining it to not attaining it. Others may find it negative and, therefore, prefer not to attain it. Still others may be neutral.

Third, what kind of behavior must the employee exhibit in order to achieve these outcomes? The outcomes are not likely to have any effect on the individual employee's performance unless the employee knows, clearly and unambiguously, what she must do in order to achieve them. For example, what is "doing well" in terms of performance appraisal? On what criteria will the employee's performance be judged?

Fourth and last, how does the employee view her chances of doing what is asked of her? After the employee has considered her own competencies and her ability to control those variables that will determine her success, what probability does she place on successful attainment?

Let's highlight some of the issues that expectancy theory has brought forward. First, it emphasizes payoffs, or rewards. As a result, we have to believe that the rewards the organization is offering align with what the employee wants. It is a theory based on self-interest, wherein each individual seeks to maximize his or her expected satisfaction. We have to be concerned with the attractiveness of rewards; this aspect requires an understanding and knowledge of what value the individual puts on organizational payoffs. We want to reward individuals with those things they value positively. Second, expectancy theory emphasizes expected behaviors. Does the person know what is expected of her and how she will be appraised? Finally, the theory is concerned with the individual's expectations. What is realistic is irrelevant. An employee's own expectations of performance, reward, and goal satisfaction outcomes, not the objective outcomes themselves, will determine her level of effort.

Don't Forget: Motivation Theories Are Culture-Bound!

Most current motivation theories were developed in the United States by Americans and about Americans. Maybe the most blatant pro-American characteristics inherent in these theories is the strong emphasis on individualism and masculinity. For instance, both goal-setting and expectancy theories emphasize goal accomplishment as well as rational and individual thought. Let's take a look at how this bias has affected a few of the motivation theories introduced in this chapter.

Maslow's hierarchy of needs theory argues that people start at the physiological level and then move progressively up the hierarchy in this order: physiological, safety, social, esteem, and self-actualization. This hierarchy, if it has any application at all, aligns with American culture. In other cultures, the order of importance might be different. In countries such as Japan, Greece, or Mexico, where uncertainty avoidance characteristics are strong, security needs would be on top of the needs hierarchy. Countries that score high on femininity characteristics—such as Denmark, Sweden, Norway, the Netherlands, and Finland—would have social needs on top. We would predict, for instance, that group work will motivate employees more when the country's culture scores high on the femininity criterion.

Another motivation concept that clearly has a U.S. bias is the achievement need. The view that a high achievement need acts as an internal motivator presupposes two cultural characteristics—a willingness to accept a moderate degree of risk (which excludes countries with strong uncertainty avoidance characteristics) and a concern with performance (which applies almost singularly to countries with strong masculinity characteristics). This combination is found in Anglo-American countries such as the United States, Canada, and Great Britain. On the other hand, these characteristics are relatively absent in countries such as Chile and Portugal.

Goal-setting theory is also certainly culture-bound. It is well adapted to the United States because its key components align reasonably well with U.S. culture. It assumes that subordinates will be reasonably independent (not too high a score on power distance), managers and subordinates will seek challenging goals (low in uncertainty avoidance), and performance is considered important by both (high in masculinity). Goal-setting theory's recommendations are not likely to increase motivation in countries in which the opposite conditions exist, such as France, Portugal, and Chile.

mplications for Managers

Many of the theories presented in this chapter have demonstrated reasonably strong predictive value. How does a manager concerned with motivating employees apply these theories? Certain general suggestions can be extracted for application, at least for managers in North America. For instance, the following recommendations are consistent with the findings in this chapter: (1) Recognize individual differences; (2) match people to jobs; (3) use goals; (4) ensure that goals are perceived as attainable; (5) individualize rewards; (6) link rewards to performance; and (7) check the system for equity. These suggestions, of course, would need to be modified to reflect cultural differences outside of North America.

The importance of motivating employees today justifies more specifics than the concepts we've just offered. The next chapter builds on the concepts we've presented here, providing a review of the more popular motivation techniques and programs.

Motivation: From Concepts to Applications

After reading this chapter, you should be able to:

1. Identify the four ingredients common to MBO programs

2. Outline the five-step problem-solving model in OB Mod

3. Explain why managers might want to use employee involvement programs

4. Define quality circles

5. Explain how ESOPs can increase employee motivation

6. Describe the link between skill-based pay plans and motivation theories

It's one thing to be able to recite the principles of motivation theories; it's another to see how, as a manager, you could use them. In this chapter, we focus on how to apply motivation concepts—that is, how to link theories to practice.

In the following pages, we'll review motivation techniques and programs that have gained varying degrees of acceptance in practice. For each of the techniques and programs we review, we'll specifically address how they build on one or more of the motivation theories covered in the previous chapter.

Management by Objectives

Goal-setting theory has an impressive base of research support. But as a manager, how do you make goal setting operational? The best answer to that question is: Install a management by objectives (MBO) program.

What Is MBO?

Management by objectives (MBO) emphasizes participatively set goals that are tangible, verifiable, and measurable. It's not a new idea. In fact, it was originally proposed by Peter Drucker more than forty years ago as a means of using goals to motivate people rather than to control them.[1] Today, no introduction to basic management concepts would be complete without a discussion of MBO.

MBO's appeal undoubtedly lies in its emphasis on converting overall organizational objectives into specific objectives for organizational units and individual members. MBO operationalizes the concept of objectives by devising a process by which objectives cascade down through the organization. As depicted in Exhibit 5-1, the organization's overall objectives are translated into specific objectives for each succeeding level (that is, divisional, departmental, individual) in the organization. But because lower-unit managers jointly participate in setting their own goals, MBO works from the "bottom up" as well as from the "top down." The result is a hierarchy of objectives that links objectives at one level to those at the next level. And for the individual employee, MBO provides specific personal performance objectives. Each person, therefore, has an identified specific contribution to make to his or her unit's performance. If all the individuals achieve their goals, then their unit's goals will be attained and the organization's overall objectives will become a reality.

There are four ingredients common to MBO programs: goal specificity, participative decision making, an explicit time period, and performance feedback. The objectives in MBO should be concise statements of expected accomplishments. It is not enough, for example, merely to state a desire to cut costs, improve service, or increase quality. Such desires have to be converted into tangible objectives that can be measured and evaluated. To cut departmental costs *by seven per-*

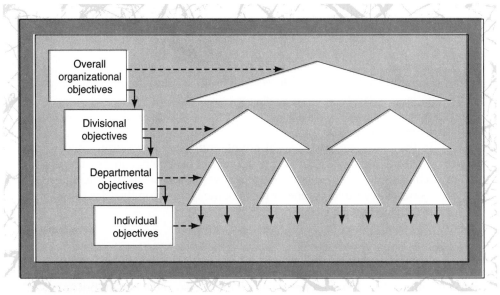

Exhibit 5-1
Cascading of Objectives

cent, to improve service by ensuring that all telephone orders are processed *within twenty-four hours of receipt,* or to increase quality by keeping returns to *less than one percent of sales* are examples of specific objectives.

The objectives in MBO are not unilaterally set by the boss and then assigned to subordinates. MBO replaces imposed goals with participatively determined goals. The superior and subordinate jointly choose the goals and agree on how they will be measured.

Each objective has a specific time period in which it is to be completed. Typically the time period is three months, six months, or a year. So managers and subordinates have not only specific objectives but also stipulated time periods in which to accomplish them.

The final ingredient in an MBO program is feedback on performance. MBO seeks to give continuous feedback on progress toward goals so that individuals can monitor and correct their own actions. Continuous feedback, supplemented by more formal periodic managerial evaluations, takes place at the top of the organization as well as at the bottom. The vice president of sales, for instance, has objectives for overall sales and for each of his or her major products. He or she will monitor ongoing sales reports to determine progress toward the sales division's objectives. Similarly, district sales managers have objectives, as does each salesperson in the field. Feedback in terms of sales and performance is provided to let all these people know how they are doing. At formal appraisal meetings, superiors and subordinates can review progress toward goals and further feedback can be provided.

Linking MBO and Goal-Setting Theory

Goal-setting theory demonstrates that hard goals result in a higher level of individual performance than do easy goals, that specific hard goals result in higher levels of performance than do no goals at all or the generalized goal of "do your best," and that feedback on one's performance leads to higher performance. Compare these findings with MBO.

MBO directly advocates specific goals and feedback. MBO implies, rather than explicitly states, that goals must be perceived as feasible. Consistent with goal setting, MBO would be most effective when the goals are difficult enough to require the person to do some stretching.

The only area of possible disagreement between MBO and goal-setting theory is related to the issue of participation—MBO strongly advocates it, whereas goal-setting theory demonstrates that assigning goals to subordinates frequently works just as well. The major benefit to using participation, however, is that it appears to induce individuals to establish more difficult goals.

MBO in Practice

How widely used is MBO? Reviews of studies that have sought to answer that question suggest that it's a popular technique. You'll find MBO programs in many business, health care, educational, government, and nonprofit organizations.[2]

MBO's popularity should not be construed to mean that it always works. There are a number of documented cases in which MBO was implemented but failed to meet management's expectations. A close look at those cases, however, indicates that the problems rarely lie with MBO's basic components. Rather, the culprits tend to be factors such as unrealistic expectations regarding results, lack of top-management commitment, and an inability or unwillingness by management to allocate rewards based on goal accomplishment. Nevertheless, MBO provides managers with the vehicle for implementing goal-setting theory.

*B*ehavior Modification

A now-classic study took place more than twenty years ago with freight packers at Emery Air Freight (now part of Federal Express).[3] Emery's management wanted packers to aggregate shipments into freight containers rather than handling many separate items. Management believed that using containers would save money. When packers were asked what percentage of shipments they put in containers, the standard reply was ninety percent. An analysis by Emery found, however, that the container use rate was only forty-five percent. In order to encourage employees to use containers, management established a program of feedback and positive reinforcements. Each packer was instructed to keep a checklist of his or her daily packings, both in containers and not. At the end of each day, the packer computed his or her container use rate. Almost unbelievably, container use jumped to more than ninety percent on the first day of the program and held to that level. Emery reported that this simple program of feedback and positive reinforcements saved the company $2 million over a three-year period.

This program at Emery Air Freight illustrates the use of behavior modification, or what has become more popularly called **OB Mod.**[4] It represents the application of reinforcement theory to individuals in the work setting.

What Is OB Mod?

The typical OB Mod program, as shown in Exhibit 5-2, follows a five-step problem-solving model: (1) Identify performance-related behaviors; (2) measure the behaviors; (3) identify behavioral contingencies; (4) develop and implement an intervention strategy; and (5) evaluate performance improvement.[5]

Everything an employee does on his or her job is not equally important in terms of performance outcomes. The first step in OB Mod, therefore, is to identify the critical behaviors that have a significant impact on the employee's job performance. These are those five to ten percent of behaviors that may account for up to seventy or eighty percent of each employee's performance. Using containers whenever possible by freight packers at Emery Air Freight is an example of a critical behavior.

The second step requires the manager to develop some baseline performance information; that is, the number of times the identified behavior is occurring under present conditions. In our freight-packing example at Emery, this would have been that forty-five percent of all shipments were containerized.

The third step is to perform a functional analysis to identify the behavioral contingencies or consequences of performance. This step tells the manager which cues emit the behavior and the consequences that are currently maintaining it. At Emery Air Freight, social norms and the greater difficulty in packing containers were the cues. Those factors encouraged the practice of packing items separately. Moreover, the consequences for continuing this behavior, before the OB Mod intervention, were social acceptance and escaping more demanding work.

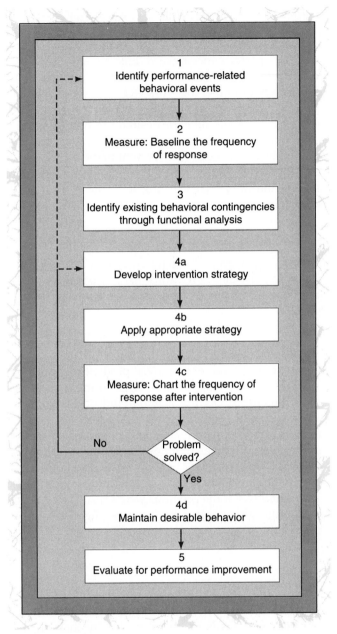

Exhibit 5-2
Steps in OB Mod

Source: Adapted by permission of the publisher from *Personnel,* July–August © 1974. Fred Luthans, American Management Association, New York. All rights reserved.

Once the functional analysis is complete, the manager is ready to develop and implement an intervention strategy to strengthen desirable performance behaviors and weaken undesirable behaviors. The appropriate strategy will entail changing some element of the performance-reward linkage—structure, processes, technology, groups, or the task—with the goal of making high-level performance more rewarding. In the Emery example, the work technology was altered to require the keeping of a checklist. The checklist plus the computation, at the end of the day, of a container use rate acted to reinforce the desired behavior of using containers.

The final step in OB Mod is to evaluate performance improvement. In the Emery intervention, the immediate improvement in the container use rate demonstrated that behavioral change took place. That it rose to ninety percent and held at that level further indicates that learning took place. That is, the employees underwent a relatively permanent change in behavior.

Linking OB Mod and Reinforcement Theory

Reinforcement theory relies on positive reinforcement, shaping, and recognizing the impact of different schedules of reinforcement on behavior. OB Mod uses these concepts to provide managers with a powerful and proven means for changing employee behavior.

OB Mod in Practice

OB Mod has been used to improve employee productivity and to reduce errors, absenteeism, tardiness, and accident rates.[6] Organizations such as General Electric, Weyerhauser, the city of Detroit, Dayton-Hudson Stores, and Xerox report impressive results using OB Mod.[7] For instance, a few years back, frustrated by customer complaints, Xerox's top management changed the basis for its executive bonus plan from traditional quotas to long-term customer satisfaction.[8] The company now surveys 40,000 customers worldwide every month to determine the percentage who are satisfied with Xerox products and service. At the start of each year, top management looks at the previous year's results and develops a goal. In 1989, the target was eighty-six percent. Each succeeding year the goal has gone up; it is now 100 percent.

*E*mployee Involvement Programs

At a General Electric lighting plant in Ohio, work teams perform many tasks and assume many of the responsibilities once handled by their supervisors. In fact, when the plant was faced with a recent decline in the demand for the tubes it produces, the workers decided first to slow production and eventually to lay themselves off. Marketing people at USAA, a large insurance company, meet in a conference room for an hour every week to discuss ways in which they can improve the quality of their work and increase productivity. Management has implemented many of their suggestions. Childress Buick, an automobile dealer in Phoenix, allows its salespeople to negotiate and finalize deals with customers without any approval from management. The laws of Germany, France, Denmark, Sweden, and Austria require companies to have elected representatives from their employee groups as members of their board of directors. The common theme throughout these examples is that they all illustrate employee involvement programs.

What Is Employee Involvement?

Employee involvement has become a convenient catchall term to cover a variety of techniques.[9] For instance, it encompasses such popular ideas as employee participation or participative management, workplace democracy, empowerment, and employee ownership. Our position is that, although each of these ideas has some unique characteristics, they all have a common core—that of employee involvement.

So what specifically do we mean by **employee involvement?** We define it as a participative process that uses the entire capacity of employees and is designed to encourage increased commitment to the organization's success.[10] The underlying logic is that involving workers in decisions that will affect them and increasing their autonomy and control over their work lives will make employees more motivated, more committed to the organization, more productive, and more satisfied with their jobs.

Does that mean that *participation* and *employee involvement* are synonyms? No. *Participation* is a more limited term. It's a subset within the larger framework of employee involvement. All of the employee involvement programs we'll describe include some form of employee participation but the term *participation*, per se, is too narrow and limiting.

Examples of Employee Involvement Programs

In this section, we'll review four forms of employee involvement: participative management, representative participation, quality circles, and employee stock ownership plans.

Participative Management. The distinct characteristic common to all **participative management** programs is the use of joint decision making. That is, subordinates actually share a significant degree of decision-making power with their immediate superiors.

Participative management has, at times, been promoted as a panacea for poor morale and low productivity. One author even argued that participative management is an ethical imperative.[11] But participative management is not appropriate for every organization or every work unit. For it to work, there must be adequate time to participate, the issues in which employees get involved must be relevant to them, employees must have the ability (intelligence, technical knowledge, communication skills) to participate, and the organization's culture must support employee involvement.[12]

Dozens of studies have been conducted on the participation-performance relationship. The findings, however, are mixed.[13] When the research is looked at carefully, it appears that participation typically has only a modest influence on variables such as employee productivity, motivation, and job satisfaction. Of course, that conclusion doesn't mean that the use of participative management can't be beneficial under the right conditions. What it says, however, is that the use of participation is no sure means for improving employee performance.

Representative Participation.   Almost every country in Western Europe has some type of legislation requiring companies to practice **representative participation.** That is, rather than participate directly in decisions, workers are represented by a small group of employees who actually participate. Representative participation has been called "the most widely legislated form of employee involvement around the world."[14]

The goal of representative participation is to redistribute power within an organization, putting labor on a more equal footing with the interests of management and stockholders.

The two most common forms that representative participation takes are works councils and board representatives. **Works councils** link employees with management. They are groups of nominated or elected employees who must be consulted when management makes decisions involving personnel. For example, in the Netherlands, if a Dutch company is taken over by another firm, the former's works council must be informed at an early stage, and if the council objects, it has thirty days to seek a court injunction to stop the takeover. **Board representatives** are employees who sit on a company's board of directors and represent the interests of the firm's employees. In some countries, large companies may be legally required to make sure that employee representatives have the same number of board seats as stockholder representatives.

The overall influence of representative participation on working employees seems to be minimal. For instance, the evidence suggests that works councils are dominated by management and have little impact on employees or the organization. And, although this form of employee involvement might increase the motivation and satisfaction of the individuals who are doing the representing, there is little evidence that this effect trickles down to the operating employees whom they represent. Overall, "the greatest value of representative participation is symbolic. If one is interested in changing employee attitudes or in improving organizational performance, representative participation would be a poor choice."[15]

Quality Circles.   "Probably the most widely discussed and undertaken formal style of employee involvement is the quality circle."[16] The quality circle concept is frequently mentioned as one of the techniques that Japanese firms use that has allowed them to make high-quality products at low costs. Originally begun in the United States and exported to Japan in the 1950s, the quality circle became quite popular in North America and Europe during the 1980s.

What is a **quality circle?** It's a work group of eight to ten employees and supervisors who have a shared area of responsibility. They meet regularly—typically once a week, on company time and on company premises—to discuss their quality problems, investigate causes of the problems, recommend solutions, and take corrective actions. They take over the responsibility for solving quality problems, and they generate and evaluate their own feedback. But management typically retains control over the final decision regarding implementation of recommended solutions. Of course, it is not presumed that employees inherently have this ability to analyze and solve quality problems. Therefore, part of the quality circle concept includes teaching participating employees group communi-

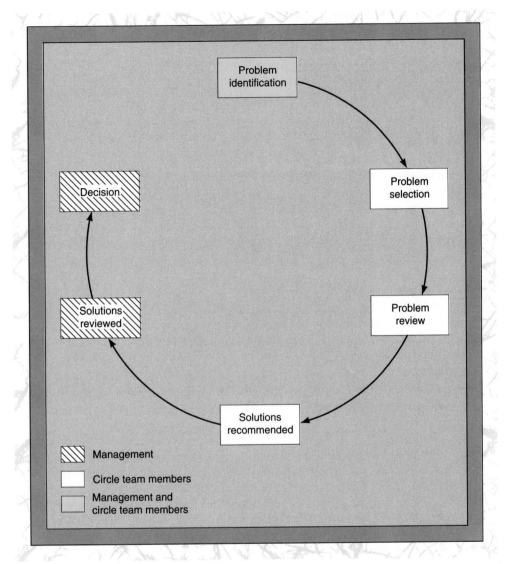

Exhibit 5-3
How a Typical Quality Circle Operates

cation skills, various quality strategies, and measurement and problem analysis techniques. Exhibit 5-3 describes a typical quality circle process.

Do quality circles improve employee productivity and satisfaction? A review of the evidence indicates that they are highly likely to positively affect productivity. They tend to show little or no effect on employee satisfaction. And, although many studies report positive results on productivity, such results are by no means guaranteed.[17] The failure of many quality circle programs to produce measurable benefits has caused a large number of them to be discontinued.

69
Chapter 5
Motivation: From Concepts
to Applications

Employee Stock Ownership Plans. The final employee involvement approach we'll discuss is **employee stock ownership plans (ESOPs).** Employee stock ownership plans are company-established benefit plans in which employees acquire stock as part of their benefits. Approximately twenty percent of Polaroid, for example, is owned by its employees. Fifty-five percent of United Airlines is owned by its employees. Avis Corporation and Weirton Steel are 100 percent owned by their employees.

In the typical ESOP, an employee stock ownership trust is created. Companies contribute either stock or cash to buy stock for the trust and allocate the stock to employees. Although employees hold stock in their company, they usually cannot take physical possession of their shares or sell them as long as they're still employed at the company.

The research on ESOPs indicates that they increase employee satisfaction. In addition, they frequently result in higher performance. For instance, one study compared 45 ESOPs against 238 conventional companies.[18] The ESOPs outperformed the conventional firms in terms of both job creation and sales growth.

Linking Employee Involvement Programs and Motivation Theories

Employee involvement draws on several motivation theories discussed in the previous chapter. For instance, Theory Y is consistent with participative management, and Theory X aligns with the more traditional autocratic style of managing people. In terms of motivation-hygiene theory, employee involvement programs could provide employees with intrinsic motivation by increasing opportunities for growth, responsibility, and involvement in the work itself.

Employee Involvement Programs in Practice

Germany, France, the Netherlands, and the Scandinavian countries have firmly established the principle of industrial democracy in Europe, and other nations, including Japan and Israel, have traditionally practiced some form of representative participation for decades. Participative management and representative participation were much slower to gain ground in North American organizations. But nowadays, employee involvement programs that stress participation have become the norm. Some managers continue to resist sharing decision-making power, but the pressure is on managers to give up their autocratic decision-making style in favor of a more participative, supportive, coaching-like role.

What about quality circles? How popular are they in practice? The names of companies that have used quality circles reads like a *Who's Who* of corporate America: Hewlett-Packard, Westinghouse, General Electric, Texas Instruments, Xerox, Eastman Kodak, Polaroid, Procter & Gamble, General Motors, Ford, IBM, Motorola, American Airlines. But, as we noted, the success of quality circles has been far from overwhelming. They were popular in the 1980s, largely because they were easy to implement. In the 1990s, many organizations have dropped their quality circles and replaced them with more comprehensive team-based structures (which we'll discuss in Chapter 13).

And what about ESOPs? They are becoming a popular form of employee involvement program. They've grown from just a handful in 1974 to around 10,000 now, covering more than 10 million employees.

Variable-Pay Programs

For more than twenty-five years, Nucor Steel has had an incentive compensation plan in place that pays bonuses of as much as 150 percent of base to employees. Bonuses are calculated on the basis of the company's profitability. P. Roy Vagelos, CEO of the pharmaceutical giant Merck & Co., took an eleven percent reduction in salary and bonus in 1993, because his pay package is closely tied to his company's performance and Merck's profits fell by eleven percent in 1993. Bob Baker, a petroleum geologist at a small Texas oil exploration firm, earned about $150,000 in 1993—more than triple his base salary. How did he make so much money? He gets performance bonuses based on his ability to find high-producing wells! The common thread in each of those examples is that they all illustrate variable-pay programs.

What Are Variable-Pay Programs?

Piece-rate plans, wage incentives, profit sharing, bonuses, and gainsharing are all forms of **variable-pay programs.** What differentiates these forms of compensation from more traditional programs is that a person is paid not only for time on the job or seniority; a portion of an employee's pay is based on some individual or organizational measure of performance or both. Unlike more traditional base-pay programs, variable pay is not an annuity. There is no guarantee that just because you made $60,000 last year you'll make the same amount this year. With variable pay, earnings fluctuate with the measure of performance.

It is precisely the fluctuation in variable pay that has made these programs attractive to management. It turns part of an organization's fixed labor costs into a variable cost, thereby reducing expenses when performance declines. In addition, when pay is tied to performance, earnings recognize contribution rather than being a form of entitlement. Low performers find, over time, that their pay stagnates, and high performers enjoy pay increases commensurate with their contribution.

Four of the more widely used of the variable-pay programs are piece-rate wages, bonuses, profit sharing, and gainsharing. Piece-rate wages have been around for nearly a century. They have long been popular as a means for compensating production workers. In **piece-rate pay plans,** workers are paid a fixed sum for each unit of production completed. A system in which an employee gets no base salary and is paid only for what he or she produces is a pure piece-rate plan. People who work ballparks selling peanuts and soda pop frequently are paid this way. They might get to keep twenty-five cents for every bag of peanuts they sell. If they sell 200 bags during a game, they make $50. If they sell only forty bags, their take is a mere $10. The harder they work and the more peanuts they sell, the more they earn. Many organizations use a modified piece-rate plan, in which employees earn a base hourly wage plus a piece-rate differential. So a legal typist might be paid $6 an hour plus twenty cents per page. Such modified plans provide a floor under an employee's earnings while still offering a productivity incentive.

Bonuses can be paid exclusively to executives or to all employees. For instance, annual bonuses in the millions of dollars are not uncommon in American corporations. Robert A. Watson received a $10 million incentive bonus in 1993 for his success in dismantling Westinghouse's financial operation. Increasingly, bonus plans are taking on a larger net within organizations to include lower-ranking employees. These plans also are tending to combine individual, group, and organizationwide performance variables. At AT&T, the biggest piece of an individual's bonus is based on overall corporate performance. But at Scott Paper, approximately seventy percent of the bonus is tied to the performance of an individual's department or division, with the remaining thirty percent linked to individual success. Bonuses amounting to ten to twenty-five percent of base salary are not unusual at Scott.

Profit-sharing plans are organizationwide programs that distribute compensation based on some established formula designed around a company's profitability. These can be direct cash outlays or, particularly in the case of top managers, allocated as stock options. For example, executives such as Michael Eisner, the CEO at Disney, can earn over $200 million in one year. Almost all of it would come from cashing in stock options previously granted on the basis of company profit performance.

The variable-pay program that has gotten the most attention in recent years is undoubtedly **gainsharing.** This is a formula-based group incentive plan. Improvements in group productivity—from one period to another—determine the total amount of money that is to be allocated. And the division of productivity savings can be split between the company and employees in any number of ways, but 50-50 is pretty typical.

Isn't gainsharing the same thing as profit sharing? They're similar but not the same thing. By focusing on productivity gains rather than on profits, gainsharing rewards specific behaviors that are less influenced by external factors than profits are. Employees in a gainsharing plan can receive incentive awards even when the organization isn't profitable.

Do variable-pay programs work? Do they increase motivation and productivity? The answer is a qualified Yes. Gainsharing, for example, has been found to improve productivity in most cases and often has a positive impact on employee attitudes. An American Management Association study of eighty-three companies that used gainsharing also found, on average, that grievances dropped eighty-three percent, absences fell eighty-four percent, and lost-time accidents decreased by sixty-nine percent.[19]

Linking Variable-Pay Programs and Expectancy Theory

Variable pay is compatible with expectancy theory predictions. Specifically, individuals should perceive a strong relationship between their performance and the rewards they receive if motivation is to be maximized. If rewards are allocated completely on nonperformance factors—such as seniority or job title—then employees are likely to reduce their effort.

The evidence supports the importance of this linkage, especially for operative employees working under piece-rate systems. For example, one study of 400 manufacturing firms found that those companies with wage incentive plans achieved forty-three to sixty-four percent greater productivity than those without such plans.[20]

Group and organizationwide incentives reinforce and encourage employees to sublimate personal goals for the best interests of their department or the organization. Group-based performance incentives are also a natural extension for organizations that are trying to build a strong team ethic. Linking rewards to team performance encourages employees to make extra efforts to help their team succeed.

Variable-Pay Programs in Practice

Variable pay is a concept that is rapidly replacing the annual cost-of-living raise. One reason, as cited above, is its motivational power—but don't ignore the cost implications. Bonuses, gainsharing, and other variable-reward programs avoid the fixed expense of permanent salary boosts.

Pay-for-performance has been "in" for compensating managers for more than a decade. The new trend has been expanding this practice to nonmanagerial employees. In 1989, forty-four percent of companies had pay-for-performance plans for employees other than senior management. That figure had increased to fifty-one percent by 1991.[21]

A 1993 survey of 382 medium-sized and large companies found that approximately three-quarters used variable pay to boost productivity.[22] Another survey found that fourteen percent of U.S. companies used performance-based bonuses to completely replace the annual raise in 1993, and that figure had increased to twenty-one percent by early 1994.[23]

Gainsharing's popularity seems to be narrowly focused among large, unionized manufacturing companies.[24] It is currently being used in about 2,000 companies including such major firms as Bell & Howell, American Safety Razor, Champion Spark Plug, Cincinnati Milacron, Eaton, Firestone Tire, Hooker Chemical, and Mead Paper.

Skill-Based Pay Plans

Organizations hire people for their skills, then typically put them in jobs and pay them on the basis of their job title or rank. So the director of corporate sales earns $120,000 a year, the regional sales managers make $75,000, and the district sales managers get $60,000. But if organizations hire people because of their competencies, why don't they pay them for those same competencies? Some organizations do.

What Are Skill-Based Pay Plans?

Skill-based pay is an alternative to job-based pay. Rather than having an individual's job title define his or her pay category, **skill-based pay** (or also sometimes called *competency-based pay*) sets pay levels on the basis of how many skills employees have or how many jobs they can do.[25] For instance, at the Polaroid Corporation, the highest pay you can earn as a machine operator is $14 an hour.

But the company has a skill-based pay plan. So if machine operators can broaden their capabilities to include additional skills such as material accounting, maintenance of equipment, and quality inspection, they can earn up to ten percent more. If they can learn some of their supervisor's skills, they can earn even more.

What's the appeal of skill-based pay plans? From management's perspective: flexibility. Filling staffing needs is easier when employee skills are interchangeable. This is particularly true in the 1990s, as many organizations cut the size of their work force. Downsizing requires more generalists and fewer specialists. Skill-based pay encourages employees to acquire a broad range of skills. But there are other benefits to skill-based pay. It facilitates communication throughout the organization because people gain a better understanding of others' jobs. It lessens dysfunctional "protection of territory" behavior. Where skill-based pay exists, you're less likely to hear the phrase, "It's not my job!" Skill-based pay also helps meet the needs of ambitious employees who confront minimal advancement opportunities. These people can increase their earnings and knowledge without a promotion in job title. Finally, skill-based pay appears to lead to performance improvements. A broad-based survey of Fortune 1000 firms found that sixty percent of those with skill-based pay rated their plans as successful or very successful in increasing organizational performance; only six percent considered them unsuccessful or very unsuccessful.[26]

What's the down side of skill-based pay? People can "top out"—learning all the skills the program calls for them to learn. Topping out can frustrate employees after they've become challenged by an environment of learning, growth, and continual pay raises. Skills can also become obsolete. Finally, skill-based plans don't address level of performance. They deal only with the issue of whether someone can perform the skill. For some skills—such as checking quality or leading a team—level of performance may be equivocal. Although it's possible to assess how well employees perform each of the skills and combine that assessment with a skill-based plan, doing so is not an inherent part of skill-based pay.

Linking Skill-Based Pay Plans to Motivation Theories

Skill-based pay plans are consistent with several motivation theories. Because they encourage employees to learn, expand their skills, and grow, they are consistent with Maslow's hierarchy of needs theory. Among employees whose lower-order needs are substantially satisfied, the opportunity to experience growth can be a motivator.

Paying people to expand their skill levels is also consistent with research on the achievement need. High achievers have a compelling drive to do things better or more efficiently. By learning new skills or improving the skills they already hold, high achievers will find their jobs more challenging.

There is also a link between reinforcement theory and skill-based pay. Skill-based pay encourages employees to develop their flexibility, to continue to learn, to cross-train, to be generalists rather than specialists, and to work cooperatively with others in the organization. To the degree that management wants employees to demonstrate such behaviors, skill-based pay should act as a reinforcer.

Skill-based pay may also have equity implications. When employees make their input-outcome comparisons, skills may provide a fairer input criterion for determining pay than factors such as seniority or education. To the degree that employees perceive skills as the critical variable in job performance, the use of skill-based pay may increase the perception of equity and help optimize employee motivation.

Skill-Based Pay in Practice

A number of studies have investigated the use and effectiveness of skill-based pay. The overall conclusion, based on these studies, is that use of skill-based pay is expanding and that it generally leads to higher employee performance and satisfaction.

The Fortune 1000 study, mentioned earlier, found a significant increase in skill-based pay plans between 1987 and 1990.[27] In 1990, fifty-one percent of large U.S. corporations used skill-based pay with at least some employees, an increase of more than twenty-five percent in just three years. But in the typical company that adopted skill-based pay, it applied to less than twenty percent of employees. Another study, covering a broader range of organizations, confirmed this trend. Among the 1,800 companies polled, ten percent were using skill-based pay in 1993, but twenty-five percent were expecting to have such a plan in place within a year.[28]

A survey of twenty-seven companies that pay employees for learning extra skills found that seventy to eighty-eight percent reported higher job satisfaction, product quality, or productivity. Some seventy to seventy-five percent cited lower operating costs or lower turnover.[29]

Skilled-based pay appears to be an idea whose time has come. As one expert noted, "Slowly, but surely, we're becoming a skill-based society where your market value is tied to what you can do and what your skill set is. In this new world where skills and knowledge are what really counts, it doesn't make sense to treat people as jobholders. It makes sense to treat them as people with specific skills and to pay them for those skills."[30]

mplications for Managers

Organizations have introduced a number of programs designed to increase employee motivation, productivity, and satisfaction. Importantly, these programs are grounded on basic motivation theories.

It's easy to criticize educators and researchers for their focus on building theories. Students and practitioners often think that these theories are unrealistic or irrelevant to solving real-life problems. This chapter makes a good rebuttal to those critics. It illustrates how tens of thousands of organizations and millions of managers, in countries around the globe, are using motivation theories to build practical incentive programs.

The five motivation programs we discussed in this chapter are not applicable to every organization or every manager's needs. But an understanding of these programs will help you design internal systems that can increase employee productivity and satisfaction.

*I*ndividual Decision Making

After reading this chapter, you should be able to:

1. Explain the six-step rational decision-making model and its assumptions

2. Identify three methods for stimulating individual creativity

3. Describe actions of the boundedly rational decision maker

4. Define *heuristics* and explain how they bias decisions

5. Explain escalation of commitment

6. Identify four decision-making styles

7. Explain the implications of stages of moral development to decision making

Individuals in organizations make decisions. Top managers, for instance, determine their organization's goals, what products or services to offer, how best to organize corporate headquarters, or where to locate a new manufacturing plant. Middle- and lower-level managers determine production schedules, select new employees, and decide how pay raises are to be allocated. The making of decisions, however, is not the sole province of managers. Nonmanagerial employees also make decisions that affect their jobs and the organizations they work for. The more obvious of these decisions might include whether to come to work on any given day, how much effort to put forward once at work, and whether to comply with a request made by the boss.

So all individuals in every organization regularly engage in **decision making;** that is, they make choices from among two or more alternatives. Undoubtedly, many of these choices are almost reflex actions, undertaken with little conscious thought. The boss asks you to complete a certain report by the end of the day and you comply, assuming the request is reasonable. In such instances, choices are still being made even though they don't require much thought. But when individuals confront new or important decisions, they can be expected to reason them out thoughtfully. Alternatives will be developed. Pros and cons will be weighed. The result is that what people do on their jobs is influenced by their decision processes.

In this chapter, we focus on two different approaches to understanding decision making. First we describe how decisions *should* be made. Then, we review a large body of evidence to show you how decisions actually are made in organizations. We conclude by offering some specific suggestions on how managers can improve their decision-making effectiveness.

How Should Decisions Be Made?

Let's begin by describing how individuals should behave in order to maximize a certain outcome. We call this the *rational decision-making process*.

The Rational Decision-Making Process

The optimizing decision maker is **rational**. That is, he or she makes consistent, value-maximizing choices within specified constraints. These choices are made following a six-step model. Moreover, specific assumptions underlie this model.

The Rational Model.   The six steps in the rational decision-making model are listed in Exhibit 6-1.[1] The model begins by *defining the problem*. A problem exists when there is a discrepancy between an existing and a desired state of affairs. If you calculate your monthly expenses and find you're spending $50 more than you allocated in your budget, you have defined a problem. Many poor decisions can be traced to the decision maker's overlooking a problem or incorrectly defining the problem.

1. Define the problem
2. Identify decision criteria
3. Weight the criteria
4. Generate alternatives
5. Rate each alternative on each criterion
6. Compute the optimal decision

Exhibit 6-1
The Six-Step Rational Decision-Making Model

Once a decision maker has defined the problem, he or she needs to *identify the decision criteria* that will be important in solving the problem. In this step, the decision maker is determining what's relevant in making the decision. This step brings the decision maker's interests, values, and personal preferences into the process. Identifying criteria is important because what one person thinks is relevant another may not. Also keep in mind that any factors not identified in this step are considered as irrelevant to the decision maker.

The criteria identified are rarely all equal in importance. So the third step requires the decision maker to *weight the previously identified criteria* in order to give them correct priority in the decision.

The fourth step requires the decision maker to *generate possible alternatives* that could succeed in resolving the problem. No attempt is made in this step to appraise these alternatives, only to list them.

Once the alternatives have been generated, the decision maker must critically analyze and evaluate each one. This is done by *rating each alternative on each criterion*. The strengths and weaknesses of each alternative become evident as they are compared with the criteria and weights established in the second and third steps.

The final step in this model requires *computing the optimal decision*. This is done by evaluating each alternative against the weighted criteria and selecting the alternative with the highest total score.

Assumptions of the Model. The rational decision-making model we just described contains a number of assumptions. Let's briefly outline them.

1. *Problem clarity.* The problem is clear and unambiguous. The decision maker is assumed to have complete information regarding the decision situation.

2. *Known options.* It is assumed that the decision maker can identify all the relevant criteria and can list all the viable alternatives. Further, the decision maker is aware of all the possible consequences of each alternative.

3. *Clear preferences.* Rationality assumes that the criteria and alternatives can be ranked and weighted to reflect their importance.

4. *Constant preferences.* It's assumed that the specific decision criteria are constant and that the weights assigned to them are stable over time.

5. *No time or cost constraints.* The rational decision maker can obtain full information about criteria and alternatives because it's assumed that there are no time or cost constraints.

6. *Maximum payoff.* The rational decision maker will choose the alternative that yields the highest perceived value.

Improving Creativity in Decision Making
The rational decision maker needs **creativity:** that is, the ability to combine ideas in a unique way or to make unusual associations between ideas. Why? Creativity allows the decision maker to more fully appraise and understand the problem, including seeing problems others can't see. However, creativity's most obvious value is in helping the decision maker identify all viable alternatives.

Creative Potential.   Most people have unleashed creative potential that they can use when confronted with a decision-making problem. But to get at that potential, they have to get out of the psychological ruts most of us get into and learn how to think about a problem in divergent ways.

We can start with the obvious. People differ in their inherent creativity. Einstein, Edison, Picasso, and Mozart were individuals of exceptional creativity. Not surprisingly, exceptional creativity is scarce. A study of lifetime creativity of 461 men and women found that fewer than one percent were exceptionally creative.[2] But ten percent were highly creative, and about sixty percent were somewhat creative. This result suggests that most of us have creative potential, if we can learn to unleash it.

Methods for Stimulating Individual Creativity.   Sometimes the simplest action can be very powerful. That seems to be true with stimulating creativity. Evidence indicates that the mere action of instructing someone to "be creative" and to avoid obvious approaches to a problem results in unique ideas.[3] This *direct instruction* method is based on evidence that people tend to accept obvious solutions and this tendency prevents them from performing up to their capabilities. So the mere statement that unique and creative alternatives are sought acts to encourage people to look for such ideas. Or overtly telling yourself that you're going to seek out creative options should lead to an increase in unique alternatives.

Another technique is *attribute listing*.[4] In attribute listing, the decision maker isolates the major characteristics of traditional alternatives. Each major attribute of the alternative is then considered in turn and is changed in every conceivable way. No ideas are rejected, no matter how ridiculous they may seem. Once this extensive list is completed, the constraints of the problem are imposed in order to eliminate all but the viable alternatives.

Creativity can also be stimulated by practicing zig-zag, or *lateral, thinking*.[5] This is a replacement for the more traditional vertical thinking, in which each step in the process follows the previous step in an unbroken sequence. Vertical thinking is often seen as rational thinking because it must be correct at every step and it deals only with what is relevant. With lateral thinking, individuals emphasize thinking sideways: not developing a pattern but restructuring a pattern. It's not sequential. For example, you could tackle a problem from the solution end rather than from the starting end, and back into various beginning states. Lateral thinking doesn't have to be correct at each step. In fact, in some cases, it may be necessary to pass through a "wrong" area in order to reach a position from which a correct path may be visible. Finally, lateral thinking is not restricted to relevant information. It deliberately uses random or irrelevant information to bring about a new way of looking at the problem.

*H*ow Are Decisions Actually Made in Organizations?

Are decision makers in organizations rational? Do they carefully assess problems, identify all relevant criteria, use their creativity to identify all viable alternatives, and painstakingly evaluate every alternative to find an optimizing choice? In some situations they do. When decision makers are faced with a simple problem

Chapter 6
Individual Decision Making

having few alternative courses of action, and when the cost of searching out and evaluating alternatives is low, the rational model provides a fairly accurate description of the decision-making process. But such situations are the exception. Most decisions in the real world don't follow the rational model. For instance, people are usually content to find an acceptable or reasonable solution to their problem rather than an optimizing one. Consequently, decision makers generally make limited use of their creativity. Choices tend to be confined to the neighborhood of the problem symptom and to the neighborhood of the current alternative. As one expert in decision making recently concluded: "Most significant decisions are made by judgment, rather than by a defined prescriptive model."[6] The following section reviews a large body of evidence to provide you with a more accurate description of how most decisions in organizations are actually made.

Bounded Rationality

When you considered which college to attend, did you look at *every* viable alternative? Did you carefully identify all the criteria that were important in your decision? Did you evaluate each alternative against the criteria in order to find the optimum college? I expect the answer to all these questions is No. Well, don't feel bad. Few people made their college choice this way. Instead of optimizing, you probably "satisficed."

When faced with a complex problem, most people respond by reducing the problem to a level at which it can be readily understood. The limited information-processing capability of human beings makes it impossible to assimilate and understand all the information necessary to optimize. So people *satisfice*; that is, they seek solutions that are satisfactory and sufficient.

Because the capacity of the human mind for formulating and solving complex problems is far too small to meet the requirements for full rationality, individuals operate within the confines of **bounded rationality.** They construct simplified models that extract the essential features from problems without capturing all of their complexity.[7] Individuals can then behave rationally within the limits of the simple model.

How does bounded rationality work for the typical individual? Once a problem is identified, the search for criteria and alternatives begins. But the list of criteria is likely to be far from exhaustive. The decision maker will identify a limited list made up of the more conspicuous choices. These are the choices that are easy to find and that tend to be highly visible. In most cases, they will represent familiar criteria and previously tried-and-true solutions. Once this limited set of alternatives is identified, the decision maker will begin reviewing them. But the review will not be comprehensive—not all of the alternatives will be carefully evaluated. Instead, the decision maker will begin with alternatives that differ only in a relatively small degree from the choice currently in effect. Following along familiar and well-worn paths, the decision maker proceeds to review alternatives only until he or she identifies an alternative that is "good enough"—one that meets an acceptable level of performance. The first alternative that meets the "good enough" criterion ends the search. So the final solution represents a satisficing choice rather than an optimum one.

One of the more interesting aspects of bounded rationality is that the order in which alternatives are considered is critical in determining which alternative is selected. Remember, in the fully rational optimizing model, all alternatives are eventually listed in a hierarchy of preferred order. Because all alternatives are considered, the initial order in which they are evaluated is irrelevant. Every potential solution gets a full and complete evaluation. But this isn't the case with bounded rationality. If we assume that a problem has more than one potential solution, the satisficing choice will be the first *acceptable* one the decision maker encounters. Decision makers use simple and limited models, so they typically begin by identifying alternatives that are obvious, ones with which they are familiar, and those not too far from the status quo. Solutions that depart least from the status quo and meet the decision criteria are most likely to be selected. A unique and creative alternative may present an optimizing solution to the problem, but it's unlikely to be chosen because an acceptable solution will be identified well before the decision maker is required to search very far beyond the status quo.

Intuition

"Sometimes you've just got to go with your gut feeling," the manager said as he tried to explain how he chose between two qualified job applicants. Was this manager wrong to use his "gut feeling"? Is using gut feelings a sign of being a poor manager? Does it necessarily result in inferior results? The answers to these questions are all *no.* Managers regularly use their intuition, and doing so may actually help improve decision making.[8]

Intuitive decision making is an unconscious process created out of distilled experience. It doesn't necessarily operate independently of rational analysis; rather, the two complement each other. Research on chess playing provides an excellent illustration of how intuition works.[9] Novice chess players and grand masters were shown an actual, but unfamiliar, chess game with about twenty-five pieces on the board. After five or ten seconds, the pieces were removed and each player was asked to reconstruct the pieces by position. On average, the grand master could put twenty-three or twenty-four pieces in their correct squares, but the novice was able to replace only six. Then the exercise was changed. This time the pieces were placed randomly on the board. Again, the novice got only about six correct, but so did the grand master! The second exercise demonstrated that the grand master didn't have any better memory than the novice. What he did have was the ability, based on the experience of having played thousands of chess games, to recognize patterns and clusters of pieces that occur on chessboards in the course of games. Studies further show that chess professionals can simultaneously play fifty or more games, in which decisions often must be made in only seconds, and exhibit only a moderately lower level of skill than when playing one game under tournament conditions, in which decisions often take half an hour or longer. Experience allows the expert to recognize a situation and draw upon previously learned information associated with that situation to quickly arrive at a decision choice. The result is that the intuitive decision maker can decide rapidly with what appears to be very limited information.

Identifying Problems

Problems don't come with flashing neon lights to identify themselves. And one person's *problem* is another person's *acceptable status quo*. So how do decision makers identify and select problems?

Problems that are visible tend to have a higher probability of being selected than ones that are important.[10] Why? We can offer at least two reasons. First, it's easier to recognize visible problems. They are more likely to catch a decision maker's attention. This reason explains why politicians are more likely to talk about the "crime problem" than the "illiteracy problem." Second, remember that we're concerned with decision making in organizations. Decision makers want to appear competent and "on top of problems." This desire motivates them to focus on problems that are visible to others.

And don't ignore the decision maker's self-interest. If a decision maker faces a conflict between selecting a problem that is important to the organization and one that is important to the decision maker, self-interest tends to win out.[11] This tendency also is related to the issue of visibility. It's usually in a decision maker's best interest to attack high-profile problems. It conveys to others that things are under control. Moreover, when the decision maker's performance is later reviewed, the evaluator is more likely to give a high rating to someone who has been aggressively attacking visible problems than to someone whose actions have been less obvious.

Developing Alternatives

Since decision makers rarely seek an optimum solution, but rather a satisficing one, we should expect to find a minimal use of creativity in the search for alternatives. And that expectation is generally on target.

Efforts will be made to try to keep the search process simple. It will tend to be confined to the neighborhood of the current alternative. More complex search behavior, which includes the development of creative alternatives, will be resorted to only when a simple search fails to uncover a satisfactory alternative.

The evidence indicates that decision making is incremental rather than comprehensive; that is, decision makers rarely formulate new and unique problem definitions and alternatives and rarely explore unfamiliar territory.[12] They avoid the difficult task of considering all the important factors, weighing their relative merits and drawbacks, and calculating the value for each alternative. Instead, they make successive limited (incremental) comparisons. This branch approach simplifies decision choices by comparing only those alternatives that differ in relatively small degree from the choice currently in effect. This approach also makes it unnecessary for the decision maker to thoroughly examine an alternative and its consequences; one need investigate only those aspects in which the proposed alternative and its consequences differ from the status quo.

What emerges from the above description is a decision maker who takes small steps toward an objective. It acknowledges the noncomprehensive nature of choice; in other words, decision makers make successive comparisons because decisions are never made forever and written in stone, but rather they are made and remade endlessly in small comparisons between narrow choices.

Making Choices

In order to avoid information overload, decision makers rely on **heuristics,** or judgmental shortcuts, in decision making.[13] There are two common categories of heuristics—availability and representativeness. Each creates biases in judgment. Another bias that decision makers often make is the tendency to escalate commitment to a failing course of action.

Availability Heuristic.   A lot more people suffer from fear of flying than from fear of driving a car. The reason is that many people think flying is more dangerous. It isn't, of course. With apologies ahead of time for this graphical example, if flying on a commercial airline was as dangerous as driving, the equivalent of two 747s, filled to capacity, would have to crash every week, killing all aboard, to match the risk of being killed in a car accident. But the media give a lot more attention to air accidents than to car accidents, so we tend to overstate the risk in flying and understate the risk in driving.

This illustration is an example of the **availability heuristic,** which is the tendency for people to base their judgments on information that is readily available to them. Events that evoke emotions, that are particularly vivid, or that have occurred recently tend to be most available in our memory. As a result, we tend to be prone to overestimating unlikely events such as an airplane crash. The availability heuristic can also explain why managers, when doing annual performance appraisals, tend to give more weight to recent behaviors of an employee than to those of six or nine months ago.

Representative Heuristic.   Literally millions of inner-city, African-American boys in the United States talk about the goal of playing basketball in the NBA. In reality, they have a better chance of becoming medical doctors than they do of playing in the NBA. But these kids are suffering from a **representative heuristic.** They tend to assess the likelihood of an occurrence by trying to match it with a preexisting category. They hear about some boy from their neighborhood ten years ago who went on to play professional basketball. Or they watch NBA games on television and think that the players are like them. We all are guilty of using this heuristic at times. Managers, for example, frequently predict the performance of a new product by relating it to a previous product's success. Or they hired three graduates from the same college who turned out to be poor performers, so they predict that a current job applicant from that college won't be a good employee.

Escalation of Commitment.   Another bias that creeps into decisions in practice is a tendency to escalate commitment when a decision stream represents a series of decisions.[14] **Escalation of commitment** is an increased commitment to a previous decision in spite of negative information. For example, a friend of mine had been dating a woman for about four years. Although he admitted that things weren't going too well in the relationship, he informed me that he was going to marry the woman. A bit surprised by his decision, I asked him why. He responded, "I have a lot invested in the relationship!" Similarly, another friend was explaining why she was working on a doctorate in education, although she disliked teaching and didn't want to continue her career in education. She told me she really wanted to be a software programmer. But then she hit me with her escalation of commitment explanation: "I already have a master's in education and I'd have to go back and complete some deficiencies if I changed to work on a degree in software programming now."

It has been well documented that individuals escalate commitment to a failing course of action when they view themselves as responsible for the failure. That is, they "throw good money after bad" to demonstrate that their initial decision wasn't wrong and to avoid having to admit they made a mistake. Escalation of commitment is also congruent with evidence that people try to appear consistent in what they say and do. Increasing commitment to previous actions conveys consistency.

Escalation of commitment has obvious implications for managerial decisions. Many an organization has suffered large losses because a manager was determined to prove that his or her original decision was right by continuing to commit resources to what was a lost cause from the beginning. In addition, consistency is a characteristic often associated with effective leaders. So managers, in an effort to appear effective, may be motivated to be consistent when switching to another course of action may be preferable. In actuality, effective managers are those who are able to differentiate between situations in which persistence will pay off and situations where it won't.

Individual Differences

Put Chad and Sean into the same decision situation and Chad almost always seems to take longer to come to a solution. Chad's final choices aren't necessarily always better than Sean's, he's just slower in processing information. In addition, if there's an obvious risk dimension in the decision, Sean seems consistently to prefer a riskier option than does Chad. What this illustrates is that all of us bring personality and other individual differences to the decisions we make. Two of these individual differences seem particularly relevant to decision making in organizations—decision-making styles and level of moral development.

Decision-Making Styles. The decision-styles model identifies four different individual approaches to making decisions.[15] It was designed to be used by managers and aspiring managers, but its general framework can be used with any individual decision maker.

The foundation of the model is the recognition that people differ along two dimensions. The first is their way of *thinking*. Some people are logical and rational. They process information serially. In contrast, some people are intuitive and creative. They perceive things as a whole. Note that these differences are above and beyond the general human characteristics—specifically, bounded rationality—discussed earlier. The other dimension addresses a person's *tolerance for ambiguity*. Some people have a high need to structure information in ways that minimize ambiguity; others are able to process many thoughts at the same time. When these two dimensions are diagrammed, they form four styles of decision making (see Exhibit 6-2). These are: Directive, Analytic, Conceptual, and Behavioral.

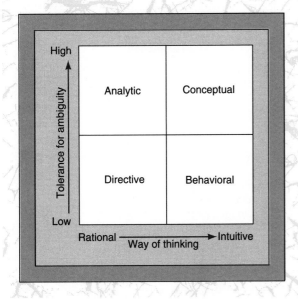

Exhibit 6-2
Decision-Styles Model

Source: A. J. Rowe, J. D. Boulgarides, and M. R. McGrath, *Managerial Decision Making;* Modules in Management Series (Upper Saddle River, NJ: Prentice Hall, 1984), p. 18.

People using the *directive* style have low tolerance for ambiguity and seek rationality. They are efficient and logical. But their concern for efficiency results in their making decisions with minimal information and with assessing few alternatives. Directive types make decisions fast, and they focus on the short run.

The *analytic* type has a much greater tolerance for ambiguity than do directive decision makers. They desire more information and consider more alternatives than do directives. Analytic managers would be best characterized as careful decision makers with the ability to adapt or cope with new situations.

Individuals with a *conceptual* style tend to be very broad in their outlook and consider many alternatives. Their focus is long-range, and they are very good at finding creative solutions to problems.

The final category—those with a *behavioral* style—characterizes decision makers who work well with others. They're concerned with the achievement of peers and subordinates. They're receptive to suggestions from others and rely heavily on meetings for communicating. This type of manager tries to avoid conflict and seeks acceptance.

Although these four categories are distinct, most managers have characteristics that fall into more than one. So it's probably best to think in terms of a manager's dominant style and his or her backup styles. Some managers rely almost exclusively on their dominant style; more flexible managers can make shifts depending on the situation.

Business students, lower-level managers, and top executives tend to score highest in the analytic style. That's not surprising, given the emphasis that formal education, particularly business education, gives to developing rational thinking. For instance, courses in accounting, statistics, and finance all stress rational analysis.

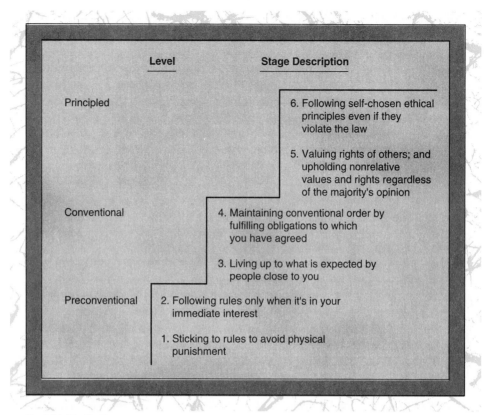

Level	Stage Description
Principled	6. Following self-chosen ethical principles even if they violate the law
	5. Valuing rights of others; and upholding nonrelative values and rights regardless of the majority's opinion
Conventional	4. Maintaining conventional order by fulfilling obligations to which you have agreed
	3. Living up to what is expected by people close to you
Preconventional	2. Following rules only when it's in your immediate interest
	1. Sticking to rules to avoid physical punishment

Exhibit 6-3
Stages of Moral Development

Source: Based on L. Kohlberg, "Moral Stages and Moralization: The Cognitive-Developmental Approach," pages 34–35 in *Moral Development and Behavior: Theory, Research, and Social Issues,* ed. T. Lickona (New York: Holt, Rinehart & Winston, 1976).

In addition to providing a framework for looking at individual differences, focusing on decision styles can be useful for helping you understand how two equally intelligent people, with access to the same information, can differ in the ways they approach decisions and the final choices they make.

Level of Moral Development. Moral development is relevant because many decisions have an ethical dimension. An understanding of this concept can help you see how different people impose different ethical standards on their decisions.

A substantial body of research confirms the existence of three levels of moral development, each comprising two stages.[16] At each successive stage, an individual's moral judgment grows less and less dependent on outside influences. The three levels and six stages are described in Exhibit 6-3.

The first level is labeled *preconventional*. At this level, individuals respond to notions of right or wrong only when personal consequences are involved, such as physical punishment, reward, or exchange of favors. Reasoning at the *conventional* level indicates that moral value resides in maintaining the conventional order and the expectations of others. In the *principled* level, individuals make a clear effort to define moral principles apart from the authority of the groups to which they belong or society in general.

Research on these stages of moral development allows us to draw several conclusions.[17] First, people proceed through the six stages in a lock-step fashion. They gradually move up a ladder, stage by stage. They don't jump steps. Second, there is no guarantee of continued development. Development can terminate at any stage. Third, most adults are at stage 4. They are limited to obeying the rules and laws of society. Finally, the higher the stage a manager reaches, the more he or she will be predisposed to make ethical decisions. For instance, a stage 3 manager is likely to make decisions that will receive approval by his or her peers; a stage 4 manager will seek to be a "good corporate citizen" by making decisions that respect the organization's rules and procedures; and a stage 5 manager is likely to challenge organizational practices that he or she believes to be wrong.

Organizational Constraints

The organization itself constrains decision makers. Managers, for instance, shape their decisions to reflect the organization's performance evaluation and reward system and organizationally imposed time constraints. Previous organizational decisions also act as precedents to constrain current decisions.

Performance Evaluation. Managers are strongly influenced in their decision making by the criteria by which they are evaluated. If a division manager believes that the manufacturing plants under his responsibility are operating best when he hears nothing negative, we shouldn't be surprised to find that his plant managers spend a good part of their time ensuring that negative information doesn't reach the division boss. Similarly, if a college dean believes that an instructor should never fail more than ten percent of her students—to fail more reflects on the instructor's ability to teach—we should expect that new instructors, who want to receive favorable evaluations, will decide not to fail too many students.

Reward Systems. The organization's reward system influences decision makers by suggesting to them what choices are preferable in terms of personal payoff. For example, if the organization rewards risk aversion, managers are likely to make conservative decisions. From the 1930s through the mid-1980s, General Motors consistently gave out promotions and bonuses to those managers who kept a low profile, avoided controversy, and were good team players. The result was that GM managers became very adept at dodging tough issues and passing controversial decisions on to committees.

System-Imposed Time Constraints. Organizations impose deadlines on decisions. For instance, department budgets need to be completed by next Friday. Or the report on new product development has to be ready for the executive committee to review by the first of the month. A host of decisions have to be made quickly in order to stay ahead of the competition and keep customers satisfied.

And almost all important decisions come with explicit deadlines. These conditions create time pressures on decision makers and often make it difficult, if not impossible, to gather all the information they might like before having to make a final choice. The rational model ignores the reality that, in organizations, decisions come with time constraints.

Historical Precedents.   Rational decision making takes an unrealistic and insulated perspective. It views decisions as independent and discrete events. But that isn't the way it is in the real world! Decisions aren't made in a vacuum. They have a context. In fact, individual decisions are more accurately characterized as points in a *stream of decisions.*

Decisions made in the past are ghosts that continually haunt current choices. For instance, commitments made in the past constrain current options. To use a social situation as an example, the decision you might make after meeting "Mr. (or Ms.) Right" is more complicated if you're married than if you're single. Prior commitments—in this case, having chosen to get married—constrain your options. In a business context, Eastman Kodak is a good example of a firm that has had to live with its past mistakes.[18] Starting in the early 1970s, Kodak's management concluded that the days of silver halide photography were numbered. They predicted other technologies, such as electronic photography, would soon replace it. But instead of approaching the problem deliberately, Kodak management panicked. They took off in all directions. And today, virtually all of Kodak's problems can be traced to the decisions made and not made since then. Government budget decisions also offer an illustration of our point. It's common knowledge that the largest determining factor of the size of any given year's budget is last year's budget.[19] Choices made today, therefore, are largely a result of choices made over the years.

Cultural Differences

The rational model does not acknowledge cultural differences. But Arabs, for instance, don't necessarily make decisions the same way that Canadians do. Therefore, we need to recognize that the cultural background of the decision maker can have significant influence on his or her selection of problems, depth of analysis, the importance placed on logic and rationality, or whether organizational decisions should be made autocratically by an individual manager or collectively in groups.[20]

Cultures, for example, differ in terms of time orientation, the importance of rationality, their belief in the ability of people to solve problems, and preference for collective decision making. Differences in time orientation help us understand why managers in Egypt will make decisions at a much slower and more deliberate pace than their American counterparts. A North American manager might make an important decision intuitively, but he or she knows that it's important to appear to proceed in a rational fashion because rationality is highly valued in the West. In countries such as Iran, where rationality is not deified, efforts to appear rational are not necessary. Some cultures emphasize solving problems; others focus on accepting situations as they are. The

United States falls into the former category; Thailand and Indonesia fall into the latter. Because problem-solving managers believe that they can and should change situations to their benefit, American managers might identify a problem long before their Thai or Indonesian counterparts would choose to recognize it as such. Decision making by Japanese managers is much more group-oriented than in the United States. The Japanese value conformity and cooperation. So before Japanese CEOs make an important decision, they collect a large amount of information, which is then used in consensus-forming group decisions.

mplications for Managers

Individuals think and reason before they act. Thus an understanding of how people make decisions can be helpful if we are to explain and predict their behavior.

Under some decision situations, people follow the optimizing model. But for most people, and most nonroutine decisions, this is probably more the exception than the rule. Few important decisions are simple or unambiguous enough for the optimizing model's assumptions to apply. So individuals look for solutions that satisfice rather than optimize, inject biases and prejudices into the decision process, and rely on intuition.

Given the evidence we've described on how decisions are actually made in organizations, what can managers do to improve their decision making? We offer five suggestions.

First, analyze the situation. Adjust your decision-making style to the national culture in which you're operating and to criteria your organization evaluates and rewards. For instance, if you're in a country that doesn't value rationality, don't feel compelled to follow the rational decision-making model or even to try to make your decisions appear rational. Similarly, organizations differ in terms of the importance they place on risk, the use of groups, and the like. Adjust your decision style to ensure it's compatible with the organization's culture.

Second, be aware of biases. We all bring biases to the decisions we make. If you understand the biases influencing your judgment, you can begin to change the way you make decisions to reduce those biases.

Third, combine rational analysis with intuition. These are not conflicting approaches to decision making. By using both, you can actually improve your decision effectiveness. As you gain managerial experience, you should feel increasingly confident in imposing your intuitive processes on top of your rational analysis.

Fourth, don't assume that your specific decision style is appropriate for every job. Just as organizations differ, so too do jobs within organizations. And your effectiveness as a decision maker will increase if you match your decision style to the requirements of the job. For instance, if you're a directive style of decision maker, you'll be more effective working with people whose jobs require quick action. This style would match up well with managing stockbrokers. An analytic style, on the other hand, would work well managing accountants, market researchers, or financial analysts.

Finally, use creativity-stimulation techniques. You can improve your overall decision-making effectiveness by searching for new solutions to problems. Stimulating creativity can be as simple as telling yourself to think creatively and to specifically look for unique alternatives. In addition, you can practice the attribute listing and lateral thinking techniques described in this chapter.

Foundations of Group Behavior

After reading this chapter, you should be able to:

1. Differentiate between formal and informal groups

2. Explain why people join groups

3. Describe how role requirements change in different situations

4. Explain the importance of the Hawthorne studies

5. Describe the importance of the Asch studies

6. Identify the implications of social loafing

7. Outline the benefits and disadvantages of cohesive groups

8. Explain the effect of diversity on group performance

9. Contrast groupthink and groupshift

The behavior of individuals in groups is something more than the sum total of each acting in his or her own way. When individuals are in groups they act differently from when they are alone. This chapter introduces basic concepts about groups and demonstrates how an understanding of groups can help explain the larger phenomenon of organizational behavior.

Defining and Classifying Groups

A **group** is defined as two or more individuals, interacting and interdependent, who come together to achieve particular objectives. Groups can be either formal or informal. By formal, we mean defined by the organization's structure, with designated work assignments establishing tasks and work groups. In formal groups, the behaviors that one should engage in are stipulated by and directed toward organizational goals. In contrast, informal groups are alliances that are neither structured nor organizationally determined. In the work environment, these groups form naturally as responses to the need for social contact.

It's possible to further subclassify groups into command, task, interest, or friendship categories. Command and task groups are dictated by the formal organization, whereas interest and friendship groups are informal alliances.

The *command group* is determined by the organizational chart. It is composed of the subordinates who report directly to a given manager. An elementary school principal and her twelve teachers form a command group, as do the director of postal audits and his five inspectors.

Task groups, also organizationally determined, represent persons working together to complete a job. However, a task group's boundaries are not limited to its immediate hierarchical superior. It can cross command relationships. For instance, if a college student is accused of a campus crime, it may require communication and coordination among the dean of academic affairs, the dean of students, the registrar, the director of security, and the student's adviser. Such a formation would constitute a task group. It should be noted that all command groups are also task groups, but because task groups can cut across the organization, the reverse need not be true.

Exhibit 7-1

Why Do People Join Groups?

Reason	Benefit
Security	By joining a group, individuals can reduce the insecurity of "standing alone." People feel stronger, have fewer self-doubts, and are more resistant to threats when they are part of a group.
Status	Inclusion in a group that is viewed as important by others provides recognition and status for its members.
Self-esteem	Groups can provide people with feelings of self-worth. That is, in addition to conveying status to those outside the group, membership can also give increased feelings of worth to the group members themselves.
Affiliation	Groups can fulfill social needs. People enjoy the regular interaction that comes with group membership. For many people, these on-the-job interactions are their primary source for fulfilling their needs for affiliation.
Power	What cannot be achieved individually often becomes possible through group action. There is power in numbers.
Goal achievement	There are times when it takes more than one person to accomplish a particular task—there is a need to pool talents, knowledge, or power in order to get a job completed. In such instances, management will rely on the use of a formal group.

People who may or may not be aligned into common command or task groups may affiliate to attain a specific objective with which each is concerned. This is an *interest group.* Employees who band together to have their vacation schedule altered, to support a peer who has been fired, or to seek increased fringe benefits represent the formation of a united body to further their common interest.

Groups often develop because the individual members have one or more common characteristics. We call these formations *friendship groups.* Social allegiances, which frequently extend outside the work situation, can be based on, for example, similar age, support for "Big Red" Nebraska football, having attended the same college, or holding similar political views.

Informal groups provide a very important function by satisfying their members' social needs. Because of interactions that result from the proximity of workstations or tasks, we find workers playing golf together, riding to and from work together, lunching together, and spending their breaks around the water cooler together. We must recognize that these types of interactions among individuals, even though informal, deeply affect their behavior and performance.

No single reason explains why individuals join groups. Most people belong to a number of groups, so it's obvious that different groups provide different benefits to their members. Exhibit 7-1 summarizes the most popular reasons why people join a group.

*B*asic Group Concepts

The following review of basic group concepts builds on the recognition that groups are not unorganized mobs. They have a structure that shapes the behavior of their members.

Roles

Laura Campbell is a buyer with Marks & Spencer, the large British retailer. Her job requires her to play a number of **roles:** that is, to engage in a set of expected behavior patterns that are attributed to occupying a given position in a social unit. For instance, Laura plays the role of a Marks & Spencer employee, a member of the headquarter's buying group, a member of the cost-improvement task force, and an adviser to the committee on diversity. Off the job, Laura Campbell finds herself in still more roles: wife, mother, Methodist, member of the Labor Party, board member at her daughter's school, singer in the St. Andrew's Chapel choir, and a member of the Surrey women's soccer league. Many of these roles are compatible; some create conflicts. For instance, a recent offer of a promotion would require Laura to relocate from London to Manchester, yet her husband and daughter want to remain in London. Can the role demands of her job be reconciled with the demands of her wife and mother roles?

Like Laura Campbell, we all are required to play a number of roles, and our behavior varies with the role we're playing. The concept of roles can help us explain why Laura's behavior at her soccer league match on Saturday, for instance, is different from her behavior when participating in a meeting of her cost-improvement task force at work—the groups impose different identities and expectations on Laura.

The understanding of role behavior would be dramatically simplified if each of us chose one role and played it out regularly and consistently. Unfortunately, we are required to play diverse roles, both on and off our jobs. Different groups impose different role requirements on people. And we can better understand an individual's behavior in specific situations if we know what role that person is playing.

On the basis of decades of role research, we can make the following conclusions:[1] (1) People play multiple roles. (2) People learn roles from the stimuli around them—friends, books, movies, television. For instance, many current lawyers had their roles shaped by role models such as Perry Mason or cast members on *L.A. Law.* (3) People have the ability to shift roles rapidly when they recognize that the situation and its demands clearly require major changes. (4) People often experience role conflict when compliance with one role requirement is at odds with another. An increasing number of people, for instance, are experiencing the stress that Laura Campbell is experiencing as a result of trying to reconcile work and family roles.

So if you're a manager, what value is a knowledge of roles? When you're dealing with employees, it helps to think in terms of what group they're predominantly identifying with at the time and what behaviors would be expected of them in that role. This perspective can often allow you to more accurately predict the employee's behavior and guide you in determining how best to handle situations with that employee.

Norms

Did you ever notice that golfers don't speak while their partners are putting on the green or that employees don't criticize their bosses in public? This is because of **norms.** That is, there are acceptable standards of behavior within a group that are shared by the group's members.[2]

Each group will establish its own set of norms. For instance, group norms might determine appropriate dress, when it's acceptable to goof off, with whom group members eat lunch, and friendships on and off the job. However, probably the most widespread norms—and the ones with which managers tend to be most concerned—deal with performance-related processes. Work groups typically provide their members with explicit cues on how hard they should work, how to get the job done, their level of output, appropriate communication channels, and the like. These norms are extremely powerful in affecting an individual employee's performance. When agreed to and accepted by the group, norms act as a means of influencing the behavior of group members with a minimum of external controls. In fact, it's not unusual to find cases in which an employee with strong abilities and high personal motivation performs at a very modest level because of the overriding influence of group norms that discourage members from producing at high levels.

A key point to remember about norms is that groups exert pressure on members to bring members' behavior into conformity with the group's standards. If people in the group violate its norms, expect group members to act to correct or even punish the violation. This is just one conclusion directly attributable to findings in the Hawthorne studies.

The Hawthorne Studies.   It is generally agreed among behavioral scientists that full-scale appreciation of the importance norms play in influencing worker behavior did not occur until the early 1930s. This enlightenment grew out of a series of studies undertaken at Western Electric Company's Hawthorne Works in Chicago between 1924 and 1932.[3] Originally initiated by Western Electric officials and later overseen by Harvard professor Elton Mayo, the Hawthorne studies concluded that a worker's behavior and sentiments were closely related, that group influences were significant in affecting individual behavior, that group standards were highly effective in establishing individual worker output, and that money was less a factor in determining worker output than were group standards, sentiments, and security. Let us briefly review the Hawthorne investigations and demonstrate the importance of these findings in explaining group behavior.

The Hawthorne researchers began by examining the relation between the physical environment and productivity. Illumination and other working conditions were selected to represent this physical environment. The researchers' initial findings contradicted their anticipated results.

They began with illumination experiments with various groups of workers. The researchers manipulated the intensity of illumination upward and downward, while at the same time noting changes in group output. Results varied, but one thing was clear: In no case was the increase or decrease in output in proportion to the increase or decrease in illumination. So the researchers introduced a control group: An experimental group was presented with varying intensity of illumination, while the controlled unit worked under a constant illumination intensity. Again, the results were bewildering to the Hawthorne researchers. As the light level was increased in the experimental unit, output rose for both the control and the experimental group. But to the surprise of the researchers, as the light level was dropped in the experimental group, productivity continued to increase in both groups. In fact, a productivity decrease was observed in the experimental group only when the light intensity had been reduced to that of moonlight. The Hawthorne researchers concluded that illumination intensity was only a minor influence among the many influences that affected an employee's productivity, but they could not explain the behavior they had witnessed.

As a follow-up to the illumination experiments, the researchers began a second set of experiments in the relay assembly test room at Western Electric. A small group of women was isolated from the main work group so that their behavior could be more carefully observed. They went about their job of assembling small telephone relays in a room laid out similarly to their normal department. The only significant difference was the placement in the room of a research assistant who acted as an observer—keeping records of output, rejects, working conditions, and a daily log sheet describing everything that happened. Observations covering a multiyear period found that this small group's output increased steadily. The number of personal absences and those due to sickness were approximately one-third of those recorded by women in the regular production department. What became evident was that this group's performance was significantly influenced by its status of being a "special" group. The women in the test room thought that being in the experimental group was fun, that they were in sort of an elite group, and that management was concerned with their interest by engaging in such experimentation.

A third study in the bank wiring observation room was introduced to ascertain the effect of a sophisticated wage incentive plan. The assumption was that individual workers would maximize their productivity when they saw that it was directly related to economic rewards. The most important finding coming out of this study was that employees did not individually maximize their outputs. Rather, their output became controlled by a group norm that determined what was a proper day's work. Output was not only being restricted, but individual workers were giving erroneous reports. The total for a week would check with the total week's output, but the daily reports showed a steady level of output regardless of actual daily production. What was going on?

Interviews determined that the group was operating well below its capability and was leveling output in order to protect itself. Members were afraid that if they significantly increased their output, the unit incentive rate would be cut, the expected daily output would be increased, layoffs might occur, or slower workers would be reprimanded. So the group established its idea of a fair output—neither too much nor too little. They helped each other out to ensure their reports were nearly level.

The norms the group established included a number of "don'ts." *Don't* be a rate-buster, turning out too much work. *Don't* be a chiseler, turning out too little work. *Don't* be a squealer on any of your peers.

How did the group enforce these norms? Their methods were neither gentle nor subtle. They included sarcasm, name–calling, ridicule, and even physical punches to the upper arm of members who violated the group's norms. Members would also ostracize individuals whose behavior was against the group's interest.

The Hawthorne studies made an important contribution to our understanding of group behavior—particularly the significant place that norms have in determining individual work behavior.

Conformity and the Asch Studies. As a member of a group, you desire continued acceptance by the group, so you are susceptible to conforming to the group's norms. There is considerable evidence that groups can place strong pressures on individual members to change their attitudes and behaviors to conform to the group's standard. Group influence was demonstrated in the now-classic studies undertaken by Solomon Asch.[4]

Asch made up groups of seven or eight people who sat in a classroom and were asked to compare two cards held by the experimenter. One card had one line, the other had three lines of varying length. As shown in Exhibit 7-2, one of the lines on the three-line card was identical to the line on the one-line card. Also, as shown in Exhibit 7-2, the difference in line length was quite obvious; under ordinary conditions, subjects made less than one percent errors. The object was to announce aloud which of the three lines matched the single line. But what happens if all the members in the group begin to give incorrect answers? Will the pressures to conform result in the unsuspecting subject (USS) altering his or her answer to align with the others? That was what Asch wanted to know. He arranged the group so that only the USS was unaware that the experiment was "fixed." The seating was prearranged so that the USS was the last to announce his or her decision.

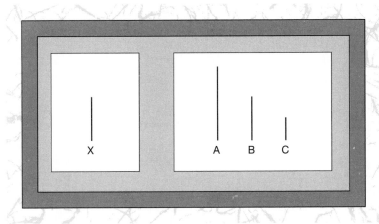

Exhibit 7-2
Examples of Cards Used in the Asch Study

The experiment began with several sets of matching exercises. All the subjects gave the right answers. On the third set, however, the first subject gave an obviously wrong answer—for example, saying "C" in Exhibit 7-2. The next subject gave the same wrong answer, and so did the others until it got to the unsuspecting subject. He knew "B" was the same as "X," yet everyone had said "C." The decision confronting the USS was this: Do you state a perception publicly that differs from the preannounced position of the others? Or do you give an answer that you strongly believe is incorrect in order to have your response agree with that of the other group members?

The results obtained by Asch demonstrated that over many experiments and many trials, subjects conformed in about thirty-five percent of the trials; that is, the subjects gave answers they knew were wrong but that were consistent with the replies of other group members.

What can we conclude from this study? The results suggest that there are group norms that press us toward conformity. We desire to be one of the group, and we avoid being visibly different. We can generalize further to say that when an individual's opinion of objective data differs significantly from that of others in the group, he or she feels extensive pressure to align his or her opinion to conform with those of the others.

Cohesiveness

Groups differ in their **cohesiveness;** that is, the degree to which members are attracted to each other and are motivated to stay in the group. For instance, some work groups are cohesive because the members have spent a great deal of time together, or the group's small size facilitates higher interaction, or the group has experienced external threats that have brought members closer together. Cohesiveness is important because it's been found to be related to the group's productivity.[5]

Studies consistently show that the relationship of cohesiveness and productivity depends on the performance-related norms established by the group. The more cohesive the group, the more its members will follow its goals. If performance-

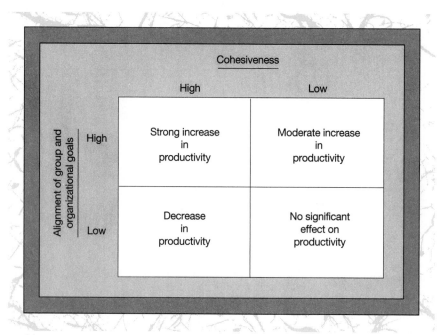

Exhibit 7-3
Relationship of Cohesiveness to Productivity

related norms are high (for example, high output, quality work, cooperation with individuals outside the group), a cohesive group will be more productive than a less cohesive group. But if cohesiveness is high and performance norms are low, productivity will be low. If cohesiveness is low and performance norms are high, productivity increases, but less than in the high cohesiveness–high norms situation. Where cohesiveness and performance-related norms are both low, there will be no significant effect on productivity. These conclusions are summarized in Exhibit 7-3.

What can you do as a manager if you want to encourage group cohesiveness? You might try one or more of the following suggestions:[6] (1) Make the group smaller; (2) encourage agreement with group goals; (3) increase the time members spend together; (4) increase the status of the group and the perceived difficulty of attaining membership in the group; (5) stimulate competition with other groups; (6) give rewards to the group rather than to members; or (7) physically isolate the group.

Size

Does the size of a group affect the group's overall behavior? The answer is a definite Yes.[7] The evidence indicates, for instance, that smaller groups are faster at completing tasks than are larger ones. If the group is engaged in problem solving, however, large groups consistently get better marks than their smaller counterparts. Translating these results into specific numbers is a bit hazardous, but we can offer some parameters. Large groups—with a dozen or more members—are good for gaining diverse input. So if the goal of the group is fact–finding, larger groups should be more effective. On the other hand, smaller groups are better at doing something productive with that input. Groups of approximately seven members, therefore, tend to be more effective for taking action.

One of the most important findings related to the size of a group has been labeled **social loafing.** Social loafing is the tendency for individuals to expend less effort when working collectively than when working individually. It directly challenges the logic that the productivity of the group as a whole should at least equal the sum of the productivity of all the individuals in that group.

A common stereotype about groups is that the sense of team spirit spurs individual effort and enhances the group's overall productivity. In the late 1920s, a German psychologist named Ringelmann compared the results of individual and group performance on a rope-pulling task.[8] He expected that the group's effort would be equal to the sum of the efforts of individuals within the group. That is, three people pulling together should exert three times as much pull on the rope as one person, and eight people should exert eight times as much pull. Ringelmann's results, however, did not confirm his expectations. Groups of three people exerted a force only two-and-a-half times the average individual performance. Groups of eight collectively achieved less than four times the solo rate.

Replications of Ringelmann's research with similar tasks have generally supported his findings.[9] Increases in group size are inversely related to individual performance. More may be better in the sense that the total productivity of a group of four is greater than that of one or two people, but the individual productivity of each group member declines.

What causes this social loafing effect? It may be due to a belief that others in the group are not carrying their fair share. If you see others as lazy or inept, you can reestablish equity by reducing your effort. Another explanation is the dispersion of responsibility. Because the results of the group cannot be attributed to any single person, the relationship between an individual's input and the group's output is clouded. In such situations, individuals may be tempted to become "free riders" and coast on the group's efforts. In other words, there will be a reduction in efficiency when individuals think that their contribution cannot be measured.

Composition

Most group activities require a variety of skills and knowledge. Given this requirement, it would be reasonable to conclude that heterogeneous groups—those composed of dissimilar individuals—would be more likely to have diverse abilities and information and should be more effective than homogeneous groups. Research studies generally substantiate that conclusion.[10]

When a group is heterogeneous in terms of gender, personalities, opinions, abilities, skills, and perspectives, there is an increased probability that the group will possess the needed characteristics to complete its tasks effectively.[11] The group may be more conflict-laden and less expedient as diverse positions are introduced and assimilated, but the evidence generally supports the conclusion that heterogeneous groups perform more effectively than do those that are homogeneous.

But does diversity created by racial or national differences have an effect? The evidence indicates that these elements of diversity interfere with group processes, at least in the short term.[12] Cultural diversity seems to be an asset on tasks that call for a variety of viewpoints. But culturally heterogeneous groups have more difficulty in learning to work with each other and solving problems. The good news is that these difficulties seem to dissipate with time. Although newly formed culturally diverse groups do not perform as well as newly formed culturally homogeneous groups, the differences disappear after about three months. The reason is that it takes diverse groups a while to learn how to work through disagreements and different approaches to solving problems.

Status

As far back as scientists have been able to trace human groupings, we have had chiefs and Indians, noblemen and peasants, haves and have-nots. This continues to be the case today. Even the smallest group will develop roles, rites, and rituals to differentiate its members. Status is an important factor in understanding behavior because it is a significant motivator and has major behavioral consequences when individuals see a disparity between what they perceive their status to be and what others perceive it to be.

Status is a prestige grading, position, or rank within a group. It may be formally imposed by a group; that is, organizationally imposed, through titles or amenities such as "the heavyweight champion of the world" or "most congenial." We are all familiar with the trappings associated with high organizational status—large offices with thick carpeting, impressive titles, high pay and fringe benefits, preferred work schedules, and so on. Whether management acknowledges the existence of a status hierarchy, organizations are filled with amenities that are not uniformly available to everyone and, hence, carry status value.

More often, we deal with status in an informal sense. Status may be informally acquired by such characteristics as education, age, gender, skill, or experience. Anything can have status value if others in the group evaluate it as status-conferring. Keep in mind that informal status is not necessarily less important than the formal variety.

In his classic restaurant study, William F. Whyte demonstrated the importance of status.[13] Whyte proposed that people work more smoothly if high-status personnel customarily originate action for lower-status personnel. He found instances in which, when those of lower status were initiating action, a conflict arose between formal and informal status systems. For example, he cited one instance in which waitresses passed their customers' orders directly on to countermen—and thus low-status servers were initiating action for high-status cooks. By the simple addition of an aluminum spindle to which the order could be hooked, a buffer was created, thus allowing the countermen to initiate action on orders when they felt ready.

Whyte also noted that in the kitchen, supply men secured food supplies from the chefs. This was, in effect, a case of low-skilled employees initiating action upon the high-skilled. Conflict was stimulated when several supply men explicitly and implicitly urged the chefs to "get a move on." Whyte observed, however, that one supply man had little trouble. He gave the chef the order and asked the chef to call him when it was ready, thus reversing the initiating process. In Whyte's analysis, he suggested several changes in procedures, which aligned interactions more closely with the accepted status hierarchy and resulted in substantial improvements in worker relations and effectiveness.

It's important for group members to believe that the status hierarchy is equitable. Any perceived inequity creates disequilibrium resulting in various types of corrective behavior. The concept of equity, presented in Chapter 4, applies to status. Individuals expect rewards to be proportionate to costs incurred in obtaining those rewards. If Sally and Betty are the two finalists for the position of head nurse in a hospital, and it is clear that Sally has more seniority and better preparation for assuming the promotion, Betty will view the selection of Sally as equitable. But if Betty is chosen because she is the daughter-in-law of the hospital director, Sally will see an injustice.

The trappings that go with formal positions are also important elements in maintaining equity. If we believe that there is an inequity between the perceived ranking of an individual and the status accoutrements he or she is given by the organization, we are experiencing status incongruence. Some examples of incongruence are the supervisor's earning less than her subordinates, the more desirable office location being held by a lower-ranking individual, or paid country club membership being provided by the company for division managers but not for vice presidents. Employees expect the things an individual has and receives to be congruent with his or her status.

Even though members of groups generally agree among themselves on status criteria and hence tend to rank individuals fairly closely, conflict can arise when individuals move between groups whose status criteria are different or when groups are formed of individuals with heterogeneous backgrounds. Businesspeople may use income, total wealth, or size of the companies they run as determinants. Government bureaucrats might use the size of their agencies. Academics may use the number of grants received or articles published. Blue-collar workers may use years of seniority, job assignments, or bowling scores. It may be difficult for an individual from one such group to perform effectively in another. Or, when such groups are forced to be interdependent, there is a potential for status differences to cause conflict as the groups attempt to reconcile and align their differing hierarchies. As we'll see in the next chapter, conflict arising from heterogeneity can be a particular problem when management creates teams made up of employees from among varied functions in the organization.

*G*roup Decision Making

The belief—characterized by juries—that two heads are better than one has long been accepted as a basic component of North American and many other countries' legal systems. This belief has expanded to the point that, today, many decisions in organizations are made by groups, teams, or committees. In this section, we review group decision making. Let's begin by comparing the strengths of group decisions against those made by individuals.

The Individual versus the Group

A major plus with individual decision making is *speed*. An individual doesn't have to convene a meeting and spend time discussing various alternatives. So when a decision is needed quickly, individuals have the advantage. Individual decisions also have *clear accountability*. You know who made the decision and, therefore, who's responsible for the decision's outcome. Accountability is more ambiguous with group decisions. A third strength of individual decisions is that they tend to convey *consistent values*. Group decisions can suffer from intragroup power struggles. This effect is best illustrated by decisions of the U.S. Congress. Decisions can vary by as much as 180 degrees from one session to the next, reflecting the makeup of members and their ability to influence their peers on any specific issue. Although individuals are not perfectly consistent in their decision making, they do tend to be more consistent than groups.

Now compare the above with the strengths of group decision making. Groups generate *more complete information and knowledge*. By aggregating the resources of several individuals, groups bring more input into the decision process. In addition to more input, groups can bring heterogeneity to the decision process. They offer *increased diversity of views*, so more approaches and alternatives can be considered. The evidence indicates that a group will almost always outperform even the best individual. So groups generate *higher–quality decisions*. Finally, groups lead to *increased acceptance of a solution*. Many decisions fail after the final choice is made because people don't accept the solution. Group members, who participated in making a decision, are more likely to enthusiastically support the decision and encourage others to accept it.

So which is better—individuals or groups? The obvious answer is, "It depends." There are times when decisions are best handled by individuals. For example, evidence indicates that individuals are preferred when the decision is relatively unimportant and doesn't require subordinate commitment to its success. Similarly, individuals should make the decision when they have sufficient information and when subordinates will be committed to the outcome even if they aren't consulted.[14]

Overall, whether individuals or groups should make a decision essentially comes down to weighing effectiveness against efficiency. In terms of effectiveness, groups are superior. They generate more alternatives, are more creative, more accurate, and produce higher–quality decisions than do individuals. But individuals are more efficient than groups. Group efficiency suffers because they consume more time and resources to achieve their solution.

Groupthink and Groupshift

Two byproducts of group decision making have received a considerable amount of attention by researchers in OB. These are the concepts of groupthink and groupshift.

Groupthink. Have you ever felt like speaking up in a meeting, classroom, or informal group, but decided against it? One reason may have been shyness. On the other hand, you may have been a victim of **groupthink,** the phenomenon that occurs when group members become so enamored of seeking concurrence that the norm for consensus overrides the realistic appraisal of alternative courses of action and the full expression of deviant, minority, or unpopular views. It describes a deterioration in an individual's mental efficiency, reality testing, and moral judgment as a result of group pressures.[15]

How do you know if a group is showing symptoms of groupthink? It tends to exhibit four characteristics: (1) Group members rationalize any resistance to the assumptions they've made; (2) members pressure any doubters to support the alternative favored by the majority; (3) to give the appearance of group consensus, doubters keep silent about misgivings and even minimize to themselves the importance of their doubts; and (4) the group interprets members' silence as a "yes" vote for the majority.

The above symptoms lead to a number of decision-making deficiencies. When groupthink occurs, you'll find one or more of the following: incomplete assessment of the problem, poor information search, selective bias in processing information, limited development of alternatives, incomplete assessment of alternatives, failure to examine risks of preferred choice, and failure to reappraise initially rejected alternatives.

Studies of decision making in U.S. government agencies have found deficient outcomes frequently preceded by symptoms of groupthink. These include unpreparedness at Pearl Harbor in 1941, the invasion of North Korea in the 1950s, the Bay of Pigs fiasco in the early 1960s, the escalation of the Vietnam War, the failed Iran hostage rescue in the late 1970s, and the decisions preceding the launch of the ill-fated space shuttle *Challenger*.

Are all groups equally vulnerable to groupthink? The evidence suggests not.[16] Researchers have focused on five variables that seem to influence when groupthink is likely to surface—the group's cohesiveness, its leader's behavior, its insulation from outsiders, time pressures, and failure to follow methodical decision-making procedures. Managers who, when leading a decision-making group, want to minimize the influence of groupthink should keep those variables in mind. First, cohesiveness can be an asset because highly cohesive groups have more discussion and bring out more information than do loose groups. But cohesiveness can also discourage dissent, so managers should be vigilant when working with a cohesive group. Second, managers should strive for an open leadership style. This includes encouraging member participation, refraining from stating one's opinion at the beginning of the meeting, encouraging divergent opinions from all group members, and emphasizing the importance of reaching a wise decision. Third, managers should avoid allowing the group to detach itself from external sources. Insulated groups tend to lose perspective and objectivity. Fourth, managers need to downplay time constraints. When group members feel severe time pressures to reach a decision, they resort to shortcuts that inevitably lead to false or superficial consensus. Finally, managers should encourage the use of methodical decision-making procedures. Following the rational decision-making process described in the previous chapter will promote constructive criticism and a full analysis of decision options.

Groupshift. Comparisons of group decisions with the individual decisions of members within the group suggest that there are differences. In some cases, the group decisions are more cautious than the individual decisions. More often, the shift is toward greater risk.[17]

What appears to happen in groups is that the discussion leads to a significant shift in the positions of members toward a more extreme position in the direction toward which they were already leaning before the discussion. So conservative types become more cautious and the more aggressive types take on more risk. The group discussion tends to exaggerate the initial position of the group.

The **groupshift** can be viewed as actually a special case of groupthink. The decision of the group reflects the dominant decision-making norm that develops during the group's discussion. Whether the shift in the group's decision is toward greater caution or more risk depends on the dominant prediscussion norm.

The greater occurrence of the shift toward risk has generated several explanations for the phenomenon. For instance, it's been suggested that the discussion creates familiarization among the members. As they become more comfortable with each other, they also become bolder and more daring. Arguably, the most plausible explanation of the shift toward risk seems to be that the group diffuses responsibility. Group decisions free any single member from accountability for the group's final choice. Greater risk can be taken because even if the decision fails, no one member can be held wholly responsible.

So, as a manager, how should you use the findings on groupshift? You should recognize that group decisions exaggerate the initial position of the individual members, that the shift has been shown more often to be toward greater risk, and that whether a group will shift toward greater risk or caution is a function of the members' prediscussion inclinations.

Selecting the Best Group Decision-Making Technique

The most common form of group decision making takes place in face-to-face interacting groups. But as our discussion of groupthink demonstrated, interacting groups often censor themselves and pressure individual members toward conformity of opinion. Brainstorming, the nominal group technique, and electronic meetings have been proposed as ways to reduce many of the problems inherent in the traditional interacting group.

Brainstorming. **Brainstorming** is meant to overcome pressures for conformity in the interacting group that retard the development of creative alternatives. It does so by utilizing an idea-generation process that specifically encourages any and all alternatives, while withholding any criticism of those alternatives.

In a typical brainstorming session, a half-dozen to a dozen people sit around a table. The group leader states the problem in a clear manner so it is understood by all participants. Members then "freewheel" as many alternatives as they can in a given length of time. No criticism is allowed, and all the alternatives are recorded for later discussion and analysis. That one idea stimulates others and that judgments of even the most bizarre suggestions are withheld until later encourage group members to "think the unusual."

Brainstorming, however, is merely a process for generating ideas. The following two techniques go further by offering methods of actually arriving at a preferred solution.

Nominal Group Technique. The nominal group restricts discussion or interpersonal communication during the decision-making process, hence the term **nominal group technique.** Group members are all physically present, as in a traditional committee meeting, but the members are required to operate independently. Specifically, the following steps take place.

1. Members meet as a group, but, before any discussion takes place, each member independently writes down his or her ideas on the problem.
2. This silent period is followed by each member's presenting one idea to the group. Each member takes his or her turn, going around the table, presenting a single idea until all ideas have been presented and recorded (typically on a flip chart or chalkboard). No discussion takes place until all ideas have been recorded.
3. The group then discusses the ideas for clarity and evaluates them.
4. Each group member silently and independently ranks the ideas. The final decision is determined by the idea with the highest aggregate ranking.

The chief advantage of this technique is that it permits the group to meet formally but does not restrict independent thinking, as so often happens in the traditional interacting group.

Electronic Meetings. The most recent approach to group decision making blends the nominal group technique with sophisticated computer technology. It's called the **electronic meeting.**

Once the technology is in place, the concept is simple. Up to fifty people sit around a horseshoe-shaped table, empty except for a series of computer terminals. Issues are presented to participants and they type their responses onto their computer screen. Individual comments, as well as aggregate votes, are displayed on a projection screen in the room.

The major advantages of electronic meetings are anonymity, honesty, and speed. Participants can anonymously type any message they want, and it flashes on the screen for all to see at the push of a participant's board key. It also allows people to be brutally honest without penalty. And it's fast, because chitchat is eliminated, discussions don't digress, and many participants can "talk" at once without stepping on one another's toes.

mplications for Managers

In order to accomplish work tasks, the individuals who make up an organization are typically united into departments, teams, committees, or other forms of work groups. In addition to these formal groups, individuals also create informal groups based on common interests or friendships. It is important for managers to look at employees as members of a group because, in reality, group behavior is not merely the summation of the individual behavior of its members. The group itself adds an additional dimension to its members' behavior.

How is it relevant to understanding group behavior to know that a Maryland woman, for example, has to reconcile her roles of mother, Methodist, Democrat, councilwoman, and police officer with the city of Baltimore? Knowledge of the role that a person is attempting to enact can make it easier for us to deal with the person, for we have insight into her expected behavior patterns. Also, knowledge of a job incumbent's role makes it easier for others to work with her, for she should behave in ways consistent with others' expectations. In other words, when a person plays out her role as it is expected to be played, the ability of others to predict her behavior improves.

Norms control group member behavior by establishing standards of right or wrong. Knowing the norms of a given group can help us explain the attitudes and behaviors of its members. Can managers control group norms? Not completely, but they can influence them. By making explicit statements about desirable behaviors, by regularly reinforcing these preferred behaviors, and by linking rewards to the acceptance of preferred norms, managers can exert some degree of influence over group norms.

Should managers seek cohesive groups? Our answer is a qualified Yes. The qualification lies in the degree of alignment between the group and the organization's goals. Managers should attempt to create work groups whose goals are consistent with those of the organization. If this is achieved, then high group cohesiveness will make a positive contribution to the group's performance.

The implications for managers of the social loafing effect on work groups are significant. When managers use collective work situations to enhance morale and teamwork, they must also provide means by which individual efforts can be identified. If they don't, management must weigh the potential losses in productivity from using groups against any possible gains in worker satisfaction.[18] This conclusion, however, has a Western bias. It's consistent with individualistic cultures, such as the United States and Canada, that are dominated by self-interest. It is not consistent with collective societies in which individuals are motivated by in-group goals. For instance, in studies comparing employees from the United States with employees from the People's Republic of China and Israel (both collectivist societies), the Chinese and Israelis showed no propensity to engage in social loafing. In fact, the Chinese and Israelis actually performed better in a group than when working alone.[19]

The managerial implications for group composition are related to staffing formal groups and using groups to make decisions. To increase the performance of work groups, you should try to choose individuals as members who can bring a diverse perspective to problems and issues. But don't be surprised if these differences negatively affect the group's performance in the short term. Be patient. As members learn to work with their differences, the group's performance will improve.

Status inequities within a group divert activity away from goal accomplishment and direct it toward resolving the inequities. When inequities exist, managers may find that group members reduce their work effort, attempt to undermine the activities of those members with higher status, or pursue similar dysfunctional behaviors. To the degree that a manager controls status accoutrements, he or she should ensure that they are distributed carefully and consistently with status equity. Inequities are likely to have a negative motivational impact on the group.

Finally, if managers use group decision making, they should particularly try to minimize groupthink. They should encourage member input, especially from those who are less active in the discussion, and avoid expressing their preferred solution early in the group's discussion. Managers might also want to consider one or more of the techniques presented, such as brainstorming or electronic meetings, as a means to lessen pressures to conform.

Understanding Work Teams

After reading this chapter, you should be able to:

1. Explain the growing popularity of teams in organizations

2. Contrast teams with groups

3. Identify three types of teams

4. Demonstrate the linkage between group concepts and high-performing teams

5. Identify ways managers can build trust among team members

6. Explain how organizations can create team players

The Boeing Company has decided that the future of aircraft design lies with replacing the firm's historical military-style hierarchy with self-regulating, cross-disciplinary work teams.[1] As a case in point, the planning and development of Boeing's new 777-200 twin jet revolved around an internal collaboration of designers, production experts, maintenance people, customer-service personnel, finance specialists, and even airline customers. Grouped into small teams of eight or ten, they were charged with the task of refining and meshing all aspects of the aircraft program right from the start. The intention was to have each team consider the aircraft as a whole and to act quickly on ideas, free from chain-of-command second-guessing.

Boeing's past practice was to develop a plane sequentially, starting at the tail and working forward to the nose. First, suggestions would come from the designers, then the production people, then customer-support personnel, and so on. In the process, refinements snowballed. Worse, development costs soared just before the plane went into production as last-minute fixes were made. The inefficiencies of this system resulted in reduced productivity and increased costs.

By using teams on the 777 project, the company was able to "front-load" development costs. That is, it was able to get the "bugs" out of the aircraft before it ever got into production. For instance, the novel folding wingtips on the new 777 had one significant shortcoming: Airlines that wanted a traditional continuous wing couldn't get one. The company initially said that the best it could offer was a wing with foldable tips locked in place. Under the old Boeing way, the airlines would have had to accept the accompanying weight penalty, because a bureaucratic chasm separated workers who designed parts from those who made them. But working closely with shop experts, 777 engineers devised a way to build the continuous wing on the same tool used to make the foldable wing— without disrupting the production work flow. Airline representatives ended up contributing more than 1,000 design changes. Similarly, Boeing's in-house maintenance experts offered hundreds of ideas that helped make the 777 cheaper to operate and faster to service.

Boeing's management believes that the use of teams will allow the company to produce better products, faster, and at lower costs. They have decided to use the teamwork approach on the 737X, a passenger jet scheduled for delivery in 1997, and Boeing's defense group is using teams to design and build the F-22 fighter that is being planned for delivery to the Air Force in 2003.

Why Have Teams Become So Popular?

Twenty years ago, the decision of companies such as Volvo, Toyota, and General Foods to introduce teams into their production processes made news because no one else was doing it. Today, it's just the opposite. It's the organization that doesn't use teams that has become newsworthy. Pick up almost any business periodical today and you'll read how teams have become an essential part of the way business is being done in companies such as General Electric, AT&T, Hewlett-Packard, Motorola, Apple Computer, Shiseido, Federal Express, Chrysler, Saab, 3M Co., John Deere, Texas Instruments, Australian Airlines, Johnson & Johnson, Dayton Hudson, Shenandoah Life Insurance Co., Florida Power & Light, and Emerson Electric. Even the world-famous San Diego Zoo has restructured its native habitat zones around cross-departmental teams.

How do we explain the current popularity of teams? The evidence suggests that teams typically outperform individuals when the tasks being done require multiple skills, judgment, and experience.[2] As organizations have restructured themselves to compete more effectively and efficiently, they have turned to teams as a way to better utilize employee talents. Management has found that teams are more flexible and responsive to changing events than are traditional departments or other forms of permanent groupings. Teams have the capability to quickly assemble, deploy, refocus, and disband.

But don't overlook the motivational properties of teams. Consistent with our discussion in Chapter 5 of the role of employee involvement as a motivator, teams facilitate employee participation in operating decisions. For instance, some assemblyline workers at John Deere are part of sales teams that call on customers.

These workers know the products better than any traditional salesperson, and by traveling and speaking with farmers, these hourly workers develop new skills and become more involved in their jobs. So another explanation for the popularity of teams is that they are an effective means for management to democratize their organizations and increase employee motivation.

Teams versus Groups: What's the Difference?

Groups and teams are not the same thing. In this section, we define and clarify the difference between a work group and a work team. In the last chapter, we defined a *group* as two or more individuals, interacting and interdependent, who have come together to achieve particular objectives. A **work group** is a group who interact primarily to share information and to make decisions to help one another perform within each member's area of responsibility.

Work groups have no need or opportunity to engage in collective work that requires joint effort. So their performance is merely the summation of all the group members' individual contributions. There is no positive synergy that would create an overall level of performance that is greater than the sum of the inputs.

A **work team** generates positive synergy through coordinated effort. Their individual efforts result in a level of performance that is greater than the sum of those individual inputs. Exhibit 8-1 highlights the differences between work groups and work teams.

These definitions help clarify why so many organizations have recently restructured work processes around teams. Management is looking for that positive synergy that will allow their organizations to increase performance.

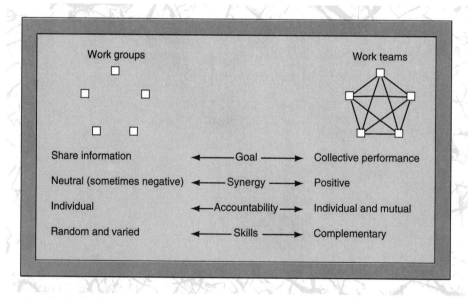

Exhibit 8-1
Comparing Work Groups and Work Teams

The extensive use of teams creates the *potential* for an organization to generate greater outputs with no increase in inputs. Notice, however, we said "potential." There is nothing inherently magical in the creation of teams that assures the achievement of this positive synergy. Merely calling a *group* a *team* doesn't automatically increase its performance. As we'll show later in this chapter, successful or high-performing teams have certain common characteristics. If management hopes to gain increases in organizational performance through the use of teams, it will need to ensure that their teams possess these characteristics.

*T*ypes of Teams

Teams can be classified on the basis of their objective. The three most common forms of teams you're likely to find in an organization are *problem-solving teams, self-managed work teams,* and *cross-functional teams* (see Exhibit 8-2).

Problem-Solving Teams

If we look back fifteen years or so, teams were just beginning to grow in popularity. And the form most of these teams took was similar. They typically were composed of five to twelve hourly employees from the same department who met for a few hours each week to discuss ways of improving quality, efficiency, and the work environment. We call these **problem-solving teams.**

In problem-solving teams, members share ideas or offer suggestions on how work processes and methods can be improved. Rarely, however, are these teams given the authority to unilaterally implement any of their suggested actions.

One of the most widely practiced applications of problem-solving teams during the 1980s was quality circles. As described in Chapter 5, these are work teams of eight to ten employees and supervisors who have a shared area of responsibility and meet regularly to discuss their quality problems, investigate causes of the problems, recommend solutions, and take corrective actions.

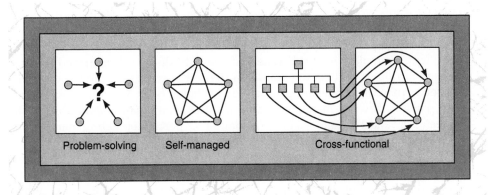

Problem-solving   Self-managed   Cross-functional

Exhibit 8-2
Three Types of Teams

Self-Managed Work Teams

Problem-solving teams were on the right track, but they didn't go far enough in getting employees involved in work-related decisions and processes. This deficiency led to experimentations with truly autonomous teams that could not only solve problems but could also implement solutions and take full responsibility for outcomes.

Self-managed work teams are generally composed of ten to fifteen people who take on the responsibilities of their former supervisors. Typically, these responsibilities include collective control over the pace of work, determination of work assignments, organization of breaks, and collective choice of inspection procedures. Fully self-managed work teams even select their own members and have the members evaluate each other's performance. As a result, supervisory positions take on decreased importance and may even be eliminated. At GE's locomotive-engine plant in Grove City, Pennsylvania, there are about 100 teams, and they make most of the plant's decisions. They arrange the maintenance, schedule the work, and routinely authorize equipment purchases. One team spent $2 million, and the plant manager never flinched. At the L-S Electrogalvanizing Co., in Cleveland, the entire plant is run by self-managed teams. They do their own scheduling, rotate jobs on their own, establish production targets, set pay scales that are linked to skills, fire co-workers, and do the hiring. "I never meet a new employee until his first day on the job," says the plant's general manager.[3]

Xerox, General Motors, Coors Brewing, PepsiCo, Hewlett-Packard, Honeywell, M&M/Mars, and Aetna Life are just a few familiar names that have implemented self-managed work teams. Approximately one in five U.S. employers now uses this form of teams, and experts predict that forty to fifty percent of all U.S. workers could be managing themselves through such teams by the decade's end.[4]

Recent business periodicals have been chock–full of articles describing successful applications of self-managed teams. Texas Instruments' defense group gives self-directed teams credit for helping it win the Malcolm Baldrige National Quality Award and for allowing it to achieve the same level of sales with twenty-five percent fewer employees. Aid Association for Lutherans, one of the largest insurance and financial service companies in the United States, claims that self-managed teams were primarily responsible for helping increase employee satisfaction and allowing the company to increase business volume by fifty percent over a four-year period while cutting work force staff by fifteen percent. The Edy's Grand Ice Cream plant in Fort Wayne, Indiana, introduced self-managed teams in 1990 and attributes to them the plant's thirty-nine percent reduction in costs and fifty-seven percent increase in productivity. Whole Foods Market, a health-food chain, claims that self-managed teams are the main reason it doubled sales between 1989 and 1992 and is able to achieve a 3.7 percent operating margin compared with the average supermarket chain's 2.6.

In spite of these impressive stories, a word of caution needs to be offered here. Some organizations have been disappointed with the results from self-managed teams. For instance, employees at Douglas Aircraft Co., which has been undergoing large layoffs, have revolted against self-managed teams.

They've come to view cooperating with the team concept as an exercise in assisting one's own executioner. The overall research on the effectiveness of self-managed work teams has not been uniformly positive.[5] For example, individuals on these teams do tend to report higher levels of job satisfaction. But, counter to conventional wisdom, employees on self-managed work teams seem to have higher absenteeism and turnover rates than do employees working in traditional work structures. Additional research is needed to determine the specific reasons for these findings.

Cross-Functional Teams

Our description of the Boeing Company's development efforts on the 777, at the opening of this chapter, illustrates the latest application of the team concept. This is the use of **cross-functional teams.** They are made up of employees from about the same hierarchical level, but from different work areas, who come together to accomplish a task.

Many organizations have used horizontal, boundary-spanning groups for years. For example, IBM created a large task force in the 1960s—made up of employees from across departments in the company—to develop the highly successful System 360. And a *task force* is really nothing other than a temporary cross-functional team. Similarly, *committees* composed of members from across departmental lines are another example of cross-functional teams.

But the popularity of cross-discipline work teams exploded in the late 1980s. All the major automobile manufacturers—including Toyota, Honda, Nissan, BMW, GM, Ford, and Chrysler—are using this form of team to coordinate complex projects. For example, the Neon, Chrylser's groundbreaking subcompact, was completely developed by a cross-functional team. The new model was delivered in a speedy forty-two months and for a fraction of what any other manufacturer's small car has cost.

Motorola's Iridium Project illustrates why so many companies have turned to cross-functional teams. This project is developing a huge network that will contain sixty-six satellites. "We realized at the beginning that there was no way we could manage a project of this size and complexity in the traditional way and still get it done on time,"[6] said the project's general manager. For the first year and a half of the project, a cross-functional team of twenty Motorola people met every morning. This number has since been expanded to include diverse expertise from people in dozens of other companies as well, such as McDonnell Douglas, Raytheon, Russia's Khrunichev Enterprise, Lockheed-Martin, Scientific-Atlanta, and General Electric.

In summary, cross-functional teams are an effective means for allowing people from diverse areas within an organization (or even between organizations) to exchange information, develop new ideas and solve problems, and coordinate complex projects. Of course, cross-functional teams are no picnic to manage. Their early stages of development are often very time-consuming as members learn to work with diversity and complexity. It takes time to build trust and teamwork, especially among people from different backgrounds, with different experiences and perspectives. Later in this chapter, we'll discuss ways managers can help facilitate and build trust among team members.

Linking Teams and Group Concepts: Toward Creating High-Performance Teams

In the previous chapter, we introduced some basic group concepts. Let's now build on that introduction and look at how our knowledge of group processes can help us create more effective or high-performance teams.[7]

Size of Work Teams

The best work teams tend to be small. When they have more than about ten to twelve members, it becomes difficult for them to get much done. They have trouble interacting constructively and agreeing on much. Large numbers of people usually can't develop the cohesiveness, commitment, and mutual account-ability necessary to achieve high performance. So in designing effective teams, managers should keep them to under a dozen. If a natural working unit is larger and you want a team effort, consider breaking the group into subteams.

Abilities of Members

To perform effectively, a team requires three different types of skills. First, it needs people with *technical expertise*. Second, it needs people with *problem-solving and decision-making skills* to be able to identify problems, generate alternatives, evaluate those alternatives, and make competent choices. Finally, teams need people with good listening, feedback, conflict-resolution, and other *interpersonal skills*.

No team can achieve its performance potential without developing all three types of skills. The right mix is crucial. Too much of one at the expense of others will lower team performance. But teams don't need to have all the complementary skills in place at their beginning. It's not uncommon for one or more members to take responsibility to learn the skills in which the group is deficient, thereby allowing the team to reach its full potential.

Allocating Roles and Promoting Diversity

In Chapter 3, we demonstrated that people differ in terms of personality traits and that employee performance is enhanced when individuals are put into jobs that are compatible with their personalities. Well, the same thing is true with regard to filling positions on a work team. Teams have different needs, and people should be selected for a team on the basis of their personalities and preferences.

High-performing teams properly match people to various roles. For example, the basketball coaches who continually win over the long term have learned how to size up prospective players, identify their strengths and weaknesses, and then assign them to positions that best fit their skills and allow them to contribute most to the overall team's performance. They recognize that winning teams need a variety of skills—for example, ball handlers, power scorers, three-point shooters, and shot blockers. Successful teams have people to fill all the key

> **Creator-Innovators:** Initiate creative ideas
> **Explorer-Promoters:** Champion ideas after they're initiated
> **Assessor-Developers:** Analyze decision options
> **Thruster-Organizers:** Provide structure
> **Concluder-Producers:** Provide direction and follow-through
> **Controller-Inspectors:** Check for details
> **Upholder-Maintainers:** Fight external battles
> **Reporter-Advisers:** Seek full information
> **Linkers:** Coordinate and integrate

Exhibit 8-3
Nine Team Roles

Source: C. Margerison and D. McCann, Team Management: Practical New Approaches (London: Mercury Books, 1990).

roles and have selected people to play in those roles on the basis of their skills and preferences.

One stream of research has identified nine potential team roles that people prefer to play[8] (see Exhibit 8-3). Let's briefly describe each and then consider their implications in creating high-performance teams.

Creator-Innovators. Creator-innovators are imaginative and good at initiating ideas or concepts. They are typically very independent and prefer to work at their own pace in their own way.

Explorer-Promoters. Explorer-promoters like to take new ideas and "champion" their cause. They are good at picking up ideas from creator-innovators and finding the resources to promote those ideas. Their primary weakness is that they may not always have the patience and control skills to ensure that the ideas are followed through in detail.

Assessor-Developers. Assessor-developers have strong analytical skills. They're at their best when given several different options to evaluate and analyze before a decision is made.

Thruster-Organizers. Thruster-organizers like to set up operating procedures to turn ideas into reality and get things done. They set goals, establish plans, organize people, and establish systems to ensure that deadlines are met.

Concluder-Producers. Like thruster-organizers, concluder-producers are also concerned with results. Only their role focuses on insisting that deadlines are kept and ensuring that all commitments are followed on through. They take pride in producing a regular output to a standard.

Controller-Inspectors. Controller-inspectors are people with a high concern for establishing and enforcing rules and regulations. They are good at examining details and making sure that inaccuracies are avoided. They want to check all the facts and figures; they want to make sure that the "*i*s are dotted" and the "*t*s are crossed."

Upholder-Maintainers. Upholder-maintainers hold strong convictions about the way things should be done. They'll defend and fight the team's battles with outsiders while at the same time strongly supporting internal team members. Upholder-maintainers are important because they provide team stability.

Reporter-Advisers. Reporter-advisers are good listeners and don't tend to press their point of view on others. They tend to favor getting more information before making decisions. As such, they perform an important role in encouraging the team to seek additional information before making decisions and in discouraging the team from making hasty decisions.

Linkers. The last role overlaps the others. It can be played by any of the previous eight. Linkers try to understand all views. They are coordinators and integrators. They dislike extremism and try to build cooperation among all team members. They recognize the various contributions that other team members can make and try to integrate people and activities despite the differences that may exist.

If forced to, most people can perform in any of these roles, but most have two or three roles they strongly prefer. Managers need to understand the individual strengths that each can bring to a team, select members with those strengths in mind, and allocate work assignments that fit with members' preferred styles. By matching individual preferences with team role demands, managers increase the likelihood that the team members will work well together. The researchers who developed this framework argue that unsuccessful teams have an unbalanced portfolio of individual talents, with too much energy being expended in one area and not enough in other areas.

Having a Commitment to a Common Purpose

Does the team have a meaningful purpose to which all members aspire? This purpose is a vision. It's broader than specific goals. Effective teams have a common and meaningful purpose that provides direction, momentum, and commitment for members.

The development team at Apple Computer that designed the Macintosh, for example, was almost religiously committed to creating a user-friendly machine that would revolutionize the way people used computers. Production teams at Saturn Corp. are driven and united by the common purpose of building an American automobile that can successfully compete in terms of quality and price with the best Japanese cars.

Members of successful teams put a tremendous amount of time and effort into discussing, shaping, and agreeing upon a purpose that belongs to them both collectively and individually. This common purpose, when accepted by the team, becomes the equivalent of what celestial navigation is to a ship captain—it provides direction and guidance under any and all conditions.

Establishing Specific Goals

Successful teams translate their common purpose into specific, measurable, and realistic performance goals. Just as we demonstrated in Chapter 4 that goals lead individuals to higher performance, goals also energize teams. These specific goals facilitate clear communication. They also help teams maintain their focus on getting results. Thermos Corp., for example, created a cross-functional team in the fall of 1990 with the specific task of designing and building an innovative barbecue grill. They agreed that they would create a new grill that looked like a handsome piece of furniture, didn't require pollutants such as charcoal lighter, and cooked food that tasted good. The team also agreed on a rock-solid deadline. They wanted to have their grill ready for the big National Hardware Show in August 1992. So they had a little less than two years to plan, design, and build their new product. And that's exactly what they did. They created the Thermos Thermal Electric Grill, which has since won four design awards and become one of the most successful new product launches in the company's history.

Leadership and Structure

Goals define the team's end targets. But high-performance teams also need leadership and structure to provide focus and direction. Defining and agreeing on a common approach, for example, assures that the team is unified on the means for achieving its goals.

Team members must agree on who is to do what and must ensure that all members share equally in the work load. In addition, the team needs to determine how schedules will be set, what skills need to be developed, how the group will resolve conflicts, and how the group will make and modify decisions. Agreeing on the specifics of work and how it fits together to integrate individual skills requires team leadership and structure. This, incidentally, can be provided directly by management or by the team members themselves as they fulfill explorer-promoter, thruster-organizer, concluder-producer, upholder-maintainer, and linker roles.

Social Loafing and Accountability

We learned in the previous chapter that individuals can hide inside a group. They can engage in "social loafing" and coast on the group's effort because their individual contributions can't be identified. High-performing teams undermine this tendency by holding themselves accountable at both the individual and team level.

Successful teams make members individually and jointly accountable for the team's purpose, goals, and approach. They are clear on both their individual and joint responsibilities.

Appropriate Performance Evaluation and Reward Systems

How do you get team members to be both individually and jointly accountable? The traditional individually oriented evaluation and reward system must be modified to reflect team performance. Individual performance evaluations, fixed hourly wages, individual incentives, and the like are not consistent with the development of high-performance teams. So, in addition to evaluating and rewarding employees for their individual contribution, management should consider group-based appraisals, profit sharing, gainsharing, small-group incentives, and other system modifications that will reinforce team effort and commitment.

Developing High Mutual Trust

High-performance teams are characterized by high mutual trust among members. That is, members believe in the integrity, character, and ability of each other. But as you know from personal relationships, trust is fragile. It takes a long time to build, can be easily destroyed, and is hard to regain. Also, since trust begets trust and distrust begets distrust, maintaining trust requires careful attention by management.

Dimensions of Trust. Recent research has identified five dimensions that underly the concept of trust (see Exhibit 8-4)[9]:

Integrity: Honesty and truthfulness
Competence: Technical and interpersonal knowledge and skills
Consistency: Reliability, predictability, and good judgment in handling situations
Loyalty: Willingness to protect and save face for a person
Openness: Willingness to share ideas and information freely

Exhibit 8-4
Dimensions of Trust

In terms of trust among team members, it has been found that the relative importance of these five dimensions is fairly constant: integrity > competence > loyalty > consistency > openness.[10] Moreover, integrity and competence are the most critical characteristics that an individual looks for in determining another's trustworthiness. Integrity seems to be rated highest because "without a perception of the other's 'moral character' and 'basic honesty,' other dimensions of trust were meaningless."[11] The high ranking of competence is probably due to the need for peer interaction by team members in order to successfully complete their job responsibilities.

How Do You Build Trust? Managers and team leaders have a significant impact on a team's trust climate. As a result, managers and team leaders need to build trust between themselves and team members. The following summarizes ways you can build trust.[12]

Demonstrate that you're working for others' interests as well as your own. All of us are concerned with our own self-interest. But if others see you using them, your job, or the organization for your personal goals to the exclusion of your team, department, and organization's interests, your credibility will be undermined.

Be a team player. Support your work team through both words and actions. Defending the team and team members when they're attacked by outsiders will demonstrate your loyalty to your work group.

Practice openness. Mistrust comes as much from what people don't know as from what they do know. Openness leads to confidence and trust. So keep people informed, explain your decisions, be candid about problems, and fully disclose relevant information.

Be fair. Before making decisions or taking actions, consider how others will perceive them in terms of objectivity and fairness. Give credit where it's due, be objective and impartial in performance evaluations, and pay attention to equity perceptions in reward distributions.

Speak your feelings. Managers and leaders who convey only hard facts come across as cold and distant. If you share your feelings, others will see you as real and human. They will know who you are and this, in turn will increase their respect for you.

Show consistency in the basic values that guide your decision making. Mistrust comes from not knowing what to expect. Take the time to think about your values and beliefs. Then let them consistently guide your decisions. When you know your central purpose, your actions will follow accordingly, and you'll project a consistency that earns trust.

Maintain confidences. You trust those you can confide in and rely on. So if people tell you something in confidence, they need to feel confident that you won't discuss it with others or betray that confidence. If people perceive you as someone who "leaks" personal confidences or someone who can't be depended upon, you won't be perceived as trustworthy.

Demonstrate competence. Develop the admiration and respect of others by demonstrating technical and professional ability and good business sense. Pay particular attention to developing and displaying your communication, team-building, and other interpersonal skills.

Turning Individuals into Team Players

To this point, we've made a strong case for the value and growing popularity of teams. But many people are not inherently "team players." They're loners or people who want to be recognized for their individual achievements. There are also a great many organizations that have historically nurtured individual accomplishments. They have created competitive work environments where only the strong survive. If these organizations adopt teams, what do they do about the selfish, "I-have-to-look-out-for-me" employees that they've created? And finally, as we discussed in Chapter 2, countries differ in terms of how they rate on individualism and collectivism. Teams fit well with countries that score high on collectivism. But what if an organization wants to introduce teams into a work population that is made up largely of individuals born and raised in a highly individualistic society? As one writer so aptly put it, in describing the role of teams in the United States: "Americans don't grow up learning how to function in teams. In school we never receive a team report card or learn the names of the team of sailors who traveled with Columbus to America."[13] This limitation would be just as true of Canadians, British, Australians, and others from highly individualistic societies.

The Challenge

The previous points are meant to dramatize that one substantial barrier to using work teams is individual resistance. An employee's success is no longer defined in terms of individual performance. To perform well as team members, individuals must be able to communicate openly and honestly, confront differences and resolve conflicts, and sublimate personal goals for the good of the team. For many employees, these abilities are difficult—sometimes impossible—to achieve. The challenge of creating team players will be greatest where (1) the national culture is highly individualistic and (2) the teams are being introduced into an established organization that has historically valued individual achievement. These conditions describe, for instance, the situation that faced managers at AT&T, Ford, Motorola, and other large U.S.-based companies. These firms prospered by hiring and rewarding corporate stars, and they bred a competitive climate that encouraged individual achievement and recognition. Employees in these types of firms can be jolted by a sudden shift to the importance of team play. One veteran employee of a large company, who had done very well by working alone, described the experience of joining a team: "I'm learning my lesson. I just had my first negative performance appraisal in twenty years."[14]

On the other hand, the challenge for management is less demanding when teams are introduced where employees have strong collectivist values—such as in Japan or Mexico—or in new organizations that use teams as their initial form for structuring work. Saturn Corp., for instance, is an American organization and owned by General Motors. But the company was designed around teams from its inception. Everyone at Saturn was initially hired with the knowledge that they would be working in teams. And the ability to be a good team player was a basic hiring qualification that all new employees had to meet.

Shaping Team Players

The following summarizes the primary options managers have for trying to turn individuals into team players.

Selection.   Some people already possess the interpersonal skills to be effective team players. When hiring team members, managers should take care to ensure that candidates can fulfill their team roles as well as having the technical skills required to fill the job.

Many job candidates, especially those socialized around individual contributions, don't have team skills. When faced with such candidates, managers basically have three options. The candidates can undergo training to "make them into team players." If this approach isn't possible or doesn't work, the other two options are to place the candidate in a unit within the organization that doesn't have teams (if one exists) or don't hire the candidate. In established organizations that decide to redesign jobs around teams, it should be expected that some employees will resist being team players and may be untrainable. Unfortunately, such people typically become casualties of the team approach.

Training.   On a more optimistic note, a large proportion of people raised on the importance of individual accomplishment can be trained to become team players. Training specialists conduct exercises that allow employees to experience the satisfaction that teamwork can provide. They typically offer workshops to help employees improve their problem-solving, communication, negotiation, conflict-management, coaching, and group-development skills. Emerson Electric's Speciality Motor Division in Missouri, for instance, has achieved remarkable success in getting its 650-member work force not only to accept, but to welcome, team training. Outside consultants were brought in to give workers practical skills for working in teams. After less than a year, employees enthusiastically accepted the value of teamwork.

Rewards.   The reward system needs to be reworked to encourage cooperative efforts rather than competitive ones. For instance, Lockheed-Martin's Space Launch Systems Company has organized its 1,400 employees into teams. Rewards are structured to return to the team members a percentage increase in the "bottom line" based on the achievement of the team's performance goals.

Promotions, pay raises, and other forms of recognition should be given to individuals for how effective they are as a collaborative team member. This doesn't mean that individual contribution is ignored; rather, it is balanced with selfless contributions to the team. Examples of behaviors that should be rewarded include training new colleagues, sharing information with teammates, helping resolve team conflicts, and mastering new skills that your team needs but in which it's deficient.

Lastly, don't forget the intrinsic rewards that employees can receive from teamwork. Teams provide camaraderie. It's exciting and satisfying to be an integral part of a successful team. The opportunity to engage in personal development and to help teammates grow can be a very satisfying and rewarding experience for employees.

mplications for Managers

Few trends have influenced jobs as much as the massive movement to introduce teams into the workplace. The shift from working alone to working on teams requires employees to cooperate with others, share information, confront differences, and sublimate personal interests for the greater good of the team.

High-performing teams have been found to have common characteristics. They tend to be small. They contain people with three different types of skills: technical, problem-solving and decision-making, and interpersonal. They properly match people to various roles. These teams have a commitment to a common purpose, establish specific goals, and have the leadership and structure to provide focus and direction. They also hold themselves accountable at both the individual and team levels by having well-designed evaluation and reward systems. Finally, high-performing teams are characterized by high mutual trust among members.

Because individualistic organizations and societies attract and reward individual accomplishment, it is more difficult to create team players in these environments than in collectivistic ones. To make the conversion, management should try to select individuals with the interpersonal skills to be effective team players, provide training to develop teamwork skills, and reward individuals for cooperative efforts.

*C*ommunication

After reading this chapter, you should be able to:

1. Define communication and list its four functions

2. Describe the communication process

3. Contrast the three common types of small-group networks

4. Identify factors affecting the use of the grapevine

5. Describe common barriers to effective communication

6. List four rules for improving cross-cultural communication

7. Outline behaviors associated with providing effective feedback

8. Identify the behaviors related to effective active listening

Probably the most frequently cited source of interpersonal conflict is poor communication.[1] Because we spend nearly seventy percent of our waking hours communicating—writing, reading, speaking, listening—it seems reasonable to conclude that one of the most inhibiting forces to successful group performance is a lack of effective communication.

No group can exist without communication: the transference of meaning among its members. It is only through transmitting meaning from one person to another that information and ideas can be conveyed. Communication, however, is more than merely imparting meaning. It must also be understood. In a group in which one member speaks only German and the others do not know

German, the individual speaking German will not be understood. Therefore, **communication** must include both the *transference* and *understanding* of meaning.

An idea, no matter how great, is useless until it is transmitted and understood by others. Perfect communication, if there were such a thing, would exist when a thought or idea was transmitted so that the mental picture perceived by the receiver was exactly the same as that envisioned by the sender. Although elementary in theory, perfect communication is never achieved in practice, for reasons we expand on later. Before making too many generalizations concerning communication and problems in communicating effectively, we need to review briefly the functions that communication performs and describe the communication process.

*f*unctions of Communication

Communication serves four major functions within a group or organization: control, motivation, emotional expression, and information.[2] Communication acts to *control* member behavior in several ways. Organizations have authority hierarchies and formal guidelines that employees are required to follow. When employees, for instance, are required to first communicate any job-related grievance to their immediate boss, to follow their job description, or to comply with company policies, communication is performing a control function. But informal communication also controls behavior. When work groups tease or harass a member who produces too much (and makes the rest of the group look bad), they are informally communicating with, and controlling, the member's behavior.

Communication fosters *motivation* by clarifying for employees what is to be done, how well they are doing, and what can be done to improve performance if it's subpar. We saw this aspect of communication operating in our review of goal-setting and reinforcement theories in Chapter 4. The formation of specific goals, feedback on progress toward the goals, and reinforcement of desired behavior all stimulate motivation and require communication.

For many employees, their work group is a primary source for social interaction. The communication that takes place within the group is a fundamental mechanism by which members show their frustrations and feelings of satisfaction. Communication, therefore, provides an avenue for *expression of emotions* and fulfillment of social needs.

The final function that communication performs is related to its role in facilitating decision making. It provides the *information* that individuals and groups need to make decisions by transmitting the data to identify and evaluate choices.

No one of these four functions should be seen as being more important than the others. For groups to perform effectively, they need to maintain some form of control over members, stimulate members to perform, provide a means for emotional expression, and make choices. You can assume that almost every communication interaction that takes place in a group or organization performs one or more of these four functions.

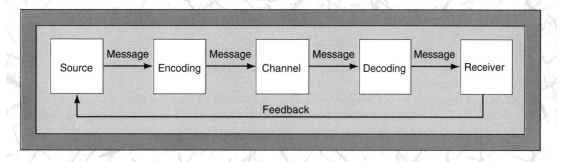

Exhibit 9-1
The Communication Process

The Communication Process

Before communication can take place, a purpose, expressed as a message to be conveyed, is needed. It passes between a source (the sender) and a receiver. The message is encoded (converted to a symbolic form) and passed by way of some medium (channel) to the receiver, who retranslates (decodes) the message initiated by the sender. The result is a transference of meaning from one person to another.

Exhibit 9-1 depicts this **communication process.** This model is made up of seven parts: (1) the communication source, (2) encoding, (3) the message, (4) the channel, (5) decoding, (6) the receiver, and (7) feedback.

The *source* initiates a message by encoding a thought. The *message* is the actual physical product from the source *encoding*. When we speak, the speech is the message. When we write, the writing is the message. When we gesture, the movements of our arms and the expressions on our faces are the message. The *channel* is the medium through which the message travels. It is selected by the source, who must determine whether to use a formal or informal channel. Formal channels are established by the organization and transmit messages that are related to the professional activities of members. They traditionally follow the authority chain within the organization. Other forms of messages, such as personal or social, follow the informal channels in the organization. The *receiver* is the object to whom the message is directed. But before the message can be received, the symbols in it must be translated into a form that can be understood by the receiver. This step is the *decoding* of the message. The final link in the communication process is a feedback loop. *Feedback* is the check on how successful we have been in transferring our messages as originally intended. It determines whether understanding has been achieved.

Direction of Communication

Communication can flow vertically or laterally. The vertical dimension can be further divided into downward and upward directions.

Downward

Communication that flows from one level of a group or organization to a lower level is a downward communication. When we think of managers communicating with subordinates, the downward pattern is the one we are usually thinking of. It's used by group leaders and managers to assign goals, provide job instructions, inform underlings of policies and procedures, point out problems that need attention, and offer feedback about performance. But downward communication doesn't have to be oral or face-to-face contact. When management sends letters to employees' homes to advise them of the organization's new sick leave policy, it is using downward communication.

Upward

Upward communication flows to a higher level in the group or organization. It's used to provide feedback to higher-ups, inform them of progress toward goals, and relay current problems. Upward communication keeps managers aware of how employees feel about their jobs, co-workers, and the organization in general. Managers also rely on upward communication for ideas on how things can be improved.

Some organizational examples of upward communication are performance reports prepared by lower management for review by middle and top management, suggestion boxes, employee attitude surveys, grievance procedures, superior-subordinate discussions, and informal "gripe" sessions in which employees have the opportunity to identify and discuss problems with their boss or representatives of higher management. For example, Federal Express prides itself on its computerized upward communication program. All 88,000 employees annually complete climate surveys and reviews of management. This program was cited as a key human resources strength by the Malcolm Baldrige National Quality Award examiners when Federal Express won the honor.[3]

Lateral

When communication takes place among members of the same work group, among members of work groups at the same level, among managers at the same level, or among any horizontally equivalent personnel, we describe it as lateral communications. Why would there be a need for horizontal communications if a group or organization's vertical communications are effective? The answer is that horizontal communications are often necessary to save time and facilitate coordination. In some cases, these lateral relationships are formally sanctioned. Often, they are informally created to short-circuit the vertical hierarchy and expedite action. So lateral communications can, from management's viewpoint, be good or bad. Since strict adherence to the formal vertical structure for all communications can impede the efficient and accurate transfer of information, lateral communications can be beneficial. In such cases, they occur with the knowledge and support of superiors. But they can create dysfunctional conflicts when the formal vertical channels are breached, when members go above or around their superiors to get things done, or when bosses find out that actions have been taken or decisions made without their knowledge.

*P*opular Ways to Communicate

How do group members transfer meaning between and among each other? There are three basic methods. People essentially rely on oral, written, and non-verbal communication.

The Obvious: Oral and Written Communication

The chief means of conveying messages is oral communication. Speeches, formal one-on-one and group discussions, and the informal rumor mill or grapevine are popular forms of oral communication.

The advantages of oral communication are speed and feedback. A verbal message can be conveyed and a response received in a minimal amount of time. If the receiver is unsure of the message, rapid feedback allows for early detection by the sender and, hence, allows for early correction.

The major disadvantage of oral communication surfaces in organizations, or whenever the message has to be passed through a number of people. The more people a message must pass through, the greater the potential distortion. If you ever played the game "telephone" at a party, you know the problem. Each person interprets the message in his or her own way. The message's content, when it reaches its destination, is often very different from that of the original. In an organization, where decisions and other communiqués are verbally passed up and down the authority hierarchy, there are considerable opportunities for messages to become distorted.

Written communications include memos, letters, electronic mail, fax transmissions, organizational periodicals, notices placed on bulletin boards, or any other device that is transmitted via written words or symbols. Why would a sender choose to use written communications? They're tangible and verifiable. Typically, both the sender and receiver have a record of the communication. The message can be stored for an indefinite period of time. If there are questions concerning the content of the message, it is physically available for later reference. This feature is particularly important for complex and lengthy communications. The marketing plan for a new product is likely to contain a number of tasks spread out over several months. By putting it in writing, those who have to initiate the plan can readily refer to it over the life of the plan. A final benefit of written communication comes from the process itself. You're usually more careful with the written word than the oral word. You're forced to think more thoroughly about what you want to convey in a written message than in a spoken one. Thus written communications are more likely to be well thought-out, logical, and clear.

Of course, written messages have their drawbacks. They're time-consuming. You could convey far more information to a college instructor in a one-hour oral exam than in a one-hour written exam. In fact, you could probably say the same thing in ten to fifteen minutes that it would take you an hour to write. So, although writing may be more precise, it also consumes a great deal of time. The other major disadvantage is feedback, or lack of it. Oral communication allows the receiver to respond rapidly to what he thinks he hears. Written communication, however, does not have a built-in feedback mechanism. The result is that the mailing of a memo is no assurance it has been received, and, if received, there is no guarantee the recipient will interpret it as the sender intended. The latter point is also relevant in oral communiqués, except it's easy in such cases merely to ask the receiver to summarize what you've said. An accurate summary presents feedback evidence that the message has been received and understood.

The Not-So-Obvious: Nonverbal Communication

Some of the most meaningful communications are not conveyed verbally or in writing. These are the "not-so-obvious" nonverbal communications. Every time we verbally give a message to someone, we also impart a nonverbal message. In some instances, the nonverbal component may stand alone. For example, in a singles bar, a glance, a stare, a smile, a frown, and a provocative body movement all convey meaning. Obviously, no discussion of communication would be complete without consideration of this not-so-obvious dimension of communication. For our purposes, we define *nonverbal communication* to include body movements, the intonations or emphasis we give to words, facial expressions, and the physical distance between the sender and receiver.

The academic study of body motions has been labeled *kinesics*. It refers to gestures, facial configurations, and other movements of the body. But it is a relatively young field, and it has been subject to far more conjecture and popularizing than the research findings support. Hence, while we acknowledge the fact that body movement is an important segment of the study of communication and behavior, conclusions must, of necessity, be guarded. Recognizing this qualification, let us briefly consider the ways body motions convey meaning.

It can be argued that every *body movement* has a meaning and no movement is accidental. For example, through body language we say, "Help me, I'm lonely"; "Take me, I'm available"; "Leave me alone, I'm depressed." And rarely do we send our messages consciously. We act out our state of being with nonverbal body language. We lift one eyebrow for disbelief. We rub our noses for puzzlement. We clasp our arms to isolate ourselves or to protect ourselves. We shrug our shoulders for indifference, wink one eye for intimacy, tap our fingers for impatience, slap our forehead for forgetfulness.

We may disagree with the specific meanings of the movements just described, but we cannot deny that body language adds to, and often complicates, verbal communication. A body position or movement does not by itself have a precise or universal meaning, but when it is linked with spoken language, it gives fuller meaning to a sender's message.

If you read the verbatim minutes of a meeting, you could not grasp the impact of what was said in the same way you could if you had been there or saw the meeting on video. Why? There is no record of nonverbal communication. The emphasis given to words or phrases is missing. To illustrate how *intonations* can change the meaning of a message, consider the student in class who asks the instructor a question. The instructor replies, "What do you mean by that?" The student's reaction will be different depending on the tone of the instructor's response. A soft, smooth tone creates a different meaning from an intonation that is abrasive with strong emphasis placed on the last word.

The *facial expression* of the instructor in the previous illustration also conveys meaning. A snarling face says something different from a smile. Facial expressions, along with intonations, can show arrogance, aggressiveness, fear, shyness, and other characteristics that would never be communicated if you read a transcript of what had been said.

The way individuals space themselves in terms of *physical distance* also has meaning. What is considered proper spacing is largely dependent on cultural norms. For example, what is considered a businesslike distance in some European countries would be viewed as intimate in many parts of North America. If someone stands closer to you than is considered appropriate, it may indicate aggressiveness or sexual interest; if farther away than usual, it may mean disinterest or displeasure with what is being said.

It is important for the receiver to be alert to these nonverbal aspects of communication. You should look for nonverbal cues as well as listen to the literal meaning of a sender's words. You should particularly be aware of contradictions between the messages. Your boss may say she is free to talk to you about a pressing budget problem, but you may see nonverbal signals suggesting that this is *not* the time to discuss the subject. Regardless of what is being said, an individual who frequently glances at her wristwatch is giving the message that she would prefer to terminate the conversation. We misinform others when we express one emotion verbally, such as trust, but nonverbally communicate a contradictory message that reads, "I don't have confidence in you." These contradictions often suggest that "actions speak louder (and more accurately) than words."

*C*ommunication Networks

The channels by which information flows are critical once we move beyond groups of two or three individuals. The way a group structures itself will determine the ease and availability with which members can transmit information.

Formal Small-Group Networks

Most studies of communication networks have taken place in groups created in a laboratory setting. As a result, the research conclusions tend to be constrained by the artificial setting and limited to small groups. Three common types of small-group networks are shown in Exhibit 9-2 (see page 130); these are the chain, wheel, and all-channel. The chain rigidly follows the formal chain of command. The wheel relies on the leader to act as the central conduit for all the group's communication. The all-channel permits all group members to actively communicate with each other. The all-channel network is most often characterized in practice by the problem-solving task force, in which all group members are free to contribute.

The effectiveness of each type of network depends on the goals of the group.[4] For instance, if speed is important, the wheel and all-channel networks are most effective. For accuracy, choose the chain or wheel. The wheel is best for allowing leaders to emerge. And if member satisfaction is important, the all-channel network is best and the wheel worst. The point is that no single network will be best for all occasions.

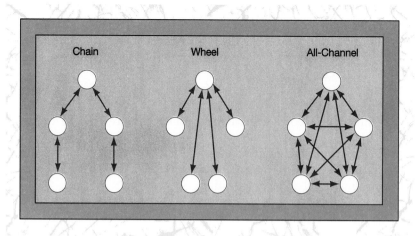

Exhibit 9-2
Three Common Small-Group Networks

The Informal Group Communication Network

The formal system is not the only communication system in a group or organization. There is also an informal system—where information flows along the well-known *grapevine* and rumors can flourish.

A classic study of the grapevine was reported forty years ago.[5] The researcher investigated the communication pattern among sixty-seven managerial personnel in a small manufacturing firm. The basic approach used was to learn from each communication recipient how he first received a given piece of information and then trace it back to its source. It was found that, although the grapevine was an important source of information, only ten percent of the executives acted as liaison individuals, that is, passed the information on to more than one other person. For example, when one executive decided to resign to enter the insurance business, eighty-one percent of the executives knew about it, but only eleven percent transmitted this information to others.

Two other conclusions from this study are also worth noting. Information on events of general interest tended to flow between the major functional groups (production, sales) rather than within them. Also, no evidence surfaced to suggest that any one group consistently acted as liaisons; rather, different types of information passed through different liaison persons.

An attempt to replicate this study among employees in a small state government office also found that only ten percent act as liaison individuals.[6] This finding is interesting, because the replication contained a wider spectrum of employees, including rank-and-file as well as managerial personnel. But the flow of information in the government office took place within, rather than between, functional groups. It was proposed that this discrepancy might be due to comparing an executive-only sample against one that also included rank-and-file workers. Managers, for example, might feel greater pressure to stay informed and thus cultivate others outside their immediate functional group. Also, in contrast to the findings of the original study, the replication found that a consistent group of individuals acted as liaisons by transmitting information in the government office.

Is the information that flows along the grapevine accurate? The evidence indicates that about seventy-five percent of what is carried is accurate.[7] But what conditions foster an active grapevine? What gets the rumor mill rolling?

It is frequently assumed that rumors start because they make titillating gossip. This is rarely the case. Rumors emerge as a response to situations that are *important* to us, where there is *ambiguity*, and under conditions that arouse *anxiety*. The fact that work situations frequently contain these three elements explains why rumors flourish in organizations. The secrecy and competition that typically prevail in large organizations—around such issues as the appointment of new bosses, the relocation of offices, downsizing decisions, and the realignment of work assignments—create conditions that encourage and sustain rumors on the grapevine. A rumor will persist either until the wants and expectations creating the uncertainty underlying the rumor are fulfilled or until the anxiety is reduced.

What can we conclude from the preceding discussion? Certainly the grapevine is an important part of any group or organization's communication network and is well worth understanding. It identifies for managers those confusing issues that employees consider important and that create anxiety. It acts, therefore, as both a filter and a feedback mechanism, picking up the issues that employees consider relevant. For employees, the grapevine is particularly valuable for translating formal communications into their group's own jargon. Maybe more important, again from a managerial perspective, it seems possible to analyze grapevine information and to predict its flow, given that only a small set of individuals (around ten percent) actively pass on information to more than one other person. By assessing which liaison individuals will consider a given piece of information to be relevant, we can improve our ability to explain and predict the pattern of the grapevine.

Barriers to Effective Communication

A number of barriers can retard or distort effective communication. In this section, we highlight a half-dozen of these barriers.

Filtering

Filtering refers to a sender's purposely manipulating information so it will be seen more favorably by the receiver. For example, when a manager tells his boss what he feels his boss wants to hear, he is filtering information.

The major determinant of filtering is the number of levels in an organization's structure. The more vertical levels in the organization's hierarchy, the more opportunities there are for filtering.

Selective Perception

We have mentioned selective perception before in this book. It appears again because the receiver, in the communication process, sees and hears things in a selective way, based on his needs, motivations, experience, background, and other personal characteristics. The receiver also projects his interests and expectations into communications as he decodes them. The employment interviewer who expects a female job candidate to put family before career is likely to *see* that priority in female candidates, regardless of whether the candidates feel that way or not. As we said in Chapter 3, we don't see reality; we interpret what we see and call it reality.

Gender Styles

Men and women use oral communication for different reasons. Consequently, gender becomes a barrier to effective communication between the sexes.

Research evidence indicates that men use talk to emphasize status, whereas women use it to create connection.[8] That is, men speak and hear a language of status and independence, and women speak and hear a language of connection and intimacy. So, for many men, conversations are primarily a means to preserve independence and maintain status in a hierarchical social order. For many women, conversations are negotiations for closeness in which people try to seek and give confirmation and support. For example, men frequently complain that women talk on and on about their problems. Women criticize men for not listening. What's happening is that when men hear a problem, they want to assert their desire for independence and control by providing solutions. Women, on the other hand, view relating a problem as a way to promote closeness. The women present the problem to gain support and connection, not to get the male's advice.

Emotions

How the receiver feels at the time of receipt of a communication message will influence how he or she interprets it. The same message received when you're angry or distraught is often interpreted differently from when you're happy. Extreme emotions such as jubilation or depression are most likely to hinder effective communication. In such instances, we are most prone to disregard our rational and objective thinking processes and substitute emotional judgments.

Language

Words mean different things to different people. Age, education, and cultural background are three of the more obvious variables that influence the language a person uses and the definitions he gives to words. The language of William F. Buckley Jr. is clearly different from that of a factory worker who has earned only a high school diploma. The latter, in fact, would undoubtedly have trouble understanding much of Buckley's vocabulary. In an organization, employees usually come from diverse backgrounds. Further, the grouping of employees into departments creates specialists who develop their own jargon or technical language. In large organizations, members are also frequently widely dispersed geographically —even operating in different countries—and individuals in each locale will use terms and phrases that are unique to their area. The existence of vertical levels can also cause language problems. For instance, differences in meaning with regard to words such as *incentives* and *quotas* have been found at different levels in management. Top managers often speak about the need for incentives and quotas, yet these terms imply manipulation and create resentment among many lower managers.

The point is that, although you and I speak a common language—English— our usage of that language is far from uniform. If we knew how each of us modified the language, communication difficulties would be minimized. The problem is that members in an organization usually don't know how those with whom they interact have modified the language. Senders tend to assume that the words and terms they use mean the same to the receiver as they do to them. This assumption is often incorrect.

Nonverbal Cues

Earlier we noted that nonverbal communication is an important way in which people convey messages. But nonverbal communication is almost always accompanied by oral communication. As long as the two are in agreement, they act to reinforce each other. My boss's words tell me he is angry, his tone and body movements indicate anger; so I can conclude, probably correctly, that he is angry. When nonverbal cues are inconsistent with the oral message, however, the receiver becomes confused, and the clarity of the message suffers.

*C*ross-Cultural Communication

Effective communication is difficult under the best of conditions. Cross-cultural factors clearly create the potential for increased communication problems.[9]

The process of encoding and decoding of messages into symbols is based on an individual's cultural background and, as a result, is not the same for all people. The greater the differences in backgrounds between sender and receiver, the greater the differences in meanings attached to particular words or behaviors. People from different cultures see, interpret, and evaluate things differently, and consequently act on them differently.

When communicating with people from a different culture, what can you do to reduce misperceptions, misinterpretations, and misevaluations? Following these four rules can be helpful:

1. *Assume differences until similarity is proved*. Most of us assume that others are more similar to us than they actually are. But people from different countries often are very different from us. So you are far less likely to err if you assume that others are different from you rather than assuming similarity until difference is proved.

2. *Emphasize description rather than interpretation or evaluation*. Interpreting or evaluating what someone has said or done, in contrast to description, is based more on the observer's culture and background than on the observed situation. So delay judgment until you've had sufficient time to observe and interpret the situation from the perspectives of all cultures involved.

3. *Practice empathy*. Before sending a message, put yourself in the receiver's shoes. What are his or her values, experiences, and frames of reference? What do you know about his or her education, upbringing, and background that can give you added insight? Try to see the other person as he or she really is.

4. *Treat your interpretation as a working hypothesis*. Once you've developed an explanation for a new situation or think you empathize with someone from a foreign culture, treat your interpretation as a hypothesis that needs further testing rather than as a certainty. Carefully assess the feedback provided by receivers to see if it confirms your hypothesis. For important decisions or communiqués, you can also check with other foreign and home-country colleagues to make sure your interpretations are on target.

mplications for Managers

Given the barriers to communication, what can managers do to minimize problems and attempt to overcome those barriers? The following suggestions should be helpful in making communication more effective.

Use Feedback

Many communication problems can be attributed directly to misunderstandings and inaccuracies. These are less likely to occur if the manager ensures that the feedback loop is utilized in the communication process (see Exhibit 9-3). This feedback can be verbal, written, or nonverbal.

If a manager asks a receiver, "Did you understand what I said?", the response represents feedback. But the "yes" or "no" type of feedback can definitely be improved upon. The manager can ask a set of questions relating to a message in order to determine whether the message was received as intended. Better yet, the manager can ask the receiver to restate the message, in his or her own words. If the manager then hears what was intended, understanding and accuracy should be enhanced. Feedback can also be more subtle than the direct asking of questions or the summarizing of the message by the receiver. General comments can give the manager a sense of a receiver's reaction to a message. In addition, performance appraisals, salary reviews, and promotion decisions represent important, but more subtle, forms of feedback.

Feedback, of course, does not have to be conveyed in words. Actions *can* speak louder than words. For instance, a sales manager sends out a directive to her staff describing a new monthly sales report that all sales personnel will need to complete. Failure of some of the salespeople to turn in the new report is a type of feedback. It should suggest to her that she needs to clarify further her initial directive. Similarly, when you give a speech to a group of people, you can tell by their eye movements and other nonverbal clues whether group members are getting your message. This benefit of feedback may explain why television performers on situation comedy shows prefer to tape their programs in front of a live audience. Immediate laughter and applause, or their absence, convey to the performers whether they are getting their message across.

The following specific suggestions can help managers to be more effective in providing feedback to others.

1. *Focus on specific behaviors.* Feedback should be specific rather than general. For example, instead of saying, "You have a bad attitude," a manager might say, "Bob, I'm concerned with your attitude toward your work. You were a half-hour late to yesterday's staff meeting, and then you told me you hadn't read the preliminary report we were discussing. Today you tell me you're taking off three hours early for a dental appointment." This tells Bob why he is being criticized.

2. *Keep feedback impersonal.* Feedback should be job-related. Never criticize someone personally because of an inappropriate action. Telling people they're "stupid," "incompetent," or the like is almost always counterproductive.

3. *Keep feedback goal-oriented.* If a manager has to say something negative, he or she should make sure it's directed toward the *recipient's* goals. A manager should ask whom the feedback is supposed to help. If the answer is essentially that "I've got something I just want to get off my chest," then he or she should not speak.

4. *Make feedback well timed.* Feedback is most meaningful to a recipient when there is a very short interval between his or her behavior and the receipt of feedback about that behavior.

5. *Ensure understanding.* Is the feedback concise and complete enough so the recipient clearly and fully understands the communication? Managers should consider having the recipient rephrase the content of the feedback to see whether it fully captures the intended meaning.

6. *Direct negative feedback toward behavior that is controllable by the recipient.* There's little value in reminding a person of a shortcoming over which he or she has no control. Negative feedback, therefore, should be directed toward behavior the recipient can do something about.

Exhibit 9-3
Improving Feedback Skills

Simplify Language

Because language can be a barrier, a manager should seek to structure messages in ways that will make them clear and understandable. Words should be chosen carefully. The manager needs to simplify his or her language and consider the audience to whom a message is directed, so that the language will be compatible with the receiver. Remember, effective communication is achieved when a message is both received and *understood*. Understanding is improved by simplifying the language used in relation to the audience intended. This means, for example, that a hospital administrator should always try to communicate in clear and easily understood terms and that the language used for conveying messages to the surgical staff should be purposely different from that used with employees in the admissions office. Jargon can facilitate understanding when it is used with other group members who speak that language, but it can cause innumerable problems when used outside that group.

Listen Actively

When someone talks, we hear. But, too often, we don't listen. Listening is an active search for meaning, whereas hearing is passive (see Exhibit 9-4). When you listen, two people, the receiver and the sender, are thinking.

The following specific suggestions can help managers to be more effective active listeners.

1. *Make eye contact.* We listen with our ears, but people judge whether we're listening by looking at our eyes. Making eye contact with the speaker focuses one's attention, reduces the potential for distractions, and encourages the speaker.

2. *Exhibit affirmative head nods and appropriate facial expressions.* The effective listener shows interest in what is being said through nonverbal signals. Affirmative head nods and appropriate facial expressions, when added to good eye contact, convey to the speaker that one is listening.

3. *Avoid distracting actions or gestures.* The other side of showing interest is avoiding actions that suggest that the manager's mind is somewhere else. Actions such as looking at one's watch, shuffling papers, or playing with a pencil make the speaker feel one is bored or uninterested.

4. *Ask questions.* The critical listener analyzes what he or she hears and asks questions. Questioning provides clarification, ensures understanding, and assures the speaker one is listening.

5. *Paraphrase.* The effective listener uses phrases such as "What I hear you saying is . . ." or "Do you mean . . . ?" Paraphrasing acts as an excellent control device to check on whether one is listening carefully. It is also a control for accuracy.

6. *Avoid interrupting the speaker.* Let the speaker complete his or her thought before responding. Don't try to guess where the speaker's thoughts are going.

7. *Don't overtalk.* Most of us would rather speak our own ideas than listen to what someone else says. Too many of us listen only because it's the price we have to pay to get people to let us talk. Talking may be more fun and silence may be uncomfortable, but it's impossible to talk and listen at the same time. The good listener recognizes this fact and doesn't overtalk.

Exhibit 9-4
Improving Active Listening Skills

Many of us are poor listeners. Why? Because it's difficult and because it's usually more satisfying to talk. Listening, in fact, is often more tiring than talking. It demands intellectual effort. Unlike hearing, active listening demands total concentration. The average person speaks at a rate of about 150 words per minute, whereas we have the capacity to listen at the rate of over 1,000 words per minute. The difference obviously leaves idle brain time and opportunities for the mind to wander.

Active listening is enhanced when the receiver develops empathy with the sender, that is, when the receiver tries to place himself in the sender's position. Because senders differ in attitudes, interests, needs, and expectations, empathy makes it easier to understand the actual content of a message. An empathetic listener reserves judgment on the message's content and carefully listens to what is being said. The goal is to improve one's ability to receive the full meaning of a communication, without having it distorted by premature judgments or interpretations.

Constrain Emotions

It would be naive to assume that a manager always communicates in a fully rational manner. Yet we know that emotions can severely cloud and distort the transference of meaning. If we're emotionally upset over an issue, we're likely to misconstrue incoming messages, and we may fail to express clearly and accurately our outgoing messages. What can the manager do? The best approach is to defer further communication until composure is regained.

Watch Your Nonverbal Cues

Assuming that actions speak louder than words, you should watch your actions to make sure they align with, and reinforce, your words. We noted that nonverbal messages carry a great deal of weight. Given this fact, the effective communicator watches his or her nonverbal cues to ensure that they, too, convey the message desired.

Use the Grapevine

You can't eliminate the grapevine. What managers should do, therefore, is use it and make it work for them. Managers can use the grapevine to transmit information rapidly, to test the reaction to various decisions before their final consummation, and as a valuable source of feedback when the managers themselves are grapevine members. Of course, the grapevine can carry damaging rumors that reduce the effectiveness of formal communication. To lessen this potentially destructive force, managers should make good use of formal channels by ensuring that they regularly carry the relevant and accurate information that employees seek.

Leadership

After reading this chapter, you should be able to:

1. Summarize the conclusions of trait theories

2. Identify the limitations of behavioral theories

3. Describe Fiedler's contingency model

4. Summarize the path-goal theory

5. List the contingency variables in the leader-participation model

6. Explain gender differences in leadership styles

7. Identify the characteristics associated with charismatic leadership

It has been accepted as a truism that good leadership is essential to business, to government, and to the countless groups and organizations that shape the way we live, work, and play. If leadership is such an important factor, the critical issue is: What makes a great leader? The tempting answer to give is: Great followers! Although there is some truth to this response, the issue is far more complex.

What Is Leadership?

Leadership is the ability to influence a group toward the achievement of goals. The source of this influence may be formal, such as that provided by the possession of managerial rank in an organization. Because management positions come with some degree of formally designated authority, an individual may assume a leadership role as a result of the position he or she holds in the organization. But not all leaders are managers, nor, for that matter, are all managers leaders. Just because an organization provides its managers with certain rights is no assurance they will be able to lead effectively. Nonsanctioned leadership, that is, the ability to influence that arises outside of the formal structure of the organization, is as important or more important than formal influence. In other words, leaders can emerge from within a group as well as being formally appointed.

Transitions in Leadership Theories

The leadership literature is voluminous, and much of it is confusing and contradictory. In order to make our way through this "forest," we consider four approaches to explaining what makes an effective leader. The first sought to find universal personality traits that leaders had to some greater degree than nonleaders. The second approach tried to explain leadership in terms of a leader's behavior. Both of these approaches proved to be false starts, based on their erroneous and oversimplified conception of leadership. The third looked to contingency models to explain the inadequacies of previous leadership theories in reconciling and bringing together the diversity of research findings. Most recently, we have returned to traits but with a different twist. Now the search is on to find the qualities or traits that are held by charismatic leaders. In this chapter, we present the contributions and limitations of each of the four approaches and conclude by attempting to ascertain the value of the leadership literature in explaining and predicting behavior.

Trait Theories

If one were to describe a leader on the basis of the general connotations presented in today's media, one might list qualities such as intelligence, charisma, decisiveness, enthusiasm, strength, bravery, integrity, self-confidence, and so on—possibly eliciting the conclusion that effective leaders must be one part Boy Scout and two parts Jesus Christ. The search for characteristics such as those listed that would differentiate leaders from nonleaders occupied the early psychologists who studied leadership.

Is it possible to isolate one or more personality traits in individuals we generally acknowledge as leaders—Winston Churchill, Susan B. Anthony, Martin Luther King Jr., John F. Kennedy, Nelson Mandela, Ted Turner—that nonleaders do not possess? We may agree that these individuals meet our definition of a leader, but they represent individuals with utterly different characteristics. If the concept of traits was to be proved valid, specific characteristics had to be found that all leaders possess.

Research efforts at isolating these traits resulted in a number of dead ends. If the search was to identify a set of traits that would always differentiate leaders from followers and effective from ineffective leaders, the search failed. Perhaps it was a bit optimistic to believe that a set of consistent and unique traits could apply across the board to all effective leaders, whether they were in charge of the Hell's Angels, the Church of Jesus Christ of Latter-Day Saints, Playboy Enterprises, the Shell Oil Company, or the Walt Disney Company.

However, attempts to identify traits consistently associated with leadership have been more successful. Six traits on which leaders differ from nonleaders include (1) drive and ambition, (2) the desire to lead and influence others, (3) honesty and integrity, (4) self-confidence, (5) intelligence, and (6) in-depth technical knowledge related to their area of responsibility.[1]

Yet traits alone are not sufficient for explaining leadership. Their primary failing is that they ignore situational factors. Possessing the appropriate traits only makes it more likely that an individual will be an effective leader. He or she still has to take the right actions. And "the right actions" in one situation are not necessarily right for a different situation. So, although there has been some resurgent interest in traits since the 1980s, a major movement away from trait theories began as early as the 1940s. Leadership research from the late 1940s through the mid-1960s emphasized the preferred behavioral styles that leaders demonstrated.

Behavioral Theories

The inability to strike gold in the "trait mines" led researchers to look at the behaviors that specific leaders exhibited. They wondered if there was something unique in the way effective leaders behave. For example, do they tend to be more democratic than autocratic?

Not only, it was hoped, would the behavioral approach provide more definitive answers about the nature of leadership but, if successful, it would have practical implications quite different from those of the trait approach. If trait research had been successful, it would have provided a basis for selecting the right person to assume a formal position in a group or organization that required leadership. In contrast, if behavioral studies were to turn up critical behavioral determinants of leadership, we could *train* people to be leaders. The difference between trait and behavioral theories, in terms of application, lies in their underlying assumptions. If trait theories were valid, then leaders were basically born: You either had it or you didn't. On the other hand, if there were specific behaviors that identified leaders, then we could teach leadership—we could design programs that implanted these behavioral patterns in individuals who desired to be effective leaders. This was surely a more exciting avenue, for it would mean that the supply of leaders could be expanded. If training worked, we could have an infinite supply of effective leaders.

A number of studies looked at behavioral styles. We briefly review the two most popular studies: the Ohio State group and the University of Michigan group. Then we see how the concepts these studies developed could be used to create a grid for looking at and appraising leadership styles.

Ohio State Studies

The most comprehensive and replicated of the behavioral theories resulted from research that began at Ohio State University in the late 1940s.[2] These studies sought to identify independent dimensions of leader behavior. Beginning with over a thousand dimensions, they eventually narrowed the list into two categories that substantially accounted for most of the leadership behavior described by subordinates. They called these two dimensions *initiating structure* and *consideration.*

Initiating structure refers to the extent to which a leader is likely to define and structure his or her role and those of subordinates in the search for goal attainment. It includes behavior that attempts to organize work, work relationships, and goals. The leader characterized as high in initiating structure could be described in terms such as "assigns group members to particular tasks," "expects workers to maintain definite standards of performance," and "emphasizes the meeting of deadlines."

Consideration is described as the extent to which a person is likely to have job relationships characterized by mutual trust, respect for subordinates' ideas, and regard for their feelings. This type of leader shows concern for his followers' comfort, well-being, status, and satisfaction. A leader high in consideration could be described as one who helps subordinates with personal problems, is friendly and approachable, and treats all subordinates as equals.

Extensive research, based on these definitions, found that leaders high in initiating structure *and* consideration (a "high-high" leader) tended to achieve high subordinate performance and satisfaction more frequently than those who rated low either on initiating structure, consideration, or both. But the high-high style did not *always* result in positive consequences. For example, leader behavior characterized as high on initiating structure led to greater rates of grievances, absenteeism, and turnover and lower levels of job satisfaction for workers performing routine tasks. Other studies found that high consideration was negatively related to performance ratings of the leader by his superior. In conclusion, the Ohio State studies suggested that the high-high style generally resulted in positive outcomes, but enough exceptions were found to indicate that situational factors needed to be integrated into the theory.

University of Michigan Studies

Leadership studies undertaken at the University of Michigan's Survey Research Center, at about the same time as those being done at Ohio State, had similar research objectives: To locate behavioral characteristics of leaders that appeared to be related to measures of performance effectiveness.[3] The Michigan group also came up with two dimensions of leadership behavior, which they labeled employee-oriented and production-oriented. Leaders who were *employee-oriented* were described as emphasizing interpersonal relations; they took a personal interest in the needs of their subordinates and accepted individual differences among members. The *production-oriented* leaders, in contrast, tended to emphasize the technical or task aspects of the job—their main concern was in accomplishing their group's tasks, and the group members were a means to that end.

The conclusions arrived at by the Michigan researchers strongly favored the leaders who were employee-oriented in their behavior. Employee-oriented leaders were associated with higher group productivity and higher job satisfaction. Production-oriented leaders tended to be associated with low group productivity and low worker satisfaction.

The Managerial Grid

A graphic portrayal of a two-dimensional view of leadership styles was developed by Robert Blake and Jane Mouton.[4] They proposed a **managerial grid** based on the styles of "concern for people" and "concern for production," which essentially represent the Ohio State dimensions of consideration and initiating structure or the Michigan dimensions of employee-oriented and production-oriented.

The grid, depicted in Exhibit 10-1, has nine possible positions along each axis, creating eighty-one different positions in which the leader's style may fall. The grid does not show results produced but rather the dominating factors in a leader's thinking in regard to getting results.

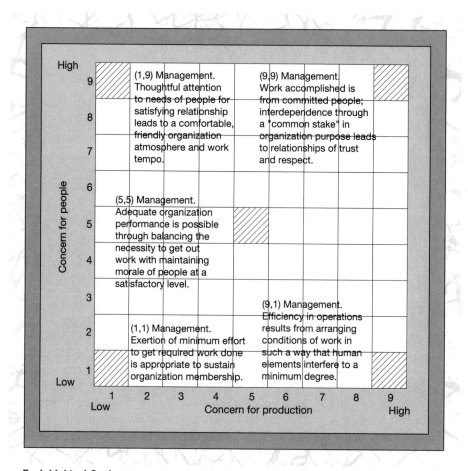

Exhibit 10-1

The Managerial Grid

Source: R. R. Blake, J. S. Mouton, L. B. Barnes, and L. E. Greiner, "Breakthrough in Organization Development," *Harvard Business Review*, November–December 1964, p. 136. Copyright © 1964 by the President and Fellows of Harvard College; all rights reserved.

On the basis of the findings from the research Blake and Mouton conducted, they concluded that managers perform best under a 9,9 style, as contrasted, for example, with a 9,1 (task-oriented) or the 1,9 (country-club type) leader. Unfortunately, the grid offers a better framework for conceptualizing leadership style than for presenting any tangible new information in clarifying the leadership quandary, since there is little substantive evidence to support the conclusion that a 9,9 style is most effective in all situations.[5]

Summary of Behavioral Theories

We have described the most popular and important of the attempts to explain leadership in terms of the behavior exhibited by the leader. Unfortunately, there was very little success in identifying consistent relationships between patterns of leadership behavior and group performance. General statements could not be made because results would vary over different ranges of circumstances. What was missing was consideration of the situational factors that influence success or failure. For example, it seems unlikely that Martin Luther King Jr. would have been a great leader of his people at the turn of the century, yet he was in the 1950s and 1960s. Would Ralph Nader have risen to lead a consumer activist group had he been born in 1834 rather than 1934, or in Costa Rica rather than Connecticut? It seems quite unlikely, yet the behavioral approaches we have described could not clarify these situational factors.

Contingency Theories

It became increasingly clear to those who were studying the leadership phenomenon that predicting leadership success was more complex than isolating a few traits or preferable behaviors. The failure to obtain consistent results led to a new focus on situational influences. The relationship between leadership style and effectiveness suggested that style x would be appropriate under condition a, whereas style y would be more suitable for condition b, and style z for condition c. But what were the conditions a, b, c, and so forth? It was one thing to say that leadership effectiveness was dependent on the situation and another to be able to isolate those situational conditions.

Many studies have attempted to isolate the critical situational factors that affect leadership effectiveness. To illustrate, some of the more popular variables have included the type of task being performed, the style of the leader's immediate supervisor, group norms, time demands, and the organization's culture.

Three contingency theories have received the bulk of attention: Fiedler, path-goal, and leader-participation. We review each in this section. We also take a look at gender as a contingency variable. Although there is no specific contingency theory that directly addresses gender, an expanding body of research compares male and female leadership styles. Given that women have been moving rapidly into organizational leadership positions in recent years, it is important to give some attention to this issue.

The Fiedler Model

The first comprehensive contingency model for leadership was developed by Fred Fiedler.[6] His model proposes that effective group performance depends on the proper match between the leader's style of interacting with his or her subordinates and the degree to which the situation gives control and influence to the leader. Fiedler developed an instrument, which he called the **least-preferred co-worker (LPC) questionnaire,** that purports to measure whether a person is task-oriented or relationship-oriented. Further, he isolated three situational criteria—leader-member relations, task structure, and position power—that he believed can be manipulated so as to create the proper match with the behavioral orientation of the leader. In a sense, the **Fiedler leadership model** is an outgrowth of trait theory, since the LPC questionnaire is a simple psychological test. Fiedler, however, went significantly beyond trait and behavioral approaches by attempting to isolate situations, relating his personality measure to his situational classification, and then predicting leadership effectiveness as a function of the two. This description of the Fiedler model is somewhat abstract. Let us now look at the model more closely.

Fiedler believed that an individual's basic leadership style is a key factor in leadership success. So he began by trying to find out what that basic style was. Fiedler created the LPC questionnaire for this purpose. It contains sixteen contrasting adjectives (such as pleasant-unpleasant, efficient-inefficient, open-guarded, supportive-hostile). The questionnaire asks the respondent to think of all the co-workers he or she has ever had and to describe the one person he or she *least enjoyed* working with by rating that person on a scale of 1 to 8 for each of the sixteen sets of contrasting adjectives. Fiedler believed that, on the basis of the answers to this LPC questionnaire, he could determine a respondent's basic leadership style. His premise was that what you say about others tells more about you than it tells the persons you're describing. If the least-preferred co-worker was described in relatively positive terms (a high LPC score), then the respondent was primarily interested in good personal relations with co-workers. That is, if you essentially described the person you are least able to work with in favorable terms, Fiedler would label you relationship-oriented. In contrast, if the least-preferred co-worker is seen in relatively unfavorable terms (a low LPC score), the respondent is primarily interested in productivity and thus would be labeled task-oriented. Notice that Fiedler assumed that an individual's leadership style is fixed, that is, either relationship-oriented or task-oriented. As we show in a moment, this assumption is important because it means that if a situation requires a task-oriented leader and the person in that leadership position is relationship-oriented, either the situation has to be modified or the leader replaced if optimum effectiveness is to be achieved. Fiedler argued that leadership style is innate to a person—you *can't* change your style to fit changing situations!

After an individual's basic leadership style has been assessed through the LPC, it is necessary to match the leader with the situation. The three situational factors or contingency dimensions identified by Fiedler are defined as follows:

1. **Leader-member relations:** The degree of confidence, trust, and respect subordinates have in their leader

2. **Task structure:** The degree to which the job assignments of subordinates are structured or unstructured

3. **Position power:** The degree of influence a leader has over power variables such as hiring, firing, discipline, promotions, and salary increases

The next step in the Fiedler model is to evaluate the situation in terms of these three contingency variables. Leader-member relations are either good or poor, task structure either high or low, and position power either strong or weak. Fiedler stated that the better the leader-member relations, the more highly structured the job, and the stronger the position power, the more control or influence the leader had. For example, a very favorable situation (in which the leader would have a great deal of control) might involve a payroll manager who is well–respected and whose subordinates have confidence in him or her (good leader-member relations), where the activities to be done—such as wage computation, check writing, report filing—are specific and clear (high task structure), and the job provides considerable freedom to reward and punish subordinates (strong position power). On the other hand, an unfavorable situation might be the disliked chairman of a voluntary United Way fund-raising team. In this job, the leader has very little control. Altogether, by mixing the three contingency variables, there are potentially eight different situations or categories in which a leader could find himself or herself.

With knowledge of an individual's LPC and an assessment of the three contingency variables, the Fiedler model proposes matching them up to achieve maximum leadership effectiveness. Fiedler studied more than 1,200 groups, comparing relationship versus task-oriented leadership styles in each of the eight situational categories. He concluded that task-oriented leaders tend to perform better than relationship-oriented leaders in situations that are *very favorable* to them and in situations that are *very unfavorable* (see Exhibit 10-2, page 146). So Fiedler would predict that, when faced with a category I, II, III, VII, or VIII situation, task-oriented leaders perform better. Relationship-oriented leaders, however, perform better in moderately favorable situations—categories IV through VI.

Given Fiedler's findings, how would you apply them? You would seek to match leaders and situations. Individuals' LPC scores would determine the type of situation for which they were best suited. That situation would be defined by evaluating the three contingency factors of leader-member relations, task structure, and position power. But remember that Fiedler viewed an individual's leadership style as being fixed. Therefore, there are really only two ways in which to improve leader effectiveness. First, you can choose the leader who best fits the situation. Analogous to a baseball game, management can reach into its bullpen and put in a right-handed pitcher or a left-handed pitcher, depending on the situational characteristics of the hitter. So, for example, if a group situation rates as highly unfavorable but is currently led by a relationship-oriented manager, the group's performance could be improved by replacing that manager with one who is task-oriented. The second alternative would be to change the situation to fit the leader. That could be done by restructuring tasks or increasing or decreasing the power that the leader has to control factors such as salary increases, promotions, and disciplinary actions. To illustrate, assume that a task-oriented leader is in a category IV situation. If this leader could increase his or her position power, then

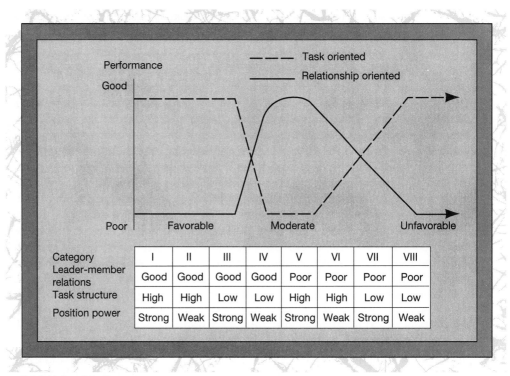

Exhibit 10-2
Findings from the Fiedler Model

the leader would be operating in category III and the leader-situation match would be compatible for high group performance.

One should not surmise that Fiedler closed all the gaps and put to rest all the questions underlying leadership effectiveness. Research finds that the Fiedler model predicts all except category II when laboratory studies are reviewed; however, when field studies are analyzed, the model produces supportive evidence for only categories II, V, VII, and VIII. So we have conflicting results depending on the type of studies used.

As a whole, reviews of the major studies undertaken to test the overall validity of the Fiedler model lead to a generally positive conclusion. That is, there is considerable evidence to support the model.[7] But additional variables are probably needed if an improved model is to fill in some of the remaining gaps. Moreover, there are problems with the LPC and the practical use of the model that need to be addressed. For instance, the logic underlying the LPC is not well understood, and studies have shown that respondents' LPC scores are not stable. Also, the contingency variables are complex and difficult for practitioners to assess. It's often difficult in practice to determine how good the leader-member relations are, how structured the task is, and how much position power the leader has.

Our conclusion is that Fiedler clearly made an important contribution toward understanding leadership effectiveness. His model has been the object of much controversy and probably will continue to be. Field studies fall short of providing full support, and the model could benefit by including additional contingency variables. But Fiedler's work continues to be a dominant input in the development of a contingency explanation of leadership effectiveness.

Path-Goal Theory

Currently, one of the most respected approaches to leadership is the path-goal theory. Developed by Robert House, **path-goal theory** is a contingency model of leadership that extracts key elements from the Ohio State leadership research on initiating structure and consideration and the expectancy theory of motivation.[8]

The essence of the theory is that it's the leader's job to assist his or her followers in attaining their goals and to provide the direction or support or both needed to ensure that their goals are compatible with the overall objectives of the group or organization. The term *path-goal* is derived from the belief that effective leaders clarify the path to help their followers get from where they are to the achievement of their work goals and make the journey along the path easier by reducing roadblocks and pitfalls.

According to path-goal theory, a leader's behavior is *acceptable* to subordinates to the degree that it is viewed by them as an immediate source of satisfaction or as a means of future satisfaction. A leader's behavior is *motivational* to the degree that it (1) makes subordinate need satisfaction contingent on effective performance and (2) provides the coaching, guidance, support, and rewards that are necessary for effective performance. To test these statements, House identified four leadership behaviors. The *directive leader* lets subordinates know what is expected of them, schedules work to be done, and gives specific guidance on how to accomplish tasks. This dimension closely parallels the Ohio State studies' initiating structure. The *supportive leader* is friendly and shows concern for the needs of subordinates. This dimension is essentially synonymous with the Ohio State studies' consideration. The *participative leader* consults with subordinates and uses their suggestions before making a decision. The *achievement-oriented leader* sets challenging goals and expects subordinates to perform at their highest level. In contrast to Fiedler's view of a leader's behavior, House assumes that leaders are flexible. Path-goal theory implies that the same leader can display any or all of these behaviors depending on the situation.

As Exhibit 10-3 (page 148) illustrates, path-goal theory proposes two classes of situational, or contingency, variables that moderate the leader behavior–outcome relationship. Those in the *environment* are outside the control of the leader (task structure, formal authority system, and work group). Factors in the second class are part of the personal characteristics of the *subordinate* (locus of control, experience, and perceived ability). Essentially, the theory proposes that leader behaviors should complement these contingency variables. So the leader will be ineffective when his or her behavior is redundant with sources of environmental structure or incongruent with subordinate characteristics.

Following are examples of hypotheses that have evolved out of path-goal theory.

- Directive leadership leads to greater satisfaction when tasks are ambiguous or stressful than when they are highly structured and well laid out.

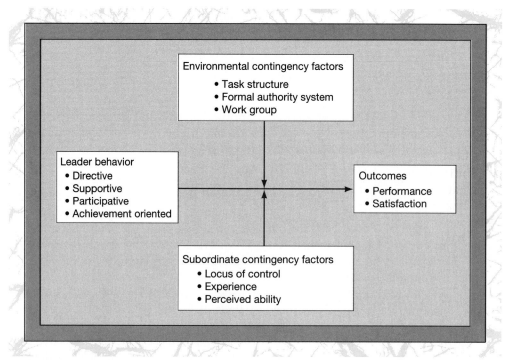

Exhibit 10-3
The Path-Goal Theory

- Supportive leadership results in high employee performance and satisfaction when subordinates are performing structured tasks. (Leadership complements environment.)
- Directive leadership is likely to be redundant among subordinates with high ability or with considerable experience.
- The clearer and more bureaucratic the formal authority relationships, the more leaders should exhibit supportive behavior and deemphasize directive behavior.
- Directive leadership will lead to higher employee satisfaction when there is substantive conflict within a work group.
- Subordinates with an internal locus of control (those who believe they control their own destiny) will be most satisfied with a participative style.
- Subordinates with an external locus of control will be most satisfied with a directive style.
- Achievement-oriented leadership will increase subordinates' expectations that effort will lead to high performance when tasks are ambiguously structured.

Research to validate hypotheses such as these is generally encouraging.[9] The evidence supports the logic underlying the theory. That is, employee performance and satisfaction are likely to be positively influenced when the leader compensates for things lacking in either the employee or the work setting. However, the leader who spends time explaining tasks when those tasks are already clear or when the employee has the ability and experience to handle them without interference is likely to be seen as redundant or even insulting.

What does the future hold for path-goal theory? Its framework has been tested and appears to have moderate to high empirical support. We can, however, expect to see more research focused on refining and extending the theory by incorporating additional moderating variables.

Leader-Participation Model

In 1973, Victor Vroom and Phillip Yetton developed a **leader-participation model** that related leadership behavior and participation in decision making.[10] Recognizing that task structures have varying demands for routine and nonroutine activities, these researchers argued that leader behavior must adjust to reflect the task structure. Vroom and Yetton's model was normative—it provided a sequential set of rules that should be followed in determining the form and amount of participation in decision making, as determined by different types of situations. The model was a decision tree incorporating seven contingencies (whose relevance could be identified by making "yes" or "no" choices) and five alternative leadership styles.

More recent work by Vroom and Arthur Jago has resulted in a revision of this model.[11] The new model retains the same five alternative leadership styles—from the leader's making the decision completely by himself or herself to sharing the problem with the group and developing a consensus decision—but expands the contingency variables to twelve. These are listed in Exhibit 10-4.

1. Importance of the decision
2. Importance of obtaining subordinate commitment to the decision
3. Whether the leader has sufficient information to make a good decision
4. How well structured the problem is
5. Whether an autocratic decision would receive subordinate commitment
6. Whether subordinates "buy into" the organization's goals
7. Whether there is likely to be conflict among subordinates over solution alternatives
8. Whether subordinates have the necessary information to make a good decision
9. Time constraints on the leader that may limit subordinate involvement
10. Whether costs to bring geographically dispersed subordinates together is justified
11. Importance to the leader of minimizing the time it takes to make the decision
12. Importance of using participation as a tool for developing subordinate decision skills

Exhibit 10-4

Contingency Variables in the Revised Leader-Participation Model

Source: Based on V. H. Vroom and A. G. Jago, *The New Leadership: Managing Participation in Organizations* (Englewood Cliffs, NJ: Prentice Hall, 1988), pp. 111–12.

Source: Adapted and reprinted from *Leadership and Decision–Making*, p. 194, by Victor H. Vroom and Philip W. Yetton, by permission of the University of Pittsburgh. © 1973 by University of Pittsburgh Press.

Research testing both the original and revised leader-participation models has been encouraging. But, unfortunately, the model is far too complex for the typical manager to use on a regular basis. In fact, Vroom and Jago have developed a computer program to guide managers through all the decision branches in the revised model.

We obviously can't do justice to the model's sophistication in this discussion. What's important, however, is that Vroom and his associates have provided us with some solid, empirically supported insights into contingency variables that you should consider when choosing your leadership style.

Gender as a Contingency Variable: Do Males and Females Lead Differently?

An extensive review of the literature suggests two conclusions regarding gender and leadership.[12] First, the similarities between men and women's leadership styles tend to outweigh the differences. Second, what differences there are seem to be that women prefer a democratic leadership style, whereas men feel more comfortable with a directive style.

The similarities among men and women leaders shouldn't be completely surprising. Almost all the studies looking at this issue have used managerial positions as being synonymous with leadership. As such, gender differences apparent in the general population don't tend to be evident. Why? Because of career self-selection and organization selection. Just as people who choose careers in law enforcement or civil engineering have a lot in common, so do individuals who choose managerial careers. People with traits associated with leadership—such as intelligence, confidence, and sociability—are likely to be perceived as leaders and encouraged to pursue careers in which they can exert leadership. This is true nowadays regardless of gender. Similarly, organizations tend to recruit and promote into leadership positions people who project leadership attributes. The result is that, regardless of gender, those who achieve formal leadership positions in organizations tend to be more alike than different.

Despite the previous conclusion, studies indicate some differences in the inherent leadership styles of women and men. Women encourage participation, share power and information, and attempt to enhance followers' self-worth. They prefer to lead through inclusion and rely on their charisma, expertise, contacts, and interpersonal skills to influence others. Men, on the other hand, are more likely to use a directive command-and-control style. They rely on the formal authority of their position for their influence base. Consistent with our first conclusion, however, these findings need to be qualified. The tendency for female leaders to be more democratic than males declines when women are in male-dominated jobs. Apparently, group norms and masculine stereotypes of leaders override personal preferences so that women abandon their feminine styles in such jobs and act more autocratically.

Given that men have historically held the great majority of leadership positions in organizations, it's tempting to assume that the existence of the noted differences between men and women would automatically work to favor men. It doesn't. In today's organizations, flexibility, teamwork, trust, and information sharing are replacing rigid structures, competitive individualism, control, and secrecy. The best managers listen, motivate, and provide support to their people.

And many women seem to do those things better than men. As a specific example, the expanded use of cross-functional teams in organizations means that effective managers must become skillful negotiators. The leadership styles women typically use can make them better than men at negotiating, as they are less likely to focus on wins, losses, and competition. They tend to treat negotiations in the context of a continuing relationship—trying hard to make the other party a winner in its own and others' eyes.

Trait Theories Updated: Charismatic Leadership

Most of the leadership theories discussed in this chapter have involved *transactional* leaders. These people guide or motivate their followers in the direction of established goals by clarifying role and task requirements. There is another type of leader who inspires followers to transcend their own self-interests for the good of the organization and who is capable of having a profound and extraordinary effect on his or her followers. These are *transformational,* or **charismatic leaders.** Ted Turner, Jesse Jackson, Mother Teresa, General Douglas MacArthur, and Franklin D. Roosevelt are of this latter type. By the force of their personal abilities they transform their followers by raising the sense of the importance and value of their tasks. "I'd walk through fire if my boss asked me" is the kind of support that charismatic leaders inspire.

What characteristics differentiate charismatic leaders from noncharismatic ones? Five attributes seem most important[13]:

Self-confidence: They have complete confidence in their judgment and ability.

A vision: This is an idealized goal that proposes a future better than the status quo. The greater the disparity between this idealized goal and the status quo, the more likely that followers will attribute extraordinary vision to the leader.

Strong convictions in that vision: Charismatic leaders are perceived as being strongly committed. They are perceived as willing to take on high personal risk, incur high costs, and engage in self-sacrifice to achieve their vision.

Extraordinary behavior: Leaders with charisma engage in behavior that is perceived as novel, unconventional, and counter to norms. When successful, these behaviors evoke surprise and admiration in followers.

Image as a change agent: Charismatic leaders are perceived as agents of radical change rather than as caretakers of the status quo.

What can we say about the charismatic leader's impact on his or her followers' attitudes and behavior? One study found that followers of charismatic leaders were more self-assured, experienced more meaningfulness in their work, reported more support from their leaders, worked longer hours, saw their leaders as more dynamic, and had higher performance ratings than the followers of noncharismatic but effective leaders.[14] Another study found that people working under charismatic leaders were more productive and satisfied than those working under leaders who relied on the more traditional transactional behaviors of initiating structure and consideration.[15] Two studies, of course, provide only limited information from which to generalize. We need more research on this subject, but the early evidence is encouraging.

$\textit{A}$ Final Thought: Sometimes Leadership Is Irrelevant!

We conclude this chapter by challenging the notion that some leadership style *will always* be effective *regardless* of the situation. Leadership may not always be important. Data from numerous studies collectively demonstrate that, in many situations, whatever behaviors leaders exhibit are irrelevant. Certain individual, job, and organizational variables can act as substitutes for leadership, negating the formal leader's ability to exert either positive or negative influence over subordinates' attitudes and effectiveness.[16]

For instance, characteristics of subordinates such as their experience, training, professional orientation, or need for independence can neutralize the effect of leadership. These characteristics can replace the need for a leader's support or ability to create structure and reduce task ambiguity. Similarly, people in jobs that are inherently unambiguous and routine or that are intrinsically satisfying may have little need for a leader. Finally, organizational characteristics such as explicit formalized goals, rigid rules and procedures, or cohesive work groups can act in the place of formal leadership.

The preceding comments should not be surprising. After all, in Chapter 3 and subsequent chapters, we introduced independent variables that have been documented to have an impact on employee performance and satisfaction. Yet supporters of the leadership concept have tended to place an undue burden on this variable for explaining and predicting behavior. It's too simplistic to consider subordinates as being guided to goal accomplishment solely on the basis of the behavior of their leader. It's important, therefore, to recognize explicitly that leadership is merely another independent variable in explaining organizational behavior. In some situations, it may contribute a lot toward explaining employee productivity, absence, turnover, and satisfaction; but in other situations, it may contribute little toward that end.

Even charismatic leadership may not be the panacea that many in the public and media think it is. Charismatic leaders may be ideal for pulling a group or organization through a crisis, but they often perform poorly after the crisis subsides and ordinary conditions return. The forceful, confident behavior that was needed during the crisis now becomes a liability. Charismatic managers are often self-possessed, autocratic, and given to thinking that their opinions have a greater degree of certainty than they merit. These behaviors then tend to drive good people away and can lead their organizations down dangerous paths.

 mplications for Managers

The topic of leadership certainly doesn't lack for theories. But from an overview perspective, what does it all mean? Let's try to identify commonalities among the leadership theories and attempt to determine what, if any, practical value the theories hold for managers.

Careful examination discloses that the concepts of "task" and "people"—often expressed in more elaborate terms that hold substantially the same meaning—permeate most of the theories. The task dimension is called just that by Fiedler, but it goes by the name of "initiating structure" for the Ohio State group, "directive" by path-goal supporters, "production orientation" by the Michigan researchers, and "concern for production" by Blake and Mouton. The people dimension gets similar treatment, going under such aliases as "consideration," "supportive," and "employee-oriented" or "relationship-oriented" leadership. Cleary, leadership behavior can be shrunk down to two dimensions—task and people—but researchers continue to differ as to whether the orientations are two ends of a single continuum (you could be high on one or the other but not on both) or two independent dimensions (you could be high or low on both).

How should we interpret the findings presented in this chapter? Some traits have shown, over time, to be modest predictors of leadership effectiveness. But the fact that a manager possessed intelligence, drive, self-confidence, or the like would by no means assure us that his or her subordinates would be productive and satisfied employees. The ability of these traits to predict leadership success is just not that strong.

The early task–people approaches (the Ohio State, Michigan, and managerial grid theories) also offer us little substance. The strongest statement one can make on the basis of these theories is that leaders who rate high in people orientation should end up with satisfied employees. The research is too mixed to make predictions regarding employee productivity or the effect of a task orientation on productivity and satisfaction.

Controlled laboratory studies designed to test the Fiedler model, in aggregate, have generally supported the theory. But field studies provide more limited support. We suggest that only category II, V, VII, and VIII situations warrant the use of the LPC instrument to assess whether this is a leader–situation match and the use of that information to predict employee productivity and satisfaction.

The path-goal model provides a framework for explaining and predicting leadership effectiveness that has developed a solid, empirical foundation. It recognizes that a leader's success depends on adjusting his or her style to the environment and to the individual characteristics of followers.

In spite of the leader-participation model's complexity, efforts to validate it have been encouraging. One investigation, for example, found that leaders who were high in agreement with the model had subordinates with higher productivity and higher satisfaction than those leaders who were low in agreement with the model. For our purposes, its greatest contribution is in identifying a set of contingency variables that you should consider before choosing a leadership style.

Power and Politics

After reading this chapter, you should be able to:

1. Define power

2. Describe the five bases of power

3. Explain what creates dependency in power relationships

4. Describe how power is central to understanding sexual harassment

5. Define political behavior

6. Describe the importance of a political perspective

7. Explain the factors contributing to political behavior in organizations

8. Identify seven techniques for managing the impression you make on others

*P*ower may be the last dirty word. It is easier for most of us to talk about money or even sex than it is to talk about power. People who have it deny it; people who want it try not to appear to be seeking it; and those who are good at getting it are secretive about how they got it.[1]

In this chapter, we show that power determines what goals a group will pursue and how the group's resources will be distributed among its members. Further, we show how group members with good political skills use their power to influence the distribution of resources in their favor.

A Definition of Power

Power refers to a capacity that A has to influence the behavior of B so that B does something he or she would not otherwise do. This definition implies (1) a *potential* that need not be actualized to be effective,

(2) a *dependence* relationship, and (3) that B has some *discretion* over his or her own behavior. Let's look at each of these points more closely.

Power may exist but not be used. It is, therefore, a capacity or potential. One can have power but not impose it.

Probably the most important aspect of power is that it is a function of dependence. The greater B's dependence on A, the greater is A's power in the relationship. Dependence, in turn, is based on alternatives that B perceives and the importance that B places on the alternatives that A controls. A person can have power over you only if he or she controls something you desire. If you want a college degree, have to pass a certain course to get that degree, and your current instructor is the only faculty member in the college who teaches that course, he or she has power over you. Your alternatives are definitely limited, and you place a high degree of importance on obtaining a passing grade. Similarly, if you're attending college on funds provided entirely by your parents, you probably recognize the power they hold over you. You are dependent on them for financial support. But once you're out of school, have a job, and are making a solid income, your parents' power is reduced significantly. Who among us, though, has not known or heard of the rich relative who is able to control a large number of family members merely through the implicit or explicit threat of writing them out of the will?

For A to get B to do something he or she otherwise would not do means B must have the discretion to make choices. At the extreme, if B's job behavior is so programmed that he is allowed no room to make choices, he obviously is constrained in his ability to do something other than what he is doing. For instance, job descriptions, group norms, organizational rules and regulations, as well as community laws and standards constrain people's choices. As a nurse, you may be dependent on your supervisor for continued employment. But, in spite of this dependence, you're unlikely to comply with her request to perform heart surgery on a patient or steal several thousand dollars from petty cash. Your job description and laws against stealing constrain your ability to make those choices.

*C*ontrasting Leadership and Power

A careful comparison of our description of power with our description of leadership in the previous chapter should bring the recognition that the two concepts are closely intertwined. Leaders use power as a way to attain group goals, and power is a means for facilitating their achievement.

What differences are there between leadership and power? One difference is related to goal compatibility. Power does not require goal compatibility, merely dependence. Leadership, on the other hand, requires some congruence between the goals of the leader and the led. The other difference deals with the direction that research on the two concepts has taken. Leadership research, for the most part, emphasizes style. It seeks answers to questions such as, How supportive should a leader be? How much decision making should be shared with subordinates? In contrast, the research on power has tended to encompass a broader area and focus on tactics for gaining compliance. It has gone beyond the individual as exerciser because power can be used by groups as well as individuals to control other individuals or groups.

Does a person have one or more of the five bases of power? Affirmative responses to the following statements can answer this question:

- The person can make things difficult for people, and you want to avoid getting him or her angry. (coercive power)
- The person is able to give special benefits or rewards to people, and you find it advantageous to trade favors with him or her. (reward power)
- The person has the right, considering his or her position and your job responsibilities, to expect you to comply with legitimate requests. (legitimate power)
- The person has the experience and knowledge to earn your respect, and you defer to his or her judgment in some matters. (expert power)
- You like the person and enjoy doing things for him or her. (referent power)

E x h i b i t 1 1 - 1

Measuring Bases of Power

Source: From, "Importance of Different Power Sources in Downward and Lateral Relations," by G. Yukl and C. M. Falbe *Journal of Applied Psychology*, June 1991, p. 417. Copyright © 1991 by the American Pyschological Association. Reprinted with permission.

*B*ases of Power

Where does power come from? What is it that gives an individual or a group influence over others? The answer to these questions is a five-category classification scheme identified by John French and Bertram Raven.[2] They proposed five types of bases, or sources, of power: coercive, reward, legitimate, expert, and referent (see Exhibit 11-1).

Coercive Power

The **coercive power** base is defined by French and Raven as being dependent on fear. One reacts to this power out of fear of the negative results that might occur if one failed to comply. It rests on the application, or the threat of application, of physical sanctions such as the infliction of pain, the generation of frustration through restriction of movement, or the controlling by force of basic physiological or safety needs.

In the 1930s, when John Dillinger went into a bank, held a gun to a teller's head, and asked for money, he was incredibly successful at getting compliance with his request. His power base was coercive. A loaded gun gives its holder power because others are fearful that they will lose something that they hold dear—their lives.

Of all the bases of power available. . . , the power to hurt others is possibly most often used, most often condemned, and most difficult to control . . . The state relies on its military and legal resources to intimidate nations, or even its own citizens. Businesses rely upon the control of economic resources. Schools and universities rely upon their rights to deny students formal education, while the church threatens individuals with loss of grace. At the personal level, individuals exercise coercive power through a reliance upon physical strength, verbal facility, or the ability to grant or withhold emotional support from others. These bases provide the individual with the means to physically harm, bully, humiliate, or deny love to others.[3]

At the organizational level, A has coercive power over B if A can dismiss, suspend, or demote B, assuming that B values his or her job. Similarly, if A can assign B work activities that B finds unpleasant or treat B in a manner that B finds embarrassing, A possesses coercive power over B.

Reward Power

The opposite of coercive power is **reward power.** People comply with the wishes or directives of another because doing so produces positive benefits; therefore, one who can distribute rewards that others view as valuable will have power over them. These rewards can be anything that another person values. In an organizational context, we think of money, favorable performance appraisals, promotions, interesting work assignments, friendly colleagues, important information, and preferred work shifts or sales territories.

Coercive and reward power are actually counterparts. If you can remove something of positive value from another or inflict something of negative value upon him or her, you have coercive power over that person. If you can give someone something of positive value or remove something of negative value, you have reward power over that person. As with coercive power, you don't need to be a manager to be able to exert influence through rewards. Rewards such as friendliness, acceptance, and praise are available to everyone in an organization. To the degree that an individual seeks such rewards, your ability to give or withhold them gives you power over that individual.

Legitimate Power

In formal groups and organizations, probably the most frequent access to one or more of the power bases is one's structural position. This is called **legitimate power.** It represents the power a person receives as a result of his or her position in the formal hierarchy of an organization.

Positions of authority include coercive and reward powers. Legitimate power, however, is broader than the power to coerce and reward. Specifically, it includes acceptance by members of an organization of the authority of a position. When school principals, bank presidents, or army captains speak (assuming that their directives are viewed to be within the authority of their positions), teachers, tellers, and first lieutenants listen and usually comply.

Expert Power

Expert power is influence wielded as a result of expertise, special skill, or knowledge. Expertise has become one of the most powerful sources of influence as the world has become more technologically oriented. As jobs become more specialized, we become increasingly dependent on "experts" to achieve goals. So, just as physicians have expertise and hence expert power—most of us follow the advice our doctor gives us—so too do computer specialists, tax accountants, solar engineers, industrial psychologists, and other specialists.

Referent Power

The last category of influence that French and Raven identified was **referent power.** Its base is identification with a person who has desirable resources or personal traits. If I admire and identify with you, you can exercise power over me because I want to please you.

Referent power develops out of admiration of another and a desire to be like that person. In a sense, then, it is a lot like charisma. If you admire someone to the point of modeling your behavior and attitudes after him or her, that person possesses referent power over you. Referent power explains why celebrities are paid millions of dollars to endorse products in commercials. Marketing research shows that people like Bill Cosby, Elizabeth Taylor, and Michael Jordan have the power to influence your choice of photo processors, perfume, and athletic shoes. With a little practice, you or I could probably deliver as smooth a sales pitch as these celebrities, but the buying public doesn't identify with you and me. In organizations, if you are articulate, domineering, physically imposing, or charismatic, you hold personal characteristics that may be used to get others to do what you want.

Dependency: The Key to Power

Earlier in this chapter we noted the important relationship between power and dependence. In this section, we show how an understanding of dependency is central to furthering our understanding of power itself.

The General Dependency Postulate

Let's begin with a general postulate: *The greater B's dependency on A, the greater power A has over B.* When you possess anything that others require but that you alone control, you make them dependent on you and, therefore, you gain power over them.[4] Dependency, then, is inversely proportional to the alternative sources of supply. If something is plentiful, possession of it will not increase your power. If everyone is intelligent, intelligence gives no special advantage. Similarly, among the super-rich, money is no longer power. But, as the old saying goes, "In the land of the blind, the one-eyed man is king!" If you can create a monopoly by controlling information, prestige, or anything that others crave, they become dependent on you. Conversely, the more you can expand your options, the less power you place in the hands of others. This principle explains, for example, why most organizations use many suppliers rather than give their business to only one. It also explains why so many of us aspire to financial independence. Financial independence reduces the power others can have over us.

What Creates Dependency?

Dependency is increased when the resource you control is *important* and *scarce.*[5]

Importance.   If nobody wants what you've got, it's not going to create dependency. To create dependency, therefore, you must control things that are perceived as important. It's been found, for instance, that organizations seek to avoid uncertainty. We should, therefore, expect that those individuals or groups who can absorb an organization's uncertainty will be understood to control an important resource. For instance, a study of industrial organizations found that the marketing departments in these firms were consistently rated as the most powerful. It was concluded by the researcher that the most critical uncertainty facing these firms was selling their products. This fact might suggest that, during a labor strike, the organization's negotiating representatives have increased power or that engineers, as a group, would be more powerful at Intel than at Procter & Gamble. These inferences appear to be generally valid. Labor negotiators do become more powerful within the personnel area and the organization as a whole during periods of labor strife. An organization such as Intel, which is a technology–driven company, is dependent on its engineers to maintain its product quality. And, at Intel, engineers are clearly the most powerful group. At Procter & Gamble, marketing is the name of the game, and marketers are the most powerful group. These examples support not only the view that the ability to reduce uncertainty increases a group's importance and, hence, its power but also that what's important is situational. It varies among organizations and undoubtedly also varies over time within any given organization.

Scarcity. As noted previously, if something is plentiful, possession of it will not increase your power. A resource needs to be perceived as scarce to create dependency. This relationship can help to explain how low-ranking members in an organization who have important knowledge not available to high-ranking members, can gain power over the high-ranking members. The need to obtain a scarce resource—in this case, important knowledge—makes the high-ranking member dependent on the low-ranking member. The relation of scarcity to dependency also helps make sense of behaviors of low-ranking members that otherwise might seem illogical, such as destroying the procedure manuals that describe how a job is done, refusing to train people in their job or even to show others exactly what they do, creating specialized language and terminology that inhibit others from understanding their jobs, or operating in secrecy so that the activity will appear more complex and difficult than it really is.

The scarcity-dependency relationship can further be seen in the power of occupational categories. Individuals in occupations in which the supply of personnel is low relative to demand can negotiate compensation and benefit packages far more attractive than can those in occupations where there is an abundance of candidates. College administrators have no problem today finding English instructors. The market for accounting teachers, in contrast, is extremely tight, with the demand high and the supply limited. The result is that the bargaining power of accounting faculty allows them to negotiate higher salaries, lighter teaching loads, and other benefits.

Power in Groups: Coalitions

Those "out of power" and seeking to be "in" will first try to increase their power individually. Why spread the spoils if one doesn't have to? But if this approach proves ineffective, the alternative is to form a coalition. There *is* strength in numbers.

The natural way to gain influence is to become a powerholder. Therefore, those who want power will attempt to build a personal power base.

But, in many instances, doing so may be difficult, risky, costly, or impossible. In such cases, efforts will be made to form a coalition of two or more "outs" who, by joining together, can each better themselves at the expense of those outside the coalition.

Historically, blue-collar workers who were unsuccessful in bargaining on their own behalf with management resorted to labor unions to bargain for them. In recent years, white-collar employees and professionals have increasingly turned to unions after finding it difficult to exert power individually to attain higher wages and greater job security.

What predictions can we make about the formation of coalitions? First, coalitions in organizations often seek to maximize their size. In political science theory, coalitions move the other way—they try to minimize their size. They tend to be just large enough to exert the power necessary to achieve their objectives. But legislatures are different from organizations in that legislators make the policy decisions that are then carried out by separate administrators or managers. Decision making in organizations does not end with merely selecting from among a set of alternatives. The decision must also be implemented. In organizations, the implementation of and commitment to the decision are at least as important as the decision itself. It's necessary, therefore, for coalitions in organizations to seek a broad constituency to support the coalition's objectives, so the coalition must be expanded to encompass as many interests as possible. Coalition expansion to facilitate consensus building, of course, is more likely to occur in organizational cultures where cooperation, commitment, and shared decision making are highly valued than in autocratic and hierarchically controlled organizations, where maximizing the coalition's size is less likely to be sought.

Another prediction about coalitions is related to the degree of interdependence within the organization. More coalitions will likely be created where there is a great deal of task and resource interdependence. In contrast, there will be less interdependence among subunits and less coalition formation activity where subunits are largely self-contained or resources are abundant.

Finally, coalition formation will be influenced by the actual tasks that workers perform. The more routine the task of a group, or the work of individual jobs, the greater the likelihood that coalitions will form. In routine situations, group members or workers are substitutable and, thus, their dependence is greater than in nonroutine situations. To offset this dependence, they can be expected to resort to a coalition. We see, therefore, that unions appeal more to low-skill and nonprofessional workers than to skilled and professional types. Of course, where the supply of skilled and professional employees is high relative to their demand or where organizations have standardized traditionally unique jobs, we would expect even these incumbents to find unionization attractive.

Power and Sexual Harassment

The issue of sexual harassment received increasing attention by corporations and the media in the 1980s because of the growing ranks of female employees, especially in nontraditional work environments. But it was the congressional hearings in the fall of 1991 in which law professor Anita Hill graphically accused Supreme

Court nominee Clarence Thomas of sexual harassment that challenged organizations to reassess their harassment policies and practices.

Legally, **sexual harassment** is defined as unwelcome advances, requests for sexual favors, and other verbal or physical conduct, whether overt or subtle, of a sexual nature. But there is a great deal of disagreement about what *specifically* constitutes sexual harassment. Organizations have made considerable progress in the last few years toward limiting overt forms of sexual harassment, including unwanted physical touching, recurring requests for dates after a clear refusal, and threats that refusing a sexual proposition will result in losing one's job. The problems today are likely to surface around the more subtle forms of sexual harassment—unwanted looks or comments; sexual artifacts, such as nude calendars, in the workplace; or misinterpretation of where the line between "being friendly" ends and "harassment" begins.

Most studies confirm that the concept of power is central to understanding sexual harassment.[6] This seems to be true whether the harassment comes from a supervisor, a co-worker, or even a subordinate. The supervisor-employee dyad best characterizes an unequal power relationship, in which position power gives the supervisor the capacity to reward and coerce. Supervisors give subordinates their assignments, evaluate their performance, make recommendations for salary adjustments and promotions, and even decide whether an employee retains his or her job. These decisions give a supervisor power. Because subordinates want favorable performance reviews, salary increases, and the like, it's clear that supervisors control resources that most subordinates consider important and scarce. It's also worth noting that individuals who occupy high-status roles (management positions, for example) sometimes believe that sexually harassing subordinates is merely an extension of their right to make demands on lower-status individuals. Because of power inequities, sexual harassment by one's boss creates great difficulty for the person being harassed. If there are no witnesses, it is one person's word against another's. Are there others this boss has harassed and, if so, will they come forward? Because of the supervisor's control over resources, many who are harassed are afraid to speak out for fear of retaliation by the supervisor.

Co-workers don't have position power, but they can have influence and use it to sexually harass peers. In fact, although co-workers appear to engage in somewhat less severe forms of harassment than do supervisors, co-workers are the most frequent perpetrators of sexual harassment in organizations. How do co-workers exercise power? Most often it's by providing or withholding information, cooperation, and support. For example, the effective performance of most jobs requires interaction and support from co-workers, especially nowadays, as work increasingly is assigned to teams. By threatening to withhold or delay providing information that's necessary for the successful achievement of your work goals, co-workers can exert power over you.

Harassment by subordinates doesn't get nearly the attention that harassment by a supervisor does, but it does occur. Persons in positions of power can be subjected to sexual harassment from persons in less powerful positions within the organization. Usually the subordinate will devalue the superior through highlighting traditional gender stereotypes that reflect negatively on the person in power (such as helplessness or passivity if the victim is a woman;

impotence or timidity if a man). Why would a subordinate engage in such practices? To gain some power over the higher-ranking person or to minimize power differentials.

The topic of sexual harassment is about power. It's about one individual's controlling or threatening another. It's wrong. It's illegal. But you can understand how sexual harassment surfaces in organizations if you analyze it in terms of power.

Politics: Power in Action

When people get together, power will be exerted. People want to carve out a niche from which to exert influence, earn rewards, and advance their careers. When employees in organizations convert their power into action, they are engaged in politics. Those with good political skills have the ability to use their bases of power effectively.

A Definition of Political Behavior

There have been no shortages of definitions for organizational politics. Essentially, however, they have focused on the use of power to affect decision making in the organization or on behaviors by members that are self-serving and organizationally nonsanctioned.[7] For our purposes, we define **political behavior** in organizations as *those activities that are not required as part of one's formal role in the organization, but that influence, or attempt to influence, the distribution of advantages and disadvantages within the organization.*[8]

This definition encompasses key elements of what most people mean when they talk about organizational politics. Political behavior is *outside* one's specified job requirements. The behavior requires some attempt to use one's *power* bases. Our definition encompasses efforts to influence the goals, criteria, or processes used for *decision making* when we state that politics is concerned with the distribution of advantages and disadvantages within the organization. Our definition is broad enough to include such varied political behaviors as withholding key information from decision makers, whistle-blowing, filing of grievances, spreading rumors, leaking confidential information about organizational activities to the media, exchanging favors with others in the organization for mutual benefit, or lobbying for or against a particular individual or decision.

The Importance of a Political Perspective

Those who fail to acknowledge political behavior ignore the reality that organizations are political systems. It would be nice if all organizations or formal groups within organizations could be described as supportive, harmonious, trusting, collaborative, or cooperative. A nonpolitical perspective can lead one to believe that employees will always behave in ways consistent with the interests of the organization. In contrast, a political view can explain much of what may seem to be irrational behavior in organizations. It can help to explain, for instance, why employees withhold information, restrict output, attempt to "build empires," publicize their successes, hide their failures, distort performance figures to make themselves look better, and engage in similar activities that appear to be at odds with the organization's desire for effectiveness and efficiency.

Factors Contributing to Political Behavior

Recent research and observation have identified a number of factors that appear to be associated with political behavior. Some are individual characteristics, derived from the unique qualities of the people whom the organization employs; others are a result of the organization's culture or internal environment.

Individual Factors. Researchers have identified certain personality characteristics, needs, and other individual factors that are likely to be related to political behavior. Employees who are authoritarian, have a high-risk propensity, or possess an external locus of control (believe that forces outside themselves control their destiny) act politically with less regard for the consequences to the organization. A high need for power, autonomy, security, or status is also a major contributor to an employee's tendency to engage in political behavior.[9]

Organizational Factors. Political activity is probably more a function of the organization's culture than of individual differences. Why? Because most organizations have a large number of employees with the characteristics we listed, yet the presence of political behavior varies widely.

Although we acknowledge the role that individual differences can play in fostering politicking, the evidence more strongly supports that certain cultures promote politics. Cultures characterized by low trust, role ambiguity, unclear performance evaluation systems, zero-sum reward allocation practices, democratic decision making, high pressures for performance, and self-serving senior managers will create opportunities for political activities to be nurtured.[10]

The less trust there is within the organization, the higher the level of political behavior. So high trust should suppress the level of political behavior.

Role ambiguity means that the prescribed behaviors of the employee are not clear. There are few limits, therefore, to the scope and functions of the employee's political actions. Since political activities are defined as those not required as part of one's formal role, the greater the role ambiguity, the more one can engage in political activity with little chance of its being visible.

The practice of performance evaluation is far from a perfected science. The more that organizations use subjective criteria in the appraisal, emphasize a single outcome measure, or allow significant time to pass between an action and its appraisal, the greater the likelihood an employee can get away with politicking. Subjective performance criteria create ambiguity. The use of a single outcome measure encourages individuals to do whatever is necessary to look good on that measure, but often at the expense of performing well on other important parts of the job that are not being appraised. The amount of time that elapses between an action and its appraisal is also a relevant factor. The longer the time period, the more unlikely it is that the employee will be held accountable for political behaviors.

The more an organization's culture emphasizes the zero-sum or win-lose approach to reward allocations, the more employees will be motivated to engage in politicking. The zero-sum approach treats the reward "pie" as fixed so that any gain one person or group achieves has to come at the expense of another person or group. If I win, you must lose! If $10,000 in annual raises is to be distributed among five employees, then any employee who gets more than $2,000 takes money away from one or more of the others. Such a practice encourages making others look bad and increasing the visibility of what you do.

Since the 1970s, there has been a general move in North America toward making organizations less autocratic. Managers are being asked to behave more democratically. They're told they should allow subordinates to advise them on decisions and they should rely to a greater extent on group input into the decision process. Such moves toward democracy, however, are not necessarily embraced by all individual managers. Many managers sought their positions in order to have legitimate power to make unilateral decisions. They fought hard and often paid high personal costs to achieve their influential positions. Sharing their power with others rubs directly against their desires. The result is that managers may use the required teams, committees, conferences, and group meetings in a superficial way—as arenas for maneuvering and manipulating.

The more pressure that employees feel to perform well, the more likely they are to engage in politicking. Holding people strictly accountable for outcomes puts great pressure on them to "look good." A person who perceives that his or her entire career is riding on next quarter's sales figures or next month's plant productivity report will be highly motivated to do whatever is necessary to make sure the numbers come out favorably.

Finally, when employees see the people on top engaging in political behavior, especially when they do so successfully and are rewarded for it, a climate is created that supports politicking. Politicking by top management, in a sense, gives permission to those lower in the organization to play politics by implying that such behavior is acceptable.

Impression Management

We know that people have an ongoing interest in how others perceive and evaluate them. For example, North Americans spend billions of dollars on diets, health club memberships, cosmetics, and plastic surgery—all intended to make them more attractive to others. Being perceived positively by others should have benefits for people in organizations. It might, for instance, help them initially to get the jobs they want in an organization and, once hired, to get favorable evaluations, superior salary increases, and more rapid promotions. In a political context, it might help sway the distribution of advantages in their favor.

The process by which individuals attempt to control the impression others form of them is called **impression management.** It's a subject that only quite recently has gained the attention of OB researchers.[11] In this section we review impression management (IM) techniques and ascertain whether they actually work in organizations.

Techniques. Most of the attention given to IM techniques has centered on seven verbal self-presentation behaviors that individuals use to manipulate information about themselves.[12] Let's briefly define them and give an example of each.

Self-descriptions: Statements made by a person that describe such personal characteristics as traits, abilities, feelings, opinions, and personal lives. An example: Job applicant to interviewer, "I got my Harvard M.B.A. even though I suffer from dyslexia."

Conformity: Agreeing with someone else's opinion in order to gain his or her approval. An example: Manager to boss, "You're absolutely right on your reorganization plan for the western regional office. I couldn't agree with you more."

Accounts: Excuses, justifications, or other explanations of a predicament-creating event aimed at minimizing the apparent severity of the predicament. An example: Sales manager to boss, "We failed to get the ad in the paper on time but no one responds to those ads anyway."

Apologies: Admitting responsibility for an undesirable event and simultaneously seeking to get a pardon for the action. An example: Employee to boss, "I'm sorry I made a mistake on the report. Please forgive me."

Acclaiming: Explanation of favorable events by someone in order to maximize the desirable implications for that person. An example: Salesperson to peer, "The sales in our division have nearly tripled since I was hired."

Flattery: Complimenting others about their virtues in an effort to make oneself appear perceptive and likable. An example: New sales trainee to peer, "You handled that client's complaint *so* tactfully! I could never have handled that as well as you did."

Favors: Doing something nice for someone to gain that person's approval. An example: Salesperson to prospective client, "I've got two tickets to the theater for tonight that I can't use. Take them. Consider it a thank-you for taking the time to talk with me."

Keep in mind that nothing in IM implies that the impressions people convey are necessarily false (although, of course, they sometimes are). You can, for instance, *actually* believe that ads contribute little to sales in your region or that you *are* the key ingredient in the tripling of your division's sales. But misrepresentation can have a high cost. If the image claimed is false, you may be discredited. If you "cry wolf" once too often, no one is likely to believe you when the wolf really comes. So one must be cautious not to be perceived as insincere or manipulative.

Are individuals more likely to misrepresent themselves or to get away with it in some situations than in others? Yes. Highly uncertain or ambiguous situations provide relatively little information for challenging a fraudulent claim and reduce the risks associated with misrepresentation.

Effectiveness. Only a few studies have been undertaken to test the effectiveness of IM techniques, and these have been essentially limited to determining whether IM behavior is related to job interview success. This makes a particularly relevant area of study since applicants clearly are attempting to present positive images of themselves and there are relatively objective outcome measures (written assessments and typically a hire–don't hire recommendation).

The evidence demonstrates that using IM behaviors seems to work.[13] In one study, for instance, interviewers felt that the applicants for a position as a customer-service representative who used IM techniques performed better in the interview than those who didn't use IM, and they seemed somewhat more inclined to hire these people.[14] Moreover, the researchers considered applicants' credentials and concluded it was the IM techniques alone that influenced the interviewers. That is, it didn't seem to matter if applicants were well or poorly qualified. If they used IM techniques, they did better in the interview. Of course, it could be argued that since the job for which applicants were being considered—customer-service representative—was a public contact position, self-presentation may be a job-relevant skill and more important than such qualifications as college major, grades, or prior work experience. Nevertheless, IM techniques seem to work in interviews.

The Ethics of Behaving Politically

We conclude our discussion of politics by providing some ethical guidelines for political behavior. While there are no clear-cut ways to differentiate ethical from unethical politicking, there are some questions you should consider.[15]

Exhibit 11-2 illustrates a decision tree to guide ethical actions. The first question you need to answer addresses self-interest versus organizational goals. Ethical actions are consistent with the organization's goals. Spreading untrue rumors about the safety of a new product introduced by your company, in order to make that product's design group look bad, is unethical. However, there may be nothing unethical if a department head exchanges favors with her division's purchasing manager in order to get a critical contract processed quickly.

The second question concerns the rights of other parties. If the department head described in the previous paragraph went down to the mailroom during her lunch hour and read through the mail directed to the purchasing manager with the intent of "getting something on him" so he would expedite a contract, she would be acting unethically. She would have violated the purchasing manager's right to privacy.

The final question that needs to be addressed is related to whether the political activity conforms to standards of equity and justice. The department head that inflates the performance evaluation of a favored employee and deflates the evaluation of a disfavored employee—then uses these evaluations to justify giving the former a big raise and nothing to the latter—has treated the disfavored employee unfairly.

Unfortunately, the answers to the questions in Exhibit 11-2 are often argued in ways to make unethical practices seem ethical. Powerful people, for example, can become very good at explaining self-serving behaviors in terms of the organization's best interests. Similarly, they can persuasively argue that unfair actions are really fair and equitable. Our point is that immoral people can justify almost any behavior. Those who are powerful, articulate, and persuasive are most vulnerable because they are likely to be able to get away with unethical practices successfully. When faced with an ethical dilemma regarding organizational politics, try to answer the questions in Exhibit 11-2 truthfully. And, if you have a strong power base, recognize the ability of power to corrupt. Remember, it's a lot easier

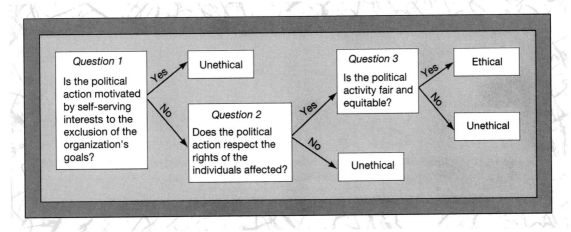

Exhibit 11-2

Is a Political Action Ethical?

Source: Adapted from G. F. Cavanagh, D. Moberg, and M. Valasquez, "The Ethics of Organizational Politics, "*Academy of Management Review*, July 1981, p. 368. Reprinted by permission.

for the powerless to act ethically, for no other reason than that they typically have very little political discretion to exploit.

 # **I** mplications for Managers

If you want to get things done in a group or organization, it helps to have power. As a manager who wants to maximize your power, you will want to increase others' dependence on you. You can, for instance, increase your power in relation to your boss by developing knowledge or a skill that he needs and for which he perceives no ready substitute. But power is a two-way street. You will not be alone in attempting to build your power bases. Others, particularly subordinates, will be seeking to make you dependent on them. The result is a continual battle. While you seek to maximize others' dependence on you, you will be seeking to minimize your dependence on others. And, of course, others you work with will be trying to do the same.

The effective manager accepts the political nature of organizations. By assessing behavior in a political framework, you can better predict the actions of others and use this information to formulate political strategies that will gain advantages for you and your work unit.

Conflict and Negotiation

After reading this chapter, you should be able to:

1. Define conflict

2. Differentiate between the traditional, human relations, and interactionist views of conflict

3. Contrast functional and dysfunctional conflict

4. Outline the conflict process

5. Describe the five conflict-handling orientations

6. Contrast distributive and integrative bargaining

7. Identify decision biases that hinder effective negotiation

8. Explain ways for individuals to improve their negotiating skills

It's been said that conflict is a theme that has occupied humans more than any other—with the exception of God and love. Only fairly recently, though, has conflict become a major area of interest and research for students of organizational behavior. The evidence suggests that this interest has been well placed: The type and intensity of conflict *does* affect group behavior.

A Definition of Conflict

There has been no shortage of definitions for conflict. In spite of the divergent meanings the term has acquired, several common themes underlie most definitions. Conflict must be *perceived* by the parties to it.

Chapter 12

Whether conflict exists is a perception issue. If no one is aware of a conflict, it is generally agreed that no conflict exists. Of course, conflicts perceived may not be real, and, conversely, many situations that otherwise could be described as conflictive are not because the group members involved do not perceive the conflict. Additional commonalities among most definitions of conflict are the concepts of *opposition, scarcity,* and *blockage* and the assumption there are two or more parties whose interests or goals appear to be incompatible. Resources—money, jobs, prestige, power, for example—are not unlimited, and their scarcity encourages blocking behavior. The parties are therefore in opposition. When one party blocks the means to a goal of another, a state of conflict exists.

Differences between definitions tend to center around *intent* and whether conflict is a term limited only to *overt* acts. The intent issue is a debate over whether blockage behavior must be a determined action or whether it could occur as a result of fortuitous circumstances. As to whether conflict can refer only to overt acts, some definitions, for example, require signs of manifest fighting or open struggle as criteria for the existence of conflict.

Our definition of conflict acknowledges awareness (perception), opposition, scarcity, and blockage. Further, we assume it to be a determined action, which can exist at either the latent or overt level. We define **conflict** as *a process in which an effort is purposely made by A to offset the efforts of B by some form of blocking that will result in frustrating B in attaining his or her goals or furthering his or her interests.*

Transitions in Conflict Thought

It is entirely appropriate to say that there has been conflict over the role of conflict in groups and organizations. One school of thought has argued that conflict must be avoided, that it indicates a malfunction within the group. We call this the *traditional view.* Another school of thought, the *human relations view,* argues that conflict is a natural and inevitable outcome in any group. It need not be evil, but rather has the potential to be a positive force in determining group performance. The third, and most recent, perspective proposes not only that conflict *can* be a positive force in a group, but explicitly argues that some conflict is *absolutely necessary* for a group to perform effectively. We label this third school the *interactionist view.* Let's take a closer look at each of these views.[1]

The Traditional View

The early approach to conflict assumed that conflict was bad. Conflict was viewed negatively, and it was used synonymously with terms such as *violence, destruction,* and *irrationality* in order to reinforce its negative connotation. Conflict, then, was to be avoided.

The traditional view was consistent with the attitudes that prevailed about group behavior in the 1930s and 1940s. From findings provided by studies such as those done at Hawthorne, it was argued that conflict was a dysfunctional outcome resulting from poor communication, a lack of openness and trust between people, and the failure of managers to be responsive to the needs and aspirations of their employees.

The view that all conflict is bad certainly offers a simple approach to looking at the behavior of people who create conflict. Since all conflict is to be avoided, we need merely direct our attention to the causes of conflict and correct these malfunctionings in order to improve group and organizational performance. Although studies now provide strong evidence to dispute that this approach to conflict reduction results in high group performance, most of us still evaluate conflict situations on the basis of this outmoded standard.

The Human Relations View

The human relations position argued that conflict was a natural occurrence in all groups and organizations. Since conflict was inevitable, the human relations school advocated acceptance of conflict. They rationalized its existence: It cannot be eliminated, and there are even times when conflict may benefit a group's performance. The human relations view dominated conflict theory from the late 1940s through the mid-1970s.

The Interactionist View

The current view toward conflict is the interactionist perspective. Whereas the human relations approach *accepted* conflict, the interactionist approach *encourages* conflict on the grounds that a harmonious, peaceful, tranquil, and cooperative group is likely to become static, apathetic, and nonresponsive to needs for change and innovation. The major contribution of the interactionist approach, therefore, is encouraging group leaders to maintain an ongoing minimal level of conflict— enough to keep the group alive, self-critical, and creative.

Given the interactionist view, which is the one we take in this chapter, it becomes evident that to say that conflict is all good or all bad is inappropriate and naive. Whether a conflict is good or bad depends on the type of conflict. Specifically, it's necessary to differentiate between functional and dysfunctional conflicts.

Differentiating Functional from Dysfunctional Conflicts

The interactionist view does not propose that *all* conflicts are good. Rather, some conflicts support the goals of the group and improve its performance; these are functional, constructive forms of conflict. There are also conflicts that hinder group performance; these are dysfunctional or destructive forms.

How does one tell if a conflict is functional or dysfunctional? The demarcation between functional and dysfunctional is neither clear nor precise. No one level of conflict can be adopted as acceptable or unacceptable under all conditions. The type and level of conflict that create healthy and positive involvement toward one group's goals may, in another group or in the same group at another time, be highly dysfunctional.

The important criterion is group performance. Since groups exist to attain a goal or goals, it is the impact of the conflict on the group, rather than on any single individual, that defines functionality. The impact of conflict on the individual and the impact on the group are rarely mutually exclusive, so the ways individuals perceive a conflict may significantly influence the effect of the conflict on the group. However, individual perceptions are not necessarily influential, and when they are not, our orientation will be to the group. In an appraisal of the functional and dysfunctional impacts of conflict on group behavior, whether the individual group members perceive the conflict as good or bad is irrelevant. A group member may perceive an action as dysfunctional because the outcome is personally dissatisfying to him or her. For our analysis, however, it would be functional if it furthered the objectives of the group.

The Conflict Process

The **conflict process** can be thought of as progressing through four stages: potential opposition, cognition and personalization, behavior, and outcomes. The process is diagrammed in Exhibit 12-1 (see page 172).

Stage I: Potential Opposition

The first step in the conflict process is the presence of conditions that create opportunities for conflict to arise. They *need not* lead directly to conflict, but one of these conditions is necessary if conflict is to arise. For simplicity's sake, these conditions (which also may be looked at as causes or sources of conflict) have been condensed into three general categories: communication, structure, and personal variables.[2]

Communication. The communicative source represents those opposing forces that arise from semantic difficulties, misunderstandings, and "noise" in the communication channels. Much of this discussion can be related to our comments on communication and communication networks in Chapter 9.

One of the major misconceptions that most of us carry around with us is that poor communication is the reason for conflicts. Such a conclusion is not unreasonable, given the amount of time each of us spends communicating. But, of course, poor communication is certainly not the source of *all* conflicts, though there is considerable evidence to suggest that problems in the communication process act to retard collaboration and stimulate misunderstanding.

A review of the research suggests that semantic difficulties, insufficient exchange of information, and noise in the communication channel are all barriers to communication and potential antecedent conditions to conflict. Specifically, evidence demonstrates that semantic difficulties arise as a result of differences in training, selective perception, and inadequate information about others. Research has further demonstrated a surprising finding: The potential for conflict increases when either too little or too much communication takes place. Apparently, an increase in communication is functional up to a point, whereupon it is possible to overcommunicate, resulting in an increase in the potential for conflict. Too much information as well as too little can lay the foundation for conflict. Further, the channel chosen for communicating can have an influence on stimulating opposition. The filtering process that occurs as information is passed between members and the divergence of communications from formal or previously established channels offer potential opportunities for conflict to arise.

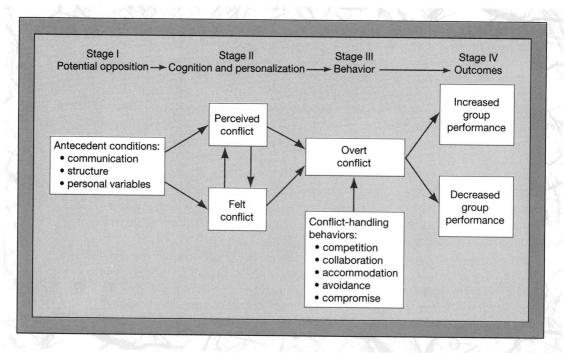

Exhibit 12-1
The Conflict Process

Structure. The term *structure* is used, in this context, to include variables such as size; degree of routinization, specialization, and standardization in the tasks assigned to group members; heterogeneity of the group; leadership styles; reward systems; and the degree of dependence between groups. Research indicates that size and specialization act as forces to stimulate conflict. The larger the group and the more specialized its activities, the greater the likelihood of conflict. Tenure and conflict have been found to be inversely related. The potential for conflict tends to be greatest where group members are younger and where turnover is high.

There is some indication that a close style of leadership, that is, tight and continuous observation with restrictive control of the others' behaviors, increases conflict potential, but the evidence is not strong. Too much reliance on participation may also stimulate conflict. Research tends to confirm that participation and conflict are highly correlated, apparently because participation encourages the promotion of differences. Reward systems, too, are found to create conflict when one member's gain is at another's expense. Finally, if a group is dependent on another group (in contrast to the two being mutually independent) or if interdependence allows one group to gain at another's expense, opposing forces are stimulated.

Personal Variables. The most important personal variables are individual value systems and individual idiosyncrasies and differences. The evidence indicates that certain personality types—for example, individuals who are highly authoritarian, dogmatic, and who demonstrate low self-esteem—lead to potential conflict. Most important, and probably the most overlooked variable in the study of social conflict, is the notion of differing value systems. That is, people differ in the importance they give to values such as freedom, pleasure, hard work, self-respect, honesty, obedience, and equality. Value differences, for example, are the best explanation of such diverse issues as prejudice, disagreements over one's contribution to the group and the rewards one deserves, or assessments of whether this particular book is any good. The fact that John dislikes blacks and Dana thinks that John's position indicates his ignorance; that an employee thinks he is worth $30,000 a year but his boss believes him to be worth $24,000; and that Ann thinks this book is interesting while Jennifer views it as "a crock" are all value judgments. And differences in value systems are important sources for creating the potential for conflict.

Stage II: Cognition and Personalization

If the conditions cited in stage I generate frustration, then the potential for opposition becomes realized in the second stage. The antecedent conditions can lead to conflict only when one or more of the parties are affected by, and cognizant of, the conflict.

As we noted in our definition of conflict, perception is required. Therefore, one or more of the parties must be aware of the existence of the antecedent conditions. However, because a conflict is perceived does not mean it is personalized. You may be aware that you and a co-worker are in disagreement. But the disagreement may not make you tense or anxious and it may not influence your affection toward this co-worker. It is at the level where conflict is felt, when individuals become emotionally involved, that parties experience anxiety, tension, frustration, or hostility.

Stage III: Behavior

We are in the third stage of the conflict process when a member engages in action that frustrates the attainment of another's goals or prevents the furthering of the other's interests. This action must be intended; that is, there must be a known effort to frustrate another. At this juncture, the conflict is out in the open.

Overt conflict covers a full range of behaviors, from subtle, indirect, and highly controlled forms of interference to direct, aggressive, violent, and uncontrolled struggle. At the low range, this overt behavior is illustrated by the student who raises his or her hand in class and questions a point the instructor has made. At the high range, strikes, riots, and wars come to mind.

Stage III is also where most conflict-handling behaviors are initiated. Once the conflict is overt, the parties will develop a method for dealing with the conflict. Conflict-handling behaviors might be initiated in stage II, but, in most cases, techniques for reducing frustration are used not as preventive measures but only when the conflict has become observable. Five conflict-handling approaches are typically available: competition, collaboration, avoidance, accommodation, and compromise.[3]

Competition. When one party seeks to achieve certain goals or to further personal interests, regardless of the impact on the parties to the conflict, he or she competes and dominates. These win-lose struggles, in formal groups or in an organization, frequently utilize the formal authority of a mutual superior as the dominant force, and each of the conflicting parties will use his or her own power base in order to resolve a victory in his or her favor.

Collaboration. When each of the parties in conflict desires to satisfy fully the concern of all parties, we have cooperation and the search for a mutually beneficial outcome. In collaboration, the behavior of the parties is aimed at solving the problem and at clarifying the differences rather than accommodating various points of view. The participants consider the full range of alternatives; the similarities and differences in viewpoints become more clearly focused; and the causes or differences become outwardly evident. Because the solution sought is advantageous to all parties, collaboration is often thought of as a win-win approach to resolving conflicts. It is, for example, a tool used frequently by marriage counselors. Behavioral scientists, who value openness, trust, and spontaneity in relationships, are also strong advocates of a collaborative approach to resolving conflicts.

Avoidance. A party may recognize that a conflict exists but react by withdrawing from or suppressing the conflict. Indifference or the desire to evade overt demonstration of a disagreement can result in withdrawal: The parties acknowledge physical separation, and each stakes out a territory that is distinct from the other's. If withdrawal is not possible or desirous, the parties may suppress, that is, withhold their differences. When group members are required to interact because of the interdependence of their tasks, suppression is a more probable outcome than withdrawal.

Accommodation. When the parties seek to appease their opponents, they may be willing to place their opponents' interests above their own. In order to maintain the relationship, one party is willing to be self-sacrificing. We refer to this behavior as accommodation. When husbands and wives have differences, it is not uncommon for one to accommodate the other by placing a spouse's interest above one's own.

Compromise. When each party to the conflict must give up something, sharing occurs, resulting in a compromised outcome. In compromising, there is no clear winner or loser. Rather, there is a rationing of the object of the conflict or, where the object is not divisible, one rewards the other by yielding something of substitute value. The distinguishing characteristic of compromise, therefore, is the requirement that each party give up something. In negotiations between unions and management, compromise is required in order to reach a settlement and agree upon a labor contract.

The Impact of Natural Culture on Conflict Behavior. Your approach to handling conflict will, to some degree, be influenced by your cultural roots. Americans, for example, have a reputation for being open, direct, and competitive. These characteristics are consistent with a society marked by relatively low uncertainty avoidance and high masculinity rankings.

As we discovered in Chapter 2, people in countries low in uncertainty avoidance feel secure and relatively free from threats of uncertainty. Their organizations, therefore, tend to be rather open and flexible. Countries high in masculinity emphasize assertiveness. The cultural climate of low uncertainty avoidance and high masculinity tends to shape a society that is open, direct, and competitive. It would also tend to create individuals who favor such conflict-handling behaviors as competition and collaboration.

This premise suggests that uncertainty avoidance and masculinity/femininity rankings would be fairly good predictors of which conflict styles are preferred in different countries. It suggests, for instance, that when one is in a Scandinavian country—which tends to rate high on femininity—avoidance or accommodation behaviors should be emphasized. The same recommendation would apply in Japan, Greece, or other countries that rate high on uncertainty avoidance, because the extensive use of formal rules and employment guarantees tends to minimize conflicts and encourage cooperation.

Stage IV: Outcomes

The interplay between the overt conflict behavior and conflict-handling behaviors results in consequences. As Exhibit 12-1 demonstrates, they may be functional in that the conflict has resulted in an improvement in the group's performance. Conversely, group performance may be hindered and the outcome then would be dysfunctional.

Functional Outcomes. How might conflict increase group performance? It is hard to visualize a situation in which open or violent aggression could be functional. But it is possible to envision how low or moderate levels of conflict could improve the effectiveness of a group. Because it is often difficult to think of instances in which conflict can be constructive, let's consider some examples and then look at the research evidence.

Conflict is constructive when it improves the quality of decisions, stimulates creativity and innovation, encourages interest and curiosity among group members, provides the medium through which problems can be aired and tensions released, and fosters an environment of self-evaluation and improvement. The evidence suggests that conflict can enhance the quality of decision making by allowing all points, particularly the ones that are unusual or held by a minority, to be weighed in important decisions. Conflict is an antidote for groupthink. It does not allow the group to rubber-stamp decisions that may be based on weak assumptions, inadequate consideration of relevant alternatives, or other debilities. Conflict challenges the status quo and therefore furthers the creation of new ideas, promotes reassessment of group goals and activities, and increases the probability that the group will respond to change.

For examples of companies that have suffered because they had too little functional conflict, you don't have to look further than Sears, Roebuck and General Motors.[4] Many of the problems that beset both of those companies throughout the 1970s and 1980s can be traced to a lack of functional conflict. They hired and promoted individuals who were "yes men," loyal to the organization to the point of never questioning company actions. Managers were, for the most part, conservative white Anglo-Saxon males raised in the midwestern United States who resisted change—they preferred looking back to past successes rather than forward to new challenges. Moreover, both firms kept their senior executives sheltered in their respective Chicago and Detroit headquarters' offices, protected from hearing anything they didn't want to hear, and a "world away" from the changes that were dramatically altering the retailing and automobile industries.

Research studies in diverse settings confirm the functionality of conflict. Consider the following findings. A comparison of six major decisions during the administrations of four U.S. presidents found that conflict reduced the chance that groupthink would overpower policy decisions. The comparisons demonstrated that conformity among presidential advisers was related to poor decisions, while an atmosphere of constructive conflict and critical thinking surrounded the well-developed decisions.[5]

There is further evidence that conflict leads to better and more innovative decisions, as well as increased group productivity. It was demonstrated that, among established groups, performance tended to improve more when there was conflict among members than when there was fairly close agreement. The investigators observed that when groups analyzed decisions that had been made by the individual members of that group, the average improvement among the high-conflict groups was seventy-three percent greater than that of those groups characterized by low-conflict conditions.[6] Other researchers have found similar results: Groups composed of members with different interests tend to produce higher-quality solutions to a variety of problems than do homogeneous groups.[7] The preceding findings suggest that conflict in the group might be an indication of strength rather than, in the traditional view, of weakness.

Dysfunctional Conflict.   The destructive consequences of conflict on a group or organization's performance are generally well known. A reasonable summary might state: Uncontrolled opposition breeds discontent, which acts to dissolve common ties and eventually leads to destruction of the group. And, of course, there is a substantial body of literature to document how the dysfunctional varieties of conflict can reduce group effectiveness. Among the more undesirable consequences are a retarding of communication, reductions in group cohesiveness, and subordination of group goals to the primacy of infighting among members. At the extreme, conflict can bring group functioning to a halt and potentially threaten the group's survival.

This discussion has returned us to the issue of what is functional and what is dysfunctional. Research on conflict has yet to identify those situations in which conflict is more likely to be constructive than destructive. However, the difference between functional and dysfunctional conflict is important enough for us to go beyond the substantive evidence and propose at least two hypotheses. The first is that extreme levels of conflict, exemplified by overt struggle or violence, are rarely, if ever, functional. Functional conflict is probably most often characterized by low to moderate levels of subtle and controlled opposition. Second, the type of group activity should be another factor determining functionality. We hypothesize that the more creative or unprogrammed the decision making of the group, the greater the probability that internal conflict will be constructive. Groups required to tackle problems demanding novel approaches—for example, in research or advertising—will benefit more from conflict than groups performing highly programmed activities, such as work teams on an automobile assembly line.

Negotiation

Negotiation permeates the interactions of almost everyone in groups and organizations. There's the obvious: Labor bargains with management. There's the not-so-obvious: Managers negotiate with subordinates, peers, and bosses; salespeople negotiate with customers; purchasing agents negotiate with suppliers. And there's the subtle: A worker agrees to answer a colleague's phone for a few minutes in exchange for some past or future benefit. In today's team-based organizations, where members are increasingly finding themselves having to work with colleagues over whom they have no direct authority and with whom they may not even share a common boss, negotiation skills become critical.

For our purposes, we define **negotiation** as a process in which two or more parties exchange goods or services and attempt to agree on the exchange rate for them.[8] In addition, we use the terms *negotiation* and *bargaining* interchangeably.

Bargaining Strategies

There are two general approaches to negotiation—*distributive bargaining* and *integrative bargaining*.[9] These are compared in Exhibit 12-2.

Distributive Bargaining. You see a used car advertised for sale in the newspaper. It appears to be just what you've been looking for. You go out to see the car. It's great and you want it. The owner tells you the asking price. You don't want to pay that much. The two of you then negotiate over the price. The negotiating

Exhibit 12-2

Distributive versus Integrative Bargaining

Bargaining Characteristic	Distributive Bargaining	Integrative Bargaining
Available amount of resources to be divided	Fixed	Variable
Primary motivations	I win; you lose	I win; you win
Primary interests	Opposed to each other	Convergent or congruent with each other
Focus of relationships	Short term	Long term

Source: Based on R. J. Lewicki and J. A. Litterer, *Negotiation*, 1985, p. 280. Copyright © Roy J. Lewicki and Joseph A. Litterer, 1985. Reprinted by permission of Richard D. Irwin, Inc.

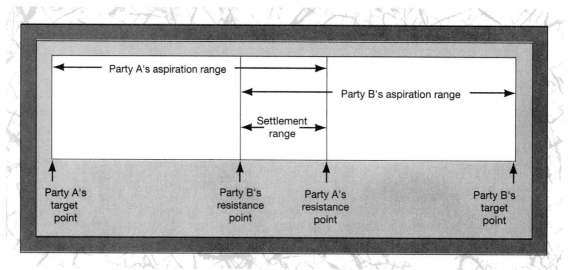

Party A's aspiration range

Party B's aspiration range

Settlement
range

Party A's
target
point

Party B's
resistance
point

Party A's
resistance
point

Party B's
target
point

Exhibit 12-3
Staking Out the Bargaining Zone

process you are engaging in is called *distributive bargaining*. Its most identifying feature is that it operates under zero-sum conditions. That is, any gain I make is at your expense, and vice versa. In the used car example, every dollar you can get the seller to cut from the car's price is a dollar you save. Conversely, every dollar more he can get from you comes at your expense. So the essence of **distributive bargaining** is negotiating over who gets what share of a fixed pie.

Probably the most widely cited example of distributive bargaining is in labor-management negotiations over wages. Typically, labor's representatives come to the bargaining table determined to get as much money as possible out of management. Every cent more that labor negotiates increases management's costs, so each party bargains aggressively and treats the other as an opponent who must be defeated.

Exhibit 12-3 depicts the distributive bargaining strategy. Parties A and B represent the two negotiators. Each has a *target point* that defines what he or she would like to achieve. Each also has a *resistance point,* which marks the lowest outcome that is acceptable—the point below which they would break off negotiations rather than accept a less favorable settlement. The area between their resistance points is the settlement range. As long as there is some overlap in their aspiration ranges, there exists a settlement area where each one's aspirations can be met.

When engaged in distributive bargaining, one's tactics focus on trying to get one's opponent to agree to one's specific target point or to get as close to it as possible. Examples of such tactics are persuading your opponent of the impossibility of getting to his or her target point and the advisability of accepting a settlement near yours; arguing that your target is fair, while your opponent's isn't; and attempting to get your opponent to feel emotionally generous toward you and thus accepting an outcome close to your target point.

Integrative Bargaining.   A sales representative for a women's sportswear manufacturer has just closed a $15,000 order from a small clothing retailer. The sales rep calls in the order to her firm's credit department. She is told the firm can't approve credit to this customer because of a past slow-pay record. The next day, the sales rep and the firm's credit manager meet to discuss the problem. The sales rep doesn't want to lose the business. Neither does the credit manager, but he also doesn't want to get stuck with an uncollectible debt. The two openly review their options. After considerable discussion, they agree on a solution that meets both their needs: The credit manager will approve the sale, but the clothing store's owner will provide a bank guarantee that will ensure payment if the bill isn't paid within sixty days.

This sales-credit negotiation is an example of **integrative bargaining.** In contrast to distributive bargaining, integrative problem solving operates under the assumption that one or more settlements exist that can create a win-win solution.

All things being equal, integrative bargaining is preferable to distributive bargaining. Why? Because the former builds long-term relationships and facilitates working together in the future. It bonds negotiators and allows each to leave the bargaining table feeling that he or she has achieved a victory. Distributive bargaining, on the other hand, leaves one party a loser. It tends to build animosities and deepen divisions when people have to work together on an ongoing basis.

Why, then, don't we see more integrative bargaining in organizations? The answer lies in the conditions necessary for this type of negotiation to succeed. These include parties who are open with information and candid about their concerns; a sensitivity by both parties to the other's needs; the ability to trust one another; and a willingness by both parties to maintain flexibility. Since many organizational cultures and interorganizational relationships are not characterized by openness, trust, and flexibility, it isn't surprising that negotiations often take on a win-at-any-cost dynamic.

Issues in Negotiation

We conclude our discussion of negotiation by reviewing three contemporary issues in negotiation: decision-making biases; the role of personality traits; and the effect of cultural differences on negotiating styles.

Decision-Making Biases That Hinder Effective Negotiation.   All of us have had negotiating experiences in which the results have been less than we had hoped for. Why? We tend to be blind to opportunities that would allow us to get as much as possible out of a negotiation. The following identifies seven decision-making biases that can blind us.[10]

1. *Irrational escalation of commitment.* People tend to continue a previously selected course of action beyond what rational analysis would recommend. Such misdirected persistence can lead to wasting a great deal of time, energy, and money. Time and money already invested are "sunk costs." They *cannot* be recovered and should *not* be considered when selecting future courses of action.

2. *The mythical fixed pie.* Bargainers assume that their gain must come at the expense of the other party. As noted with integrative bargaining, that needn't be the case. There are often win-win solutions. By assuming a zero-sum game, you preclude opportunities to find options that can allow multiple victories.

3. *Anchoring and adjustments.* People often have a tendency to anchor their judgments on irrelevant information, such as an initial offer. Many factors influence the initial positions people take when entering a negotiation. They are often meaningless. Effective negotiators don't let an initial anchor minimize the amount of information and the depth of thinking they use to evaluate a situation, and they don't give too much weight to their opponent's initial offer too early in the negotiation.

4. *Framing negotiations.* People tend to be overly affected by the way information is presented to them. For instance, in a labor-management contract negotiation, assume that your employees are currently making $15 an hour but the union is seeking a $4 raise. You are prepared to go to $17. The union's response is likely to be different if you can successfully frame this as a $2 an hour gain (in comparison to the current wage) rather than a $2 an hour loss (when compared against the union's demand).

5. *Availability of information.* Negotiators often rely too much on readily available information while ignoring more relevant data. Things or events that people have often encountered are usually easy to remember—they're "available" in their memory. It's also easy to remember or imagine vivid events. Information that is easily recalled, because it's familiar or vivid, may be interpreted as being reliable when it's not. Effective negotiators learn to distinguish what's emotionally familiar to them from what is reliable and relevant.

6. *The winner's curse.* A friend went in to a local dealership to buy a new, luxury sports car. The list price was $42,300. My friend estimated that the dealer probably paid around $35,000 for the car. My friend was prepared to go as high as $41,000, but he made an initial offer of $38,000. To his surprise, the dealer accepted his offer. Two hours later he was driving home in his new car. That night he couldn't sleep. In spite of the fact that he had paid $3,000 less than he expected, he felt that he still may have paid too much. He was experiencing "winner's curse," or the regret one feels after closing a negotiation. Because your opponent accepted your offer, you become concerned that you offered too much. This postnegotiation reaction is not unusual. In most negotiations, one side (usually the seller) has much better information than the other. Yet people often tend to act in a negotiation as if their opponent is inactive and ignore the valuable information that can be learned by thinking about the other side's decisions. You can reduce the "curse" by gaining as much information as possible and putting yourself in your opponent's shoes.

7. *Overconfidence.* Many of the previous biases can combine to inflate a person's confidence in his or her judgment and choices. When people hold certain beliefs and expectations, they tend to ignore information that contradicts them. The result is that negotiators tend to be overconfident. Overconfidence, in turn, lessens the incentive to compromise. Considering the suggestions of qualified advisers or seeking objective assessment about your position from a neutral party are two ways to temper this tendency.

The Role of Personality Traits in Negotiation. Can you predict an opponent's negotiating tactics if you know something about his or her personality? It's tempting to answer Yes to that question. For instance, you might assume that high risk takers would be aggressive bargainers who make few concessions. Surprisingly, the evidence doesn't support that assumption.[11]

Overall assessments of the personality-negotiation relationship find that personality traits have no significant direct effect on either the bargaining process or negotiation outcomes. This conclusion is important. It suggests that you should concentrate on the issues and the situational factors in each bargaining episode and not on your opponent and his or her characteristics.

Cultural Differences in Negotiations. Although there appears to be no significant direct relationship between an individual's personality and negotiation style, cultural background does seem to be relevant. Negotiating styles clearly vary among national cultures.[12]

The French like conflict. They frequently gain recognition and develop their reputations by thinking and acting against others. As a result, the French tend to take a long time in negotiating agreements, and they aren't overly concerned about whether their opponents like or dislike them.[13] The Chinese also draw out negotiations but for a different reason. They believe that negotiations never end. Just when you think you've pinned down every detail and reached a final solution with a Chinese executive, that executive might smile and start the process all over again. Like the Japanese, the Chinese negotiate to develop a relationship and a commitment to work together rather than to tie up every loose end.[14] Americans are known around the world for their impatience and their desire to be liked. Astute negotiators from other countries often turn these characteristics to their advantage by dragging out negotiations and making friendship conditional on the final settlement.

The cultural context of the negotiation significantly influences the amount and type of preparation for bargaining, the relative emphasis on task versus interpersonal relationships, the tactics used, and even where the negotiation should be conducted. To further illustrate some of these differences, let's look at two studies comparing the influence of culture on business negotiations.

The first study compared North Americans, Arabs, and Russians.[15] Among the factors that were looked at were their negotiating style, how they responded to an opponent's arguments, their approach to making concessions, and how they handled negotiating deadlines. North Americans tried to persuade by relying on facts and appealing to logic. They countered opponents' arguments with objective facts. They made small concessions early in the negotiation to establish a relationship and usually reciprocated opponents' concessions. North Americans treated deadlines as very important. The Arabs tried to persuade by appealing to emotion. They countered opponents' arguments with subjective feelings. They made concessions throughout the bargaining process and almost always reciprocated opponents' concessions. Arabs approached deadlines very casually. The Russians based their arguments on asserted ideals. They made few, if any, concessions. Any concession offered by an opponent was viewed as a weakness and was almost never reciprocated. Finally, the Russians tended to ignore deadlines.

The second study looked at verbal and nonverbal negotiation tactics exhibited by North Americans, Japanese, and Brazilians during half-hour bargaining sessions.[16]

Some of the differences were particularly interesting. For instance, the Brazilians on average said No eighty-three times, compared with five times for the Japanese and nine times for the North Americans. The Japanese displayed more than five periods of silence lasting longer than ten seconds during each thirty-minute session. North Americans averaged 3.5 such periods; the Brazilians had none. The Japanese and North Americans interrupted their opponent about the same number of times, but the Brazilians interrupted two-and-a-half to three times more often than the North Americans and the Japanese. Finally, while the Japanese and the North Americans had no physical contact with their opponents during negotiations except for handshaking, the Brazilians touched each other almost five times every half-hour.

mplications for Managers

Managing Conflict

Many people assume that conflict is related to lower group and organizational performance. This chapter has demonstrated that this assumption is often false. Conflict can be either constructive or destructive to the functioning of a group or unit. When it's too high or too low, it hinders performance. An optimal level is one in which there is enough conflict to prevent stagnation, stimulate creativity, allow tensions to be released, and initiate the seeds for change, yet not so much as to be disruptive.

What advice can we give to managers faced with excessive conflict and the need to reduce it? Don't assume that there's one conflict-handling approach that will always be best! You should select the resolution technique appropriate for each situation. The following provide some guidelines.[17]

Use *competition* when quick, decisive action is vital (in emergencies); on important issues, where unpopular actions need implementing (in cost cutting, enforcing unpopular rules, discipline); on issues vital to the organization's welfare when you know you're right; and against people who take advantage of noncompetitive behavior.

Use *collaboration* to find an integrative solution when both sets of concerns are too important to be compromised; when your objective is to learn; to merge insights from people with different perspectives; to gain commitment by incorporating concerns into a consensus; and to work through feelings that have interfered with a relationship.

Use *avoidance* when an issue is trivial or when more important issues are pressing; when you perceive no chance of satisfying your concerns; when potential disruption outweighs the benefits of resolution; to let people cool down and regain perspective; when gathering information supersedes immediate decision; when others can resolve the conflict more effectively; and when issues seem tangential or symptomatic of other issues.

Use *accommodation* when you find you are wrong and to allow a better position to be heard, to learn, and to show your reasonableness; when issues are more important to others than to yourself and to satisfy others and maintain cooperation; to build social credits for later issues; to minimize loss when you are outmatched and losing; when harmony and stability are especially important; and to allow subordinates to develop by learning from mistakes.

Use *compromise* when goals are important but not worth the effort of potential disruption of more assertive approaches; when opponents with equal power are committed to mutually exclusive goals; to achieve temporary settlements to complex issues; to arrive at expedient solutions under time pressure; and as a backup when collaboration or competition is unsuccessful.

Toward Improving Negotiation Skills

The following recommendations should help improve your effectiveness at negotiating.[18]

Research Your Opponent. Acquire as much information as you can about your opponent's interests and goals. What constituencies must he or she appease? What is his or her strategy? This knowledge will help you to better understand your opponent's behavior, predict responses to your offers, and help you to frame solutions in terms of his or her interests.

Begin with a Positive Overture. Research shows that concessions tend to be reciprocated and lead to agreements. As a result, begin bargaining with a positive overture—perhaps a small concession—and then reciprocate your opponent's concessions.

Address the Problem, Not Personalities. Concentrate on the negotiation issues not on the personal characteristics of your opponent. When negotiations get tough, avoid the tendency to attack your opponent. It's your opponent's ideas or position that you disagree with, not him or her personally. Separate the people from the problem, and don't personalize differences.

Pay Little Attention to Initial Offers. Treat initial offers as merely a point of departure. Everyone has to have an initial position. They tend to be extreme and idealistic. Treat them as such.

Emphasize Win-Win Solutions. If conditions are supportive, look for an integrative solution. Frame options in terms of your opponent's interests, and look for solutions that can allow both you and your opponent to declare a victory.

Create an Open and Trusting Climate. Skilled negotiators are good listeners, ask questions, focus their arguments directly, are not defensive, and have learned to avoid words and phrases that can irritate an opponent (e.g., "generous offer," "fair price," "reasonable arrangement"). In other words, they are good at creating the open and trusting climate necessary for reaching an integrative settlement.

Foundations of Organization Structure

After reading this chapter, you should be able to:

1. Identify the six key elements that define an organization's structure

2. Describe a simple structure

3. Explain the characteristics of a bureaucracy

4. Describe a matrix organization

5. Explain the characteristics of a "virtual" organization

6. Summarize why managers want to create boundaryless organizations

7. List the factors that favor different organization structures

8. Explain the behavioral implications of different organization structures

The theme of this chapter is that organizations have different structures and that these structures have a bearing on employee attitudes and behavior. More specifically, in the following pages, we'll define the key components that make up an organization's structure, present half a dozen or so structural design options, identify the contingency factors that make certain structural designs preferable in different situations, and conclude by considering the different effects that various organization structures have on employee behavior.

Exhibit 13-1

Six Key Questions That Managers Need to Answer in Designing the Proper Organization Structure

The Key Question Is	The Answer Is Provided by
1. To what degree are tasks subdivided into separate jobs?	Work specialization
2. On what basis will jobs be grouped together?	Departmentalization
3. To whom do individuals and groups report?	Chain of command
4. How many individuals can a manager efficiently and effectively direct?	Span of control
5. Where does decision-making authority lie?	Centralization and decentralization
6. To what degree will there be rules and regulations to direct employees and managers?	Formalization

What Is Organization Structure?

An **organization structure** defines how job tasks are formally divided, grouped, and coordinated. For instance, Johnson & Johnson has historically grouped activities into semi-autonomous companies organized around products and allowed managers of these companies considerable decision-making latitude.

There are six key elements that managers need to address when they design their organization's structure. These are work specialization, departmentalization, chain of command, span of control, centralization and decentralization, and formalization.[1] Exhibit 13-1 presents each of these elements as answers to an important structural question. The following sections describe these six elements of structure.

Work Specialization

Early in this century, Henry Ford became rich and famous by building automobiles on an assembly line. Every Ford worker was assigned a specific, repetitive task. For instance, one person would just put on the right front wheel and someone else would install the right front door. By breaking jobs up into small standardized tasks, which could be performed over and over again, Ford was able to produce cars at the rate of one every ten seconds, while using employees who had relatively limited skills.

Ford demonstrated that work can be performed more efficiently if employees are allowed to specialize. Today we use the term **work specialization** or *division of labor* to describe the degree to which tasks in the organization are subdivided into separate jobs.

The essence of work specialization is that, rather than an entire job being done by one individual, it is broken down into steps, each step being completed by a separate individual. In essence, individuals specialize in doing part of an activity rather than the entire activity.

By the late 1940s, most manufacturing jobs in industrialized countries were being done with high work specialization. Management saw this as a means to make the most efficient use of its employees' skills. In most organizations, some tasks require highly developed skills; others can be performed by the untrained. If all workers were engaged in each step of, say, an organization's manufacturing process, all would have to have the skills necessary to perform both the most demanding and the least demanding jobs. The result would be that, except when performing the most skilled or highly sophisticated tasks, employees would be working below their skill levels. And, since skilled workers are paid more than unskilled workers and their wages tend to reflect their highest level of skill, paying highly skilled workers to do easy tasks represents an inefficient use of organizational resources.

Managers also looked for other efficiencies that could be achieved through work specialization. Employee skills at performing a task successfully increase through repetition. Less time is spent in changing tasks, in putting away one's tools and equipment from a prior step in the work process, and in getting ready for another. Equally important, training for specialization is more efficient from the organization's perspective. It is easier and less costly to find and train workers to do specific and repetitive tasks than to do a broad range of diverse tasks. This is especially true of highly sophisticated and complex operations. For example, could Cessna produce one Citation jet a year if one person had to build the entire plane alone? Finally, work specialization increases efficiency and productivity by encouraging the creation of special inventions and machinery.

For much of the first half of this century, managers viewed work specialization as an unending source of increased productivity. And, up to a point, they were probably right. Because specialization was not widely practiced, its introduction almost always generated higher productivity. But, by the 1960s, there was increasing evidence that a good thing can be carried too far. The point had been reached in some jobs at which the human diseconomies from specialization—which surface as boredom, fatigue, stress, low productivity, poor quality, increased absenteeism, and high turnover—more than offset the economic advantages (see Exhibit 13-2). In such cases, productivity could be increased by enlarging, rather than narrowing, the scope of job activities. In addition, some companies found that by giving employees a variety of activities to do, allowing them to do a whole and complete job, and putting them into teams with interchangeable skills, they often achieved significantly higher output with increased employee satisfaction.

Most managers today see work specialization as neither obsolete nor an unending source of increased productivity. Rather, managers recognize the economies it provides in certain types of jobs and the problems it creates when it's carried too far. You'll find, for example, high work specialization being used by McDonald's to efficiently make and sell hamburgers and fries and by medical specialists in most health maintenance organizations. On the other hand, companies such as the Saturn Corporation have had success by broadening the scope of jobs and reducing specialization.

Departmentalization

Once you've divided jobs up through work specialization, you need to group these jobs together so that common tasks can be coordinated. The basis by which jobs are grouped together is called **departmentalization.**

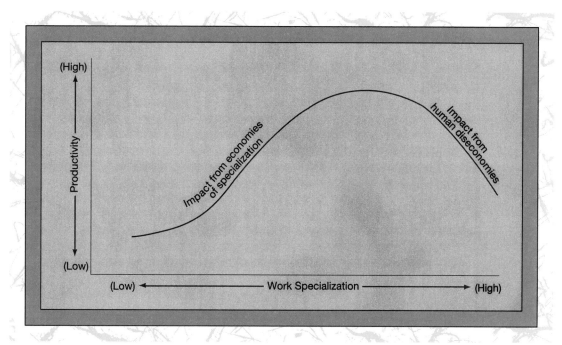

Exhibit 13-2
Economies and Diseconomies of Work Specialization

One of the most popular ways to group activities is by *functions* performed. A manufacturing manager might organize his or her plant by separating engineering, accounting, manufacturing, personnel, and purchasing specialists into common departments. Of course, departmentalization by function can be used in all types of organizations. Only the functions change to reflect the organization's objectives and activities. A hospital might have departments devoted to research, patient care, accounting, and so forth. The major advantage to this type of grouping is obtaining efficiencies from putting like specialists together. Functional departmentalization seeks to achieve economies of scale by placing people with common skills and orientations into common units.

Tasks can also be departmentalized by the type of *product* the organization produces. At Sun Petroleum Products, for instance, each of the three major product areas in the corporation (fuels, lubricants and waxes, and chemicals) is placed under the authority of a vice president who is a specialist in, and responsible for, everything having to do with his or her product line. Each, for example, would have his or her own manufacturing and marketing group. The major advantage to this type of grouping is increased accountability for product performance, since all activities related to a specific product are under the direction of a single manager. If an organization's activities were service-related rather than product-related, each service would be autonomously grouped. For instance, an accounting firm could have departments for tax, management consulting, auditing, and the like. Each would offer a common array of services under the direction of a product or service manager.

Another way to departmentalize is on the basis of *geography* or territory. The sales function, for instance, may have western, southern, midwestern, and eastern regions. Each of these regions is, in effect, a department organized around geography. If an organization's customers are scattered over a large geographical area, then this form of departmentalization can be valuable.

At a Reynolds Metals aluminum tubing plant in upstate New York, production is organized into five departments: casting; pressing; tubing; finishing; and inspecting, packing, and shipping. This is an example of *process* departmentalization because each department specializes in one specific phase in the production of aluminum tubing. The metal is cast in huge furnaces; sent to the press department, where it is extruded into aluminum pipe; transferred to the tube mill, where it is stretched into various sizes and shapes of tubing; moved to finishing, where it is cut and cleaned; and finally arrives in the inspect, pack, and ship department. Because each process requires different skills, this method offers a basis for the homogeneous categorizing of activities.

A final category of departmentalization is to use the particular type of *customer* the organization seeks to reach. The sales activities in an office supply firm, for instance, can be broken down into three departments to service retail, wholesale, and government customers. A large law office can segment its staff on the basis of whether they service corporate or individual clients. The assumption underlying customer departmentalization is that customers in each department have a common set of problems and needs that can best be met by having specialists for each.

Large organizations may use all of the forms of departmentalization that we've described. A major Japanese electronics firm, for instance, organizes each of its divisions along functional lines and its manufacturing units around processes; it departmentalizes sales around seven geographical regions and divides each sales region into four customer groupings. Two general trends, however, seem to be gaining momentum in the 1990s. First, customer departmentalization is growing in popularity. In order to better monitor the needs of customers and to be better able to respond to changes in those needs, many organizations have given greater emphasis to customer departmentalization. The second trend is that rigid functional departmentalization is being complemented by teams that cross over traditional departmental lines. As we described in Chapter 8, as tasks have become more complex and more diverse skills are needed to accomplish those tasks, management has turned to cross-functional teams.

Chain of Command

In the 1970s, the chain-of-command concept was a basic cornerstone in the design of organizations. As you'll see, it has far less importance today. But contemporary managers should still consider its implications when they decide how best to structure their organizations.

The **chain of command** is an unbroken line of authority that extends from the top of the organization to the lowest eschelon and clarifies who reports to whom. It answers questions for employees such as, "Who do I go to if I have a problem?" and "Who am I responsible to?"

You can't discuss the chain of command without discussing two complementary concepts: authority and unity of command. **Authority** refers to the rights inherent in a managerial position to give orders and expect the orders to be obeyed. To facilitate coordination, organizations give each managerial position a place in the chain of command, and each manager is given a degree of authority in order to meet his or her responsibilities. The **unity of command principle** helps preserve the concept of an unbroken line of authority. It states that a person should have one and only one superior to whom he or she is directly responsible. If the unity of command is broken, a subordinate might have to cope with conflicting demands or priorities from several superiors.

Times change and so do the basic tenets of organizational design. The concepts of chain of command, authority, and unity of command have substantially less relevance today because of advancements in computer technology and the trend toward empowering employees. A low-level employee today can access information in seconds that, twenty years ago, was available only to top managers. Similarly, computer technology increasingly allows employees anywhere in an organization to communicate with anyone else without going through formal channels. Moreover, the concepts of authority and maintaining the chain of command are increasingly less relevant as operating employees are being empowered to make decisions that previously were reserved for management. Add to this trend the popularity of self-managed and cross-functional teams and the creation of new structural designs that include multiple bosses, and the unity-of-command concept takes on less relevance. There are, of course, still many organizations that find they can be most productive by enforcing the chain of command. There just seem to be fewer of them nowadays.

Span of Control

How many subordinates can a manager efficiently and effectively direct? This question of **span of control** is important because, to a large degree, it determines the number of levels and managers an organization has. All things being equal, the wider or larger the span, the more efficient the organization. An example can illustrate the validity of this statement.

Assume that we have two organizations, both of which have approximately 4,100 operative-level employees. As Exhibit 13-3 illustrates, if one has a uniform span of four and the other a span of eight, the wider span would have two fewer levels and approximately 800 fewer managers. If the average manager made $40,000 a year, the wider span would save $32 million a year in management salaries! Obviously, wider spans are more efficient in terms of cost. But at some point wider spans reduce effectiveness. That is, when the span becomes too large, employee performance suffers because supervisors no longer have the time to provide the necessary leadership and support.

Small spans have their advocates. By keeping the span of control to five or six employees, a manager can maintain close control. But small spans have three major drawbacks. First, as already described, they're expensive because they add levels of management. Second, they make vertical communication in the organization more complex. The added levels of hierarchy slow down decision making

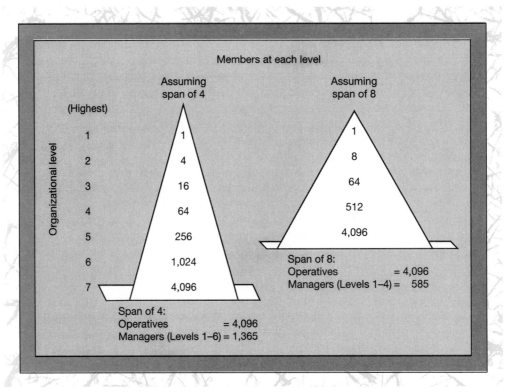

Members at each level

Organizational level		Assuming span of 4	Assuming span of 8
(Highest)			
	1	1	1
	2	4	8
	3	16	64
	4	64	512
	5	256	4,096
	6	1,024	
	7	4,096	

Span of 8:
Operatives = 4,096
Managers (Levels 1–4) = 585

Span of 4:
Operatives = 4,096
Managers (Levels 1–6) = 1,365

Exhibit 13-3
Contrasting Spans of Control

and tend to isolate upper management. Third, small spans of control encourage overly tight supervision and discourage employee autonomy.

The trend in recent years has been toward larger spans of control. Wide spans are consistent with recent efforts by companies to reduce costs, cut overhead, speed up decision making, increase flexibility, get closer to customers, and empower employees. However, to ensure that performance doesn't suffer because of these wider spans, organizations have been investing heavily in employee training. Managers recognize that they can handle a wider span when employees know their jobs inside and out or can turn to their co-workers when they have questions.

Centralization and Decentralization

In some organizations, top managers make all the decisions. Lower-level managers merely carry out top management's directives. At the other extreme are organizations in which decision making is pushed down to those managers who are closest to "the action." The former organizations are highly centralized; the latter are decentralized.

The term **centralization** refers to the degree to which decision making is concentrated at a single point in the organization. The concept includes only formal authority; that is, the rights inherent in one's position. Typically, it's said that if top management makes the organization's key decisions with little or no input from lower-level personnel, then the organization is centralized. In contrast, the more that lower-level personnel provide input or are actually given the discretion to make decisions, the more *decentralization* there is.

An organization characterized by centralization is an inherently different structural animal from one that is decentralized. In a decentralized organization, action can be taken more quickly to solve problems, more people provide input into decisions, and employees are less likely to feel alienated from those who make the decisions that affect their work lives.

Consistent with recent management efforts to make organizations more flexible and responsive, there has been a marked trend toward decentralizing decision making. In large companies, lower-level managers are closer to the action and typically have more detailed knowledge about problems than do top managers. Big retailers such as Sears and J.C. Penney have given their store managers considerably more discretion in choosing what merchandise to stock so that their stores can compete more effectively against local merchants. Similarly, the Bank of Montreal has grouped its 1,164 Canadian branches into 236 "communities"—that is, a group of branches within a limited geographical area.[2] Each community is led by a community area manager, who typically works within a twenty-minute drive of the other branches. This area manager can respond faster and more intelligently to problems in his community than could some senior executive in Montreal. IBM Europe's chairman, Renato Riverso, has similarly sliced the Continent into some 200 autonomous business units, each with its own profit plan, employee incentives, and customer focus. "We used to manage from the top, like an army," says Riverso. "Now, we're trying to create entities that drive themselves."[3]

Formalization

Formalization refers to the degree to which jobs within the organization are standardized. If a job is highly formalized, then the job incumbent has a minimum amount of discretion over what is to be done, when it is to be done, and how he or she should do it. Employees can be expected always to handle the same input in exactly the same way, resulting in a consistent and uniform output. There are explicit job descriptions, lots of organizational rules, and clearly defined procedures covering work processes in organizations that have a high degree of formalization. Where formalization is low, job behaviors are relatively nonprogrammed and employees have a great deal of freedom to exercise discretion in their work. An individual's discretion on the job is inversely related to the amount of behavior in that job that is preprogrammed by the organization; therefore, the greater the standardization, the less input the employee has into how his or her work is to be done. Standardization not only eliminates the possibility of employees' engaging in alternative behaviors, but it removes the need for employees even to consider alternatives.

The degree of formalization can vary widely among organizations and within organizations. Certain jobs, for instance, are well known to have little formalization. College book travelers—the representatives of publishers who call on professors to inform them of their company's new publications—have a great deal of freedom in their jobs. They have no standard sales "spiel," and the extent of rules and procedures governing their behavior may be little more than the requirement that they submit a weekly sales report and some suggestions on what to emphasize for the various new titles. At the other extreme, employees in clerical and editorial positions in the same publishing houses are required to "clock in" at their workstations by 8:00 A.M. or be docked a half-hour of pay and, once at that workstation, to follow a set of precise procedures dictated by management.

Common Organizational Designs

We now turn to describing three of the more common organizational designs found in use. They're the *simple structure*, the *bureaucracy*, and the *matrix structure*.

The Simple Structure

What do a small retail store, an electronics firm run by a hard-driving entrepreneur, a new Planned Parenthood office, and an airline in the midst of a companywide pilot's strike have in common? They probably all have a simple structure.

The **simple structure** is characterized most by what it is not rather than what it is. The simple structure is not elaborate.[4] It has a low degree of departmentalization, wide spans of control, and little formalization. The simple structure is a "flat" organization; it usually has only two or three vertical levels, a loose body of employees, and one individual in whom the decision-making authority is centralized. It's most widely practiced in small businesses in which the manager and the owner are one and the same. But it is also the preferred structure in time of temporary crisis because it centralizes control.

The strength of the simple structure lies in its simplicity. It's fast, flexible, inexpensive to maintain, and accountability is clear. One major weakness is that it's difficult to maintain in anything other than small organizations. It becomes increasingly inadequate as an organization grows because its low formalization and high centralization tend to create information overload at the top. As size increases, decision making typically becomes slower and can eventually come to a standstill as the single executive tries to continue making all the decisions. This outcome proves to be the undoing of many small businesses. When an organization begins to employ fifty or a hundred people, it's very difficult for the owner-manager to make all the choices. If the structure isn't changed and made more elaborate, the firm often loses momentum and can eventually fail. The simple structure's other weakness is that it's risky—everything depends on one person. One heart attack can literally destroy the organization's information and decision-making center.

The Bureaucracy

Standardization! That's the key concept that underlies all bureaucracies. Take a look at the bank where you keep your checking account; the department store where you buy your clothes; or the government offices that collect your taxes, enforce health regulations, or provide local fire protection. They all rely on standardized work processes for coordination and control.

The **bureaucracy** is characterized by highly routine operating tasks achieved through specialization, very formalized rules and regulations, tasks that are grouped into functional departments, centralized authority, narrow spans of control, and decision making that follows the chain of command.

The primary strength of the bureaucracy lies in its ability to perform standardized activities in a highly efficient manner. Putting like specialties together in functional departments results in economies of scale, minimum duplication of personnel and equipment, and employees who have the opportunity to talk "the same language" among their peers. Further, bureaucracies can get by nicely with less talented—and, hence, less costly—middle- and lower-level managers. The pervasiveness of rules and regulations substitutes for managerial discretion. Standardized operations, coupled with high formalization, allow decision making to be centralized. There is little need, therefore, for innovative and experienced decision makers below the level of senior executives.

One of the major weaknesses of bureaucracy is that specialization creates subunit conflicts. Functional unit goals can override the overall goals of the organization. The other major weakness of bureaucracy is something we've all experienced at one time or another when having to deal with people who work in these organizations: obsessive concern with following the rules. When cases arise that don't precisely fit the rules, there is no room for modification. The bureaucracy is efficient only as long as employees confront problems that they have previously encountered and for which programmed decision rules have already been established.

The peak of bureaucracy's popularity was probably in the 1950s and 1960s. At that time, for instance, just about every major corporation in the world—firms such as IBM, General Electric, Volkswagen, Matsushita, and Royal Dutch Shell—was organized as a bureaucracy. Although the bureaucracy is out of fashion in the 1990s—largely because it has difficulty responding rapidly to change—the majority of large organizations still take on basic bureaucratic characteristics, particularly specialization and high formalization. However, spans of control have generally been widened, authority has become more decentralized, and functional departments have been supplemented with an increased use of teams. Another trend is toward breaking bureaucracies up into smaller, though fully functioning, minibureaucracies. Each of these smaller versions, with 150 to 250 people, has its own mission and profit goals. It's been estimated that about fifteen percent of large corporations have taken this direction.[5] For instance, Eastman Kodak has transformed over 100 production units into separate businesses.

The Matrix Structure

Another popular organizational design option is the **matrix structure.** It is used in advertising agencies, aerospace firms, research and development laboratories, construction companies, hospitals, government agencies, universities, management consulting firms, and entertainment companies. Essentially, the matrix combines two forms of departmentalization—functional and product.

The strength of functional departmentalization lies in putting like specialists together. Grouping specialists minimizes the number necessary while allowing

Programs Academic Departments	Undergraduate	Master's	Ph. D.	Research	Executive Development	Community Service
Accounting						
Administrative Studies						
Finance						
Information and Decision Sciences						
Marketing						
Organizational Behavior						
Quantitative Methods						

Exhibit 13-4
Matrix Structure for a College of Business Administration

specialized resources to be pooled and shared across products. Its major weakness is that it is difficult to coordinate the specialists' tasks so that their diverse projects are completed on time and within budget. Product departmentalization, on the other hand, has exactly the opposite strengths and weaknesses. It facilitates coordination of specialists so that they can meet deadlines and budget targets, and further, it provides clear responsibility for all activities related to a product. But activities and costs are duplicated. The matrix attempts to gain the strengths of each while avoiding their weaknesses.

The most obvious structural characteristic of the matrix is that it breaks the unity-of-command concept. Employees in the matrix have two bosses—their functional department managers and their product managers. Therefore, the matrix has a dual chain of command.

Exhibit 13-4 shows the matrix form as used in a college of business administration. The academic departments of accounting, administrative studies, marketing, and so forth are functional units. In addition, specific programs (that is, products) are overlaid on the functions. In this way, members in a matrix structure have a dual assignment—to their functional department and to their product groups. For instance, a professor of accounting teaching an undergraduate course reports to the director of undergraduate programs as well as to the chairperson of the accounting department.

The strength of the matrix lies in its ability to facilitate coordination when the organization has multiple complex and interdependent activities. As an organization gets larger, its information-processing capacity can become overloaded. In a bureaucracy, complexity results in increased formalization. The direct and frequent contact between different specialties in the matrix can make for better communication and more flexibility. Information permeates the organization and more quickly reaches those people who need to take account of it. Further, the matrix reduces bureaupathologies. The dual lines of authority reduce tendencies of departmental members to become so busy protecting their little worlds that the organization's overall goals become secondary.

There is also another advantage to the matrix. It facilitates the efficient allocation of specialists. When individuals with highly specialized skills are lodged in one functional department or product group, their talents are monopolized and underutilized. The matrix achieves the advantages of economies of scale by providing the organization with both the best resources and an effective way of ensuring their efficient deployment.

The major disadvantages of the matrix lie in the confusion it creates, its propensity to foster power struggles, and the stress it places on individuals. When you dispense with the unity-of-command concept, ambiguity is significantly increased, and ambiguity often leads to conflict. For example, it's frequently unclear who reports to whom, and it is not unusual for product managers to fight over getting the best specialists assigned to their products. Confusion and ambiguity also create the seeds of power struggles. Bureaucracy reduces the potential for power grabs by defining the rules of the game. When those rules are "up for grabs," power struggles between functional and product managers result. For individuals who desire security and absence of ambiguity, this work climate can produce stress. Reporting to more than one boss introduces role conflict, and unclear expectations introduce role ambiguity. The comfort of bureaucracy's predictability is replaced by insecurity and stress.

*N*ew Options

Since the early 1980s, senior managers in a number of organizations have been working to develop new structural options that can better help their firms compete effectively. In this section, we'll describe three such structural designs: the *team structure,* the *virtual organization,* and the *boundaryless organization.*

The Team Structure

As described in Chapter 8, teams have become an extremely popular means around which to organize work activities. An organization that uses teams as its central coordination device has a **team structure.** The primary characteristics of the team structure are that it breaks down departmental barriers and decentralizes decision making to the level of the work team.

In smaller companies, the team structure can define the entire organization. For instance, Imedia, a thirty-person marketing firm in New Jersey, is organized completely around teams that have full responsibility for most operational issues and client services.[6]

More often, particularly among larger organizations, the team structure complements what is typically a bureaucracy. The organization is thus able to achieve the efficiency of bureaucracy's standardization while gaining the flexibility that teams provide.

The Virtual Organization

Why own when you can rent? That's the essence of the **virtual organization**—a small, core organization that outsources major business functions. In structural terms, the virtual organization is highly centralized, with little or no departmentalization.

Companies such as Nike, Reebok, Liz Claiborne, Emerson Radio, and Dell Computer are just a few of the thousands of companies that have found that they can do hundreds of millions of dollars in business without owning manufacturing facilities. Dell Computer, for instance, owns no plants and merely assembles computers from outsourced parts. National Steel Corp. contracts out its mailroom operations. AT&T farms out its credit-card processing. Mobil Corp. has turned over maintenance of its refineries to another firm.

What's going on here? A quest for maximum flexibility. These "virtual" organizations have created networks of relationships that allow them to contract out manufacturing, distribution, marketing, or any other business function that management feels can be done better or cheaper by others.

The virtual organization stands in sharp contrast to the typical bureaucracy that has many vertical levels of management and where control is sought through ownership. In such organizations, research and development are done in-house, production occurs in company-owned plants, and sales and marketing are performed by the company's own employees. To support all these levels, management has to employ extra personnel including accountants, human resource specialists, and lawyers. The virtual organization, however, outsources many of these functions and concentrates on what it does best.

Exhibit 13-5 shows a virtual organization in which management outsources all of the primary functions of the business. The core of the organization is a small group of executives. Their job is to oversee directly any activities that are done in-house and to coordinate relationships with the other organizations that manufacture, distribute, and perform other crucial functions for the virtual organization. The dotted lines in Exhibit 13-5 represent those relationships, typically maintained under contracts. In essence, managers in virtual structures spend most of their time coordinating and controlling external relations, typically by way of computer-network links.

The major advantage to the virtual organization is its flexibility. For instance, it allowed someone with an innovative idea and little money—such as Michael Dell and his Dell Computer firm in its early years—to successfully compete against large companies such as IBM. The primary drawback to this structure is that it reduces management's control over key parts of its business.

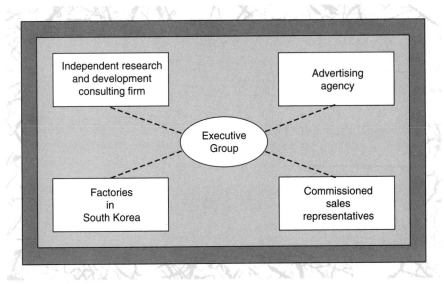

Exhibit 13-5
Structure of a Virtual Organization

The Boundaryless Organization

General Electric chairman, Jack Welch, coined the term **boundaryless organization** to describe his idea of what he wanted GE to become. Welch wanted to turn his company into a "$60 billion family grocery store."[7] That is, in spite of its monstrous size, he wanted to eliminate *vertical* and *horizontal* boundaries within GE and to break down *external* barriers between the company and its customers and suppliers. The boundaryless organization seeks to eliminate the chain of command, have limitless spans of control, and replace departments with empowered teams.

GE hasn't yet achieved this boundaryless state—and probably never will— but it has made significant progress. So have other companies such as Hewlett-Packard, AT&T, and Motorola. Let's take a look at what a boundaryless organization would look like and what some firms are doing to make it a reality.

By removing *vertical* boundaries, management flattens the hierarchy. Status and rank are minimized. And the organization looks more like a silo than a pyramid. Cross-hierarchical teams (which include top executives, middle managers, supervisors, and operative employees), participative decision-making practices, and the use of 360-degree performance appraisals (peers and others above and below the employee evaluate his or her performance) are examples of what GE is doing to break down vertical boundaries.

Functional departments create *horizontal* boundaries. The way to reduce these barriers is to replace functional departments with cross-functional teams and to organize activities around processes. For instance, some AT&T units are now doing annual budgets based not on functions or departments but on processes such as the maintenance of a worldwide telecommunications network. Another way management can cut through horizontal barriers is to use lateral

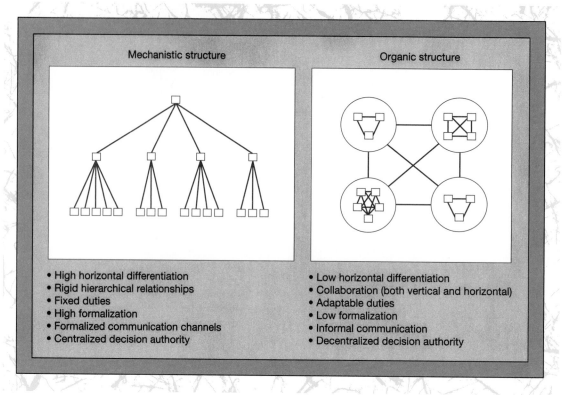

Mechanistic structure

- High horizontal differentiation
- Rigid hierarchical relationships
- Fixed duties
- High formalization
- Formalized communication channels
- Centralized decision authority

Organic structure

- Low horizontal differentiation
- Collaboration (both vertical and horizontal)
- Adaptable duties
- Low formalization
- Informal communication
- Decentralized decision authority

Exhibit 13-6
Mechanistic Versus Organic Structures

transfers and rotate people into and out of different functional areas. This approach turns specialists into generalists.

When fully operational, the boundaryless organization also breaks down barriers to *external* constituencies and barriers created by geography. Globalization, strategic alliances, customer-organization linkages, and telecommuting are all examples of practices that reduce external boundaries. For instance, firms such as NEC Corp., Boeing, and Apple Computer each have strategic alliances or joint partnerships with dozens of companies. These alliances blur the distinction between one organization and another as employees work on joint projects.

The one common technological thread that makes the boundaryless organization possible is networked computers. They allow people to communicate across intraorganizational and interorganizational boundaries.

Why Do Structures Differ?

The organization structures described so far ranged from the highly structured and standardized bureaucracy to the loose and amorphous boundaryless organization. Exhibit 13-6 reconceptualizes the preceding discussions by presenting two extreme models of organization structure. One extreme we'll call the **mechanistic model.** It is generally synonymous with the bureaucracy in that it has extensive departmentalization, high formalization, a limited information network (mostly downward communication), and little participation by low-level members in decision making. At the other extreme is the **organic model.** This model looks a lot like the boundaryless organization. It is flat, uses cross-hierarchical and cross-functional teams, has low formalization, possesses a comprehensive information network (using lateral and upward communication as well as downward), and involves high participation in decision making.

What are the forces that determine whether an organization will be structured after the mechanistic model or the organic model? With these two models in mind, we're now prepared to address that question.[8]

Strategy

An organization's structure is a means to help management achieve its objectives. Since objectives are derived from the organization's overall strategy, it is only logical that strategy and structure should be closely linked. More specifically, structure should follow strategy. If management makes a significant change in its organization's strategy, the structure will need to be modified to accommodate and support that change.

Most current strategy frameworks focus on three strategy dimensions—innovation, cost minimization, and imitation—and the structural design that works best with each.[9] To what degree does an organization introduce major new products or services? An innovation strategy does not mean a strategy merely for simple or cosmetic changes from previous offerings but rather one for meaningful and unique innovations. Obviously, not all firms pursue innovation. This strategy may appropriately characterize 3M Co., but it certainly is not a strategy pursued by Reader's Digest.

An organization that is pursuing a cost-minimization strategy tightly controls costs, refrains from incurring unnecessary innovation or marketing expenses, and cuts prices in selling a basic product. This would describe the strategy pursued by Wal-Mart or the sellers of generic grocery products.

Organizations following an imitation strategy try to capitalize on the best of both of the previous strategies. They seek to minimize risk and maximize opportunity for profit. Their strategy is to move into new products or new markets only after viability has been proved by innovators. They take the successful ideas of innovators and copy them. Manufacturers of mass-marketed fashion goods that are rip-offs of designer styles follow the imitation strategy. This label also probably characterizes such well-known firms as IBM and Caterpillar. They essentially follow their smaller and more innovative competitors with superior products, but only after their competitors have demonstrated that the market is there.

So how do we link strategy and structure? Innovators need the flexibility of the organic structure, while cost minimizers seek the efficiency and stability of the mechanistic structure. Imitators combine the two structures. They use a mechanistic structure in order to maintain tight controls and low costs in their current activities, while at the same time they create organic subunits in which to pursue new undertakings.

Organization Size

There is considerable evidence to support the notion that an organization's size significantly affects its structure.[10] For instance, large organizations—those typically employing 2,000 or more people—tend to have more specialization, more departmentalization, more vertical levels, and more rules and regulations than do small organizations. But the relationship isn't linear. Rather, size affects structure at a decreasing rate. The impact of size becomes less important as an organization expands. Why? Essentially, once an organization has around 2,000 employees, it's already fairly mechanistic. An additional 500 employees will not have much impact. On the other hand, adding 500 employees to an organization that has only 300 members is likely to result in a shift toward a more mechanistic structure.

Technology

The term **technology** refers to how an organization transfers its inputs into outputs. Every organization has at least one technology for converting financial, human, and physical resources into products or services. The Ford Motor Co., for instance, predominantly uses an assemblyline process to make its products. On the other hand, colleges may use a number of instruction technologies—the ever-popular formal lecture method, the case analysis method, the experiential exercise method, the programmed learning method, and so forth. In this section we show that organization structures adapt to their technology.

Numerous studies have been carried out on the technology-structure relationship.[11] The details of those studies are quite complex, so we'll go straight to "the bottom line" and summarize what we know. The common theme that differentiates technologies is their *degree of routineness.* By this term we mean that technologies tend toward either routine or nonroutine activities. The former are characterized by automated and standardized operations. Nonroutine activities are customized. They include such varied operations as furniture restoring, custom shoemaking, and genetic research.

What relationships have been found between technology and structure? Although the relationship is not overwhelmingly strong, we find that routine tasks are associated with taller and more departmentalized structures. The relationship between technology and formalization, however, is stronger. Studies consistently show routineness to be associated with the presence of rule manuals, job descriptions, and other formalized documentation.

Environmental Uncertainty

An organization's environment is composed of those institutions or forces that are outside the organization and potentially affect the organization's performance. The environment has acquired a large following as a key determinant of structure.

Why should an organization's structure be affected by its environment? Because of environmental uncertainty. Some organizations face relatively static environments; other organizations face very dynamic environments. Static environments create significantly less uncertainty for managers than do dynamic ones.

And, since uncertainty is a threat to an organization's effectiveness, management will try to minimize it. One way to reduce environmental uncertainty is through adjustments in the organization's structure.[12]

There is substantial evidence that relates the degree of environmental uncertainty to different structural arrangements. Essentially, the more dynamic and uncertain the environment, the greater the need for flexibility. Hence, the organic structure will lead to higher organizational effectiveness. Conversely, in stable and predictable environments, the mechanistic form will be the structure of choice.

Organization Structure and Employee Behavior

We opened this chapter by implying that an organization's structure can have profound effects on its members. In this section, we directly assess just what those effects might be. A review of the evidence linking organization structures to employee performance and satisfaction leads to a pretty clear conclusion—you can't generalize! Not everyone prefers the freedom and flexibility of organic structures. Some people are most productive and satisfied when work tasks are standardized and ambiguity is minimized—that is, in mechanistic structures. So any discussion of the effect of organizational design on employee behavior has to address individual differences. To illustrate this point, let's consider employee preferences for work specialization, span of control, and centralization.[13]

The evidence generally indicates that *work specialization* contributes to higher employee productivity but at the price of reduced job satisfaction. However, this statement ignores individual differences and the type of job tasks people do.

As we noted previously, work specialization is not an unending source of higher productivity. Problems start to surface, and productivity begins to suffer, when the human diseconomies of doing repetitive and narrow tasks overtake the economies of specialization. As the work force has become more highly educated and desirous of jobs that are intrinsically rewarding, the point at which productivity begins to decline seems to be reached more quickly than in decades past.

Undoubtedly people today are less tolerant of overly specialized jobs than were their parents or grandparents, but it would be naive to ignore the reality that there is still a segment of the work force that prefers the routine and repetitiveness of highly specialized jobs. Some individuals want work that makes minimal intellectual demands and provides the security of routine. For these people, high work specialization is a source of job satisfaction. The empirical question, of course, is whether this group represents two percent of the work force or fifty-two percent. Given that there is some self-selection operating in the choice of careers, we might conclude that negative behavioral outcomes from high specialization are most likely to surface in professional jobs occupied by individuals with high needs for personal growth and diversity.

A review of the research indicates that it is probably safe to say there is no evidence to support a relationship between *span of control* and employee performance. It is intuitively attractive to argue that large spans lead to higher employee performance because they provide more distant supervision and more opportunity for personal initiative, but the research fails to support this notion. At this point, it is impossible to state that any particular span of control is best for producing high performance or high satisfaction among subordinates. The reason is, again, probably individual differences. That is, some people like to be left alone, whereas others prefer the security of a boss who is quickly available at all times. Several of the contingency theories of leadership discussed in Chapter 10 would lead us to expect factors such as employees' experience and abilities and the degree of structure in their tasks to explain when wide or narrow spans of control are likely to contribute to their performance and job satisfaction. However, there is some evidence indicating that a *manager's* job satisfaction increases as the number of subordinates he or she supervises increases.

We find fairly strong evidence linking *centralization* and job satisfaction. In general, organizations that are less centralized have a greater amount of participative decision making. And the evidence suggests that participative decision making is positively related to job satisfaction. But, again, individual differences surface. The decentralization-satisfaction relationship is strongest with employees who have low self-esteem. Because such individuals have little confidence in their abilities, they place a fairly high value on shared decision making, which means that they're not held solely responsible for decision outcomes.

Our conclusion: To maximize employee performance and satisfaction, individual differences—such as experience, personality, and the work task—should be taken into account.

mplications for Managers

An organization's internal structure contributes to explaining and predicting employee behavior. That is, in addition to individual and group factors, the structural relationships in which people work have an important bearing on their attitudes and behavior.

What's the basis for the argument that structure has an impact on both attitudes and behavior? To the degree that an organization's structure reduces ambiguity for employees and clarifies such concerns as "What am I supposed to do?" "How am I supposed to do it?" "Who do I report to?" and "Who do I go to if I have a problem?", it shapes their attitudes and facilitates and motivates them to higher levels of performance.

Of course, structure also constrains employees to the extent that it limits and controls what they do. For example, organizations structured around high levels of formalization and specialization, strict adherence to the chain of command, limited delegation of authority, and narrow spans of control give employees little autonomy. Controls in such organizations are tight, and behavior will tend to vary within a narrow range. In contrast, organizations that are structured around limited specialization, low formalization, wide spans of control, and the like provide employees greater freedom and, thus, will be characterized by greater behavioral diversity.

Chapter 14

Technology and Work Design

After studying this chapter, you should be able to:

1. Contrast reengineering and total quality management

2. Describe the implications of flexible manufacturing systems for people who work within them

3. Identify who is affected by worker obsolescence

4. Explain the job characteristics model

5. Contrast the social information-processing model with the job characteristics model

6. Describe how a job can be enriched

7. Explain the argument that jobs may be becoming obsolete

Technology is completely changing most organizations. In this chapter, we focus on how technologies of operations and information are influencing management and work processes, the effect of technology on worker obsolescence, and how managers can design jobs and work schedules to maximize employee performance.

Technology in the Workplace

We introduced the term technology in the previous chapter's discussion of why structures differ. We said it was how an organization transfers its inputs into outputs. In recent years, the term has become widely used by economists, managers, consultants, and business analysts to describe machinery and equipment that use sophisticated electronics and computers to produce those outputs.

The common theme among new technologies in the workplace is that they substitute machinery for human labor in transforming inputs into outputs. This substitution of capital for labor has been going on essentially nonstop since the Industrial Revolution in the mid-1800s. For instance, the introduction of electricity allowed textile factories to introduce mechanical looms that could produce cloth far faster and cheaper than was previously possible when the looms were powered by individuals. But it has been the computerization of equipment and machinery in the last quarter-century that has been the prime mover in reshaping the twentieth-century workplace. Automated teller machines, for example, have replaced tens of thousands of human tellers in banks. Ninety-eight percent of the spot welds on new Ford Tauruses are performed by robots, not by people. Many cars now come equipped with on-board computers that take only seconds to diagnose problems that used to take mechanics hours to diagnose. IBM has built a plant in Austin, Texas, that can produce laptop computers without the help of a single worker. Everything from the time parts arrive at the IBM plant to the final packing of finished products is completely automated.

This book is concerned with the behavior of people at work. No coverage of this topic, today, would be complete without discussing how recent advances in technology are changing the workplace and affecting the work lives of employees. In this section, we'll look at four specific issues related to technology and work. These are total quality management and continuous improvement processes, reengineering, flexible manufacturing systems, and worker obsolescence.

Quality and Continuous Improvement Processes

In Chapter 1, we described total quality management (TQM) as a philosophy of management that's driven by the constant attainment of customer satisfaction through the continuous improvement of all organizational processes. Managers in many organizations, especially in North America, have been criticized for accepting a level of performance that is below perfection. TQM, however, argues that *good* isn't *good enough!* To dramatize this point, assume that a 99.9 percent error-free performance represents the highest standard of excellence. By that standard, the U.S. Post Office would lose 2,000 pieces of mail an hour, or U.S. doctors would perform 500 incorrect surgical procedures each week, or there would be two plane crashes a day at O'Hare Airport in Chicago![1]

TQM programs seek to achieve continuous process improvements so that variability is constantly reduced. When you eliminate variations, you increase the uniformity of the product or service. Increasing uniformity, in turn, results in lower costs and higher quality. For instance, Advanced Filtration Systems Inc., of Champaign, Illinois, cut the number of product defects—as determined by a customer quality audit—from 26.5 per 1,000 units to zero over a four-year period. During that same period, monthly unit production tripled and the number of workers declined by twenty percent.

Continuous improvement runs counter to the typical American management approach of seeing work projects as being linear—with a beginning and an end.

For example, American managers have traditionally looked at cutting costs as a short-term project. They set a goal of cutting costs by twenty percent, achieved it, and then said: "Whew! Our cost cutting is over." The Japanese, on the other hand, have regarded cost cutting as something that never ends. The search for continuous improvement creates a race without a finish line.

As tens of thousands of organizations introduce TQM and continuous process improvement, how will employees be affected? They will no longer be able to rest on their previous accomplishments and successes. So some people may experience increased stress from a work climate that no longer accepts complacency with the status quo. A race with no finish line can never be won—a situation that creates constant tension. This tension may be positive for the organization (remember *functional conflict* from Chapter 12?), but the pressures from an unrelenting search for process improvements can create anxiety and stress in some employees. Probably the most significant implication for employees is that management will look to them as the prime source for improvement ideas. Employee involvement programs, therefore, are part and parcel of TQM. Empowered work teams who have hands-on involvement in process improvement, for instance, are widely used in those organizations that have introduced TQM.

Reengineering Work Processes

We also introduced reengineering in Chapter 1. We described it as considering how you would do things if you could start all over from scratch. The term **reengineering** comes from the process of taking apart an electronics product and designing a better version. Michael Hammer applied the term to organizations. When he found companies using computers simply to automate outdated processes, rather than finding fundamentally better ways of doing things, he realized that the principles of reengineering could be applied to business. So, as applied to organizations, reengineering means that management should start with a clean sheet of paper—rethinking and redesigning those processes by which the organization creates value and does work, ridding itself of operations that have become antiquated.[2]

Key Elements. Three key elements of reengineering are identifying an organization's distinctive competencies, assessing core processes, and reorganizing horizontally by process. An organization's **distinctive competencies** define what it is that the organization does better than its competition. Examples might include better store locations, a more efficient distribution system, higher-quality products, more knowledgeable sales personnel, or superior technical support. Dell Computer, for instance, differentiates itself from its competitors by emphasizing high-quality hardware, comprehensive service and technical support, and low prices. Why is identifying distinctive competencies so important? Because it guides decisions regarding what activities are crucial to the organization's success.

Management also needs to assess the core processes that clearly add value to the organization's distinctive competencies. These are the processes that transform materials, capital, information, and labor into products and services that the customer values. When the organization is viewed as a series of processes, ranging from strategic planning to after-sales customer support, management can determine to what degree each adds value. Not surprisingly, this *process value analysis* typically uncovers a whole lot of activities that add little or nothing of value and whose only justification is "we've always done it this way."

Reengineering requires management to reorganize around horizontal processes. This means using cross-functional and self-managed teams. It means focusing on processes rather than functions. So, for instance, the vice president of marketing might become the "process owner of finding and keeping customers."[3] It also means cutting out levels of middle management. As Hammer points out, "Managers are not value-added. A customer never buys a product because of the caliber of management. Management is, by definition, indirect. So if possible, less is better. One of the goals of reengineering is to minimize the necessary amount of management."[4]

Reengineering versus TQM. Is reengineering just another term for TQM? No! They do have some common characteristics.[5] They both, for instance, emphasize processes and satisfying the customer. After that, they diverge radically, as is evident in their goals and the means they use for achieving their goals.

TQM seeks incremental improvements; reengineering looks for quantum leaps in performance. That is, the former is essentially about improving something that is basically okay; the latter is about taking something that is irrelevant, throwing it out, and starting over. And the means the two approaches use are totally different. TQM relies on bottom-up, participative decision making in both the planning of a TQM program and its execution. Reengineering, on the other hand, is initially driven by top management. When reengineering is complete, the workplace is largely self-managed. But getting there is a very autocratic, non-democratic process. Reengineering's supporters argue that it has to be this way because the level of change that the process demands is highly threatening to people and they aren't likely to accept it voluntarily. When top management commits to reengineering, employees have no choice. As Hammer is fond of saying, "You either get on the train, or we'll run over you with the train."[6]

Implications for Employees. Reengineering is rapidly gaining momentum in business and industry.[7] A recent survey found that, among manufacturing firms, forty-four percent of respondents indicated they are now reengineering or considering doing so. Among utilities and insurance companies, the responses were forty-eight and fifty-two percent, respectively.

Some of the companies that have implemented reengineering in at least some of their divisions include Motorola, Xerox, Ford, Banc One, Banca di America e di Italia, AT&T, Siemens, KPMG Peat Marwick, Hallmark, and the Commonwealth Life Insurance group. Hallmark, for instance, cut the time it takes to get a new product to market down from two years to a few months.[8] And Commonwealth now has 1,100 people doing the work that 1,900 used to do, even though its business has risen twenty-five percent.[9]

Reengineering's popularity isn't surprising. In today's highly competitive global marketplace, companies are being forced to reengineer their work processes in order to survive. And employees will "have to get on the train."

Lots of people are going to lose their jobs as a direct result of reengineering efforts. Just how many depends on the pace at which organizations adopt the new techniques. Some experts say that reengineering will eliminate between a million and 2.5 million jobs each year for the foreseeable future.[10] Regardless of the number, the impact won't be uniform throughout an organization. Staff support jobs, especially middle managers, will be most vulnerable. So, too, will clerical jobs in service industries. For instance, one knowledgeable observer predicts that reengineering will reduce employment in commercial banks and thrift institutions by thirty to forty percent by the year 2000.[11]

Those employees that keep their jobs after reengineering will find that they aren't the same jobs any longer. These new jobs will typically require a wider range of skills, include more interaction with customers and suppliers, offer greater challenge, contain increased responsibilities, and provide higher pay. However, the three– to five–year period it takes to implement reengineering is usually tough on employees. They suffer from uncertainty and anxiety associated with taking on new tasks and having to discard long-established work practices and formal social networks.

Flexible Manufacturing Systems

They look like something out of a science fiction movie in which remote-controlled carts deliver a basic casting to a computerized machining center. With robots positioning and repositioning the casting, the machining center calls upon its hundreds of tools to perform various operations that turn the casting into a finished part. Completed parts, each a bit different from the others, are finished at a rate of one every ninety seconds. Neither skilled machinists nor conventional machine tools are used. Nor are there any costly delays for changing dies or tools in this factory. A single machine can make dozens or even hundreds of different parts in any order management wants. Welcome to the world of **flexible manufacturing systems.**

In a global economy, manufacturing organizations that can respond rapidly to change have a competitive advantage. They can, for instance, better meet the diverse needs of customers and deliver products faster than their competitors. When customers were willing to accept standardized products, fixed assembly lines made sense. But nowadays, flexible technologies are increasingly necessary to compete effectively.

The unique characteristic of flexible manufacturing systems is that by integrating computer-aided design, engineering, and manufacturing, they can produce low-volume products for customers at a cost comparable to what had been previously possible only through mass production. Flexible manufacturing systems are, in effect, repealing the laws of economies of scale. Management no longer has to mass-produce thousands of identical products to achieve low per-unit production costs. With flexible manufacturing, when management wants to produce a new part, it doesn't change machines—it just changes the computer program.

Some automated plants can build a wide variety of flawless products and switch from one product to another on cue from a central computer. John Deere, for instance, has a $1.5 billion automated factory that can turn out 10 basic tractor models with as many as 3,000 options without plant shutdowns for retooling. National Bicycle Industrial Co., which sells its bikes under the Panasonic brand, uses flexible manufacturing to produce any of 11,231,862 variations on 18 models of racing, road, and mountain bikes in 199 color patterns and an almost unlimited number of sizes. This capability allows Panasonic to provide almost customized bikes at mass-produced prices.

How do flexible manufacturing systems affect the people who have to work within them? They require a different breed of industrial employee.[12] Workers in flexible manufacturing plants need more training and higher skills than assemblyline workers. There are fewer employees, so each has to be able to do a greater variety of tasks. For instance, at a flexible Carrier plant in Arkansas, which makes compressors for air conditioners, all employees undergo six weeks of training before they start their jobs. This training includes learning to read blueprints, math such as fractions and metric calculations, statistical process-control methods, some computer skills, and solving the problems involved in dealing with fellow workers. In addition to higher skills, employees in flexible plants are typically organized into teams and given considerable decision-making discretion. Consistent with the objective of high flexibility, these plants tend to have organic structures. They decentralize authority into the hands of the operating teams.

Worker Obsolescence

Changes in technology have cut the shelf life of most employees' skills. A factory worker or clerical employee in the 1950s could learn one job and be reasonably sure that his or her skills would be adequate to do that job for most of his or her work life. That certainly is no longer true. New technologies driven by computers, reengineering, TQM, and flexible manufacturing systems are changing the demands of jobs and the skills employees need to do them.

Repetitive tasks—like those traditionally performed on assembly lines and by low-skilled office clerks—will continue to be automated. And a good number of jobs will be upgraded. For instance, as most managers and professionals take on the task of writing their own memos and reports using word-processing software, the traditional secretary's job will be upgraded to become more of an administrative assistant. Secretaries who aren't equipped to take on these expanded roles will be displaced.

Reengineering , as we previously noted, is producing significant increases in employee productivity. The redesign of work processes is achieving higher output with fewer workers. And these reengineered jobs require different skills. Employees who are computer illiterate, have poor interpersonal skills, or can't work autonomously will increasingly find themselves ill-prepared for the demands of new technologies.

Finally, keep in mind that the obsolescence phenomenon doesn't exclude the managerial ranks. Those middle managers who merely acted as conduits in the chain of command between top management and the operating floor are being eliminated. And those managers who believe that employees respond only to directive leadership, tight controls, and intimidation will either change or find themselves on the street. The new model for effective managers will be one that emphasizes good listening, coaching, motivation, and team-support skills.

Work Design

The way that tasks are combined to create individual jobs has a direct influence on employee performance and satisfaction. In this section, we'll look at task characteristics theories and work redesign. Then we'll conclude this section by suggesting that, as we approach the twenty-first century, we need to begin completely rethinking what a job is. In ten or twenty years, it's very possible that few of us will be doing anything that looks like what we have traditionally called *a job*.

Task Characteristics Theories

Most of us acknowledge these two facts: (1) Jobs are different, and (2) some are more interesting and challenging than others. These facts have not gone unnoticed by OB researchers. They have responded by developing task characteristics theories that seek to identify task characteristics of jobs, how these characteristics are combined to form different jobs, and the relationship of these task characteristics to employee motivation, satisfaction, and performance.

There are several task characteristics theories. We'll review the three most important—requisite task attributes theory, the job characteristics model, and the social information-processing model.

Requisite Task Attributes Theory.   The task characteristics approach began with the pioneering work of Arthur Turner and Paul Lawrence in the mid-1960s.[13] They developed a research study to assess the effect of different kinds of jobs on employee satisfaction and absenteeism. They predicted that employees would prefer jobs that were complex and challenging; that is, such jobs would increase satisfaction and result in lower absence rates. They defined job complexity in terms of six task characteristics: (1) variety, (2) autonomy, (3) responsibility, (4) knowledge and skill, (5) required social interaction, and (6) optional social interaction. The higher a job scored on these characteristics, according to Turner and Lawrence, the more complex it was.

Their findings confirmed their absenteeism prediction. Employees in high-complexity tasks had better attendance records. But they found no general correlation between task complexity and satisfaction—until they broke their data down by the background of employees. When individual differences in the form of urban versus rural background were taken into account, employees from urban settings were shown to be more satisfied with low-complexity jobs. Employees with rural backgrounds reported higher satisfaction in high-complexity jobs. Turner and Lawrence concluded that workers in larger communities had a variety of nonwork interests and thus were less involved in and motivated by their work. In contrast, workers from smaller towns had fewer nonwork interests and were more receptive to the complex tasks of their jobs.

Turner and Lawrence's requisite task attributes theory was important for at least three reasons. First, they demonstrated that employees did respond differently to different types of jobs. Second, they provided a preliminary set of task attributes by which jobs could be assessed. And third, they focused

EXHIBIT 14-1

Examples of High and Low Job Characteristics

Characteristic	Example
Skill variety	
High variety	The owner-operator of a garage who does electrical repair, rebuilds engines, does body work, and interacts with customers
Low variety	A bodyshop worker who sprays paint eight hours a day
Task Identity	
High identity	A cabinetmaker who designs a piece of furniture, selects the wood, builds the object, and finishes it to perfection
Low identity	A worker in a furniture factory who operates a lathe solely to make table legs
Task significance	
High significance	Nursing the sick in a hospital intensive care unit
Low significance	Sweeping hospital floors
Autonomy	
High autonomy	A telephone installer who schedules his or her own work for the day, makes visits without supervision, and decides on the most effective techniques for a particular installation
Low autonomy	A telephone operator who must handle calls as they come according to a routine, highly specified procedure
Feedback	
High feedback	An electronics factory worker who assembles a radio and then tests it to determine if it operates properly
Low feedback	An electronics factory worker who assembles a radio and then routes it to a quality control inspector who tests it for proper operation and makes needed adjustments

Source: J. R. Hackman and G. R. Oldham, *Work Redesign,* (Reading, MA: Addison Wesley, 1980). Reprinted with permission.

attention on the need to consider the influence of individual differences on employees' reaction to jobs.

The Job Characteristics Model. Turner and Lawrence's requisite task attributes theory laid the foundation for what is today the dominant framework for defining task characteristics and understanding their relationship to employee motivation, performance, and satisfaction. That is J. Richard Hackman and Greg Oldham's **job characteristics model (JCM).**[14]

According to the JCM, any job can be described in terms of five core job dimensions, defined as follows:

1. *Skill variety:* The degree to which the job requires a variety of different activities so the worker can use a number of different skills and talent
2. *Task identity:* The degree to which the job requires completion of a whole and identifiable piece of work
3. *Task significance:* The degree to which the job has a substantial impact on the lives or work of other people

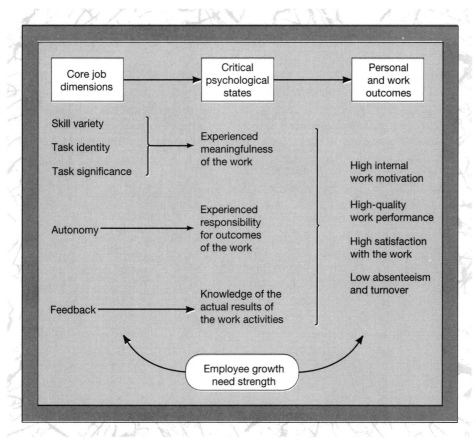

Exhibit 14-2

The Job Characteristics Model

Source: J. R. Hackman and J. L. Suttle eds., *Improving Life at Work,* (Glenview, IL: Scott, Foresman and Company, 1977, p. 129).

4. *Autonomy:* The degree to which the job provides substantial freedom, independence, and discretion to the individual in scheduling the work and in determining the procedures to be used in carrying it out

5. *Feedback:* The degree to which carrying out the work activities required by the job results in the individual's obtaining direct and clear information about the effectiveness of his or her performance

Exhibit 14-1 offers examples of job activities that rate high and low for each characteristic.

Exhibit 14-2 presents the model. Notice how the first three dimensions—skill variety, task identity, and task significance—combine to create meaningful work. That is, if these three characteristics exist in a job, we can predict that the incumbent will view the job as being important, valuable, and worthwhile. Notice, too, that jobs that possess autonomy give the job incumbent a feeling of personal responsibility for the results and that, if a job provides feedback, the employee will know how effectively he or she is performing. From a motivational stand-point, the model says that internal rewards are obtained by an individual when she *learns* (knowledge of results) that she *personally* (experienced responsibility) has performed well on a task that she *cares* about (experienced meaningfulness).[15] The more that these three psychological states are present, the greater will be the employee's motivation, performance, and satisfaction and the lower his or her absenteeism and likelihood of leaving the organization. As Exhibit 14-2 shows, the links between the job dimensions and the outcomes are moderated or adjusted by the strength of the individual's growth need: that is, by the employee's desire for self-esteem and self-actualization. This means that individuals with a high growth need are more likely to experience the psychological states when their jobs are enriched than are their counterparts with a low growth need. Moreover, they will respond more positively to the psychological states when they are present than will individuals with a low growth need.

The job characteristics model has been well researched. Most of the evidence supports the general framework of the theory—that is, there is a multiple set of job characteristics, and these characteristics affect behavioral outcomes.[16] But there is still considerable debate around the five specific core dimensions in the JCM and the validity of growth need strength as a moderating variable.

Where does this leave us? Given the current state of evidence, we can make the following statements with relative confidence: (1) People who work on jobs with high-core job dimensions are generally more motivated, satisfied, and pro-ductive than are those who do not. (2) Job dimensions operate through the psy-chological states in influencing personal and work outcome variables rather than influencing the outcomes directly.[17]

Social Information-Processing Model.   Would it surprise you to know that two people can have the same job yet view it differently? Probably not! As made clear in our discussion of perception in Chapter 3, people respond to their jobs *as they perceive them* rather than to the *objective* jobs themselves. This is the central thesis in our third task characteristics theory. It's called the **social information-processing (SIP) model.**[18]

The SIP model argues that employees adopt attitudes and behaviors in response to the social cues provided by others with whom they have contact. These others can be co-workers, supervisors, friends, family members, or cus-tomers. For instance, Gary Ling got a summer job working in a British Columbia sawmill. Since jobs were scarce and this one paid particularly well, Gary arrived on his first day of work highly motivated. Two weeks later, however, his motiva-tion was quite low. What had happened was that his co-workers consistently bad-mouthed their jobs. They said the work was boring, that having to clock in and out proved management didn't trust them, and that supervisors never listened to their opinions. The objective characteristics of Gary's job had not changed in the two-week period; rather, Gary had reconstructed reality on the basis of messages he had received from others.

A number of studies generally confirm the validity of the SIP model.[19] For instance, it has been shown that employee motivation and satisfaction can be manipulated by such subtle actions as a co-worker or boss commenting on the existence or absence of job features like difficulty, challenge, and autonomy.

So managers should give as much (or more) attention to employees' perceptions of their jobs as they give to the actual characteristics of those jobs. They might, for example, spend more time telling employees how interesting and important their jobs are. And managers should also not be surprised that newly hired employees and people transferred or promoted to a new position are more likely to be receptive to social information than are those with greater seniority.

Work Redesign

What are some of the options managers have at their disposal if they want to redesign or change the makeup of employee jobs? The following discusses three of those options: job rotation, job enlargement, and job enrichment.

Job Rotation. If employees suffer from overroutinization of their work, one alternative is to use **job rotation** (or what many now call *cross-training*). When an activity is no longer challenging, the employee is rotated to another job, at the same level, that has similar skill requirements.

G.S.I. Transcomm Data Systems Inc. in Pittsburgh uses job rotation to keep its staff of 110 people from getting bored.[20] Over a recent two-year period, nearly twenty percent of Transcomm's employees made lateral job switches. Management believes the job rotation program has been a major contributor to cutting employee turnover from twenty-five percent to less than seven percent a year. Brazil's Semco SA makes extensive use of job rotation. "Practically no one," says Semco's president, "stays in the same position for more than two or three years. We try to motivate people to move their areas completely from time to time so they don't get stuck to the technical solutions, to ways of doing things in which they have become entrenched."[21] Mike Conway, CEO of America West Airlines, describes how his company fully cross-trains their customer service representatives. He says America West does it "to give the employees a better job, to give them more job variety. It's more challenging, and for those who are interested in upward mobility, it exposes them to about sixteen different areas of the company versus the one they would be exposed to if we specialized."[22]

The strengths of job rotation are that it reduces boredom and increases motivation through diversifying the employee's activities. Of course, it can also have indirect benefits for the organization since employees with a wider range of skills give management more flexibility in scheduling work, adapting to changes, and filling vacancies. On the other hand, job rotation is not without its drawbacks. Training costs are increased, and productivity is reduced by moving a worker into a new position just when his or her efficiency at the prior job was creating organizational economies. Job rotation also creates disruptions. Members of the work group have to adjust to the new employee. The supervisor may also have to spend more time answering questions and monitoring the work of the recently rotated employee. Finally, job rotation can demotivate intelligent and ambitious trainees who seek specific responsibilities in their chosen specialty.

Job Enlargement. More than thirty years ago, the idea of expanding jobs horizontally, or what we call **job enlargement,** grew in popularity. Increasing the number and variety of tasks that an individual performed resulted in jobs with more diversity. Instead of only sorting the incoming mail by department, for instance, a mail sorter's job could be enlarged to include physically delivering the mail to the various departments or running outgoing letters through the postage meter.

Efforts at job enlargement met with less than enthusiastic results.[23] As one employee who experienced such a redesign on his job remarked, "Before I had one lousy job. Now, through enlargement, I have three!" However, there have been some successful applications of job enlargement. For example, U.S. Shoe Co. created modular work areas to replace production lines in over half of its factories. In these work areas, workers perform two or three shoemaking steps instead of only one, as in traditional production lines. The result has been footwear produced more efficiently and with greater attention to quality.

So, although job enlargement attacked the lack of diversity in overspecialized jobs, it did little to instill challenge or meaningfulness to a worker's activities. Job enrichment was introduced to deal with the shortcomings of enlargement.

Job Enrichment. **Job enrichment** refers to the vertical expansion of jobs. It increases the degree to which the worker controls the planning, execution, and evaluation of his or her work. An enriched job organizes tasks so as to allow the worker to do a complete activity, increases the employee's freedom and independence, increases responsibility, and provides feedback, so an individual will be able to assess and correct his or her own performance.

How does management enrich an employee's job? The following suggestions, based on the job characteristics model, specify the types of changes in jobs that are most likely to lead to improving their motivating potential (see Exhibit 14-3).

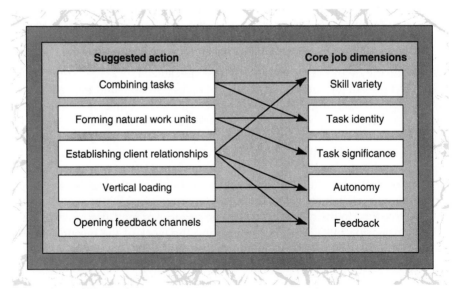

Exhibit 14-3
Guidelines for Enriching a Job

Source: J. R. Hackman and J. L. Suttle, eds., *Improving Life at Work.* (Glenview, IL: Scott, Foresman and Company, 1977, p. 138).

1. *Combine tasks.* Managers should seek to take existing and fractionalized tasks and put them back together to form a new and larger module of work. This measure increases skill variety and task identity.

2. *Create natural work units.* The creation of natural work units means that the tasks an employee does form an identifiable and meaningful whole. This measure increases employee "ownership" of the work and improves the likelihood that employees will view their work as meaningful and important rather than as irrelevant and boring.

3. *Establish client relationships.* The client is the user of the product or service that the employee works on (and may be an "internal customer" as well as someone outside the organization). Wherever possible, managers should try to establish direct relationships between workers and their clients to increase skill variety, autonomy, and feedback for the employee.

4. *Expand jobs vertically.* Vertical expansion gives employees responsibilities and control that were formerly reserved to management. It seeks to partially close the gap between the "doing" and the "controlling" aspects of the job, and it increases employee autonomy.

5. *Open feedback channels.* Feedback lets employees know not only how well they are performing their jobs but also whether their performance is improving, deteriorating, or remaining at a constant level. Ideally, feedback about performance should be received directly as the employee does the job, rather than from management on an occasional basis.[24]

Lawrence Buettner used the previous suggestions to design a job enrichment program for his international-trade banking department at First Chicago Corporation.[25] His department's chief product is commercial letters of credit—essentially a bank guarantee to stand behind huge import and export transactions. When he took over the department of 300 employees, he found paperwork crawling along a document "assembly line," with errors creeping in at each handoff. And employees did little to hide the boredom they were experiencing in their jobs. Buettner replaced the narrow, specialized tasks that employees were doing with enriched jobs. Each clerk is now a trade expert who can handle a customer transaction from start to finish. After 200 hours of training in finance and law, the clerks became full-service advisers who could turn around documents in a day while advising clients on such arcane matters as bank procedures in Turkey and U.S. munitions export controls. And the results? Productivity has more than tripled, employee satisfaction has soared, and transaction volume has risen more than ten percent a year. In addition, increased skills have translated into higher pay for the employees who are performing the enriched jobs. These trade-service representatives, some of whom had come to the bank directly out of high school, now earn from $25,000 to $50,000 a year.

The First Chicago example shouldn't be taken as a blanket endorsement of job enrichment. The overall evidence generally shows that job enrichment reduces absenteeism and turnover costs and increases satisfaction; but on the critical issue of productivity the evidence is inconclusive.[26] In some situations, such as at First Chicago, job enrichment increases productivity; in others, it decreases it. Even when productivity goes down, however, there does seem to be consistently more conscientious use of resources and a higher quality of product or service.

Changing the Way We Look at Jobs: A Provocative Perspective

The changes we've described throughout this book led one observer to predict that the whole notion of *jobs* may be becoming obsolete.[27] Before 1800, very few people had a job. People worked hard raising food or making things at home. They had no regular hours, no job descriptions, no bosses, and no employee benefits. Instead, they put in long hours on shifting clusters of tasks, in a variety of locations, on a schedule set by the sun and the weather and the needs of the day. It was the Industrial Revolution and the creation of large manufacturing companies that brought about the concept of what we have come to think of as *jobs.* But the conditions that created "the job" are disappearing. Customized production is pushing out mass production; most workers now handle information, not physical products; and competitive conditions are demanding rapid response to changing markets. While economists and social analysts continue to talk about the disappearance of jobs in certain countries or industries, they're missing a more relevant point: What's actually disappearing is *the job itself.*

In a fast-moving economy, jobs are rigid solutions to an elastic problem. We can rewrite a person's job description occasionally, but not every week. When the work that needs doing changes constantly—which increasingly describes today's world—organizations can't afford the inflexibility that traditional jobs bring with them.

In twenty-five years or so it's possible that very few people will have jobs as we have come to know them. In place of jobs, there will be part-time and temporary work situations. Organizations will be transformed from a structure built out of jobs into a field of work needing to be done. And these organizations will be essentially made up of "hired guns"—contingent employees (temporaries, part-timers, consultants, and contract workers) who join project teams created to complete a specific task. When that task is finished, the team disbands. People will work on more than one team at a time, keep irregular hours, and may never meet their co-workers face-to-face. Computers, pagers, cellular phones, modems, and the like will allow people to work for multiple employers, at the same time, in locations throughout the world. Few of these employees will be working from nine to five at specific work spots. And they'll have little of the security that their grandfathers—who worked for U.S. Steel, General Motors, Sears, Bank of America, or similar large bureaucracies—had. In place of security and predictability, they'll have flexibility and autonomy. They'll be able to put together their own place-time combinations to support their diverse work, family, lifestyle, and financial needs.

Is this jobless scenario realistic? There are certainly pressures in the environment to encourage employers to move in this direction. On the other hand, we should expect labor unions and others with a vested interest in the status quo to fight hard to protect the security and predictability that traditional jobs provide. Yet there are already companies—for instance, Intel and Microsoft—who are moving toward creating these jobless work environments. Employees in these firms are typically assigned to a project when they're hired. As the project changes over time, employee responsibilities and tasks change with it. As projects evolve and new projects are developed, employees are added to and dropped from various projects. At any given time, most employees are working on multiple projects, under several team leaders, keeping different schedules, being in various places, and performing several different tasks. These employees don't look to job descriptions or a supervisor for direction. Instead, they take their cues for what they should do from the changing demands of the specific project they're working on.

mplications for Managers

Technology is changing people's jobs and their work behavior. TQM and its emphasis on continuous process improvement can increase employee stress as individuals find that performance expectations are constantly being increased. Reengineering is eliminating millions of employees and completely reshaping the jobs of those who remain. Flexible manufacturing systems require employees to learn new skills and accept increased responsibilities. And technology is making many job skills obsolete and shortening the life span of almost all skills—technical, administrative, and managerial.

An understanding of work design can help managers design jobs that positively affect employee motivation. For instance, jobs that score high on the JCM increase an employee's control over key elements in his or her work. Therefore, jobs that offer autonomy, feedback, and similar complex task characteristics help to satisfy the individual goals of those employees who desire greater control over their work. Of course, consistent with the social information-processing model, the perception that task characteristics are complex is probably more important in influencing an employee's motivation than are the objective task characteristics themselves. The key, then, is to provide employees with cues that suggest that their jobs score high on factors such as skill variety, task identity, autonomy, and feedback.

Chapter 15

Performance Appraisal and Reward Systems

After reading this chapter, you should be able to:

1. Explain the purposes of performance appraisal

2. Identify the advantages of using behaviors rather than traits in appraising performance

3. Explain the most popular performance evaluation criteria

4. Identify who, in addition to a boss, can do performance evaluations

5. Describe the potential problems in performance appraisal and actions that can correct those problems

6. Explain why managers often dislike giving performance reviews

7. Outline the various types of rewards

8. Explain the links between performance appraisals, rewards, and employee behavior

Would you study differently for a course if your goal was *to learn as much as you can about the subject* rather than *to make a high grade on the tests in the course?* When I ask that question of students, I frequently get an affirmative answer. When I inquire further, I typically am told that making a high grade is only partially determined by knowledge of the material. You also need to know what the instructor thinks is important. I have been told by many a student, "If you want to do well in a course, you do best to study what the instructor tests for." In some cases, that approach will also result in learning as much as you can about the subject. But in many courses, studying to make a high grade means studying much differently than if you were studying for general knowledge.

Let me propose another question. Assume you are taking two similar classes, both with enrollments of about twenty students. In one class, the grade is determined totally by your scores on the midterm and final. In the other class, the midterm and final each count only twenty-five percent, with the remaining fifty percent being allocated for class participation. Would your in-class behavior be different in the two classes? I would predict that most students would talk more—ask questions, answer questions, offer examples, elaborate on points made by the instructor—in the class where participation was so highly weighted.

The previous paragraphs are meant to illustrate how the system's appraisal and reward practices influence behavior. Studying and in-class behavior are modified to take into consideration the criteria that the instructor appraises and the linking of those appraisals to desirable rewards (high grades). It's not unusual, in fact, for the more experienced student to behave five different ways in five different classes in order to obtain five high grades. The reason studying and in-class behaviors vary is certainly in large measure directly attributable to the different performance appraisal and reward systems that instructors use.

What applies in the school context also applies to employees at work. In this chapter, we show how performance appraisal and reward systems influence the attitudes and behaviors of people in organizations.

Performance Appraisal

Why do organizations appraise the performance of their employees? *How* do they appraise? *What* potential problems can arise to subvert the intentions of objective appraisals? *How* can managers overcome these problems? These are the key questions addressed in this section.

Purposes of Performance Appraisal

Performance appraisal serves a number of purposes in organizations.[1] First, management uses appraisals for general personnel decisions. Appraisals provide information for such important decisions as promotions, transfers, and terminations. Second, appraisals identify training and development needs. They pinpoint employee skills and competencies that are currently inadequate but can be remedied if appropriate programs are developed. Third, performance appraisals can be used as a criterion against which selection and development programs are validated. Newly hired employees who perform poorly can be identified through performance appraisal. Similarly, the effectiveness of training and development programs can be determined by assessing how well those employees who have participated do on their performance appraisals. Fourth, appraisals also fulfill the purpose of providing feedback to employees on how the organization views their performance. Finally, performance appraisals are used as the basis for reward allocations. Decisions about who gets merit pay increases and other rewards are typically determined by performance appraisals.

Each of these functions of performance appraisal is important. Yet their importance to us depends on the perspective we're taking. Several are clearly most relevant to personnel management decisions. But our interest is in organizational behavior. As a result, we emphasize performance appraisal in its role as a determinant of reward allocations.

Performance Appraisal and Motivation

In Chapter 4, considerable attention was given to the expectancy model of motivation. We argued that this model currently offers the best explanation of what conditions the amount of effort an individual will exert on his or her job. A vital component of this model is performance, specifically the effort-performance and performance-reward linkages. Do people see effort as leading to performance, and performance to the rewards that they value? Clearly, they have to know what is expected of them. They need to know how their performance will be measured. Further, they must feel confident that if they exert an effort within their capabilities it will result in a satisfactory performance as defined by the criteria by which they are being measured. Finally, they must feel confident that if they perform as they are being asked, they will achieve the rewards they value.

In brief, if the objectives that employees are seeking are unclear, if the criteria for measuring those objectives are vague, and if the employees lack confidence that their efforts will lead to a satisfactory appraisal of their performance, or believe there will be an unsatisfactory payoff by the organization when their performance objectives are achieved, we can expect individuals to work considerably below their potential.

What Do We Evaluate?

The criteria or criterion that management chooses to evaluate, when appraising employee performance, will have a major influence on what employees do. Two examples illustrate this point.

In a public employment agency, which served workers seeking employment and employers seeking workers, employment interviewers were appraised by the number of interviews they conducted. The interviewers' actions were consistent with the thesis that the evaluating criteria influence behavior. Interviewers were more concerned with the number of interviews they conducted than with the number of clients they placed in jobs.[2]

A management consultant specializing in police research noticed that, in one community, officers would come on duty for their shift, get into their police cars, drive to the highway that cut through the town, and speed back and forth along this highway for their entire shift. Clearly this fast cruising had little to do with good police work, but this behavior made sense once the consultant learned that the community's City Council used mileage on police vehicles as an evaluative measure of police effectiveness.[3]

These examples demonstrate the importance of criteria in performance evaluation, but they beg the question, What *should* management evaluate? The three most popular sets of criteria are individual task outcomes, behaviors, and traits.

Individual Task Outcomes.   If ends count, rather than means, then management should evaluate an employee's task outcomes. Using task outcomes, a plant manager could be judged on criteria such as quantity produced, scrap generated, and cost per unit of production. Similarly, a salesperson could be assessed on overall sales volume in his or her territory, dollar increase in sales, and number of new accounts established.

Behaviors.   In many cases, it's difficult to identify specific outcomes that can be directly attributable to an employee's actions. This is particularly true of personnel in staff positions and individuals whose work assignments are intrinsically part of a group effort. In the latter case, the group's performance may be readily evaluated, but the contribution of each group member may be difficult or impossible to identify clearly. In such instances, it is not unusual for management to evaluate the employee's behavior. Using the previous examples, behaviors of a plant manager that could be used for performance evaluation purposes might include promptness in submitting his or her monthly reports or the leadership style that the manager exhibits. Pertinent salesperson behaviors could be average number of contact calls made per day or sick days used per year.

Traits.   The weakest set of criteria, yet one that is still widely used by organizations, is individual traits. We say they are weaker than either task outcomes or behaviors because they are furthest removed from the actual performance of the job itself. Traits such as having "a good attitude," showing "confidence," being "dependable" or "cooperative," "looking busy," or possessing "a wealth of experience" may or may not be highly correlated with positive task outcomes, but only the naive would ignore the reality that such traits are frequently used in organizations as criteria for assessing an employee's level of performance.

Who Should Do the Evaluating?

Who should evaluate an employee's performance? The obvious answer would seem to be: his or her immediate boss. By tradition, a manager's authority typically has included appraising subordinates' performance. The logic behind this tradition seems to be that since managers are held responsible for their subordinates' performance, it only makes sense that these managers should evaluate that performance. But that logic may be flawed. Others may actually be able to do the job better.

Immediate Superior.   As we implied, about ninety-five percent of all performance evaluations at the lower and middle levels of the organization are conducted by the employee's immediate boss.[4] Yet a number of organizations are recognizing the drawbacks to using this source of evaluation. For instance, many bosses feel unqualified to evaluate the unique contributions of each of their subordinates. Others resent being asked to "play God" with their employees' careers. In addition, in the 1990s, when many organizations are using self-managed teams, telecommuting, and other organizing devices that distance bosses from their employees, an employee's immediate superior may not be a reliable judge of that employee's performance.

Peers.   Peer evaluations are one of the most reliable sources of appraisal data. Why? First, peers are close to the action. Daily interactions provide them with a comprehensive view of an employee's job performance. Second, using peers as raters results in several independent judgments, whereas a boss can offer only a single evaluation. And the average of several ratings is often more reliable than a single evaluation. On the down side, peer evaluations can suffer from co-workers' unwillingness to evaluate one another and from biases of friendship or animosity.

Self-Evaluation. Having employees evaluate their own performance is consistent with values such as self-management and empowerment. Self-evaluations get high marks from employees themselves; they tend to lessen employees' defensiveness about the appraisal process; and they make excellent vehicles for stimulating job performance discussions between employees and their superiors. As you might guess, however, they suffer from overinflated assessment and self-serving bias. Moreover, self-evaluations are often low in agreement with superiors' ratings.[5] Because of these serious drawbacks, self-evaluations are probably better suited to developmental uses than evaluative purposes.

Immediate Subordinates. A fourth judgment source is an employee's immediate subordinates. For instance, Datatec Industries, a maker of in-store computer systems, uses this form of appraisal.[6] The company's president says it's consistent with the firm's core values of honesty, openness, and employee empowerment.

Immediate subordinates' evaluations can provide accurate and detailed information about a manager's behavior because the evaluators typically have frequent contact with the manager. The obvious problem with this form of rating is fear of reprisal from bosses given unfavorable evaluations. Therefore, respondent anonymity is crucial if these evaluations are to be accurate.

The Comprehensive Approach: 360-Degree Evaluations. The latest approach to performance evaluation is the use of 360-degree evaluations. It provides for performance feedback from the full circle of daily contacts that an employee might have, ranging from mailroom personnel to customers to bosses to peers. The number of appraisals can be as few as three or four evaluations or as many as twenty-five, with most organizations collecting five to ten per employee.

A recent survey found that twenty-six percent of U.S. companies use some form of 360-degree feedback as part of the review process.[7] Included were companies such as Alcoa, Du Pont, Levi Strauss, Honeywell, UPS, Sprint, Amoco, AT&T, and W.L. Gore & Associates.

What's the appeal of 360-degree evaluations? They fit well into organizations that have introduced teams, employee involvement, and TQM programs. By relying on feedback from co-workers, customers, and subordinates, these organizations are hoping to give everyone more of a sense of participation in the review process and to gain more accurate readings on employee performance.

Performance Appraisal Methods

Obviously, performance appraisals are important. But how do you evaluate an employee's performance? That is, what are the specific techniques for appraisal? The following reviews the major performance appraisal methods.

Written Essays.   Probably the simplest method of appraisal is to write a narrative describing an employee's strengths, weaknesses, past performance, potential, and suggestions for improvement. The written essay requires no complex forms or extensive training to complete. But the results often reflect the ability of the writer. A good or bad appraisal may be determined as much by the evaluator's writing skill as by the employee's actual level of performance.

Critical Incidents.   Critical incidents focus the evaluator's attention on those behaviors that are key in making the difference between executing a job effectively or ineffectively. That is, the appraiser writes down anecdotes that describe what the employee did that was especially effective or ineffective. The key here is that only specific behaviors, and not vaguely defined personality traits, are cited. A list of critical incidents provides a rich set of examples from which the employee can be shown those behaviors that are desirable and those that call for improvement.

Graphic Rating Scales.   One of the oldest and most popular methods of appraisal is the use of **graphic rating scales.** In this method, a set of performance factors, such as quantity and quality of work, depth of knowledge, cooperation, loyalty, attendance, honesty, and initiative, are listed. The evaluator then goes down the list and rates each on incremental scales. The scales typically specify five points, so a factor such as *job knowledge* might be rated 1 ("poorly informed about work duties") to 5 ("has complete mastery of all phases of the job").

Why are graphic rating scales so popular? Though they don't provide the depth of information that essays or critical incidents do, they are less time-consuming to develop and administer. They also allow for quantitative analysis and comparison.

Behaviorally Anchored Rating Scales.   Behaviorally anchored rating scales have received a great deal of attention in recent years. These scales combine major elements from the critical incident and graphic rating scale approaches: The appraiser rates the employees on the basis of items along a continuum, but the points are examples of actual behavior on the given job rather than general descriptions or traits.

Behaviorally anchored rating scales specify definite, observable, and measurable job behavior. Examples of job-related behavior and performance dimensions are found by asking participants to give specific illustrations of effective and ineffective behavior regarding each performance dimension. These behavioral examples are then translated into a set of performance dimensions, each dimension having varying levels of performance. The results of this process are behavioral descriptions, such as anticipates, plans, executes, solves immediate problems, carries out orders, and handles emergency situations.

Multiperson Comparisons.   Multiperson comparisons evaluate one individual's performance against that of one or more others. It is a relative rather than an absolute measuring device. The three most popular comparisons are group order ranking, individual ranking, and paired comparisons.

The group order ranking requires the evaluator to place employees into a particular classification, such as top one-fifth or second one-fifth. This method is often used in recommending students to graduate schools. Evaluators are asked to rank the student in the top five percent, the next five percent, the next fifteen percent, and so forth. But when used by managers to appraise employees, managers deal with all their subordinates. Therefore, if a rater has twenty subordinates, only four can be in the top fifth and, of course, four must also be relegated to the bottom fifth.

The individual ranking approach rank orders employees from best to worst. If the manager is required to appraise thirty subordinates, this approach assumes that the difference between the first and second employee is the same as that between the twenty-first and twenty-second. Even though some of the employees may be closely grouped, this approach allows for no ties. The result is a clear ordering of employees, from the highest performer down to the lowest.

The paired comparison approach compares each employee with every other employee and rates each as either the superior or the weaker member of the pair. After all paired comparisons are made, each employee is assigned a summary ranking based on the number of superior scores he or she achieved. This approach ensures that each employee is compared against every other, but it can obviously become unwieldy when many employees are being compared.

Multiperson comparisons can be combined with one of the other methods to blend the best from both absolute and relative standards. For example, a college might use the graphic rating scale and the individual ranking method to provide more accurate information about its students' performance. A student's relative rank in the class could be noted next to an absolute grade of A, B, C, D, or F. A prospective employer or graduate school could then look at two students who each got a B in their different financial accounting courses and draw considerably different conclusions about each where next to one grade it says "ranked fourth out of twenty-six," while the other says "ranked seventeenth out of thirty." Obviously, the latter instructor gives out a lot more high grades!

Potential Problems

Although organizations may seek to make the performance appraisal process free from personal biases, prejudices, or idiosyncrasies, potential problems can creep into the process. To the degree that the following factors are prevalent, an employee's evaluation is likely to be distorted.

Single Criterion. The typical employee's job is made up of a number of tasks. An airline flight attendant's job, for example, includes welcoming passengers, seeing to their comfort, serving meals, and offering safety advice. If performance on this job were assessed by a single criterion measure—for example, the time it took to provide food and beverages to a hundred passengers—the result would be a limited evaluation of that job. More important, flight attendants whose performance appraisal included assessment on only this single criterion would be motivated to ignore those other tasks composing the job. Similarly, if a football quarterback were appraised only on his percentage of completed passes, he would be likely to throw short passes and only in situations where he felt assured they would be caught. Our point is that when employees are appraised on a single job criterion, even though successful performance on that job requires good performance on several criteria, employees will concentrate on the single criterion to the exclusion of other relevant factors.

Leniency Error.   Every appraiser has his or her own value system that acts as a standard against which appraisals are made. Relative to the true or actual performance of an individual, some evaluators mark high and others low. The former is referred to as positive leniency error and the latter as negative leniency error. When evaluators are positively lenient in their appraisal, an individual's performance becomes overstated, that is, rated higher than it actually should be. Similarly, a negative leniency error understates performance, giving the individual a lower appraisal.

If all individuals in an organization were appraised by the same person, there would be no problem. Although there would be an error factor, it would be applied equally to everyone. The difficulty arises when we have different raters with different leniency errors making judgments. For example, Jones and Smith are performing the same job for different supervisors, but they have absolutely identical job performance. If Jones' supervisor tends to err toward positive leniency, while Smith's supervisor errs toward negative leniency, we might be confronted with two dramatically different evaluations.

Halo Error.   The **halo error** is the tendency for an evaluator to let the assessment of an individual on one trait influence his or her appraisal of that person on other traits. For example, if an employee tends to be trustworthy and dependable, we might become biased toward that individual and rate him or her high on many other desirable attributes.

People who design teaching appraisal forms for college students to fill out in evaluating the effectiveness of their instructors each semester must confront the halo effect. Students tend to rate a faculty member as outstanding on all criteria when they are particularly appreciative of a few things he or she does in the classroom. Similarly, a few bad habits such as showing up late for lectures or being slow in returning papers might result in students' appraising the instructor as lousy across the board.

Similarity Error.   When evaluators rate other people by giving special consideration to those qualities that they perceive in themselves, they are making a similarity error. For example, evaluators who perceive themselves as aggressive may appraise others by looking for aggressiveness. Those who demonstrate this characteristic tend to benefit, while others are penalized. Again, this error would tend to be canceled out if the same evaluator appraised all the people in the organization. But reliability obviously suffers when various evaluators are using their own similarity criteria.

Low Differentiation. It is possible that, regardless of whom the appraiser evaluates and what traits are used, all of his evaluations seem similar. This evaluator's ability to appraise objectively and accurately might be impeded by social differentiation. It has been suggested that evaluators can be classified as either high differentiators, who use all or most of the scale, or low differentiators, who use a limited range of the scale. Low differentiators tend to ignore or suppress differences, perceiving the universe as more uniform than it really is. High differentiators, on the other hand, tend to utilize all available information to the utmost extent and thus are better able to perceive anomalies and contradictions. If multiple evaluations made by one person are very similar, they should be carefully inspected. They may have been made by a low differentiator. The people working for a low differentiator are likely to be appraised as significantly more homogeneous than they really are.

Forcing Information to Match Nonperformance Criteria. Although the practice is rarely advocated, sometimes the formal appraisal takes place *after* the decision about the individual's performance has been made! This may sound illogical, but it shows that subjective, yet formal, decisions are often arrived at before objective information to support that decision has been gathered.[8] For example, if the evaluator believes the appraisal should not be based on performance, but rather on seniority, he or she may be unknowingly adjusting each performance appraisal to bring it into line with the employee's seniority rank. In this and other cases, the evaluator is increasing or decreasing performance appraisals to align with the nonperformance criteria actually being used.

Overcoming the Problems

The fact that organizations can encounter problems with performance appraisals should not lead managers to give up on the process. Steps can be taken to overcome most of the problems we have identified.[9]

Use Multiple Criteria. Since successful performance on most jobs requires doing a number of things well, all those things should be identified and evaluated. The more complex the job, the more criteria that will need to be identified and evaluated. But everything need not be assessed. The critical activities that lead to effective or ineffective performance are the ones that need to be appraised.

Deemphasize Traits. Many traits often considered to be related to good performance may, in fact, have little or no performance relationship. Traits such as loyalty, initiative, courage, reliability, and self-expression are intuitively appealing characteristics in employees. But the relevant question is, Are individuals who are appraised as high on those traits better performers than those who rate low? We can't answer that question. We know there are employees who rate high on these characteristics and are poor performers. We can find others who are excellent performers but do not score well on traits like these. Our conclusion is that traits such as loyalty and initiative may be prized by managers, but there is no evidence to support that certain traits will be adequate synonyms for performance in a large cross section of jobs.

Another weakness in traits is the judgment itself. What is "loyalty"? When is an employee "reliable"? What one considers loyalty, another may not. So traits suffer from weak agreement among evaluators.

Emphasize Behavior.   Whenever possible, it is better to use measures based on behavior rather than traits for appraisals. Why? They can deal with the two major objections to traits. First, because measures based on behavior focus on specific examples—both good and bad—of performance we avoid the problem of using inappropriate substitutes for actual performance. Second, because we are appraising specific examples of behavior, we increase the likelihood that two or more evaluators will see the same thing. You might consider a given employee as friendly, while I rate her as standoffish. But when asked to rate her in terms of specific behaviors, we might both agree that she "frequently says 'Good morning' to customers," "rarely gives advice or assistance to co-workers," and "almost always avoids idle chatter with co-workers."

Document Performance Behaviors in a Diary.   By keeping a diary of specific critical incidents for each employee, evaluators tend to make more accurate judgments. Diaries, for instance, tend to reduce leniency and halo errors because they encourage the evaluator to focus on performance-related behaviors rather than traits.

Use Multiple Evaluators.   As the number of evaluators increases, the probability of attaining accurate information increases. If rater error tends to follow a normal curve, an increase in the number of appraisers will tend to show the majority congregating about the middle. You see this approach being used in athletic competitions in such sports as diving and gymnastics. A multiple set of evaluators judge a performance, the highest and lowest scores are dropped, and the final performance appraisal is derived from the cumulative scores of those remaining. The logic of multiple evaluators applies to organizations as well.

If an employee has had ten supervisors, nine having rated her excellent and one poor, we can discount the value of the one poor appraisal. Therefore, by moving employees about within the organization to gain several evaluations, we increase the probability of achieving valid and reliable appraisals.

Appraise Selectively.   Appraisers should evaluate in only those areas in which they have some expertise. If raters make appraisals on *only* those dimensions on which they are in a good position to rate, we increase interrater agreement and make the evaluation a more valid process. This approach also recognizes that different organizational levels often have different orientations toward rates and observe them in different settings. In general, therefore, we would recommend that appraisers should be as close as possible, in terms of organizational level, to the individual being evaluated. Conversely, the more levels that separate the evaluator and evaluatee, the less opportunity the evaluator has to observe the individual's behavior and, not surprisingly, the greater the possibility for inaccuracies.

The specific application of these concepts would result in having immediate supervisors or co-workers as the major contributors to the appraisal and having them evaluate those factors that they are best qualified to judge. For example, when professors are evaluating secretaries within a university, they could use criteria such as judgment, technical competence, and conscientiousness, whereas peers (other secretaries) could use criteria such as job knowledge, organization, cooperation with co-workers, and responsibility. Such an approach is both logical and reliable, since people are appraising only those dimensions about which they are in a good position to make judgments.

Train Appraisers. If you can't *find* good appraisers, the alternative is to *make* good appraisers. By training appraisers, we can make them more accurate raters. Common errors such as halo and leniency have been minimized or eliminated in workshops in which managers can practice observing and rating behaviors. These workshops typically run from one to three days, but allocating many hours to training may not always be necessary. One case has been cited in which both halo and leniency errors were decreased immediately after exposing evaluators to explanatory training sessions lasting only five minutes.[10] But the effects of training do appear to diminish over time, so regular training refresher sessions may be needed.

Don't Forget Performance Feedback!

A few years back, a nationwide motel chain advertised that when it came to motel rooms, "the best surprise is no surprise." This logic also holds for performance appraisals. Employees like to know how they are doing. They expect feedback. Typically, they get it in the annual review. But this review frequently creates problems. In some cases, it's a problem merely because managers put off such reviews, particularly if the appraisal is negative. The annual review is additionally troublesome if the manager saves up information related to performance and unloads it during the appraisal review. In such instances, it is not surprising that the manager may try to avoid addressing stressful issues that, even if confronted, may only be denied or rationalized by the employee. Much of this problem can be avoided by giving feedback to employees on an ongoing basis, for example, providing daily output reports with comparative data on actual units produced and the goal for the day, or bringing up problems as they occur rather than allowing them to accumulate for the annual review.

Regardless of whether feedback is provided annually or on an ongoing basis, management needs to offer performance feedback to employees. Yet, appraising another person's performance is one of the most emotionally charged of all management activities. The impression subordinates receive about their assessment has a strong impact on their self-esteem and, importantly, on their subsequent performance. Of course, conveying good news is considerably less difficult for both the manager and the subordinate than revealing that performance has been below expectations. In this context, the discussion of the evaluation can have negative as well as positive motivational consequences. Statistically speaking, half of all employees are below the median, yet evidence tells us that the average employee's estimate of his or her own performance level generally falls

1. Don't let problems fester until the annual review. Give daily or weekly feedback. The annual review is not the place to spring surprises.

2. Separate performance feedback reviews from pay reviews. In their eagerness to find out how much of a pay increase they are to receive, employees tend to tune out appraisals of their performance when the two reviews are combined.

3. Allow employees to engage in self-evaluation. Ask them how they are doing, how you and the organization can help them perform better, and how much cooperation they get from their peers.

4. When you have to be critical, focus the criticism on specific examples of behavior rather than on the individual personally.

5. Treat the review as only a point in an ongoing process. Use it to achieve agreement about what constitutes satisfactory performance in the future.

Exhibit 15-1

A Manager's Guide to More Effective Performance Appraisal Reviews

Source: Based on B. Brophy, "The Rite of Annual Reviews," *U.S. News & World Report,* February 2, 1986, p. 59.

around the seventy-fifth percentile.[11] A survey of more than 800,000 high school seniors also found that people seem to see themselves as better than average. Seventy percent rated themselves above average on leadership, and when asked to rate themselves on "ability to get along with others," none rated himself or herself below average. Sixty percent rated themselves in the top ten percent, and twenty-five percent saw themselves among the top one percent! Similarly, a survey of 500 clerical and technical employees found that fifty-eight percent rated their own performance as falling in the top ten percent of their peers doing comparable jobs, and a total of eighty-one percent placed themselves in the top twenty percent.[12]

The inevitable conclusion is that employees tend to be unrealistic and inflate the assessment of their own performance. This tendency puts the manager in the uncomfortable position of recognizing that even good news may not be good enough! Suggestions for making the best of a tough situation are listed in Exhibit 15-1.

What about Team Performance Evaluations?

Performance evaluation concepts have been almost exclusively developed with only individual employees in mind. This fact reflects the belief that individuals are the core building block around which organizations are built. But as we've described throughout this book, more and more organizations are restructuring themselves around teams. How should those organizations using teams evaluate performance? Four suggestions have been offered for designing a system that supports and improves the performance of teams.[13]

1. *Tie the team's results to the organization's goals.* It's important to find measurements that apply to important goals that the team is supposed to accomplish.

2. *Begin with the team's customers and the work process the team follows to satisfy their needs.* The final product the customer receives can be evaluated in terms of the customer's requirements. The transactions between teams can be evaluated on the basis of delivery and quality. And the process steps can be evaluated on the basis of waste and cycle time.

3. *Measure both team and individual performance.* Define the roles of each team member in terms of accomplishments that support the team's work process. Then assess each member's contribution and the team's overall performance.

4. *Train the team to create its own measures.* Having the team define its objectives and those of each member ensures that everyone understands his or her role on the team and helps the team develop into a more cohesive unit.

Performance Appraisal in a Global Context

We previously examined the role that performance appraisal plays in motivation and in affecting behavior. Caution must be used, however, in generalizing across cultures. Why? Because many cultures are not particularly concerned with performance appraisal, or, if they are, they don't look at it in the same way as we do in the United States or Canada.

To illustrate these points let's look at three cultural dimensions discussed in Chapter 2: a person's relationship to the environment, time orientation, and focus of responsibility.

American and Canadian organizations hold people responsible for their actions because people in these countries believe they can dominate their environment. In Middle Eastern countries, on the other hand, performance appraisals aren't likely to be widely used, because managers in these countries tend to see people as subjugated to their environment.

Some countries, such as the United States, have a short-term time orientation. Performance appraisals are likely to be frequent in such a culture, conducted at least once a year. In Japan, however, where people hold a long-term time frame, performance appraisals may occur only at five- or ten-year intervals.

Israel's culture values group activities much more than does the culture of the United States or Canada. So North American managers focus on the individual in performance appraisals, and their counterparts in Israel are likely to emphasize group contributions and performance.

Reward Systems

Our knowledge of motivation tells us that people do what they do to satisfy needs. Before they do anything, they look for the payoff or reward. Because many of these rewards—salary increases, promotions, and preferred job assignments, to name a few—are organizationally controlled, we should consider rewards as an important force influencing the behavior of employees.

Determinants of Rewards

Most organizations believe that their reward systems are designed to reward merit. The problem lies in defining merit. One person's merit may be another person's favoritism. Some define merit as being "deserving"; to others, merit is being "excellent." And there is no clear definition for either of those terms. A consideration of "deserving" may take into account such factors as intelligence, effort, or seniority. If "excellence" refers to performance, how do we measure it? Quantifiable and meaningful performance measures of most white-collar and service jobs, and of many blue-collar jobs, have eluded us.

In the next several pages we briefly assess the role of performance as a prerequisite for rewards and then discuss other popular criteria by which rewards are distributed. In Chapter 4, we argued that motivation will be highest when performance and rewards are closely linked. But, in reality, performance is only *one* of many criteria on which organizational rewards are based.

Performance.   Performance is the measurement of results. It asks the simple question: Did you get the job done? To reward people in the organization, therefore, requires some agreed-upon criterion for defining their performance. Whether this criterion is valid in representing performance is not relevant to our definition; as long as rewards are allocated on the basis of factors that are directly linked to doing the job successfully, we are using performance as the determinant. For many jobs, productivity is used as a single criterion. But as jobs become less standardized and routine, productivity becomes more difficult to measure, and hence, defining performance becomes increasingly complex.

Yet senior managers in corporations or those who oversee distinct business units increasingly are paying attention to linking rewards (particularly pay) to performance. Companies as diverse as American Broadcasting; Security Pacific National Bank; Sears, Roebuck; and Dow Chemical are measuring the economic performance of their business units, comparing the results against those of the competition, and awarding rewards accordingly.

Effort.   It is not uncommon for a report card in grammar school to include effort as one of the categories used in grading students. Organizations rarely make their rewarding of effort that explicit, yet it is certainly a major determinant in the reward distribution.

The rewarding of effort represents the classical example of rewarding means rather than ends. In organizations where performance is generally of low caliber, rewarding effort may be the only criterion by which to differentiate rewards. For example, a major eastern university was attempting to increase its research efforts and had designated obtaining funded research grants as a critical benchmark toward this end. Once this objective had been selected, all faculty members were informed that rewards for the coming year were going to be based on performance in obtaining grants. Unfortunately, after the first year of the program, even though approximately twenty percent of the faculty had made grant applications, none were approved. When the time came for performance evaluation and the distribution of rewards, the dean chose to give the majority of the funds available for pay raises to those faculty members who had applied for grants. Here is a case in which performance, defined in terms of obtaining funded research grants, was zero, so the dean chose to allocate rewards on the basis of effort.

This practice is more common than you might think. Effort can count *more than* actual performance when it is believed that those who try should be encouraged. The employee who is clearly perceived by her superiors to be working less than her optimum can often expect to be rewarded less than some other employee who, while producing less, is giving out a greater effort. Even if it is clearly stated that performance is what will be rewarded, people who make evaluations and distribute rewards are only human. Therefore, they are not immune to sympathizing with those who try hard, but with minimal success, and allowing this sympathy to influence their evaluation and reward decisions.

Seniority.   Seniority, job rights, and tenure dominate most civil service systems in the United States. They do not play as important a role in business corporations, but the length of time on the job is still a major factor in determining the allocation of rewards. Seniority's greatest virtue is that, relative to other criteria, it is easy to determine. We may disagree whether the quality of Smith's work is higher or lower than that of Jones', but we would probably not have much debate over who has been with the organization longer. So seniority represents an easily quantifiable criterion that can be substituted for performance.

Skills Held.   Another practice not uncommon in organizations is to allocate rewards on the basis of the skills of the employee. Regardless of whether the skills are used, those individuals who possess the highest levels of skill or talent will be rewarded commensurately.

When individuals enter an organization, their skill level is usually a major determinant of the compensation they will receive. In such cases, the marketplace or competition has acted to make skills a major element in the reward package. These externally imposed standards can evolve from the community or from occupational categories themselves. In other words, the relationship of demand and supply for particular skills in the community can significantly influence the rewards the organization must expend to acquire those skills. Also, the demand-supply relationship for an entire occupational category throughout the country can affect rewards.

Job Difficulty.   The complexity of the job can be a criterion by which rewards are distributed. For example, jobs that are highly repetitive and quickly learned may be viewed as less deserving of rewards than those that are more complex and sophisticated. Jobs that are difficult to perform or are undesirable because of stress or unpleasant working conditions may have to carry with them higher rewards in order to attract workers to them.

Discretionary Time.   The greater the discretion called for on a job, the greater the impact of mistakes and the greater the need for good judgment. In a job that has been completely programmed—that is, where each step has been accorded a procedure and there is no room for decision making by the incumbent—there is little discretionary time. Such jobs require less judgment, and lower rewards can be offered to attract people to take these positions. As discretionary time increases, greater judgmental abilities are needed, and rewards must commensurately be expanded.

Types of Rewards

The types of rewards that an organization can allocate are more complex than is generally thought. Obviously, there is direct compensation. But there are also indirect compensation and nonfinancial rewards. Each of these types of rewards can be distributed on an individual, group, or organizationwide basis. Exhibit 15-2 presents an outline for looking at rewards.

Intrinsic rewards are those that individuals receive for themselves. They are largely a result of the worker's satisfaction with his or her job. As noted in the previous chapter, techniques such as job enrichment or any efforts to redesign or restructure work to increase its personal worth to the employee may make his or her job more intrinsically rewarding.

A. Intrinsic rewards
    1. Participative decision making
    2. More responsibility
    3. Opportunities for personal growth
    4. Greater job freedom and discretion
    5. More interesting work
    6. Diversity of activities
B. Extrinsic rewards
    1. Direct compensation
        a. Basic salary or wage
        b. Overtime and holiday premiums
        c. Performance bonuses
        d. Profit sharing
        e. Stock options
    2. Indirect compensation
        a. Protection programs
        b. Pay for time not worked
        c. Services and perquisites
    3. Nonfinancial rewards
        a. Preferred office furnishings
        b. Assigned parking spaces
        c. Impressive titles
        d. Preferred lunch hours
        e. Preferred work assignments
        f. Own secretary

Exhibit 15-2
Types of Rewards

As previously noted, extrinsic rewards include direct compensation, indirect compensation, and nonfinancial rewards. Of course, an employee expects some form of direct compensation: a basic wage or salary, overtime and holiday premium pay, bonuses based on performance, profit sharing, or possible opportunities to receive stock options. Employees expect their direct compensation generally to align with their assessment of their contribution to the organization and, in addition, expect it to be relatively comparable with the direct compensation given to other employees with similar abilities, responsibilities, and performance.

The organization will provide employees with indirect compensation: insurance, paid holidays and vacations, services, and perquisites. Inasmuch as these are generally made uniformly available to all employees at a given job level, regardless of performance, they are really not motivating rewards. However, where indirect compensation is controllable by management and is used to reward performance, then it clearly needs to be considered as a motivating reward. To illustrate, if a company-paid membership in a country club is not available to all middle- and upper-level executives, but only to those who have shown particular performance ratings, then it is a motivating reward. Similarly, if company-owned automobiles and aircraft are made available to certain employees on the basis of their performance rather than their "entitlement," we should view these indirect compensations as motivating rewards for those who might deem these forms of compensation as attractive.

As with direct compensation, indirect compensation may be viewed in an individual, group, or organizational context. If rewards are to be linked closely with performance, however, we should expect individual rewards to be emphasized. On the other hand, if a certain group of managers within the organization has made a significant contribution to the effective performance of the organization, a blanket reward such as a membership in a social club might be appropriate.

The classification of nonfinancial rewards tends to be a smorgasbord of desirable "things" that are potentially at the disposal of the organization. The creation of nonfinancial rewards is limited only by managers' ingenuity and ability to assess "payoffs" that individuals in the organization find desirable and that are within the managers' discretion.

The old saying "One man's meat is another man's poison" certainly applies to rewards. What one employee views as highly desirable, another finds superfluous. Therefore *any* reward may not get the desired result; however, where selection has been done assiduously, the benefits to the organization by way of higher worker performance should be impressive.

Some workers are very status-conscious. A paneled office, a carpeted floor, a large walnut desk, or a private bathroom may be just the office furnishings that stimulate an employee toward top performance. Status-oriented employees may also value an impressive job title, their own secretary, or a well-located parking space with their name clearly painted underneath the Reserved sign.

Some employees value having their lunch at, say, 1 P.M. to 2 P.M. If lunch is normally from 11 A.M. to noon, the benefit of being able to take their lunch at another, more desirable time can be viewed as a reward. Having a chance to work with congenial colleagues or getting a desired work assignment are rewards that are within the discretion of management and, when carefully aligned to individual needs, can provide stimulus for improved performance.

Implications for Managers

Managers choose how employees are appraised and rewarded. Because these decisions affect the behavior of employees, care should be taken to ensure that the organization's appraisal and reward systems encourage the kinds of behaviors that management desires.

People do not work gratis. They expect payoffs: salary, benefits, promotion opportunities, recognition, social contact, and so forth. If employees perceive that their efforts are accurately appraised, and if they further perceive that the rewards they value are closely linked to their appraisals, management will have optimized the motivational properties from the organization's appraisal and reward procedures and policies. More specifically, on the basis of the contents of this chapter and our discussion of motivation in Chapters 4 and 5, we can conclude that rewards are likely to lead to effective performance and satisfaction when they are (1) perceived as equitable by the employee, (2) tied to performance, and (3) tailored to the needs of the individual. These conditions should foster a minimum of dissatisfaction among employees, reduced absenteeism and turnover, and increased organizational commitment. If these conditions don't exist, the probability of withdrawal behavior increases, and the prevalence of marginal or barely adequate performance increases. If workers perceive that their efforts are not recognized or rewarded, and if they view their alternatives as limited, they may continue working but perform at a level considerably below their capabilities.

Organizational Culture

After reading this chapter, you should be able to:

1. Define the common characteristics making up organizational culture

2. Contrast strong and weak cultures

3. Identify the functional and dysfunctional effects of organizational culture on people

4. List the factors that maintain an organization's culture

5. Clarify how culture is transmitted to employees

6. Contrast organizational culture with national culture

7. Explain the paradox of diversity

Just as individuals have personalities, so too do organizations. In Chapter 3, we found that individuals have relatively enduring and stable traits that help us predict their attitudes and behaviors. In this chapter, we propose that organizations, like people, can be characterized as, for example, rigid, friendly, warm, innovative, or conservative. These traits, in turn, can then be used to predict attitudes and behaviors of the people within these organizations.

The theme of this chapter is that there is a systems variable in organizations that, although hard to define or describe precisely, nevertheless exists and that employees generally describe in common terms. We call this variable *organizational culture*. Just as tribal cultures have totems and taboos that dictate how each member will act toward fellow members and outsiders, organizations have cultures that govern how members behave. Just what organizational culture is, how it has an impact on employee attitudes and behavior, where it comes from, and whether it can be managed are discussed in the following pages.

Defining Organizational Culture

There seems to be wide agreement that **organizational culture** refers to a system of shared meaning held by members that distinguishes the organization from other organizations.[1] This system of shared meaning is, on closer examination, a set of key characteristics that the organization values. Recent research suggests that seven primary characteristics, in aggregate, capture the essence of an organization's culture.[2]

1. *Innovation and risk taking:* The degree to which employees are encouraged to be innovative and take risks
2. *Attention to detail:* The degree to which employees are expected to exhibit precision, analysis, and attention to detail
3. *Outcome orientation:* The degree to which management focuses on results or outcomes rather than on the techniques and processes used to achieve those outcomes
4. *People orientation:* The degree to which management decisions take into consideration the effect of outcomes on people within the organization
5. *Team orientation:* The degree to which work activities are organized around teams rather than individuals
6. *Aggressiveness:* The degree to which people are aggressive and competitive rather than easygoing
7. *Stability:* The degree to which organizational activities emphasize maintaining the status quo in contrast to growth

Each of these characteristics exists on a continuum from low to high. Appraising the organization on these seven characteristics, then, gives a composite picture of the organization's culture. This picture becomes the basis for feelings of shared understanding that members have about the organization, how things are done in it, and the way members are supposed to behave. Exhibit 16-1 demonstrates how these characteristics can be mixed to create highly diverse organizations.

Culture Is a Descriptive Term

Organizational culture is concerned with how employees perceive the seven characteristics, not whether they like them. That is, it is a descriptive term. This point is important because it differentiates the concept of organizational culture from that of job satisfaction.

Research on organizational culture has sought to measure how employees see their organization: Are there clear objectives and performance expectations? Does the organization reward innovation? Does it encourage competitiveness?

Organization A

This organization is a manufacturing firm. Managers are expected to fully document all decisions, and "good managers" are those who can provide detailed data to support their recommendations. Creative decisions that incur significant change or risk are not encouraged. Because managers of failed projects are openly criticized and penalized, managers try not to implement ideas that deviate much increase from the status quo. One lower-level manager quoted an often-used phrase in the company: "If it ain't broke, don't fix it."

Employees in this firm are required to follow extensive rules and regulations. Managers supervise employees closely to ensure there are no deviations. Management is concerned with high productivity, regardless of the impact on employee morale or turnover.

Work activities are designed around individuals. There are distinct departments and lines of authority, and employees are expected to minimize formal contact with other employees outside their functional area or line of command. Performance evaluations and rewards emphasize individual effort, although seniority tends to be the primary factor in the determination of pay raises and promotions.

Organization B

This organization is also a manufacturing firm. Here, however, management encourages and rewards risk taking and change. Decisions based on intuition are valued as much as those that are well rationalized. Management prides itself on its history of experimenting with new technologies and its success in regularly introducing innovative products. Managers or employees who have a good idea are encouraged to "run with it," and failures are treated as "learning experiences." The company prides itself on being market-driven and rapidly responsive to the changing needs of its customers.

There are few rules and regulations for employees to follow, and supervision is loose because management believes that its employees are hardworking and trustworthy. Management is concerned with high productivity but believes that this comes through treating its people right. The company is proud of its reputation as being a good place to work.

Job activities are designed around work teams, and team members are encouraged to interact with people across functions and authority levels. Employees talk positively about the competition between teams. Individuals and teams have goals, and bonuses are based on achievement of those outcomes. Employees are given considerable autonomy in choosing the means by which the goals are attained.

Exhibit 16-1
Contrasting Organizational Cultures

In contrast, research on job satisfaction seeks to measure affective responses to the work environment. It is concerned with how employees feel about the organization's expectations, reward practices, methods for handling conflict, and the like. Although the two terms undoubtedly have characteristics that overlap, keep in mind that the term *organizational culture* is descriptive, whereas *job satisfaction* is evaluative.

Do Organizations Have Uniform Cultures?

Organizational culture represents a common perception held by the organization's members. This feature was made explicit when we defined culture as a system of *shared* meaning. We should expect, therefore, that individuals with different backgrounds or at different levels in the organization will tend to describe the organization's culture in similar terms.

Acknowledgment that organizational culture has common properties does not mean, however, that there cannot be subcultures within any given culture. Most large organizations have a dominant culture and numerous sets of subcultures. A *dominant culture* expresses the core values that are shared by a majority of the organization's members. When we talk about an *organization's* culture, we are referring to its dominant culture. It is this macro view of culture that gives an organization its distinct personality. *Subcultures* tend to develop in large organizations to reflect common problems, situations, or experiences that members face. These subcultures are likely to be defined by department designations and geographical separation. The purchasing department, for example, can have a subculture that is uniquely shared by members of that department. It will include the core values of the dominant culture plus additional values unique to members of the purchasing department. Similarly, an office or unit of the organization that is physically separated from the organization's main operations may take on a different personality. Again, the core values are essentially retained but modified to reflect the separated unit's distinct situation.

If organizations had no dominant culture and were composed only of numerous subcultures, the value of organizational culture as an independent variable would be significantly lessened. Why? Because there would be no uniform interpretation of what represented appropriate or inappropriate behavior. It is the shared meaning aspect of culture that makes it such a potent device for guiding and shaping behavior.

Strong versus Weak Cultures

It has become increasingly popular to differentiate between strong and weak cultures. The argument is that strong cultures have a greater impact on employee behavior and are more directly related to reduced turnover.

A **strong culture** is characterized by the organization's core values being both intensely held and widely shared.[3] The more members that accept the core values and the greater their commitment to those values, the stronger the culture is. Consistent with this definition, a strong culture will obviously have a greater influence on the behavior of its members than will a weak culture. Religious organizations, cults, and Japanese companies are examples of organizations that have very strong cultures. When a David Koresh can entice dozens of his Branch Davidian members in Waco, Texas, to voluntarily die in flames, we see a behavioral influence considerably greater than that typically attributed to leadership. The culture of the Branch Davidians had a degree of sharedness and intensity that allowed for extremely high behavioral control. Of course, the same strong cultural influence that led to the tragedy in Waco can be directed positively to create immensely successful organizations such as Microsoft, Mary Kay Cosmetics, and Sony.

A specific result of a strong culture should be low employee turnover. A strong culture demonstrates high agreement among members about what the organization stands for. Such unanimity of purpose builds cohesiveness, loyalty, and organizational commitment. These, in turn, lessen the propensity for employees to leave the organization.

Culture versus Formalization

A strong organizational culture increases behavioral consistency. In this sense, we should recognize that a strong culture can act as a substitute for formalization.

In Chapter 13, we discussed how formalization's rules and regulations act to regulate employee behavior. High formalization in an organization creates predictability, orderliness, and consistency. A strong culture achieves the same end without the need for written documentation. Therefore, we should view formalization and culture as two different roads to a common destination. The stronger an organization's culture, the less management need be concerned with developing formal rules and regulations to guide employee behavior. Those guides will be internalized in employees when they accept the organization's culture.

What Does Culture Do?

We've alluded to organizational culture's impact on behavior. We've also explicitly argued that a strong culture should be associated with reduced turnover. In this section, we more carefully review the functions that culture performs and assess whether culture can be a liability for an organization.

Culture's Functions

Culture performs several functions within an organization. First, it has a boundary-defining role; that is, it creates distinctions between one organization and others. Second, it conveys a sense of identity for organization members. Third, culture facilitates the generation of commitment to something larger than one's individual self-interest. Fourth, it enhances social system stability. Culture is the social glue that helps hold the organization together by providing appropriate standards for what employees should say and do. Finally, culture serves as a sense-making and control mechanism that guides and shapes the attitudes and behavior of employees. This last function is of particular interest to us. As the following quotation makes clear, culture defines the rules of the game:

> Culture by definition is elusive, intangible, implicit, and taken for granted. But every organization develops a core set of assumptions, understandings, and implicit rules that govern day-to-day behavior in the workplace. . . . Until newcomers learn the rules, they are not accepted as full-fledged members of the organization. Transgressions of the rules on the part of high-level executives or front-line employees result in universal disapproval and powerful penalties. Conformity to the rules becomes the primary basis for reward and upward mobility.[4]

As we show later in this chapter, who is offered a job, who is appraised as a high performer, and who gets a promotion are strongly influenced by the individual-organization fit, that is, whether the applicant or employee's attitudes and behavior are compatible with the culture. It is not a coincidence that employees at Disneyland and Disney World appear to be almost universally attractive, clean, and wholesome, with bright smiles. That's the image Disney seeks. The company selects employees who will maintain that image.

And both the informal norms and formal rules and regulations ensure that Disney employees, once on the job, will act in a relatively uniform and predictable way.

Culture as a Liability

We are treating culture in a nonjudgmental manner. We haven't said that it's good or bad, only that it exists. Many of its functions, as outlined, are valuable for both the organization and the employee. Culture enhances organizational commitment and increases the consistency of employee behavior. These clearly are benefits to an organization. From an employee's standpoint, culture is valuable because it reduces ambiguity. It tells employees how things are done and what's important. But we shouldn't ignore the potentially dysfunctional aspects of culture, especially of a strong culture.

Culture is a liability when the shared values do not agree with those that will further the organization's effectiveness. This situation is most likely to occur when the organization's environment is dynamic. When the environment is undergoing rapid change, the organization's entrenched culture may no longer be appropriate. Consistency of behavior is an asset to an organization in a stable environment. It may, however, burden the organization and hinder its ability to respond to changes in the environment.

Creating and Sustaining Culture

An organization's culture doesn't pop out of thin air. Once established, it rarely fades away. What forces influence the creation of a culture? What reinforces and sustains those forces once they are in place?

How a Culture Begins

An organization's current customs, traditions, and general way of doing things are largely due to what it has done before and the degree of success it had with those endeavors. So the ultimate source of an organization's culture is its founders![5]

The founders of an organization traditionally have a major impact in establishing the early culture. They have a vision of what the organization should be. They are unconstrained by previous customs of doing things or ideologies. The small size that typically characterizes any new organization further facilitates the founders' imposing their vision on all organizational members. Because the founders have the original idea, they also typically have biases on how to get the idea fulfilled. The organization's culture results from the interaction between the founders' biases and assumptions and what the original members learn subsequently from their own experiences.

Henry Ford at the Ford Motor Company, Thomas Watson at IBM, J. Edgar Hoover at the FBI, ChungJu Yung at Hyundi, Walt Disney at Walt Disney Company, Sam Walton at Wal-Mart, and David Packard at Hewlett-Packard are just a few obvious examples of individuals who had immeasurable impact in shaping their organization's culture. For instance, Watson's views on research and development, product innovation, employee dress attire, and compensation policies still influence practices at IBM, though he died in 1956. The Walt Disney Company continues to focus on Walt Disney's original vision of a company that created fantasy entertainment. Wal-Mart's commitment to frugality, simplicity, and value comes directly from the late Sam Walton.

Keeping a Culture Alive

Once a culture is in place, practices within the organization act to maintain it by exposing employees to a set of similar experiences.[6] For example, many of an organization's human resource practices reinforce its culture. The selection process, performance evaluation criteria, reward practices, training and career development activities, and promotion procedures ensure that those hired fit in with the culture, reward those who support it, and penalize (and even expel) those who challenge it. Three forces play a particularly important part in sustaining a culture—selection practices, the actions of top management, and socialization methods. Let's take a closer look at each.

Selection.   The explicit goal of the selection process is to identify and hire individuals who have the knowledge, skills, and abilities to perform the jobs within the organization successfully. But, typically, more than one candidate will meet any given job's requirements. The final decision about who is hired will be significantly influenced by the decision maker's judgment of how well the candidates will fit into the organization. It would be naive to ignore this subjective aspect of the decision to hire. This attempt to ensure a proper match, whether purposely or inadvertently, results in the hiring of people who have common values (ones essentially consistent with those of the organization) or at least a good portion of those values. The selection process also gives applicants information about the organization. Candidates who perceive a conflict between their values and those of the organization can self-select themselves out of the applicant pool. Selection, therefore, becomes a two-way street, allowing either employer or applicant to abrogate a marriage if there appears to be a mismatch. In this way, the selection process sustains an organization's culture by selecting out those individuals who might attack or undermine its core values.

Applicants for entry-level positions in brand management at Procter & Gamble (P&G) experience an exhaustive application and screening process. Their interviewers are part of a cadre who have been selected and trained extensively via lectures, videotapes, films, practice interviews, and role plays to identify applicants who will successfully fit in at P&G. Applicants are interviewed in depth for such qualities as their ability to "turn out high volumes of excellent work," "identify and understand problems," and "reach thoroughly substantiated and well-reasoned conclusions that lead to action." P&G values rationality and seeks applicants who think rationally. College applicants receive two interviews and a general knowledge test on campus before being flown to Cincinnati for three more one-on-one interviews and a group interview at lunch. Each encounter seeks corroborating evidence of the traits that the firm believes are correlated highly with "what counts" for success at P&G.

Applicants for positions at Compaq Computer are carefully chosen for their ability to fit into the company's teamwork-oriented culture. As one executive put it, "We can find lots of people who are competent. . . . The No. 1 issue is whether they fit into the way we do business."[7] At Compaq, that means job candidates who are easy to get along with and who feel comfortable with the company's consensus management style. Compaq's extensive interview process increases the likelihood that loners and persons with big egos will be screened out; it's not unusual for a new hire to be interviewed by fifteen people who represent all departments of the company and a variety of seniority levels.

Top Management. The actions of top management also have a major impact on an organization's culture. Through what they say and how they behave, senior executives establish norms that filter down through the organization as to whether risk taking is desirable, how much freedom managers should give their subordinates, what is appropriate dress, what actions will pay off in terms of pay raises, promotions, and other rewards, and the like.

For example, look at Xerox Corp. Its chief executive from 1961 to 1968 was Joseph C. Wilson. An aggressive, entrepreneurial type, he oversaw Xerox's staggering growth on the basis of its 914 copier, one of the most successful products in American history. Under Wilson, Xerox had an entrepreneurial environment, with an informal, high-camaraderie, innovative, bold, risk-taking culture. Wilson's replacement as CEO was C. Peter McColough, a Harvard MBA with a formal management style. He instituted bureaucratic controls and a major change in Xerox's culture. By the time McColough stepped down in 1982, Xerox had become stodgy and formal, with lots of politics and turf battles and layers of watchdog managers. His replacement was David T. Kearns, who believed that the culture he had inherited hindered Xerox's ability to compete. To increase the company's competitiveness, Kearns trimmed Xerox down by cutting 15,000 jobs, delegated decision making downward, and refocused the organization's culture around a simple theme: Boost the quality of Xerox products and services. By his actions and those of his senior managerial cadre, Kearns conveyed to everyone at Xerox that the company valued and rewarded quality and efficiency. When Kearns retired in 1990, Xerox still had its problems. The copier business was mature and Xerox had fared badly in developing computerized office systems. The current CEO, Paul Allaire, has again sought to reshape Xerox's culture. Specifically, he has reorganized the corporation around a worldwide marketing department, has unified product development and manufacturing divisions, and has replaced half of the company's top management team with outsiders. Allaire seeks to reshape Xerox's culture to focus on innovative thinking and outhustling the competition.

Socialization. No matter how good a job the organization does in recruiting and selection, new employees are not fully indoctrinated in the organization's culture. Because they are least familiar with the organization's culture, new employees are potentially the most likely to disturb the beliefs and customs that are in place. The organization will, therefore, want to help new employees adapt to its culture. This adaptation process is called **socialization.**

All Marines must go through boot camp, where they prove their commitment. Of course, at the same time, the Marine trainers are indoctrinating new recruits in the "Marine way." The success of any cult depends on effective socialization. New Moonies undergo a "brainwashing" ritual that substitutes group

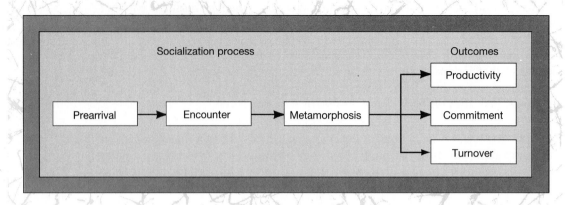

Exhibit 16-2
A Socialization Model

loyalty and commitment in place of family. New Disneyland employees spend their first two full days of work watching films and listening to lectures on how Disney employees are expected to look and act.

As we discuss socialization, keep in mind that the most critical socialization stage is at the time of entry into the organization. This is when the organization seeks to mold the outsider into an employee in "good standing." Employees who fail to learn the essential or pivotal role behaviors risk being labeled nonconformists or rebels and, ultimately being expelled. But the organization will be socializing every employee, though maybe not explicitly, throughout his or her career in the organization. This continual process further contributes to sustaining the culture.

Socialization can be conceptualized as a process made up of three stages: prearrival, encounter, and metamorphosis. The first stage encompasses all the learning that occurs before a new member joins the organization. In the second stage, the new employee sees what the organization is really like and confronts the likelihood that expectations and reality may diverge. In the third stage, the relatively long-lasting changes take place. The new employee masters the skills required for his or her job, successfully performs his or her new roles, and makes the adjustments to his or her work group's values and norms. This three-stage process has an impact on the new employee's work productivity, commitment to the organization's objectives, and his or her decision to stay with the organization. Exhibit 16-2 depicts this process.

The *prearrival stage* occurs before the employee joins the organization, so that he or she arrives with an established set of values, attitudes, and expectations. These cover both the work to be done and the organization. For instance, in many jobs, particularly professional work, new members will have undergone a considerable degree of prior socialization in training and in school. One major purpose of a business school, for example, is to socialize business students into the attitudes and behaviors that business firms want. If business executives believe that successful employees value the profit ethic, are loyal, will work hard, want to achieve, and willingly accept directions from their superiors, they can hire individuals out of business schools who have been premolded in this pattern. But prearrival socialization goes beyond the specific job. The selection process itself is used in most

Formal vs. Informal: The more a new employee is segregated from the ongoing work setting and differentiated in some way to make explicit his or her newcomer's role, the more formal socialization is. Specific orientation and training programs are examples. Informal socialization puts the new employee directly into his or her job, with little or no special attention.

Individual vs. Collective: New members can be socialized individually. Many professional offices socialize new employees in this way. New members can also be grouped together and processed through an identical set of experiences, as in military boot camp.

Fixed vs. Variable: The time schedule in which newcomers make the transition from outsider to insider can be fixed or variable. A fixed schedule establishes standardized stages of transition, such as those used in rotational training programs. It also includes probationary periods, such as the six-year "tenure or out" procedure commonly used with new assistant professors in colleges. Variable schedules give no advanced notice of their transition timetable. For example, this describes the typical promotion system, where one is not advanced to the next stage until he or she is "ready."

Serial vs. Random: Serial socialization is characterized by the use of role models who train and encourage the newcomer. Apprenticeship and mentoring programs are examples. In random socialization, role models are deliberately withheld. The new employee is left on his or her own to figure things out.

Investiture vs. Divestiture: Investiture socialization assumes that the newcomer's qualities and qualifications are the necessary ingredients for job success, so those qualities and qualifications are confirmed and supported. Divestiture socialization tries to strip away certain characteristics of the recruit. Fraternity and sorority "pledges" go through divestiture socialization to shape them into the proper role.

Exhibit 16-3
Entry Socialization Options

Source: Based on J. Van Maanen, "People Processing: Strategies of Organizational Socialization," *Organizational Dynamics*, Summer 1978, pp. 19–36; and E. H. Schein, "Organizational Culture," *American Psychologist*, February 1990, p. 116.

organizations to inform prospective employees about the organization as a whole and to ensure the inclusion of the right type—those who will fit in. "Indeed, the ability of the individual to present the appropriate face during the selection process determines his ability to move into the organization in the first place. Thus, success depends on the degree to which the aspiring member has correctly anticipated the expectations and desires of those in the organization in charge of selection."[8]

Entry into the organization begins the *encounter stage.* Now the individuals confront the possible dichotomy between their expectations—about their job, co-workers, boss, and the organization in general—and reality. If expectations prove to have been more or less accurate, the encounter stage merely provides a reaffirmation of the perceptions gained earlier. But this is often not the case. Where expectations and reality differ, new employees must undergo socialization that will detach them from previous assumptions and replace those assumptions with another set that the organization deems desirable. At the extreme, new members may become totally disillusioned with the actualities of their job and resign. Proper selection should significantly reduce the probability of the latter occurrence.

Finally, new members must work out any problems discovered during the encounter stage. To do so, they may have to go through changes; hence, we call this the *metamorphosis stage.* The choices presented in Exhibit 16-3 are alternatives

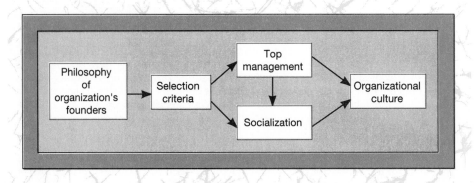

Exhibit 16-4
How Organizational Cultures Form

organizations can use to bring about the desired metamorphosis. But what is a desirable metamorphosis? We can say that metamorphosis and the entry socialization process are complete when new members have become comfortable with the organization and their job. They have internalized the norms of the organization and their work group, and they understand and accept those norms. New members feel accepted by their peers as trusted and valued individuals. They are self-confident that they have the competence to complete the job successfully. They understand the system—not only their own tasks, but the rules, procedures, and informally accepted practices as well. Finally, they know how they will be evaluated, that is, what criteria will be used to measure and appraise their work. They know what is expected of them and what constitutes a job well done. As Exhibit 16-2 shows, successful metamorphosis should have a positive impact on the new employees' productivity and their commitment to the organization and reduce their propensity to leave the organization.

Summary: How Cultures Form

Exhibit 16-4 summarizes how an organization's culture is established and sustained. The original culture is derived from the founder's philosophy. This, in turn, strongly influences the criteria used in hiring. The actions of the current top management set the general climate of what is acceptable behavior and what is not. How employees are to be socialized will depend on the degree of success achieved in matching new employees' values to those of the organization in the selection process and top management's preference for socialization methods.

How Employees Learn Culture

Culture is transmitted to employees in a number of forms, the most potent being stories, rituals, material symbols, and language.

Stories

During the days when Henry Ford II was chairman of the Ford Motor Co., one would have been hard-pressed to find a manager who hadn't heard the story about Mr. Ford's reminding his executives, when they got too arrogant, that "It's my name that's on the building." The message was clear: Henry Ford II ran the company!

Nordstrom employees are fond of the following story. It strongly conveys the company's policy toward customer returns: When this specialty retail chain was in its infancy, a customer came in and wanted to return a set of automobile tires. The salesclerk was not sure how to handle the problem. As the customer and salesclerk spoke, Mr. Nordstrom walked by and overheard the conversation. He immediately interceded, asking the customer how much he had paid for the tires. Mr. Nordstrom then instructed the clerk to take the tires back and provide a full cash refund. After the customer had received his refund and left, the perplexed clerk looked at the boss. "But, Mr. Nordstrom, we don't sell tires!" "I know," replied the boss, "but we do whatever we need to do to make the customer happy. I mean it when I say we have a no-questions-asked return policy." Nordstrom then picked up the telephone and called a friend in the auto parts business to see how much he could get for the tires.

Stories such as these circulate through many organizations. They typically contain a narrative of events about the organization's founders, rule breaking, rags-to-riches successes, reductions in the work force, relocation of employees, reactions to past mistakes, and organizational coping. These stories anchor the present in the past and provide explanations and legitimacy for current practices.

Rituals

Rituals are repetitive sequences of activities that express and reinforce the key values of the organization, what goals are most important, which people are important and which are expendable. College faculty members undergo a lengthy ritual in their quest for permanent employment—tenure. Typically, the faculty member is on probation for six years. At the end of that period, the member's colleagues must make one of two choices: extend a tenured appointment or issue a one-year terminal contract. What does it take to obtain tenure? It usually requires satisfactory teaching performance, service to the department and university, and scholarly activity. But, of course, what satisfies the requirements for tenure in one department at one university may be appraised as inadequate in another. The key is that the tenure decision, in essence, asks those who are tenured to assess whether the candidate has demonstrated, in six years of performance, that he or she fits in. Colleagues who have been socialized properly will have proved themselves worthy of being granted tenure. Every year, hundreds of faculty members at colleges and universities are denied tenure. In some cases, this action is a result of poor performance across the board. More often, however, the decision can be traced to the faculty member's not doing well in those areas that the tenured faculty believe are important. The instructor who spends dozens of hours each week preparing for class and achieves outstanding evaluations by students but neglects his or her research and publication activities may be passed over for tenure.

What has happened, simply, is that the instructor has failed to adapt to the norms set by the department. The astute faculty member will assess early on in the probationary period what attitudes and behaviors his or her colleagues want and will then proceed to give them what they want. And, of course, by demanding certain attitudes and behaviors, the tenured faculty will have made significant strides toward standardizing tenure candidates.

One of the best-known corporate rituals is Mary Kay Cosmetics' annual award meeting. Looking like a cross between a circus and a Miss America pageant, the meeting takes place over a couple of days in a large auditorium, on a stage in front of a large, cheering audience, with all the participants dressed in glamorous evening clothes. Saleswomen are rewarded with an array of flashy gifts—gold and diamond pins, fur stoles, pink Cadillacs—based on success in achieving sales quotas. This "show" acts as a motivator by publicly recognizing outstanding sales performance. In addition, the ritual aspect reinforces Mary Kay's personal determination and optimism, which enabled her to overcome personal hardships, found her own company, and achieve material success. It conveys to her salespeople that reaching their sales quota is important and that through hard work and encouragement they too can achieve success.

Material Symbols

Fullers and Lampreia are two of Seattle's most highly rated and expensive restaurants. But, although they're less than ten blocks apart, the two restaurants convey a very different feel. Fullers is formal to the point of being "stuffy." It has a museum-level decor. The staff is formally attired, serious, focused, and stiff. In contrast, Lampreia is casual and low-key. It has a stylish but minimalist decor. The staff's casual dress and style are consistent with the decor.

Both Fullers and Lampreia consistently receive honors for their food and service; require reservations days, and sometimes weeks, ahead of time; and cost at least $80 for dinner for two. Yet the restaurants have two different cultures as reflected in things such as the decor and the employees' attire. Moreover, these material symbols convey messages to new employees. At Fullers, the message is that we're serious, formal, and conservative. The message at Lampreia, on the other hand, is that we're relaxed and open.

Messages can also be conveyed by material symbols bestowed on executives. Some corporations provide their top executives with chauffeur-driven limousines and unlimited use of the corporate jet. Executives at other firms may get a car and jet transportation paid for by the company, but the car is a Chevrolet (with no driver) and the plane seat is in the economy section of a commercial airliner.

Other examples of material symbols include the size of offices, the elegance of furnishings, executive perks, the existence of employee lounges or on-site dining facilities, and the presence of reserved parking spaces for certain employees. These material symbols convey to employees who is important, the degree of egalitarianism desired by top management, and the kinds of behavior (for example, risk-taking, conservative, authoritarian, participative, individualistic, social) that are appropriate.

Language

Many organizations and units within organizations use language as a way to identify members of a culture or subculture. By learning this language, members attest to their acceptance of the culture and, in so doing, help to preserve it.

The following are examples of terminology used by employees at Knight-Ridder Information, a California-based data redistributor: *accession number* (a number assigned each individual record in a data base); *KWIC* (a set of key-words-in-context); and *relational operator* (searching a data base for names or key terms in some order). Librarians are a rich source of terminology foreign to people outside their profession. They sprinkle their conversations liberally with acronyms such as ARL (Association for Research Libraries), OCLC (a center in Ohio that does cooperative cataloging), and OPAC (for on-line patron accessing catalog). When Louis Gerstner left RJR Nabisco to head up IBM, he had to learn a whole new vocabulary, which included: *the Orchard* (IBM's Armonk, New York, corporate headquarters, which was once an apple orchard); *big iron* (mainframe computers); *hypo* (a high-potential employee); *a one performer* (an employee with IBM's top performance rating); and *PROFS* (Professional Office Systems, IBM's internal electronic mail system).[9]

Organizations, over time, often develop unique terms to describe equipment, offices, key personnel, suppliers, customers, or products that are related to its business. New employees are frequently overwhelmed with acronyms and jargon that, after six months on the job, have become fully part of their language. Once learned, this terminology acts as a common denominator that unites members of a given culture or subculture.

Does an Organization's Culture Override a Country's National Culture?

In places throughout this book we've argued that national differences—that is, national culture—must be taken into account if accurate predictions are to be made about organizational behavior in different countries. But does national culture override an organization's culture? Is an IBM facility in Germany, for example, more likely to reflect German ethnicity or IBM's corporate culture?

The research indicates that national culture has a greater impact on employees than does their organization's culture.[10] German employees at an IBM facility in Munich, therefore, will be influenced more by German culture than by IBM's culture. Organizational culture does have a great influence on the behavior of people at work, but national culture has even more.

The preceding conclusion has to be qualified to reflect the self-selection that goes on at the hiring stage. IBM, for example, may be less concerned with hiring the "typical Italian" for its Italian operations than in hiring an Italian who fits within the IBM way of doing things. Italians who have a high need for autonomy are more likely to go to Olivetti than to IBM. Why? Because Olivetti's organizational culture is informal and nonstructured. It allows employees considerably more freedom than IBM. In fact, Olivetti seeks to hire individuals who are impatient, risk-taking, and innovative—qualities in job candidates that IBM's Italian operations would purposely seek to exclude in new hires.

Organizational Culture and the Paradox of Diversity

We briefly mention here a contemporary challenge for managers. Socializing new employees who, because of race, gender, ethnic, or other differences, are not like the majority of the organization's members creates what we call the *paradox of diversity.* Management wants new employees to accept the organization's core cultural values. Otherwise, these employees are unlikely to fit in or be accepted. But at the same time, management wants to openly acknowledge and demonstrate support for the differences that these employees bring to the workplace.

Strong cultures put considerable pressure on employees to conform. They limit the range of values and styles that are acceptable. Obviously, this creates a dilemma. Organizations hire diverse individuals because of the alternative strengths these people bring to the workplace, yet these diverse behaviors and strengths are likely to diminish in strong cultures as people attempt to fit in.

Management's challenge in this paradox of diversity is to balance two conflicting goals: Get employees to accept the organization's dominant values and encourage the acceptance of differences. Too much attention to investiture rites is likely to create employees who are misfits. On the other hand, too much emphasis on divestiture rites may eliminate those unique strengths that people of different backgrounds bring to the organization.

mplications for Managers

There seems to be little doubt that culture has a strong influence on employee behavior. But what can management do to design a culture that molds employees in the way management wants?

When an organization is just being established, management has a great deal of influence. There are no established traditions. The organization is small. There are few, if any, subcultures. Everyone knows the founder and is directly touched by his or her vision of what the organization is. Not surprisingly, under these conditions management has the opportunity to create a culture that will best facilitate the achievement of the organization's goals.

However, when the organization is well established, so too is its dominant culture. Given that this culture is made up of relatively stable and permanent characteristics, it becomes very resistant to change. It took time to form; and once established, it tends to become entrenched. Strong cultures are particularly resistant to change because employees become so committed to them. So, if a given culture, over time, becomes inappropriate to an organization and a handicap to management, there may be little management can do to change it, especially in the short run. Under the most favorable conditions, cultural changes have to be measured in years, not weeks or months.

What would those "favorable conditions" be that *might* facilitate changing a culture? The evidence suggests that cultural change is most likely to take place when most or all of the following conditions exist:[11]

A dramatic crisis: This can be the shock that undermines the status quo and calls into question the relevance of the current culture. Examples might be a surprising financial setback, the loss of a major customer, or a dramatic technological breakthrough by a competitor.

Turnover in leadership: New top leadership, who can provide an alternative set of key values, may be perceived as more capable of responding to the crisis. This would definitely encompass the organization's chief executive, but also might need to include all senior management positions.

Young and small organization: The younger the organization is, the less entrenched will be its culture. Similarly, it's easier for management to communicate its new values when the organization is small.

Weak culture: The more widely held a culture is and the higher the agreement among members on its values, the more difficult it will be to change. Weak cultures are more amenable to change than strong ones.

Keep in mind that even if these conditions exist, there is no assurance that the culture will change. Moreover, any significant change will take a long time. So, an organization's culture should be treated as an important influence on employee behavior, especially in the short and intermediate term, and something over which management has little influence.

Chapter 17

Organizational Change and Development

After reading this chapter, you should be able to:

1. Describe forces that act as stimulants to change
2. Define planned change
3. Summarize Lewin's three-step change model
4. Explain sources of resistance to change
5. List techniques for overcoming resistance to change
6. Define organizational development (OD)
7. Identify symptoms of work stress
8. Summarize sources of innovation

This chapter is about organizational change. We describe environmental forces that are requiring managers to implement comprehensive change programs. We compare two views on change. We also consider why people and organizations often resist change and how this resistance can be overcome. Finally, we present the concept of organizational development as a systemwide approach to change and introduce several contemporary issues in organizational change.

Forces for Change

More and more organizations today face a dynamic and changing environment that requires organizations to adapt. Exhibit 17-1 summarizes six specific forces that are acting as stimulants for change.

Exhibit 17-1

Forces for Change

Force	Examples
Nature of the work force	More cultural diversity Increase in professionals Many new entrants with inadequate skills
Technology	More computers and automation TQM programs Reengineering programs
Economic shocks	Security market crashes Interest-rate fluctuations Foreign currency fluctuations
Competition	Global competitors Mergers and consolidations Growth of specialty retailers
Social trends	Increase in college attendance Delayed marriages by young people Increase in divorce rate
World politics	Collapse of Soviet Union Iraq's invasion of Kuwait Overthrow of Haitian dictator

Throughout this book, we've discussed the changing *nature of the work force.* For instance, almost every organization is having to adjust to a multicultural environment. Human resource policies and practices have to change in order to attract and keep this more diverse work force. And many companies are having to spend large amounts of money on training to upgrade reading, math, computer, and other skills of employees.

As noted in Chapter 14, *technology* is changing jobs and organizations. The substitution of computer control for direct supervision, for instance, is resulting in wider spans of control for managers and flatter organizations. Sophisticated information technology is also making organizations more responsive. Companies such as AT&T, Motorola, General Electric, and Chrysler can now develop, make, and distribute their products in a fraction of the time it took them a decade ago. And, as organizations have had to become more adaptable, so too have their employees. As we noted in our discussion of groups and organizational design, many jobs are being reshaped. Individuals doing narrow, specialized, and routine jobs are being replaced by work teams whose members can perform multiple tasks and actively participate in team decisions.

We live in an "age of discontinuity." In the 1950s and 1960s, the past was a pretty good indication of the future. Tomorrow was essentially an extended trend line from yesterday. That's no longer true. Beginning in the early 1970s, with the overnight quadrupling of world oil prices, *economic shocks* have continued to impose changes on organizations. In recent years, for instance, the U.S. dollar has declined sharply against Japanese and German currencies. And, as U.S. interest rates rose rapidly in 1994, the price of bonds collapsed. Then, in 1995, interest rates turned around and incurred a dramatic decline. While these economic shocks affect some industries and firms harder than others, they can be critical when they hit.

As a case in point, many mortgage-brokerage firms had to lay off large numbers of employees in 1994 because as interest rates rose the market for new home loans and refinancings dried up.

Competition is changing. In today's global economy, competitors are as likely to come from across the ocean as from across town. Heightened competition also makes it necessary for established organizations to defend themselves against both traditional competitors who develop new products and services and small, entrepreneurial firms with innovative offerings. Successful organizations will be the ones that can change in response to the competition. They'll be fast on their feet, capable of developing new products rapidly and getting them to market quickly. They'll rely on short production runs, short product cycles, and an ongoing stream of new products. In other words, they'll be flexible. They'll require an equally flexible and responsive work force that can adapt to rapidly and even radically changing conditions.

Take a look at *social trends* during the 1970s and 1980s. They suggest changes for the 1990s that organizations have to adjust for. For instance, there has been a clear trend in marriage and divorce during the past two decades. Young people are delaying marriage, and half of all marriages are ending in divorce. One obvious result of this social trend is an increasing number of single households and demand for housing by singles. If you're in the house-building business, this is an important factor in determining the size and design of homes. Similarly, the expansion of single households has increased demand for single-portion quantities of frozen meals, which is highly relevant to organizations such as ConAgra's Healthy Choice division or Pillsbury's Green Giant.

In Chapter 2, we argued strongly for the importance of seeing OB in a global context. We then reinforced the argument in other chapters. Business schools have been preaching a global perspective since the early 1980s, but no one—not even the strongest proponents of globalization—could have imagined how *world politics* would change in recent years. A few examples make the point: the fall of the Berlin Wall, the reunification of Germany, Iraq's invasion of Kuwait, and the breakup of the Soviet Union. Almost all major U.S. defense contractors, for instance, have had to rethink their business and make serious changes in response to the demise of the Soviet Union and a shrinking Pentagon budget. Since 1991, Hughes Aircraft has laid off more than 21,000 employees; Lockheed Martin has cut 15,000 workers; and McDonnell Douglas has eliminated more than 10,000 jobs.

Managing Planned Change

A group of employees in a small retail women's clothing store confronted the owner: "The air pollution in this store from cigarette smoke has gotten awful," said their spokeswoman. "We won't continue to work here if you allow smoking in the store. We want you to post no smoking signs on the entrance doors and not allow any employee to smoke on the floor. If people have to smoke, they can go into the mall." The owner listened thoughtfully to the group's ultimatum and agreed to their request. The next day the owner posted the no smoking signs and advised all of her employees of the new rule.

A major automobile manufacturer spent several billion dollars to install state-of-the-art robotics. One area that would receive the new equipment was quality control. Sophisticated computer-controlled equipment would be put in place to significantly improve the company's ability to find and correct defects. Since the new equipment would dramatically change the jobs of the people working in the quality control area, and since management anticipated considerable employee resistance to the new equipment, executives were developing a program to help people become familiar with the equipment and to deal with any anxieties they might be feeling.

Both of the previous scenarios are examples of **change.** That is, both were concerned with making things different. However, only the second scenario described a *planned change.* Many changes in organizations are like the one that occurred in the retail clothing store—they just happen. Some organizations treat all change as an accidental occurrence. We're concerned with change activities that are proactive and purposeful. In this chapter, we address change as an intentional, goal-oriented activity.

What are the goals of **planned change?** Essentially there are two. First, it seeks to improve the ability of the organization to adapt to changes in its environment. Second, it seeks to change employee behavior.

If an organization is to survive, it must respond to changes in its environment. When competitors introduce new products or services, government agencies enact new laws, important sources of supply go out of business, or similar environmental changes take place, the organization needs to adapt. Efforts to introduce work teams, decentralized decision making, and new organizational cultures are examples of planned change activities directed at responding to changes in the environment.

Since an organization's success or failure is essentially due to the things that employees do or fail to do, planned change also is concerned with changing the behavior of individuals and groups within the organization. Later in this chapter, we review techniques that organizations can use to get people to behave differently in the tasks they perform and in their interaction with others.

Who in organizations is responsible for managing change activities? The answer is **change agents.** Change agents can be managers or nonmanagers, employees of the organization, or outside consultants. For major change efforts, internal management often will hire the services of outside consultants to provide advice and assistance. Because they are from the outside, these individuals can offer an objective perspective often unavailable to insiders. Outside consultants, however, are disadvantaged because they usually have an inadequate understanding of the organization's history, culture, operating procedures, and personnel. Outside consultants also may be prone to initiating more drastic changes—which can be a benefit or a disadvantage—because they do not have to live with the repercussions after the change is implemented. In contrast, internal staff specialists or managers, when acting as change agents, may be more thoughtful (and possibly cautious) because they must live with the consequences of their actions.

Two Views

The organization is like a large ship traveling across the calm Mediterranean Sea to a specific port. The ship's captain has made this exact trip hundreds of times before with the same crew. Every once in a while, however, a storm will appear, and the crew has to respond. The captain will make the appropriate adjustment—that is, implement changes—and, having maneuvered through the storm, will return to calm waters. Implementing change in organizations should therefore be seen as a response to a break in the status quo and needed only in occasional situations.

The organization is more akin to a forty-foot raft than to a large ship. Rather than sailing a calm sea, this raft must traverse a raging river made up of an uninterrupted flow of permanent white-water rapids. To make things worse, the raft is manned by ten people who have never worked together, none have traveled the river before, much of the trip is in the dark, the river is dotted by unexpected turns and obstacles, the exact destination of the raft is not clear, and at irregular frequencies the raft needs to pull to shore, where new crew members are added and others leave. Change is a natural state and managing change is a continual process.

These two similes present very different approaches to understanding and responding to change. Let's take a closer look at each one.[1]

The "Calm Waters" Simile

Until very recently, the "calm waters" simile dominated the thinking of practicing managers and academics. It's best illustrated in Kurt Lewin's three-step description of the change process.[2] (See Exhibit 17-2.) According to Lewin, successful change requires *unfreezing* the status quo, *changing* to a new state, and *refreezing* the new change to make it permanent. The status quo can be considered an equilibrium state. Moving from this equilibrium requires unfreezing, which can be achieved in one of three ways:

1. The *driving forces,* which direct behavior away from the status quo, can be increased.
2. The *restraining forces,* which hinder movement from the existing equilibrium, can be decreased.
3. The two approaches can be *combined.*

Once unfreezing has been accomplished, the change itself can be implemented. However, the mere introduction of change does not ensure that it will take hold. The new situation therefore needs to be *refrozen* so it can be sustained

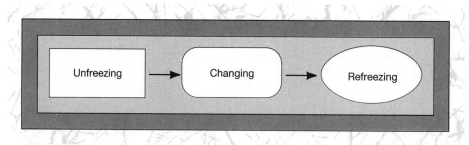

Exhibit 17-2

Lewin's Description of the Change Process

over time. Unless this last step is attended to, there is a very strong chance the change will be short-lived and employees will revert to the previous equilibrium state. The objective of refreezing, then, is to stabilize the new situation by balancing the driving and restraining forces.

Note how Lewin's three-step process treats change as a break in the organization's equilibrium state. The status quo has been disturbed, and change is necessary to establish a new equilibrium state. This view might have been appropriate to the relatively calm environment that most organizations faced in the 1950s, 1960s, and early 1970s. But one can argue that "calm waters" no longer describe the kind of seas that current managers have to negotiate.

The "White-Water Rapids" Simile

The "white-water rapids" simile is consistent with the discussion in Chapter 13 of uncertain and dynamic environments. It is also consistent with the dynamics associated with going from an industrial society to a world dominated by information and ideas.

To get a feeling for what managing change might be like when you have to continually maneuver in uninterrupted rapids, consider attending a college that has the following curriculum. Courses vary in length. Unfortunately, when you sign up, you don't know how long a course will last. It might go for two weeks or thirty weeks. Furthermore, the instructor can end a course any time he or she wants, with no prior warning. If that isn't bad enough, the length of the class changes each time it meets—sometimes it lasts twenty minutes, other times it runs for three hours—and determination of when the next class meeting will take place is set by the instructor during this class. Oh yes, there's one more thing. The exams are all unannounced, so you have to be ready for a test at any time.

To succeed in this college, you'd have to be incredibly flexible and able to respond quickly to every changing condition. Students who were overstructured, rigid, or slow on their feet wouldn't survive.

A growing number of managers are coming to accept that their job is much like what a student would face in such a college. Stability and predictability don't exist. Nor are disruptions in the status quo only occasional and temporary, followed by a return to calm waters. Many of today's managers never get out of the rapids. They face constant change, bordering on chaos. These managers are being forced to play a game they've never played before, governed by rules that are created as the game progresses.

Putting the Two Views in Perspective

Does *every* manager face a world of constant and chaotic change? No, but the set of managers who don't is dwindling rapidly.

Managers in businesses such as women's high-fashion clothing and computer software have long confronted a world that looks like white-water rapids. They used to look with envy at their counterparts in industries such as auto manufacturing, oil exploration, banking, fast-food restaurants, office equipment, publishing, telecommunications, and air transportation because these managers historically faced a stable and predictable environment. That might have been true in the 1960s, but it's not true now!

Few organizations today can treat change as the occasional disturbance in an otherwise peaceful world. Even these few do so at great risk. Too much is changing too fast for any organization or its managers to be complacent. Most competitive advantages last less than eighteen months. A firm such as People Express was described in business periodicals as the model "new look" firm, then went bankrupt a short time later. As Tom Peters aptly noted, the old saw "If it ain't broke, don't fix it" no longer applies. In its place, he suggests "If it ain't broke, you just haven't looked hard enough. Fix it anyway."[3]

Resistance to Change

One of the most well-documented findings from studies of individual and organizational behavior is that organizations and their members resist change. In a sense, this resistance is positive. It provides a degree of stability and predictability to behavior. If there weren't some resistance, organizational behavior would take on characteristics of chaotic randomness. Resistance to change can also be a source of functional conflict. For example, resistance to a reorganization plan or a change in a product line can stimulate a healthy debate over the merits of the idea and result in a better decision. But there is a definite down side to resistance to change. It hinders adaptation and progress.

Resistance to change doesn't necessarily surface in standardized ways. Resistance can be overt, implicit, immediate, or deferred. It is easiest for management to deal with resistance when it is overt and immediate. For instance, a change is proposed and employees quickly respond by voicing complaints, engaging in a work slowdown, threatening to go on strike, or the like. The greater challenge is managing resistance that is implicit or deferred. Implicit resistance efforts are subtle—loss of loyalty to the organization, loss of motivation to work, increased errors or mistakes, increased absenteeism due to "sickness"—and hence difficult to recognize. Similarly, deferred actions cloud the link between the source of the resistance and the reaction to it. A change may produce what appears to be only a minimal reaction at the time it is initiated but surfaces weeks, months, or even years later. Or a single change, in and of itself, has little impact. But it becomes the straw that breaks the camel's back. Reactions to change can build up and then explode in some response that seems totally out of proportion to the change action it follows. The resistance, of course, has merely been deferred and stockpiled. What surfaces is a response to an accumulation of changes.

Let's look at the sources of resistance. For analytical purposes, we've categorized them by individual and organizational sources. In the real world, the sources often overlap.

Individual Resistance

Individual sources of resistance to change reside in basic human characteristics such as perceptions, personalities, and needs. The following summarizes five reasons why individuals may resist change.

Habit. Every time you go out to eat do you try a different restaurant? Probably not. If you're like most people, you find a couple of places you like and return to them on a somewhat regular basis.

As human beings, we're creatures of habit. Life is complex enough; we don't need to consider the full range of options for the hundreds of decisions we have to make every day. To cope with this complexity, we all rely on habits, or programmed responses. When we are confronted with change, this tendency to respond in our accustomed ways becomes a source of resistance. When your department is moved to a new office building across town, you're likely to have to change many habits: waking up ten minutes earlier, taking a new route to work, finding a new parking place, adjusting to the new office layout, developing a new lunchtime routine, and so on.

Security. People who have a high need for security are likely to resist change because it threatens their feeling of safety. When Sears announces it's laying off 50,000 people or Ford introduces new robotic equipment, many employees at these firms may fear that their jobs are in jeopardy.

Economic Factors. Another source of individual resistance is concern that changes will lower one's income. Changes in job tasks or established work routines also can arouse economic fears if people are concerned they won't be able to perform the new tasks or routines to their previous standards, especially when pay is closely tied to productivity.

Fear of the Unknown. Changes substitute ambiguity and uncertainty for the known. Regardless of how much you may dislike attending college, at least you know what is expected of you. When you leave college and venture out into the world of full-time employment, regardless of how much you want to get out of college, you have to trade the known for the unknown.

Employees in organizations hold the same dislike for uncertainty. If, for example, the introduction of TQM requires that production workers learn statistical process control techniques, some may fear they'll be unable to do so. They may, therefore, develop a negative attitude toward TQM or behave dysfunctionally if required to use statistical techniques.

Selective Information Processing. As we learned in Chapter 3, individuals shape their world through their perceptions. Once they have created this world, they resist changing it. So individuals are guilty of selectively processing information in order to keep their perceptions intact. They hear what they want to hear. They ignore information that challenges the world they've created. The production workers who are faced with the introduction of TQM may ignore the arguments their bosses make in explaining why a knowledge of statistics is necessary or the potential benefits the change will provide them.

Organizational Resistance

Organizations, by their very nature, are conservative.[4] They actively resist change. You don't have to look far to see evidence of this phenomenon. Government agencies want to continue doing what they have been doing for years, whether the need for their service changes or remains the same. Organized religions are deeply entrenched in their history. Changing church doctrine requires great persistence and patience. Educational institutions, which exist to open minds and challenge established doctrine, are themselves extremely resistant to change. Most school systems are using essentially the same teaching technologies today as they were fifty years ago. Most business firms, too, appear highly resistant to change. Six major sources of organizational resistance have been identified.[5]

Structural Inertia.   Organizations have built-in mechanisms to produce stability. For example, the selection process systematically selects certain people in and certain people out. Training and other socialization techniques reinforce specific role requirements and skills. Formalization provides job descriptions, rules, and procedures for employees to follow.

   The people who are hired into an organization are chosen for fit; they are then shaped and directed to behave in certain ways. When an organization is confronted with change, this structural inertia acts as a counterbalance to sustain stability.

Limited Focus of Change.   Organizations are made up of interdependent subsystems. You can't change one without affecting the others. For example, if management changes the technological processes without simultaneously modifying the organization's structure to match, the change in technology is not likely to be accepted. So limited changes in subsystems tend to get nullified by the larger system.

Group Inertia.   Even if individuals want to change their behavior, group norms may act as a constraint. An individual union member, for instance, may be willing to accept changes in his job suggested by management. But if union norms dictate resisting any unilateral change made by management, he's likely to resist.

Threat to Expertise.   Changes in organizational patterns may threaten the expertise of specialized groups. The introduction of decentralized personal computers, which allow managers to gain access to information directly from a company's mainframe, is an example of a change that was strongly resisted by many information systems departments in the early 1980s. Why? Because decentralized, end-user computing was a threat to the specialized skills held by those in the centralized information systems departments.

Threat to Established Power Relationships.   Any redistribution of decision-making authority can threaten long-established power relationships within the organization. Introduction of participative decision making or autonomous work teams are examples of changes that often are seen as threats to the power of supervisors and middle managers.

Threat to Established Resource Allocations.   Those groups in the organization that control sizable resources often see change as a threat. They tend to be content with the way things are. Will the change, for instance, mean a reduction in their budgets or a cut in their staff size? Those who most benefit from the current allocation of resources are often threatened by changes that may affect future allocations.

Overcoming Resistance to Change

Six tactics have been suggested for use by change agents in dealing with resistance to change.[6] Let's review them briefly.

Education and Communication.   Resistance can be reduced through communicating with employees to help them see the logic of a change. This tactic basically assumes that the source of resistance lies in misinformation or poor communication: If employees receive the full facts and get any misunderstandings cleared up, resistance will subside. Employees can be educated through one-on-one discussions, memos, group presentations, or reports. Does this approach work? It does, provided that the source of resistance is inadequate communication and that management-employee relations are characterized by mutual trust and credibility. If those conditions do not exist, the change is unlikely to succeed. In addition, the time and effort that this tactic involves must be considered against its advantages, particularly when the change affects a large number of people.

Participation.   It's difficult for individuals to resist a change decision in which they participated. Before a change is made, those opposed can be brought into the decision process. If the participants have the expertise to make a meaningful contribution, their involvement can reduce resistance, obtain commitment, and increase the quality of the change decision. Against these advantages are the negatives: potential for a poor solution and great time consumption.

Facilitation and Support.   Change agents can offer a range of supportive efforts to reduce resistance. When employee fear and anxiety are high, employee counseling and therapy, new skills training, or a short paid leave of absence may facilitate adjustment. The drawback of this tactic is that, like education and participation, it is time-consuming. It also is expensive, and its implementation offers no assurance of success.

Negotiation.   Another way for the change agent to deal with potential resistance to change is to exchange something of value for a lessening of the resistance. For instance, if only a few powerful individuals are resisting, a specific reward package can be negotiated that will meet their individual needs. Negotiation, as a tactic, may be necessary when resistance comes from a powerful source. Yet one cannot ignore its potentially high costs. In addition, there is the risk that, once a change agent negotiates to avoid resistance, he or she is open to the possibility of being blackmailed by other individuals in positions of power.

Manipulation and Cooptation.   **Manipulation** refers to covert attempts to influence. Twisting and distorting facts to make them appear more attractive, withholding undesirable information, or creating false rumors to get employees to accept a change are all examples of manipulation. If corporate management threatens to close down a particular manufacturing plant if that plant's employees fail to accept an across-the-board pay cut, and if the threat is actually untrue, management is using manipulation. **Cooptation,** on the other hand, is a form of both manipulation and participation. It seeks to buy off the leaders of a resistance group by giving them a key role in the change decision. The leaders' advice is sought, not to seek a better decision, but to get their endorsement.

Both manipulation and cooptation are relatively inexpensive and easy ways to gain the support of adversaries, but the tactics can backfire if the targets become aware they are being tricked or used. Once discovered, the change agent's credibility may drop to zero.

Coercion. Last on the list of tactics is **coercion,** that is, the application of direct threats or force on the resisters. If the corporate management mentioned in the previous discussion were really determined to close the manufacturing plant if employees did not acquiesce to a pay cut, then coercion would be the label attached to their change tactic. Other examples of coercion include threats of transfer, loss of promotions, negative performance evaluations, or a poor letter of recommendation. The advantages and drawbacks of coercion are approximately the same as those mentioned for manipulation and cooptation.

*M*anaging Change through Organizational Development

Organizational development refers to systematic, planned change. It's not an easily definable single concept. Rather, **organizational development (OD)** is a term used to encompass a collection of change techniques or interventions, from organizationwide changes in structure and systems to psychotherapeutic counseling sessions with groups and individuals, undertaken in response to changes in the external environment that seek to improve organizational effectiveness and employee well-being.

Organizational development is built on humanistic-democratic values. In addition, OD characteristics that distinguish it from more traditional change approaches include (1) an emphasis on the work team as the key unit for learning more effective modes of organizational behavior, (2) an emphasis on participation and collaborative management, (3) an emphasis on changing the organization's culture, (4) the use of behavioral scientists as change agents, and (5) a view of the change effort as an ongoing process.[7]

What are some of the OD techniques and interventions for bringing about change? In this section, we review the more popular intervention techniques. We have categorized them under structural, task-technology, and people-focused interventions.

Structural Interventions

Structural OD interventions emphasize making organizations more organic and egalitarian. We can see this emphasis in OD programs that include major structural reorganization, introduction of new reward systems, and efforts to change organizational cultures.

Structural Reorganization. Formal structures are not chiseled in stone. The structural configuration that was right for a firm in 1987 can put it at a competitive disadvantage in 1997. So structural reorganization may be necessary. Recent trends indicate that structures are becoming flatter, more decentralized, and more organic. Notice that these trends are all consistent with OD values.

Change agents favor flatter organizations for at least three reasons. First, they provide economic benefits. By widening spans of control and cutting the number of vertical levels, the organization reduces administrative overhead costs because there are fewer managers. Second, fewer vertical levels improve communication. Third, wider spans of control typically give employees greater autonomy, since managers can't directly oversee their subordinates as closely.

Decentralized decision making is a popular intervention favored by OD change agents. Pushing authority downward creates power equalization. It allows people closest to and most knowledgeable about an issue to make decisions regarding that issue. Decentralization also gives lower-level employees greater control over their work.

The trend in OD structural interventions has been toward making organizations more organic. Change agents are trying to make organizations less bureaucratic so they can respond more quickly to changes in the environment as discussed in Chapter 13. If bureaucratic structures are necessary to maintain competitive efficiency, OD change agents have often favored adding organic subunits to gain flexibility. IBM, for instance, developed its personal computer (PC) in a small organic unit located in Florida, far from the company's headquarters in New York. Once the PC was designed by the Florida group, responsibility for the product was subsumed by the company's large and efficient production and marketing bureaucracies.

Major structural reorganizations are typically quite disruptive and threatening to the people affected. As a result, OD change agents favor employees' active participation in the reorganization process.

New Reward Systems.   Change agents enthusiastically endorse operant conditioning's notion that behavior is a function of its consequences. So they often focus on the organization's reward system.

In general, during the postwar era organizations did a poor job of linking rewards to employee performance. Production workers increasingly were paid by the hour rather than by output. Clerical and managerial personnel received a monthly salary that often had little direct relationship to productivity. In recent years, organizations have moved to enact "pay-for-performance" programs. Organizational development change agents have been actively involved in helping to develop and implement these programs. Although individual-based bonus plans are most popular, OD change agents typically favor plans that emphasize group and organizational performance in order to facilitate teamwork and cooperation.

Changing Organizational Culture.   The challenges involved in changing an organization's culture were addressed in the previous chapter. Among those who argue that change is possible, it is still clear that it's a long-term process. Regardless of the difficulty, many major corporations—for example, AT&T, Xerox, Scott Paper, and Ford Motor Company—have undertaken the task. Interestingly, consistent with OD values, the changes have been almost exclusively toward introducing new cultural values that support less management control, increased tolerance for risk and conflict, and opening up communication channels. Many large and historically successful organizations have learned the hard way that cultures can become obsolete and create serious impediments for responding to a changing environment. The emphasis has moved toward making organizational cultures more flexible, more responsive, and more focused on customer needs, service, and quality.

What are organizations that are taking on the task doing? They're reorganizing; replacing and reassigning people in key positions; changing their reward systems; creating new stories, symbols, and rituals; and modifying their selection and socialization processes to hire and support individuals who will espouse the new values.

Task-Technology Interventions

Task-technology interventions emphasize changing either the actual jobs that people do or the technological processes and tools they use to perform those jobs. Sometimes they emphasize both. Included in this category are job redesign, sociotechnical systems, and quality-of-worklife programs.

Job Redesign.   We discussed job redesign in Chapter 14. Examples of job redesign interventions include job rotation, enlargement, enrichment, and autonomous work teams.

Job redesign is similar to structural reorganization except, instead of focusing the change effort at the level of the organization, the focus is at the job level. As a result, in contrast to organizational redesign, job redesign is more widely practiced and can be implemented by lower-level supervisors as well as by senior-level managers.

Change agents have actively promoted the redesign of jobs along the lines suggested by the job characteristics model. That is, they have sought to increase the skill variety, task identity, and significance, autonomy, and feedback of jobs.

Successful job redesign interventions that follow the job characteristics model share several qualities. They have cultures that support employee autonomy and participation; they have low formalization that allows flexibility in redesigning tasks; and they either are nonunionized organizations or have the support of the union.

Sociotechnical Systems.   The accomplishment of any task requires a technology and a social system. The technology consists of the tools, techniques, procedures, skills, knowledge, and devices used by employees to do their jobs. The social system comprises the people who work in the organization and their interrelationships. Proponents of a *sociotechnical systems* approach to change argue that any successful work design must jointly optimize the social and the technological demands of the job.

When originally introduced in the 1950s, the sociotechnical systems perspective was one of the first to recognize that the needs of both the organization *and* the individual employee had to be considered in the design of work. Technology constrains the social system by shaping the behaviors required to operate it. However, if job designers ignore the personalities and attitudes of workers, their interaction patterns, their relationships with their supervisors, and the like, then the best-designed technical system will fail to achieve its full potential.

What should change agents who want to use sociotechnical systems as a guide in redesigning jobs do? Probably the best place to begin is to conceptualize work design as organizing *groups* of workers rather than *individuals* alone. Then the various technologies that are within the feasible set for achieving the group's objectives can be evaluated to find the proper match.

Quality of Worklife.   The term **quality of worklife (QWL)** describes a process by which an organization responds to employee needs by developing mechanisms to allow them to share fully in making the decisions that design their lives at work. It may help to think of QWL as an umbrella concept that encompasses literally dozens of specific interventions that have a common goal of humanizing the workplace.

Although QWL encompasses a large number of interventions, one author has divided them into eight specific categories:[8]

1. Adequate and fair compensation
2. A safe and healthy environment
3. Jobs that develop human capacities
4. A chance for personal growth and security
5. A social environment that provides personal identity, freedom from prejudice, a sense of community, and upward mobility
6. Rights of personal privacy, dissent, and due process
7. A work role that minimizes infringement on personal leisure and family needs
8. Socially responsible organizational actions

Any comprehensive list of QWL programs would encompass job redesign, participative management, and flextime, as well as programs that offer employees the opportunity to purchase equity in their firms or programs that provide protection against arbitrary action by their supervisors.

People-Focused Interventions

The vast majority of OD intervention efforts have been directed at changing the attitudes and behaviors of organizational members through the processes of communication, decision making, and problem solving. This group of interventions could include corporate training programs and management development, but OD has emphasized five specific people-focused interventions: sensitivity training, survey feedback, process consultation, team building, and intergroup development.

Sensitivity Training.   It can go by a variety of names—**sensitivity training,** laboratory training, encounter groups, or T-groups (training groups)—but all refer to a method of changing behavior through unstructured group interaction. Members are brought together in a free and open environment in which participants discuss themselves and their interactive processes. The discussion is loosely directed by a professional behavioral scientist. The group is process-oriented; individuals learn by observing and participating rather than by being told. The professional creates the opportunity for participants to express their ideas, beliefs, and attitudes. He or she does not accept—in fact, overtly rejects—any leadership role.

The objectives of the T-groups are to provide the subjects with increased awareness of their own behavior and how others perceive them, greater sensitivity to the behavior of others, and increased understanding of group processes. Specific results sought include increased ability to empathize with others, improved listening skills, greater openness, increased tolerance of individual differences, and improved conflict resolution skills.

If individuals lack awareness of how others perceive them, then the successful T-group can effect more realistic self-perceptions, greater group cohesiveness, and a reduction in dysfunctional interpersonal conflicts. Further, it will ideally result in a better integration between the individual and the organization.

Survey Feedback.   One tool for assessing attitudes held by organizational members, identifying discrepancies among member perceptions, and resolving these differences is the **survey feedback** approach. Everyone in an organization can participate in survey feedback, but of key importance is the organizational family—the manager of any given unit and those employees who report directly to him or her. A questionnaire is usually completed by all members in the organization or unit. Organizational members may be asked to suggest questions or may be interviewed to determine what issues are relevant. The questionnaire typically asks members for their perceptions and attitudes on a broad range of topics, including decision-making practices; communication effectiveness; coordination between units; and satisfaction with the organization, job, peers, and their immediate supervisor.

The data from this questionnaire are tabulated with data pertaining to an individual's specific "family" and to the entire organization and distributed to employees. These data then become the springboard for identifying problems and clarifying issues that may be creating difficulties for people. In some cases, the manager may be counseled by an external change agent about the meaning of the responses to the questionnaire and may even be given suggested guidelines for leading the organizational family in group discussion of the results. Particular attention is given to the importance of encouraging discussion and ensuring that discussions focus on issues and ideas and not on attacking individuals.

Finally, group discussion in the survey feedback approach should result in members' identifying possible implications of the questionnaire's findings. Are people listening? Are new ideas being generated? Can decision making, interpersonal relations, or job assignments be improved? Answers to such questions, it is hoped, will result in the group's agreeing on commitments to various actions that will remedy the problems identified.

Process Consultation.   No organization operates perfectly. Managers often sense that their unit's performance can be improved, but they are unable to identify what can be improved and how it can be improved. The purpose of **process consultation** is for an outside consultant to assist a client, usually a manager, to perceive, understand, and act on process events with which he or she must deal. These might include work flow, informal relationships among unit members, and formal communication channels.

Process consultation (PC) is similar to sensitivity training in its assumption that organizational effectiveness can be improved by dealing with interpersonal problems and in its emphasis on involvement. But PC is more task-directed than sensitivity training. Consultants in PC are there to give the clients insight into what is going on around them, within them, and between them and other people. They do not solve the organization's problems. Rather, the consultant is a guide or coach who advises on the process to help the clients solve their own problems.

The consultant works with the client in *jointly* diagnosing what processes need improvement. The emphasis is on *jointly*, because the client develops a skill at analyzing processes within his or her unit that can be continually called on long after the consultant is gone. In addition, having the client actively participate in both the diagnosis and the development of alternatives enhances understanding of the process and the remedy and reduces resistance to the action plan chosen.

Importantly, the process consultant need not be an expert in solving the particular problem that is identified. The consultant's expertise lies in diagnosis and developing a helping relationship. If the specific problem uncovered requires technical knowledge outside the client and consultant's expertise, the consultant helps the client locate such an expert and then instructs the client in how to get the most out of this expert resource.

Team Building. Organizations are made up of people working together to achieve a common end. Since people are frequently required to work in groups, considerable attention has been focused in OD on *team building*. Team building can be applied within groups (intragroup) or between groups (intergroup). Here, we emphasize the intragroup level and leave intergroup development to the next section.

Intragroup development concerns organizational families (command groups), committees, cross-functional teams, and task groups. The activities that form **team building** can typically include goal setting, development of interpersonal relations among team members, role analysis to clarify each member's role and responsibilities, and team process analysis. Of course, team building may emphasize or exclude certain activities, depending on the purpose of the development effort and the specific problems with which the team is confronted. Basically, however, team building attempts to use high interaction among group members to increase trust and openness.

It may be beneficial to begin by having members attempt to define the goals and priorities of the group. This exercise will bring to the surface different perceptions of what the group's purpose may be. Next, members can evaluate the group's performance—how effective are they in structuring priorities and achieving their goals? This step should identify potential problem areas. This self-critique of means and ends can be done with the total group present, or, if large size impinges on a free interchange of views, may initially take place in smaller groups followed up by the sharing of their findings with the total group.

Team building can also address the clarification of each member's role in the group. Previous ambiguities can be brought to the surface. It may offer some individuals one of the few opportunities they have had to think through what their job is all about and what specific tasks they are expected to carry out if the group is to optimize its effectiveness.

Still another team-building activity can be similar to that performed by the process consultant—that is, to analyze key processes that go on within the team to identify the way work is performed and how these processes might be improved to make the team more effective.

Intergroup Development. A major area of concern in OD is the dysfunctional conflict that exists between groups. As a result, change efforts have been directed toward improving intergroup relations.

Intergroup development seeks to change the attitudes, stereotypes, and perceptions that groups have of each other. For example, in one company the engineers saw the accounting department as composed of shy and conservative types and the human resources department as having a bunch of "smiley-types who sit around and plan company picnics." Such stereotypes can have an obvious negative impact on the coordinative efforts between the departments.

Although there are a number of approaches for improving intergroup relations, a popular method emphasizes problem solving. In this method, members of each group meet independently to develop lists of their perception of themselves, the other group, and how they believe the other group perceives them. The groups then share their lists, after which similarities and differences are discussed. Differences are clearly articulated, and the groups look for the causes of the disparities.

Are the groups' goals at odds? Were perceptions distorted? On what basis were stereotypes formulated? Have some differences been caused by misunderstandings of intentions? Have words and concepts been defined differently by each group? Answers to questions like these clarify the exact nature of the conflict. Once the causes of the difficulty have been identified, the groups can move to the integration phase and work to develop solutions that will improve relations between the groups.

Subgroups, with members from each of the conflicting groups, can now be created for further diagnosis and to begin to formulate alternative actions that will improve relations.

Contemporary Issues in Organizational Change

For many employees, change creates stress. As a result, many managers are asking, *How do I reduce stress among my work staff?* "Innovate or die" is another popular phrase in management circles. *What can managers do to help their organizations become more innovative?* In the following pages, we address these two questions.

Work Stress

Stress is a dynamic condition in which an individual is confronted with an opportunity, constraint, or demand related to what he or she desires and for which the outcome is perceived to be both uncertain and important.[9] Stress is not necessarily bad in and of itself. Although stress is often discussed in a negative context, it also has a positive value, particularly when it offers a potential gain. For example, it often helps athletes or stage performers achieve a superior performance in a critical situation. However, stress is more often associated with constraints and demands. A constraint prevents you from doing what you desire; demands refer to the loss of something desired. When you take a test at school or you undergo your annual performance review at work, you feel stress because you confront opportunity, constraints, and demands. A good performance review may lead to a promotion, greater responsibilities, and a higher salary. But a poor review may prevent you from getting the promotion. An extremely poor review might cause you to be fired.

Symptoms of Stress. What signs indicate that an employee's stress level might be too high? Stress shows itself in a number of ways. For instance, an employee who is experiencing a high level of stress may develop high blood pressure, ulcers, irritability, difficulty in making routine decisions, loss of appetite, accident proneness, and the like. These symptoms can be subsumed under three general categories: physiological, psychological, and behavioral.

Most of the early concern with stress was directed at physiological symptoms, primarily because the topic was researched by specialists in the health and medical sciences. This research led to the conclusion that stress could create changes in metabolism, increase heart and breathing rates, increase blood pressure, bring on headaches, and induce heart attacks. The link between stress and particular physiological symptoms is not clear. There are few, if any, consistent relationships. This inability to pair stress with particular symptoms is attributed to the complexity of the symptoms and the difficulty in measuring them objectively. But physiological symptoms have the least direct relevance to managers.

Of greater importance are the psychological symptoms. Stress can cause dissatisfaction. Job-related stress can cause job-related dissatisfaction. Job dissatisfaction, in fact, is the simplest and most obvious psychological effect of stress. But stress shows itself in other psychological states—for instance, tension, anxiety, irritability, boredom, and procrastination. Behavioral stress symptoms include changes in productivity, absence, and turnover, as well as changes in eating habits, increased smoking or consumption of alcohol, rapid speech, fidgeting, and sleep disorders.

Reducing Stress. Not all stress is dysfunctional. Moreover, realistically, stress can never be totally eliminated from a person's life, either off the job or on. As we review stress reduction techniques, keep in mind that our concern is with reducing the part of stress that is dysfunctional.

In terms of organizational factors, any attempt to lower stress levels has to begin with employee *selection*. Management needs to make sure that an employee's abilities match the requirements of the job. When employees are in over their heads, their stress levels will typically be high. An objective job preview during the selection process will also lessen stress by reducing ambiguity. Improved organizational communications will keep ambiguity-induced stress to a minimum. Similarly, a goal-setting program will clarify job responsibilities and provide clear performance objectives. Job redesign is also a way to reduce stress. If stress can be traced directly to boredom or work overload, jobs should be redesigned to increase challenge or reduce the work load. Redesigns that increase opportunities for employees to participate in decisions and to gain social support have also been found to lessen stress.

Stress that arises from an employee's personal life creates two problems. First, it is difficult for the manager to directly control. Second, there are ethical considerations. Specifically, does the manager have any right to intrude—even in the most subtle ways—in the employee's personal life? If a manager believes it is ethical and the employee is receptive, there are a few approaches the manager can consider. Employee *counseling* can provide stress relief. Employees often want to talk to someone about their problems; and the organization—through its managers, in-house personnel counselors, or free or low-cost outside professional help—can meet that need. For employees whose personal lives suffer from a lack of planning and organization that, in turn, creates stress, the offering of a *time management program* may prove beneficial in helping them sort out their priorities. Still another approach is organizationally sponsored *physical activity programs.* Some large corporations employ physical fitness specialists who provide employees with exercise advice, teach relaxation techniques, and show individual employees physical activities they can use to keep their stress levels down.

Stimulating Innovation

3M Company has set the standard for guiding managers in how to make their organizations more innovative.[10] 3M has developed a reputation for being able to stimulate innovation over a long period of time. It has a stated objective that twenty-five percent of each division's profits are to come from products developed in the preceding five years. In one recent year alone, 3M launched more than 200 new products.

What's the secret of 3M's success? What can other organizations do to duplicate 3M's track record for innovation? There is no guaranteed formula, but certain characteristics surface again and again when researchers study innovative organizations. We group them into structural, cultural, and human resource categories. Our message to change agents is that they should consider introducing these characteristics into their organization if they want to create an innovative climate.

Structural Variables.   Structural variables have been the most studied potential source of innovation. Findings on the structure-innovation relationship lead to the following conclusions:[11] First, organic structures positively influence innovation. Because they're lower in vertical differentiation, formalization, and centralization, organic organizations facilitate the flexibility, adaptation, and cross-fertilization that make the adoption of innovations easier. Second, long tenure in management is associated with innovation. Managerial tenure apparently provides legitimacy and knowledge of how to accomplish tasks and obtain desired outcomes. Third, innovation is nurtured where there are slack resources. Having an abundance of resources allows an organization to afford to purchase innovations, bear the cost of instituting innovations, and absorb failures. Finally, interunit communication is high in innovative organizations. These organizations are high users of committees, task forces, cross-functional, and other mechanisms that facilitate interaction across departmental lines.

Cultural Variables.   Innovative organizations tend to have similar cultures. They encourage experimentation. They reward both successes and failures. They celebrate mistakes. Unfortunately, in too many organizations, people are rewarded for the *absence* of failures rather than for the *presence* of successes. Such cultures extinguish risk taking and innovation. People will suggest and try new ideas only when they feel that such behaviors exact no penalties.

Human Resource Variables. Innovative organizations actively train and develop their members to keep them current. They offer high job security so that employees won't fear getting fired for making mistakes, and they encourage individuals to become champions of change. Once a new idea is developed, champions of change actively and enthusiastically promote the idea, build support, overcome resistance, and ensure that the innovation is implemented.

Summary. Given the status of 3M as a premier product innovator, we would expect it to have most or all of the properties we've identified. And it does. The company is so highly decentralized that it has many of the characteristics of small organic organizations. All of 3M's scientists and managers are challenged to "keep current." Idea champions are created and encouraged by allowing scientists and engineers to spend up to fifteen percent of their time on projects of their own choosing. The company encourages its employees to take risks—and it rewards the failures as well as the successes. And very importantly, 3M doesn't hire and fire with the business cycle. For instance, during the most recent recession, while almost all major companies cut costs by firing employees, 3M initiated no layoffs. When reductions in staff have been necessary, 3M has averted layoffs by relying on early retirement incentives and transfers of full-time employees to jobs filled by temporary or part-time workers.

 mplications for Managers

The need for change encompasses almost all of the concepts within organizational behavior. Think about attitudes, perceptions, teams, leadership, motivation, organizational design, and the like. It is impossible to think about these concepts without inquiring about change.

If environments were perfectly static, if employees' skills and abilities were always up-to-date and incapable of deteriorating, and if tomorrow was always exactly the same as today, organizational change would have little or no relevance to managers. But the real world is turbulent, requiring organizations and their members to undergo dynamic change if they are to perform at competitive levels.

In the past, managers could treat change as an occasional disturbance in their otherwise peaceful and predictable world. Such a world no longer exists for most managers. Today's managers are increasingly finding that their world is one of constant and chaotic change. In this world, managers must continually act as change agents.

$\mathcal{E}$pilogue

The end of a book typically has the same meaning to an author that it has to the reader: It generates feelings of both accomplishment and relief. As both of us rejoice at having completed our tour of the essential concepts in organizational behavior, this is a good time to examine where we've been and what it all means.

The underlying theme of this book has been that the behavior of people at work is *not* a random phenomenon. Employees are complex entities, but their attitudes and behavior can nevertheless be explained and predicted with a reasonable degree of accuracy. Our approach has been to look at organizational behavior at three levels: the individual, the group, and the organization system.

We started with the individual and reviewed the major psychological contributions to understanding why individuals act as they do. We found that many of the individual differences among employees can be systematically labeled and categorized, and therefore generalizations can be made. For example, we know that individuals with a conventional type of personality are better matched to certain jobs in corporate management than are people with investigative personalities. So placing people into jobs that are compatible with their personality types should result in higher-performing and more satisfied employees.

Next, our analysis moved to the group level. We argued that the understanding of group behavior is more complex than merely multiplying what we know about individuals by the number of members in the group, because people act differently when in a group than when alone. We demonstrated how roles, norms, leadership styles, power relationships, and other similar group factors affect the behavior of employees.

Finally, we overlaid systemwide variables on our knowledge of individual and group behavior to further improve our understanding of organizational behavior. Major emphasis was given to showing how an organization's structure, technological processes, work design, performance appraisal and reward systems, and culture affect both the attitudes and behavior of employees.

It may be tempting to criticize the stress this book placed on theoretical concepts. But as noted psychologist Kurt Lewin is purported to have said, "There is nothing so practical as a good theory." Of course, it is also true that there is nothing so *impractical* as a good theory that leads nowhere. To avoid presenting theories that led nowhere, this book included a wealth of examples and illustrations. And we regularly stopped to inquire about the implications of theory for the practice of management. The result has been the presentation of numerous concepts that, individually, offer some insights into behavior, but which, when taken together, provide a complex system to help you explain, predict, and control organizational behavior.

E nd Notes

CHAPTER 1

1. See M. Hammer and J. Champy, *Reengineering the Corporation: A Manifesto for Business Revolution* (New York: HarperBusiness, 1993); and J. Champy, *Reengineering Management* (New York: HarperBusiness, 1995).

2. See, for instance, R. R. Thomas Jr., "From Affirmative Action to Affirming Diversity," *Harvard Business Review*, March–April 1990, pp. 107–17; and I. Wielawski, "Diversity Makes Both Dollars and Sense," *Los Angeles Times*, May 16, 1994, p. II-3.

3. J. Dreyfuss, "Get Ready for the New Work Force," *Fortune*, April 23, 1990, p. 168.

4. B. Dumaine, "The New Non-Manager Managers," *Fortune*, February 22, 1993, pp. 80–84.

5. B. S. Moskal, "Company Loyalty Dies, A Victim of Neglect," *Industry Week*, March 1, 1993, pp. 11–12.

CHAPTER 2

1. E. Lazar, "Values Must Blend in Overseas Operations," *Personnel Journal*, February 1993, pp. 67–70.

2. D. A. Ricks, M. Y. C. Fu, and J. S. Arpas, *International Business Blunders* (Columbus, OH: Grid, 1974); and C. F. Valentine, "Blunders Abroad," *Nation's Business*, March 1989, p. 54.

3. See, for instance, J. B. Ford and E. D. Honeycutt Jr., "Japanese National Culture as a Basis for Understanding Japanese Business Practices," *Business Horizons*, November–December 1992, pp. 27–34.

4. J. Child, "Culture, Contingency and Capitalism in the Cross-National Study of Organizations," pp. 303–56 in *Research in Organizational Behavior*, vol. 3, ed. L. L. Cummings and B. M. Staw (Greenwich, CT: JAI Press, 1981).

5. Ibid.

6. G. Hofstede, *Culture's Consequences: International Differences in Work-Related Values* (Beverly Hills, CA: Sage, 1980).

7. F. Kluckhohn and F. L. Strodtbeck, *Variations in Value Orientations* (Evanston, IL: Row, Peterson, 1961).

8. G. Hofstede, *Culture's Consequences;* "The Cultural Relativity of Organizational Practices and Theories," *Journal of International Business Studies*, Fall 1983, pp. 75–89; *Cultures and Organizations: Software of the Mind* (London: McGraw-Hill, 1991); and "Cultural Constraints in Management Theories," *Academy of Management Executive*, November 1993, pp. 81–94.

9. Hofstede, "The Cultural Relativity of Organizational Practices and Theories," p. 85.

10. N. J. Adler, "Cross-Cultural Management Research: The Ostrich and the Trend," *Academy of Management Review*, April 1983, pp. 226–32. These findings have also been confirmed in L. Godkin, C. E. Braye, and C. L. Caunch, "U.S.-Based Cross-Cultural Management Research in the Eighties," *Journal of Business and Economic Perspectives*, Fall 1989, pp. 37–45; and T. K. Peng, M. F. Peterson, and Y. P. Shyi, "Quantitative Methods in Cross-National Management Research: Trends and Equivalence Issues," *Journal of Organizational Behavior* 12, no. 2 (1991), pp. 87–107.

CHAPTER 3

1. E. A. Locke, "The Nature and Causes of Job Satisfaction," pp. 1319–28, in *Handbook of Industrial and Organizational Psychology*, ed. M. D. Dunnette (Chicago: Rand McNally, 1976).

2. See, for instance, A. H. Brayfield and W. H. Crockett, "Employee Attitudes and Employee Performance," *Psychological Bulletin*, September 1955, pp. 396–428; V. H. Vroom, *Work and Motivation* (New York: Wiley, 1964); and M. M. Petty, G. W. McGee,

273

273

End Notes

and J. W. Cavender, "A Meta-Analysis of the Relationship between Individual Job Satisfaction and Individual Performance," *Academy of Management Review*, October 1984, pp. 712–21.

3. L. Festinger, *Theory of Cognitive Dissonance* (Stanford, CA: Stanford University Press, 1957).

4. A. W. Wicker, "Attitude versus Action: The Relationship of Verbal and Overt Behavioral Responses to Attitude Objects," *Journal of Social Issues*, Autumn 1969, pp. 41–78.

5. R. B. Cattell, "Personality Pinned Down," *Psychology Today*, July 1973, pp. 40–46.

6. See A. J. Vaccaro, "Personality Clash," *Personnel Administrator*, September 1988, pp. 88–92; and R. R. McCrae and P. T. Costa Jr., "Reinterpreting the Myers-Briggs Type Indicator from the Perspective of the Five-Factor Model of Personality," *Journal of Personality*, March 1989, pp. 17–40.

7. G. N. Landrum, *Profiles of Genius* (New York: Prometheus, 1993).

8. J. M. Digman, "Personality Structure: Emergence of the Five–Factor Model," pp. 417–40 in *Annual Review of Psychology*, vol. 41, ed. M. R. Rosenzweig and L. W. Porter (Palo Alto, CA: Annual Reviews, 1990).

9. M. R. Barrick and M. K. Mount, "The Big Five Personality Dimensions and Job Performance: A Meta-Analysis," *Personnel Psychology* 44 (1991), pp. 1–26; and M. R. Barrick and M. K. Mount, "Autonomy as a Moderator of the Relationships between the Big Five Personality Dimensions and Job Performance," *Journal of Applied Psychology*, February 1993, pp. 111–18.

10. J. L. Holland, *Making Vocational Choices: A Theory of Vocational Personalities and Work Environments*, 2nd ed. (Englewood Cliffs, NJ: Prentice-Hall, 1985); A. R. Spokane, "A Review of Research on Person-Environment Congruence in Holland's Theory of Careers," *Journal of Vocational Behavior*, June 1985, pp. 306–43; and T. J. Tracey and J. Rounds, "Evaluating Holland's and Gati's Vocational-Interest Models: A Structural Meta-Analysis," *Psychological Bulletin*, March 1993, pp. 229–46.

11. H. H. Kelley, "Attribution in Social Interaction," pp. 1–26 in *Attribution: Perceiving the Causes of Behavior*, ed. E. Jones et al. (Morristown, NJ: General Learning Press, 1972).

12. E. L. Thorndike, *Educational Psychology: The Psychology of Learning* (New York: Columbia University Press, 1913); and B. F. Skinner, *Beyond Freedom and Dignity* (New York: Knopf, 1971).

CHAPTER 4

1. A. Maslow, *Motivation and Personality* (New York: Harper & Row, 1954).

2. D. McGregor, *The Human Side of Enterprise* (New York: McGraw-Hill, 1960).

3. F. Herzberg, B. Mausner, and B. Snyderman, *The Motivation to Work* (New York: Wiley, 1959).

4. D. C. McClelland, *The Achieving Society* (New York: Van Nostrand Reinhold, 1961); J. W. Atkinson and J. O. Raynor, *Motivation and Achievement* (Washington, DC: Winston, 1974); and D. C. McClelland, *Power: The Inner Experience* (New York: Irvington, 1975).

5. E. A. Locke, "Toward a Theory of Task Motivation and Incentives," *Organizational Behavior and Human Performance*, May 1968, pp. 157–89; M. E. Tubbs, "Goal-Setting: A Meta-Analysis Examination of the Empirical Evidence," *Journal of Applied Psychology*, August 1986, pp. 474–83; and E. A. Locke and G. P. Latham, *A Theory of Goal Setting and Task Performance* (Englewood Cliffs, NJ: Prentice Hall, 1990).

6. F. Luthans and R. Kreitner, *Organizational Behavior Modification and Beyond: An Operant and Social Learning Approach* (Glenview, IL: Scott, Foresman, 1984).

7. J. S. Adams, "Inequity in Social Exchanges," pp. 267–300 in *Advances in Experimental Social Psychology*, ed. L. Berkowitz (New York: Academic Press, 1965); R. P. Vecchio, "Models of Psychological Inequity," *Organizational Behavior and Human Performance*, October 1984, pp. 266–82; and R. T. Mowday, "Equity Theory Predictions of Behavior in Organizations," pp. 111–31 in *Motivation and Work Behavior*, 5th ed., ed. R. Steers and L. W. Porter (New York: McGraw-Hill, 1991).

8. V. H. Vroom, *Work and Motivation* (New York: Wiley, 1964); and R. J. House, H. J. Shapiro, and M. A. Wahba, "Expectancy Theory as a Predictor of Work Behavior and Attitudes: A Re-Evaluation of Empirical Evidence," *Decision Sciences*, January 1974, pp. 481–506.

CHAPTER 5

1. P. F. Drucker, *The Practice of Management* (New York: Harper & Row, 1954).

2. See, for instance, F. Schuster and A. F. Kendall, "Management by Objectives, Where We Stand—A Survey of the Fortune 500," *Human Resource Management*, Spring 1974, pp. 8–11; and R. Rodgers and J. E. Hunter, "A Foundation of Good Management Practice in Government: Management by Objectives," *Public Administration Review*, January–February 1992, pp. 27–39.

3. "At Emery Air Freight: Positive Reinforcement Boosts Performance," *Organizational Dynamics*, Winter 1973, pp. 41–50.

4. F. Luthans and R. Kreitner, *Organizational Behavior Modification and Beyond: An Operant and Social Learning Approach* (Glenview, IL: Scott, Foresman, 1985).

5. F. Luthans and R. Kreitner, "The Management of Behavioral Contingencies," *Personnel*, July–August 1974, pp. 7–16.

6. Luthans and Kreitner, *Organizational Behavior Modification and Beyond*, Chapter 8.

7. See W. C. Hamner and E. P. Hamner, "Behavior Modification on the Bottom Line," *Organizational Dynamics*, Spring 1976, pp. 12–24; and "Productivity Gains from a Pat on the Back," *Business Week*, January 23, 1978, pp. 56–62.

8. M. P. Heller, "Money Talks, Xerox Listens," *Business Month*, September 1990, pp. 91–92.

9. J. L. Cotton, *Employee Involvement* (Newbury Park, CA: Sage, 1993), pp. 3, 14.

10. Ibid., p. 3.

11. M. Sashkin, "Participative Management Is an Ethical Imperative," *Organizational Dynamics*, Spring 1984, pp. 5–22.

12. R. Tannenbaum, I. R. Weschler, and F. Massarik, *Leadership and Organization: A Behavioral Science Approach* (New York: McGraw-Hill, 1961), pp. 88–100.

13. See E. Locke and D. Schweiger, "Participation in Decision Making: One More Look," pp. 265–339 in *Research in Organizational Behavior*, vol. 1, ed. B. M. Staw (Greenwich, CT: JAI Press, 1979); J. L. Cotton, D. A. Vollrath, K. L. Froggatt, M. L. Lengnick-Hall, and K. R. Jennings, "Employee Participation: Diverse Forms and Different Outcomes," *Academy of Manage-*

ment Review, January 1988, pp. 8–22; and J. A. Wagner III, "Participation's Effects on Performance and Satisfaction: A Reconsideration of Research Evidence," *Academy of Management Review*, April 1994, pp. 312–20.

14. Cotton, *Employee Involvement*, p. 114.

15. Ibid., p. 140.

16. Ibid., p. 59.

17. Ibid., p. 76.

18. C. M. Rosen and M. Quarrey, "How Well Is Employee-Ownership Working?" *Harvard Business Review*, September–October 1987, pp. 126–32.

19. See Cotton, *Employee Involvement*, pp. 89–113; and W. Imberman, "Boosting Plan Performance with Gainsharing," *Business Horizons*, November–December 1992, p. 79.

20. M. Fein, "Work Measurement and Wage Incentives," *Industrial Engineering*, September 1973, pp. 49–51.

21. J. S. Lublin, "A New Track," *Wall Street Journal*, April 22, 1992, p. R5.

22. K. Hannon, "Variable-Pay Programs: Where the Real Raises Are," *Working Woman*, March 1994, p. 48.

23. Ibid., p. 50.

24. D. Beck, "Implementing a Gainsharing Plan: What Companies Need to Know," *Compensation & Benefits Review*, January–February 1992, p. 23.

25. E. E. Lawler III, G. E. Ledford Jr., and L. Chang, "Who Uses Skill-Based Pay, and Why," *Compensation & Benefits Review*, March–April 1993, p. 22.

26. Ibid.

27. Ibid.

28. F. R. Bleakley, "Many Companies Try Management Fads, Only to See Them Flop," *Wall Street Journal*, July 6, 1993, p. A6.

29. "Skill-Based Pay Boosts Worker Productivity and Morale," *Wall Street Journal*, June 23, 1992, p. A1.

30. M. Rowland, "It's What You Can Do That Counts," *New York Times*, June 6, 1993, p. F17.

CHAPTER 6

1. For a review of the rational model, see E. F. Harrison, *The Managerial Decision-Making Process*, 4th ed. (Boston: Houghton Mifflin, 1995), pp. 75–113.

2. C. G. Morris, *Psychology: An Introduction*, 8th ed. (Englewood Cliffs, NJ: Prentice Hall, 1993), p. 341.

3. M. A. Colgrove, "Stimulating Creative Problem Solving: Innovative Set," *Psychological Reports*, 22 (1968), pp. 1205–11.

4. See M. Stein, *Stimulating Creativity*, vol. 1 (New York: Academic Press, 1974).

5. E. deBono, *Lateral Thinking: Creativity Step by Step* (New York: Harper & Row, 1971).

6. M. Bazerman, *Judgment in Managerial Decision Making*, 3rd ed. (New York: Wiley, 1994), p. 5.

7. See H. A. Simon, *Administrative Behavior*, 3rd ed. (New York: Free Press, 1976); and J. Forester, "Bounded Rationality and the Politics of Muddling Through," *Public Administration Review*, January–February 1984, pp. 23–31.

8. See K. R. Hammond, R. M. Hamm, J. Grassia, and T. Pearson, "Direct Comparison of the Efficacy of Intuitive and Analytical Cognition in Expert Judgment," *IEEE Transactions on Systems, Man and Cybernetics*, SMC-17, 1987, pp. 753–70; W. H. Agor, ed., *Intuition in Organizations* (Newbury Park, CA: Sage, 1989); and O. Behling and N. L. Eckel, "Making Sense Out of Intuition," *Academy of Management Executive*, February 1991, pp. 46–47.

9. As described in H. A. Simon, "Making Management Decisions: The Role of Intuition and Emotion," *Academy of Management Executive*, February 1987, pp. 59–60.

10. See, for example, M. D. Cohen, J. G. March, and J. P. Olsen, "A Garbage Can Model of Organizational Choice," *Administrative Science Quarterly*, March 1972, pp. 1–25.

11. See J. G. Thompson, *Organizations in Action* (New York: McGraw-Hill, 1967), p. 123.

12. C. E. Lindholm, "The Science of 'Muddling Through,'" *Public Administration Review*, Spring 1959, pp. 79–88.

13. A. Tversky and D. Kahneman, "Judgment under Uncertainty: Heuristics and Biases," *Science*, September 1974, pp. 1124–31.

14. See B. M. Staw, "The Escalation of Commitment to a Course of Action," *Academy of Management Review*, October 1981, pp. 577–87; and D. R. Bobocel and J. P. Meyer, "Escalating Commitment to a Failing Course of Action: Separating the Roles of Choice and Justification," *Journal of Applied Psychology*, June 1994, pp. 360–63.

15. A. J. Rowe, J. D. Boulgarides, and M. R. McGrath, *Managerial Decision Making*, Modules in Management Series (Chicago: SRA, 1984), pp. 18–22.

16. L. Kohlberg, *Essays in Moral Development: The Philosophy of Moral Development*, vol. 1 (New York: Harper & Row, 1981); and L. Kohlberg, *Essays in Moral Development: The Psychology of Moral Development*, vol. 2 (New York: Harper & Row, 1984).

17. See, for example, J. Weber, "Managers' Moral Reasoning: Assessing Their Responses to Three Moral Dilemmas," *Human Relations*, July 1990, pp. 687–702; and S. B. Knouse and R. A. Giacalone, "Ethical Decision-Making in Business: Behavioral Issues and Concerns," *Journal of Business Ethics*, May 1992, pp. 369–77.

18. S. N. Chakravarty and A. Feldman, "The Road Not Taken," *Forbes*, August 30, 1993, pp. 40–41.

19. A. Wildavsky, *The Politics of the Budgetary Process* (Boston: Little, Brown & Co., 1964).

20. N. J. Adler, *International Dimensions of Organizational Behavior*, 2nd ed. (Boston: Kent Publishing, 1991), pp. 160–68.

CHAPTER 7

1. See, for example, R. K. Merton, *Social Theory and Social Structure* (New York: Free Press, 1968); and S. E. Jackson and R. S. Schuler, "A Meta-Analysis and Conceptual Critique of Research on Role Ambiguity and Role Conflict in Work Settings," *Organizational Behavior and Human Decision Processes*, August 1985, pp. 16–78.

2. D. C. Feldman, "The Development and Enforcement of Group Norms," *Academy of Management Review*, January 1984, pp. 47–53; and J. R. Hackman, "Group Influences on Individuals in Organizations," pp. 235–50 in *Handbook of Industrial and Organizational Psychology*, vol. 3, 2nd ed. ed. M. D. Dunnette and L. M. Hough (Palo Alto, CA: Consulting Psychologists Press, 1992).

3. E. Mayo, *The Human Problems of an Industrial Civilization* (New York: Macmillan, 1933); and F. J. Roethlisberger and W. J. Dickson, *Management and the Worker* (Cambridge, MA: Harvard University Press, 1939).

4. S. E. Asch, "Effects of Group Pressure upon the Modification and Distortion of Judgments," pp. 177–90 in *Groups, Leadership and Men,* ed. H. Guetzkow (Pittsburgh, PA: Carnegie Press, 1951).

5. I. Summers, T. Coffelt, and R. E. Horton, "Work-Group Cohesion," *Psychological Reports,* October 1988, pp. 627–36; and B. Mullen and C. Copper, "The Relation between Group Cohesiveness and Performance: An Integration," *Psychological Bulletin,* March 1994, pp. 210–27.

6. Based on J. L. Gibson, J. M. Ivancevich, and J. H. Donnelly Jr., *Organizations* 8th ed (Burr Ridge, IL: Irwin, 1994), p. 323.

7. E. J. Thomas and C. F. Fink, "Effects of Group Size," *Psychological Bulletin,* July 1963, pp. 371–84; A. P. Hare, *Handbook of Small Group Research* (New York: Free Press, 1976); and M. E. Shaw, *Group Dynamics: The Psychology of Small Group Behavior,* 3rd ed. (New York: McGraw Hill, 1981).

8. W. Moede, "Die Richtlinien der Leistungs-Psychologie," *Industrielle Psychotechnik* 4 (1927), pp. 193–207. See also D. A. Kravitz and B. Martin, "Ringelmann Rediscovered: The Original Article," *Journal of Personality and Social Psychology,* May 1986, pp. 936–41.

9. See, for example, J. A. Shepperd, "Productivity Loss in Performance Groups: A Motivation Analysis," *Psychological Bulletin,* January 1993, pp. 67–81; and S. J. Karau and K. D. Williams, "Social Loafing: A Meta-Analysis Review and Theoretical Integration," *Journal of Personality and Social Psychology,* October 1993, pp. 681–706.

10. See, for example, P. S. Goodman, E. C. Ravlin, and L. Argote, "Current Thinking about Groups: Setting the Stage for New Ideas," pp. 15–16 in *Designing Effective Work Groups,* ed. P. S. Goodman and associates (San Francisco: Jossey-Bass, 1986); and R. A. Guzzo and G. P. Shea, "Group Performance and Intergroup Relations in Organizations," pp. 288–90 in Dunnette and Hough, *Handbook of Industrial & Organizational Psychology.*

11. M. E. Shaw, *Contemporary Topics in Social Psychology* (Morristown, NJ: General Learning Press, 1976), p. 356.

12. W. E. Watson, K. Kumar, and L. K. Michaelsen, "Cultural Diversity's Impact on Interaction Process and Performance: Comparing Homogeneous and Diverse Task Groups," *Academy of Management Journal,* June 1993, pp. 590–602.

13. W. F. Whyte, "The Social Structure of the Restaurant," *American Journal of Sociology,* January 1954, pp. 302–08.

14. V. H. Vroom and A. G. Jago, *The New Leadership: Managing Participation in Organizations* (Englewood Cliffs, NJ: Prentice Hall, 1988).

15. See I. L. Janis, *Groupthink* (Boston: Houghton Mifflin, 1982); S. Smith, "Groupthink and the Hostage Rescue Mission," *British Journal of Political Science* 15 (1984), pp. 117–23; and G. Moorhead, R. Ference, and C. P. Neck, "Group Decision Fiascoes Continue: Space Shuttle *Challenger* and a Revised Framework," *Human Relations,* May 1991, pp. 539–50.

16. C. R. Leana, "A Partial Test of Janis' Groupthink Model: Effects of Group Cohesiveness and Leader Behavior on Defective Decision Making," *Journal of Management,* Spring 1985, pp. 5–17; G. Moorhead and J. R. Montanari, "An Empirical Investigation of the Groupthink Phenomenon," *Human Relations,* May 1986, pp. 399–410; and C. P. Neck and G. Moorhead, "Groupthink Remodeled: The Importance of Leadership, Time Pressure, and Methodical Decision-Making Procedures," *Human Relations,* May 1995, pp. 537–57.

17. See, for example, N. Kogan and M. A. Wallach, "Risk Taking as a Function of the Situation, the Person, and the Group," in *New Directions in Psychology,* vol. 3 (New York: Holt, Rinehart and Winston, 1967); and M. A. Wallach, N. Kogan, and D. J. Bem, "Group Influence on Individual Risk Taking," *Journal of Abnormal and Social Psychology* 65 (1962), pp. 75–86.

18. S. G. Harkins and K. Szymanski, "Social Loafing and Group Evaluation," *Journal of Personality and Social Psychology,* December 1989, pp. 934–41.

19. See P. C. Earley, "Social Loafing and Collectivism: A Comparison of the United States and the People's Republic of China," *Administrative Science Quarterly,* December 1989, pp. 565–81; and P. C. Earley, "East Meets West Meets Mideast: Further Explorations of Collectivistic and Individualistic Work Groups," *Academy of Management Journal,* April 1993, pp. 319–48.

CHAPTER 8

1. Based on B. Acohido, "Boeing Workforce Tries New Direction," *Dallas Morning News,* May 5, 1991, p. H8; D. Jones Yang, "When the Going Gets Tough, Boeing Gets Touchy-Feely," *Business Week,* January 17, 1994, pp. 65–66; and W. J. Cook, "The End of the Plain Plane," *U.S. News & World Report,* April 11, 1994, pp. 43–46.

2. See, for example, D. Tjosvold, *Working Together to Get Things Done: Managing for Organizational Productivity* (Lexington, MA: Lexington Books, 1986); Tjosvold, *Team Organization: An Enduring Competitive Advantage* (Chichester, England: Wiley, 1991); J. Lipnack and J. Stamps, *The TeamNet Factor* (Essex Junction, VT: Oliver Wight, 1993); and J. R. Katzenbach and D. K. Smith, *The Wisdom of Teams* (Boston: Harvard Business School Press, 1993).

3. J. Hillkirk, "Self-Directed Work Teams Give TI Lift," *USA Today,* December 20, 1993, p. 8B; and M. A. Verespej, "Worker-Managers," *Industry Week,* May 16, 1994, p. 30.

4. J. S. Lublin, "Trying to Increase Worker Productivity, More Employers Alter Management Style," *Wall Street Journal,* February 13, 1992, p. B1.

5. See, for instance, T. D. Wall, N. J. Kemp, P. R. Jackson, and C. W. Clegg, "Outcomes of Autonomous Workgroups: A Long-Term Field Experiment," *Academy of Management Journal,* June 1986, pp. 280–304; and J. L. Cordery, W. S. Mueller, and L. M. Smith, "Attitudinal and Behavioral Effects of Autonomous Group Working: A Longitudinal Field Study," *Academy of Management Journal,* June 1991, pp. 464–76.

6. T. B. Kinni, "Boundary-Busting Teamwork," *Industry Week,* March 21, 1994, p. 73.

7. This section is largely based on K. Hess, *Creating the High-Performance Team* (New York: Wiley, 1987); and Katzenbach and Smith, *The Wisdom of Teams,* pp. 43–64.

8. Based on C. Margerison and D. McCann, *Team Management: Practical New Approaches* (London: Mercury Books, 1990).

9. P. L. Schindler and C. C. Thomas, "The Structure of Interpersonal Trust in the Workplace," *Psychological Reports,* October 1993, pp. 563–73.

10. Ibid.

11. Ibid.

12. Based on F. Bartolome, "Nobody Trusts the Boss Completely—Now What?" *Harvard Business Review,* March–April 1989, pp. 135–42; and P. Pascarella, "15 Ways to Win People's Trust," *Industry Week,* February 1, 1993, pp. 47–51.

13. D. Harrington-Mackin, *The Team Building Tool Kit* (New York: AMACOM, 1994), p. 53.

14. T. D. Schellhardt, "To Be a Star among Equals, Be a Team Player," *Wall Street Journal,* April 20, 1994, p. B1.

CHAPTER 9

1. See, for example, K. W. Thomas and W. H. Schmidt, "A Survey of Managerial Interests with Respect to Conflict," *Academy of Management Journal,* June 1976, p. 317.

2. W. G. Scott and T. R. Mitchell, *Organization Theory: A Structural and Behavioral Analysis* (Homewood, IL: Richard D. Irwin, 1976).

3. B. Smith, "FedEx's Key to Success," *Management Review,* July 1993, pp. 23–24.

4. A. Bavelas and D. Barrett, "An Experimental Approach to Organizational Communication," *Personnel,* March 1951, p. 370.

5. K. Davis, "Management Communication and the Grapevine," *Harvard Business Review,* September–October 1953, pp. 43–49.

6. H. Sutton and L. W. Porter, "A Study of the Grapevine in a Governmental Organization," *Personnel Psychology,* Summer 1968, pp. 223–30.

7. K. Davis, cited in R. Rowan, "Where Did That Rumor Come From?" *Fortune,* August 13, 1979, p. 134.

8. D. Tannen, *You Just Don't Understand: Women and Men in Conversation* (New York: Ballantine Books, 1991).

9. This section is based on N. J. Adler, *International Dimensions of Organizational Behavior,* 2nd ed. (Boston: PWS-Kent, 1991), pp. 83–84.

CHAPTER 10

1. S. A. Kirkpatrick and E. A. Locke, "Leadership: Do Traits Matter?" *Academy of Management Executive,* May 1991, pp. 48–60.

2. R. M. Stogdill and A. E. Coons, eds., *Leader Behavior: Its Description and Measurement,* Research

Monograph No. 88 (Columbus: Ohio State University, Bureau of Business Research, 1951); and B. M. Fisher, "Consideration and Initiating Structure and Their Relationships with Leader Effectiveness: A Meta-Analysis," pp. 201–05 in *Proceedings of the 48th Academy of Management Conference,* ed. F. Hoy (Anaheim, CA: 1988).

3. R. Kahn and D. Katz, "Leadership Practices in Relation to Productivity and Morale," in *Group Dynamics: Research and Theory,* 2nd ed., ed. D. Cartwright and A. Zander (Elmsford, NY: Row, Peterson, 1960).

4. R. R. Blake and J. S. Mouton, *The Managerial Grid* (Houston: Gulf, 1964).

5. See, for example, L. L. Larson, J. G. Hunt, and R. N. Osborn, "The Great Hi-Hi Leader Behavior Myth: A Lesson from Occam's Razor," *Academy of Management Journal,* December 1976, pp. 628–41; and P. C. Nystrom, "Managers and the Hi-Hi Leader Myth," *Academy of Management Journal,* June 1978, pp. 325–31.

6. F. E. Fiedler, *A Theory of Leadership Effectiveness* (New York: McGraw-Hill, 1967).

7. C. A. Schriesheim, B. J. Tepper, and L. A. Tetrault, "Least Preferred Co-Worker Score, Situational Control, and Leadership Effectiveness: A Meta-Analysis of Contingency Model Performance Predictions," *Journal of Applied Psychology,* August 1994, pp. 561–73.

8. R. J. House, "A Path-Goal Theory of Leader Effectiveness," *Administrative Science Quarterly,* September 1971, pp. 321–38.

9. See J. C. Wofford and L. Z. Liska, "Path-Goal Theories of Leadership: A Meta-Analysis," *Journal of Management,* Winter 1993, pp. 857–76.

10. V. H. Vroom and P. W. Yetton, *Leadership and Decision Making* (Pittsburgh: University of Pittsburgh Press, 1973).

11. V. H. Vroom and A. G. Jago, *The New Leadership: Managing Participation in Organizations* (Englewood Cliffs, NJ: Prentice Hall, 1988).

12. The material in this section is based on J. Grant, "Women as Managers: What They Can Offer to Organizations," *Organizational Dynamics,* Winter 1988, pp. 56–63; S. Helgesen, *The Female Advantage: Women's Ways of Leadership* (New York: Doubleday, 1990); A. H. Eagly and B. T. Johnson, "Gender and Leadership Style: A Meta-Analysis," *Psychological Bulletin,* September 1990, pp. 233–56; A. H. Eagly and S. J. Karau, "Gender and the Emergence of Leaders: A Meta-Analysis," *Journal of Personality and Social Psychology,* May 1991, pp. 685–710; and A. H. Eagly, M. G. Makhijani, and B. G. Klonsky, "Gender and the Evaluation of Leaders: A Meta-Analysis," *Psychological Bulletin,* January 1992, pp. 3–22.

13. J. A. Conger and R. N. Kanungo, "Behavioral Dimensions of Charismatic Leadership," pp. 78–97 in *Charismatic Leadership,* J. A. Conger, R. N. Kanungo, and Associates (San Francisco: Jossey-Bass, 1988).

14. R. J. House, J. Woycke, and E. M. Fodor, "Charismatic and Noncharismatic Leaders: Differences in Behavior and Effectiveness," pp. 103–04 in Conger, Kanungo, and associates, *Charismatic Leadership;* and D. A. Waldman, B. M. Bass, and F. J. Yammarino, "Adding to Contingent-Reward Behavior: The Augmenting Effect of Charismatic Leadership," *Group & Organization Studies,* December 1990, pp. 381–94.

15. J. M. Howell and P. J. Frost, "A Laboratory Study of Charismatic Leadership," *Organizational Behavior and Human Decision Processes,* April 1989, pp. 243–69.

16. See, for instance, S. Kerr and J. M. Jermier, "Substitutes for Leadership: Their Meaning and Measurement," *Organizational Behavior and Human Performance,* December 1978, pp. 375–403; and P. M. Podsakoff, B. P. Niehoff, S. B. MacKenzie, and M. L. Williams, "Do Substitutes for Leadership Really Substitute for Leadership? An Empirical Examination of Kerr and Jermier's Situational Leadership Model," *Organizational Behavior and Human Decision Processes,* February 1993, pp. 1–44.

CHAPTER 11

1. R. M. Kanter, "Power Failure in Management Circuits," *Harvard Business Review,* July–August 1979, p. 65.

2. J. R. P. French Jr. and B. Raven, "The Bases of Social Power," pp. 150–67 in *Studies in Social Power,* ed. D. Cartwright (Ann Arbor: University of Michigan, Institute for Social Research, 1959).

3. D. Kipnis, *The Powerholders* (Chicago: University of Chicago Press, 1976), pp. 77–78.

4. R. E. Emerson, "Power-Dependence Relations," *American Sociological Review* 27, (1962), pp. 31–41.

5. H. Mintzberg, *Power In and Around Organizations* (Englewood Cliffs, NJ: Prentice Hall, 1983), p. 24.

6. This discussion is based on J. N. Cleveland and M. E. Kerst, "Sexual Harassment and Perceptions of Power: An Under-Articulated Relationship," *Journal of Vocational Behavior*, February 1993, pp. 49–67.

7. D. J. Vredenburgh and J. G. Maurer, "A Process Framework of Organizational Politics," *Human Relations*, January 1984, pp. 47–66.

8. D. Farrell and J. C. Petersen, "Patterns of Political Behavior in Organizations," *Academy of Management Review,* July 1982, p. 405.

9. See, for example, G. Biberman, "Personality and Characteristic Work Attitudes of Persons with High, Moderate, and Low Political Tendencies," *Psychological Reports,* October 1985, pp. 1303–10; and G. R. Ferris, G. S. Russ, and P. M. Fandt, "Politics in Organizations," pp. 155–56 in *Impression Management in the Organization,* ed. R. A. Giacalone and P. Rosenfeld (Hillsdale, NJ: Erlbaum, 1989).

10. See, for example, Farrell and Petersen, "Patterns of Political Behavior in Organizations," p. 409; P. M. Fandt and G. R. Ferris, "The Management of Information and Impressions: When Employees Behave Opportunistically," *Organizational Behavior and Human Decision Processes,* February 1990, pp. 140–58; and Ferris, Russ, and Fandt, "Politics in Organizations," p. 147.

11. See, for instance, B. R. Schlenker, *Impression Management: The Self-Concept, Social Identity, and Interpersonal Relations* (Monterey, CA: Brooks/Cole, 1980); and D. C. Gilmore and G. R. Ferris, "The Effects of Applicant Impression Management Tactics on Interviewer Judgments," *Journal of Management,* December 1989, pp. 557–64.

12. Based on Schlenker, *Impression Management;* W. L. Gardner and M. J. Martinko, "Impression Management in Organizations," *Journal of Management,* June 1988, p. 332; and R. B. Cladini, "Indirect Tactics of Image Management: Beyond Basking," pp. 45–71 in Giacalone and Rosenfeld, *Impression Management in the Organization.*

13. R. A. Baron, "Impression Management by Applicants during Employment Interviews: The 'Too Much of a Good Thing' Effect," pp. 204–15 in *The Employment Interview: Theory, Research, and Practice,* ed. R. W. Eder and G. R. Ferris (Newbury Park, CA: Sage, 1989); Gilmore and Ferris, "The Effects of Applicant Impression Management Tactics on Interviewer Judgments"; and A. L. Kristof and C. K. Stevens, "Applicant Impression Management Tactics: Effects on Interviewer Evaluations and Interview Outcomes," pp. 127–31 in *Proceedings of the National Academy of Management Conference,* ed. D. P. Moore (Dallas: August 1994).

14. Gilmore and Ferris, "The Effects of Applicant Impression Management Tactics on Interviewer Judgments."

15. G. F. Cavanagh, D. J. Moberg, and M. Valasquez, "The Ethics of Organizational Politics," *Academy of Management Review,* July 1981, pp. 363–74.

CHAPTER 12

1. S. P. Robbins, *Managing Organizational Conflict: A Nontraditional Approach* (Englewood Cliffs, NJ: Prentice Hall, 1974).

2. This section is based on Robbins, *Managing Organizational Conflict,* pp. 31–55.

3. K. W. Thomas, "Conflict and Negotiation Processes in Organizations," pp. 651–717 in *Handbook of Industrial and Organizational Psychology,* vol. 3, 2nd ed., ed. M. D. Dunnette and L. M. Hough (Palo Alto, CA: Consulting Psychologists Press, 1992).

4. See, for instance, C. J. Loomis, "Dinosaurs?" *Fortune,* May 3, 1993, pp. 36–42.

5. I. L. Janis, *Victims of Groupthink* (Boston: Houghton Mifflin, 1972).

6. J. Hall and M. S. Williams, "A Comparison of Decision-Making Performances in Established and Ad-Hoc Groups," *Journal of Personality and Social Psychology,* February 1966, p. 217.

7. R. L. Hoffman, "Homogeneity of Member Personality and Its Effect on Group Problem Solving," *Journal of Abnormal and Social Psychology,* January 1959, pp. 27–32; R. L. Hoffman and N. R. F. Maier, "Quality and Acceptance of Problem Solutions by Members of Homogeneous and Heterogeneous Groups," *Journal of Abnormal and Social Psychology,* March 1961, pp. 401–07.

8. J. A. Wall Jr., *Negotiation: Theory and Practice* (Glenview, IL: Scott, Foresman, 1985).

9. R. E. Walton and R. B. McKersie, *A Behavioral Theory of Labor Negotiations: An Analysis of a Social Interaction System* (New York: McGraw-Hill, 1965).

10. M. H. Bazerman and M. A. Neale, *Negotiating Rationally* (New York: Free Press, 1992), pp. 67–68.

11. J. A. Wall Jr. and M. W. Blum, "Negotiations," *Journal of Management,* June 1991, pp. 276–78.

12. See N. J. Adler, *International Dimensions of Organizational Behavior,* 2nd ed. (Boston: PWS-Kent, 1991), pp. 179–217.

13. K. D. Schmidt, *Doing Business in France* (Menlo Park, CA: SRI International, 1987).

14. S. Lubman, "Round and Round," *Wall Street Journal,* December 10, 1993, p. R3.

15. E. S. Glenn, D. Witmeyer, and K. A. Stevenson, "Cultural Styles of Persuasion," *Journal of Intercultural Relations,* Fall 1977, pp. 52–66.

16. J. Graham, "The Influence of Culture on Business Negotiations," *Journal of International Business Studies,* Spring 1985, pp. 81–96.

17. K. W. Thomas, "Toward Multidimensional Values in Teaching: The Example of Conflict Behaviors," *Academy of Management Review,* July 1977, p. 487.

18. Based on R. Fisher and W. Ury, *Getting to Yes: Negotiating Agreement without Giving In* (Boston: Houghton Mifflin, 1981); Wall and Blum, "Negotiations," pp. 295–96; and Bazerman and Neale, *Negotiating Rationally.*

CHAPTER 13

1. See, for instance, R. L. Daft, *Organization Theory and Design,* 5th ed. (St. Paul, MN: West Publishing, 1995).

2. A. Ross, "BMO's Big Bang," *Canadian Business,* January 1994, pp. 58–63.

3. J. B. Levine, "For IBM Europe, 'This Is the Year of Truth,'" *Business Week,* April 19, 1993, p. 45.

4. H. Mintzberg, *Structure in Fives: Designing Effective Organizations* (Englewood Cliffs, NJ: Prentice Hall, 1983), p. 157.

5. Cited in *At Work,* May–June 1993, p. 3.

6. L. Brokaw, "Thinking Flat," *INC.,* October 1993, p. 88.

7. "GE: Just Your Average Everyday $60 Billion Family Grocery Store," *Industry Week,* May 2, 1994, pp. 13–18.

8. This analysis is referred to as a contingency approach to organizational design. See, for instance, J. M. Pennings, "Structural Contingency Theory: A Reappraisal," pp. 267–309 in *Research in Organizational Behavior,* vol. 14, ed. B. M. Staw and L. L. Cummings (Greenwich, CT: Jai Press, 1992).

9. See R. E. Miles and C. C. Snow, *Organizational Strategy, Structure, and Process* (New York: McGraw-Hill, 1978); and D. C. Galunic and K. M. Eisenhardt, "Renewing the Strategy-Structure-Performance Paradigm," pp. 215–55 in *Research in Organizational Behavior,* vol. 16, ed. B. M. Staw and L. L. Cummings, (Greenwich, CT: Jai Press, 1994).

10. See, for instance, P. M. Blau and R. A. Schoenherr, *The Structure of Organizations* (New York: Basic Books, 1971); and R. Z. Gooding and J. A. Wagner III, "A Meta-Analytic Review of the Relationship between Size and Performance: The Productivity and Efficiency of Organizations and Their Subunits," *Administrative Science Quarterly,* December 1985, pp. 462–81.

11. See J. Woodward, *Industrial Organization: Theory and Practice* (London: Oxford University Press, 1965); C. Perrow, "A Framework for the Comparative Analysis of Organizations," *American Sociological Review,* April 1967, pp. 194–208; and C. C. Miller, W. H. Glick, Y. Wang, and G. P. Huber, "Understanding Technology–Structure Relationships: Theory Development and Meta-Analytic Theory Testing," *Academy of Management Journal,* June 1991, pp. 370–99.

12. See F. E. Emery and E. Trist, "The Causal Texture of Organizational Environments," *Human Relations,* February 1965, pp. 21–32; and P. Lawrence and J. W. Lorsch, *Organization and Environment: Managing Differentiation and Integration* (Boston: Harvard Business School, Division of Research, 1967).

13. See, for instance, L. W. Porter and E. E. Lawler III, "Properties of Organization Structure in Relation to Job Attitudes and Job Behavior," *Psychological Bulletin,* July 1965, pp. 23–51; and L. R. James and A. P. Jones, "Organization Structure: A Review of Structural Dimensions and Their Conceptual Relationships with Individual Attitudes and Behavior," *Organizational Behavior and Human Performance,* June 1976, pp. 74–113.

CHAPTER 14

1. See, for example, D. Ciampa, *Total Quality* (Reading, MA: Addison-Wesley, 1992); and W. H. Schmidt and J. P. Finnegan, *The Race without a Finish Line* (San Francisco: Jossey-Bass, 1992).

2. M. Hammer and J. Champy, *Reengineering the Corporation: A Manifesto for Business Revolution* (New York: HarperBusiness, 1993).

3. R. Karlgaard, "ASAP Interview: Mike Hammer," *Forbes ASAP,* September 13, 1993, p. 70.

4. Ibid.

5. "The Age of Reengineering," *Across the Board,* June 1993, p. 29.

6. Quoted in Ibid., p. 33.

7. "The Bigger Picture: Reorganizing Work," *Industry Week,* August 2, 1993, p. 24.

8. "The Age of Reengineering," p. 31.

9. A. Ehrbar, "'Reengineering' Gives Firms New Efficiency, Workers the Pink Slip," *Wall Street Journal,* March 16, 1993, p. A1.

10. Ibid.

11. Ibid.

12. See E. Norton, "Small, Flexible Plants May Play Crucial Role in U.S. Manufacturing," *Wall Street Journal,* January 13, 1993, p. A1.

13. A. N. Turner and P. R. Lawrence, *Industrial Jobs and the Worker* (Boston: Harvard University Press, 1965).

14. J. R. Hackman and G. R. Oldham, "Motivation through the Design of Work: Test of a Theory," *Organizational Behavior and Human Performance,* August 1976, pp. 250–79.

15. See B. T. Loher, R. A. Noe, N. L. Moeller, and M. P. Fitzgerald, "A Meta-Analysis of the Relation of Job Characteristics to Job Satisfaction," *Journal of Applied Psychology,* May 1985, pp. 280–89; Y. Fried and G. R. Ferris, "The Validity of the Job Characteristics Model: A Review and Meta-Analysis," *Personnel Psychology,* Summer 1987, pp. 287–322; and S. J. Zaccaro and E. F. Stone, "Incremental Validity of an Empirically Based Measure of Job Characteristics," *Journal of Applied Psychology,* May 1988, pp. 245–52.

16. J. R. Hackman, "Work Design," pp. 132–33 in *Improving Life at Work,* ed. J. R. Hackman and J. L. Suttle (Santa Monica, CA: Goodyear, 1977).

17. Ibid., pp. 96–162.

18. G. R. Salancik and J. Pfeffer, "A Social Information Processing Approach to Job Attitudes and Task Design," *Administrative Science Quarterly,* June 1978, pp. 224–53; and J. G. Thomas and R. W. Griffin, "The Power of Social Information in the Workplace," *Organizational Dynamics,* Autumn 1989, pp. 63–75.

19. See, for instance, J. Thomas and R. W. Griffin, "The Social Information Processing Model of Task Design: A Review of the Literature," *Academy of Management Journal,* October 1983, pp. 672–82; and M. D. Zalesny and J. K. Ford, "Extending the Social Information Processing Perspective: New Links to Attitudes, Behaviors, and Perceptions," *Organizational Behavior and Human Decision Processes,* December 1990, pp. 205–46.

20. B. G. Posner, "Role Changes," *INC.,* February 1990, pp. 95–98.

21. C. Garfield, "Creating Successful Partnerships with Employees," *At Work,* May/June 1992, p. 8.

22. Ibid.

23. See, for instance, data on task enlargement described in M. A. Campion and C. L. McClelland, "Follow-Up and Extension of the Interdisciplinary Costs and Benefits of Enlarged Jobs," *Journal of Applied Psychology,* June 1993, pp. 339–51.

24. J. R. Hackman, "Work Design," pp. 132–33.

25. *U.S. News & World Report,* May 31, 1993, p. 63.

26. See, for example, J. R. Hackman and G. R. Oldham, *Work Redesign* (Reading, MA: Addison-Wesley, 1980); J. B. Miner, *Theories of Organizational Behavior* (Hinsdale, IL: Dryden Press, 1980), pp. 231–66; R. W. Griffin, "Effects of Work Redesign on Employee Perceptions, Attitudes, and Behaviors: A Long-Term Investigation," *Academy of Management Journal,* June 1991, pp. 425–35; and J. L. Cotton, *Employee Involvement* (Newbury Park, CA: Sage, 1993), pp. 141–72.

27. W. Bridges, *JobShift* (Reading, MA: Addison-Wesley, 1995).

CHAPTER 15

1. See J. N. Cleveland, K. R. Murphy, and R. E. Williams, "Multiple Uses of Performance Appraisal: Prevalence and Correlates," *Journal of Applied Psychology,* February 1989, pp. 130–35.

2. P. M. Blau, *The Dynamics of Bureaucracy*, rev. ed. (Chicago: University of Chicago Press, 1963).

3. "The Cop-Out Cops," *National Observer*, August 3, 1974.

4. G. P. Latham and K. N. Wexley, *Increasing Productivity through Performance Appraisal* (Reading, MA: Addison-Wesley, 1981), p. 80.

5. See review in R. D. Bretz Jr., G. T. Milkovich, and W. Read, "The Current State of Performance Appraisal Research and Practice: Concerns, Directions, and Implications," *Journal of Management*, June 1992, p. 326.

6. "Appraisals: Reverse Reviews," *INC.*, October 1992, p. 33.

7. R. J. Newman, "Job Reviews Go Full Circle," *U.S. News & World Report*, November 1, 1993, pp. 42–43.

8. See D. J. Woehr and J. Feldman, "Processing Objective and Question Order Effects on the Causal Relation between Memory and Judgment in Performance Appraisal: The Tip of the Iceberg," *Journal of Applied Psychology*, April 1993, pp. 232–41.

9. See, for example, W. M. Fox, "Improving Performance Appraisal Systems," *National Productivity Review*, Winter 1987–88, pp. 20–27.

10. H. J. Bernardin, "The Effects of Rater Training on Leniency and Halo Errors in Student Rating of Instructors," *Journal of Applied Psychology*, June 1978, pp. 301–08.

11. R. J. Burke, "Why Performance Appraisal Systems Fail," *Personnel Administration*, June 1972, pp. 32–40.

12. "How Do I Love Me? Let Me Count the Ways," *Psychology Today*, May 1980, p. 16.

13. J. Zigon, "Making Performance Appraisal Work for Teams," *Training*, June 1994, pp. 58–63.

CHAPTER 16

1. See, for example, E. H. Schein, *Organizational Culture and Leadership* (San Francisco: Jossey-Bass, 1985), p. 168.

2. C. A. O'Reilly III, J. Chatman, and D. F. Caldwell, "People and Organizational Culture: A Profile Comparison Approach to Assessing Person-Organization Fit," *Academy of Management Journal*, September 1991, pp. 487–516.

3. Y. Wiener, "Forms of Value Systems: A Focus on Organizational Effectiveness and Cultural Change and Maintenance," *Academy of Management Review*, October 1988, p. 536.

4. T. E. Deal and A. A. Kennedy, "Culture: A New Look through Old Lenses," *Journal of Applied Behavioral Science*, November 1983, p. 501.

5. E. H. Schein, "The Role of the Founder in Creating Organizational Culture," *Organizational Dynamics*, Summer 1983, pp. 13–28.

6. See, for example, J. R. Harrison and G. R. Carroll, "Keeping the Faith: A Model of Cultural Transmission in Formal Organizations," *Administrative Science Quarterly*, December 1991, pp. 552–82.

7. "Who's Afraid of IBM?" *Business Week*, June 29, 1987, p. 72.

8. J. Van Maanen and E. H. Schein, "Career Development," p. 59 in *Improving Life at Work*, ed. J. R. Hackman and J. L. Suttle (Santa Monica, CA: Goodyear, 1977).

9. Ibid.

10. N. J. Adler, *International Dimensions of Organizational Behavior*, 2nd ed. (Boston: PWS-Kent, 1991), pp. 58–60.

11. See, for example, R. H. Kilmann, M. J. Saxton, and R. Serpa, eds, *Gaining Control of the Corporate Culture* (San Francisco: Jossey-Bass, 1985).

CHAPTER 17

1. These similes were developed by P. B. Vaill, *Managing as a Performing Art: New Ideas for a World of Chaotic Change* (San Francisco: Jossey-Bass, 1989).

2. K. Lewin, "Group Decision and Social Change," pp. 459–73 in *Readings in Social Psychology*, 2nd ed., ed. G. E. Swanson, T. M. Newcome, and E. L. Hartley (New York: Holt, 1952).

3. T. Peters, *Thriving on Chaos* (New York: Alfred A. Knopf, 1987), p. 3.

4. R. H. Hall, *Organizations: Structures, Processes, and Outcomes*, 4th ed. (Englewood Cliffs, NJ: Prentice Hall, 1987), p. 29.

5. D. Katz and R. L. Kahn, *The Social Psychology of Organizations*, 2nd ed. (New York: Wiley, 1978), pp. 714–15.

6. J. P. Kotter and L. A. Schlesinger, "Choosing Strategies for Change," *Harvard Business Review*, March–April 1979, pp. 106–14.

7. Adapted from W. L. French and C. H. Bell Jr., *Organization Development: Behavioral Science Interventions for Organization Improvement*, 4th ed. (Englewood Cliffs, NJ: Prentice Hall, 1990), pp. 17–21.

8. R. E. Walton, "Improving the Quality of Work Life," *Harvard Business Review*, May–June 1974, p. 12.

9. Adapted from R. S. Schuler, "Definition and Conceptualization of Stress in Organizations," *Organizational Behavior and Human Performance*, April 1980, p. 189.

10. This discussion of 3M is based on K. Labich, "The Innovators," *Fortune*, June 6, 1988, p. 49; R. Mitchell, "Masters of Innovation," *Business Week*, April 10, 1989, p. 58; K. Kelly, "The Drought Is Over at 3M," *Business Week*, November 7, 1994, pp. 140–41; and T. Stevens, "Tool Kit for Innovators," *Industry Week*, June 5, 1995, pp. 28–31.

11. F. Damanpour, "Organizational Innovation: A Meta-Analysis of Effects of Determinants and Moderators," *Academy of Management Journal*, September 1991, pp. 555–90.

Index/Glossary

Ability, 114
Absenteeism, 2
Accommodation, 174
Achievement need *The drive to excel, to achieve in relation to a set of standards, to strive to succeed,* 52-54
Achievement-oriented leader, 147
Activity orientation, cultural dimension, 24
Advanced Filtration Systems, Inc., 204
Aetna Life, 112
Affilition need *The desire for friendly and close interpersonal relationships,* 52-53, 59
Agreeableness, 35
Aid Association for Lutherans, 112
Alcoa, 222
Allaire, P., 243
America West Airlines, 213
American Airlines, 70
American Broadcasting Co., 231
American Safety Razor, 73
American Telephone & Telegraph (AT&T), 10, 35, 72, 109, 120, 196, 197, 206, 222, 253, 263
Amoco, 222
Anchoring, 180
Anthony, S.B., 139
Anthropology *The study of societies to learn about human beings and their activities,* 3-5
Apple Computer, 35, 109, 116, 198
Appraisal, performance (*see* Performance, appraisal)
Asch, S.E., 96-97
Assumed similarity *The tendency for people to judge others as if they were like themselves,* 41
Attitude-behavior relationship, 33-34
Attitudes *Evaluative statements—either favorable or unfavorable—concerning objects, people, or events,* 30-34, 43-44
Attribution theory *When individuals observe behavior, they attempt to determine whether it is internally or externally caused,* 40-41
Authoritarianism *A personality attribute that measures the belief that there should be status and power differences among people in organizations,* 36-37
Authority *The rights inherent in a managerial position to give orders and expect the orders to be obeyed,* 189

Autonomy, 211
Availability heuristic *The tendency for people to base their judgments on information that is readily available to them,* 83
Avis Corporation, 70
Avoidance, 174

Baker, B., 71
Banc One, 206
Banca di America e di Italia, 206
Bank of America, 216
Bank of Montreal, 191
Bargaining strategies, 177-79
Barclays, 11
Barnes, L.B., 142
Behavior (*see* Organizational Behavior (OB))
Behavior modification, 64-66
Behavioral leadership theories, 140-43
Behaviorally anchored rating scales *An appraisal method where actual job-related behaviors are rated along a continuum,* 223
Bell & Howell, 73
Biases, decision-making, 83-84, 89, 179-80
Big-5 model *The five basic dimensions underlying personality are extraversion, agreeableness, conscientiousness, emotional stability, and openness to experience,* 35-36
Bi-modal work force, motivating, 11-13
Blake, R.R., 142-43
BMW, 113
Board representatives *A form of representative participation; employees sit on a company's board of directors and represent the interests of the firm's employees,* 68
Body language, 128
Boeing, 10, 108-09, 113, 198
Boulgarides, J.D., 85
Boundaryless organization *An organization that seeks to eliminate the chain of command, have limitless spans of control, and replace departments with empowered teams,* 197-98
Bounded rationality *A decision-making approach whereby individuals construct simplified models that*

extract the essential features from problems without capturing all their complexity, 80-81

Brainstorming *An idea-generating process that specifically encourages any and all alternatives, while withholding any criticism of those alternatives,* 104

Branch Davidians, 239

Brophy, B., 229

Buckley, W.F., Jr., 132

Buettner, L., 215

Bureaucracy *A structure with highly routine operating tasks achieved through specialization, very formalized rules and regulations, tasks that are grouped into functional departments, centralized authority, narrow spans of control, and decison making that follows the chain of command,* 192-93

Burger King, 9

Cable News Network, 21

Calm-waters simile, 256-57

Campbell, L., 93-94

Carrier, 208

Caterpillar Corporation, 10, 199

Cavanagh, G.F., 167

CBS Records, 18

Centralization *The degree to which decision making is concentrated at a single point in the organization,* 190-91, 202

Cessna Aircraft, 186

Chain of command *An unbroken line of authority that extends from the top of the organization to the lowest eschelon and clarifies who reports to whom,* 188-89

Champion Spark Plug, 73

Chandler, A.D., Jr., 199

Change *Making things different,* 255
  agents *Persons who act as catalysts and assume the responsibility for managing change activities,* 255
  contemporary issues in, 268-71
  forces for, 252-54
  implications for managers, 271
  innovation and, 10
  managing, 254-55, 262-68
  planned, 254-55
  process, 256-57
  resistance to, 258-62
  views of, 255-58
  (*see also* Organizational development (OD))

Change agent, 151

Charismatic leadership *Inspires followers to transcend their own self-interests for the good of the organization; capable of having a profound and extraordinary effect on followers,* 151-52

Childress Buick, 66

Christ, J., 139

Chrysler Corporation, 10, 109, 113, 253

Churchill, W., 139

Church of Jesus Christ of Latter-Day Saints, 140

Cincinnati Milacron, 73

Citicorp, 18, 35

Claiborne, Liz, 196

Coalitions, 159-60

Coca-Cola, 18

Coercion *The application of direct threats or force,* 262

Coercive power *Power that is based on fear,* 156-57

Cognitive dissonance *Any incompatibility between two or more attitudes or between behavior and attitudes,* 32-33, 44

Cohesiveness *The degree to which members of a group are attracted to each other and motivated to stay in the group,* 97-98

Collaboration, 174

Collectivism *A national culture attribute that describes a tight social framework in which people expect others in groups of which they are a part to look after them and protect them,* 26-28

Command group, 92

Commitment, escalation of, 83-84, 179

Committees, 113

Commonwealth Life Insurance group, 206

Communication *The transference and understanding of meaning,* 123-37
  barriers, 131-33
  as conflict source, 171
  cross-cultural, 133-34
  downward, 126
  functions of, 124
  globalization and different styles of, 133-34
  grapevine, 130-31, 137
  informal, 130-31
  lateral, 126
  managing, 134-37
  networks, 129-31
  nonverbal, 128-29, 133, 137
  oral, 127
  to overcome resistance to change, 261
  process *The steps between a source and a receiver that result in the transference and understanding of meaning,* 125
  upward, 126
  written, 127-28

Compaq Computer, 242-43

Competencies, distinctive (*see* Distinctive competencies)

Competency-based pay (*see* Skill-based pay)

Competition, 174, 253, 254

Composition, group, 99-100, 106

Compromise, 174

ConAgra, 254

Conflict *A process in which an effort is purposely made by A to offset the efforts of B by some form of blocking that will result in frustrating B in attaining his or her*

goals or furthering his or her interests, 168-77
    behavior creating, 171-73
    cognition and personalization of, 173
    dysfunctional, 170-71, 176-77
    functional, 170-71, 175-76
    human relations view of, 170
    interactionist view of, 170
    managing, 182-83
    process *Four stages: potential opposition or incompatibility; cognition and personalization; intentions; and outcomes,* 171-77
    sources of, 171-73
    traditional view of, 169-70
Conformity *Adjusting one's behavior to align with the norms of the group,* 96-97
Conscientiousness, 36
Consideration *The extent to which a leader is likely to have job relationships characterized by mutual trust, respect for subordinates' ideas, and regard for their feelings,* 141
Contingency theory(ies)
    of leadership, 143-51
    of organizational design, 198-201
Contingent employees, 10-11
Controlling behavior, 5-6
Conway, M., 213
Cooptation *Buying off the leaders of a resistance group by giving them a key role in the change decision,* 261
Coors Brewing, 112
Cosby, B., 158
Cost-minimization strategy, 199
Creativity *The ability to combine ideas in a unique way or to make unusual associations between ideas,* 78-79, 82, 90
Critical incidents, 223
Cross-cultural communication, 133-34
Cross-functional teams *Employees from about the same hierarchical level, but from different work areas, who come together to accomplish a task,* 113
Cross-training, 213
Culture (*see* National culture(s) *and* Organizational culture)
Culture-bound, OB concepts as, 29
Customer departmentalization, 188

Datatec Industries, 222
Dayton Hudson Stores, 66, 109
Decentralization, 190-91
Decision making *Making choices from among two or more alternatives,* 76
    biases in, 83-84, 89, 179-80
    group, 101-05, 107
    implications for managers, 89-90
    individual, 76-90
    organizational constraints on, 87-88

participative, 67
rational, 77-78
styles, 84-86, 89-90
Deere, John, 109-10, 207
Dell Computer, 196, 205
Dell, M., 196
Departmentalization *The basis by which jobs are grouped together,* 186-88
Dependency, 155, 158-59
Detroit, city of, 66
Digital Equipment Corp., 8
Difficulty of job, as reward criterion, 232
Dillinger, J., 156
Directive leader, 147
Discretionary time, as reward criterion, 232-33
Disney, Walt. Co., 72, 140, 240-42, 244
Dissonance, cognitive, 32-33
Distinctive competencies *Defines what it is that the organization is more superior at delivering than its competition,* 205
Distributive bargaining *Negotiation that seeks to divide up a fixed amount of resources; a win-lose situation,* 177-78
Diversity (*see also* Gender *and* Women)
    of group members, 99-100
    paradox of, 250
    on teams, 114-16
    work force, 8-9,
Division of labor (*see* Work specialization)
Domino's Pizza, 10
Douglas Aircraft Co., 112
Dow Chemical, 231
Du Pont, E.I., 222
Dysfunctional conflict, 170-71, 176-77

Eaton, 73
Eastern Airlines, 10
Eastern Europe, 19-20
Eastman Kodak, 70, 88, 193
Economic factors, resisting change and, 259
Economic shocks, 253-54
Education, resistance to change and, 261
Edy's Grand Ice Cream, 112
Effort, as reward criterion, 231-32
Eisner, M., 72
Electronic meeting *A group decision-making technique that allows participants to comment and vote on issues by using networked computers,* 105
Emerson Electric, 109, 121
Emerson Radio, 196
Emery Air Freight, 64, 66
Emotional stability, 36
Emotions in communication, 132, 136-37
Employee involvement *A participative process that uses the entire capacity of employees and is designed to*

encourage increased commitment to the organization's success, 67-71

Employee-oriented leaders, 67-71, 141

Employee stock ownership plans (ESOPs) *Company–established benefit plans in which employees acquire stock as part of their benefits*, 70

Empowerment, 9-10

Environment
    relationship to, 23
    as structural determinant, 200-01

Equity, status and, 101

Equity theory *Individuals compare their job inputs and outcomes with those of others and then respond so as to eliminate any inequities*, 55-57, 74-75

Escalation of commitment *An increased commitment to a previous decision in spite of negative information*, 83-84, 179

Essays, written, 223

Esteem needs, 48

Ethical development, 86-87

Ethical dilemmas *Situations where organizational members are required to define right and wrong conduct*, 13

Ethics and ethical behavior, 13-14, 166-67

Ethnocentric views *The belief that one's cultural values and customs are superior to all others*, 20, 21

European Union *The 15 nations composed of France, Denmark, Belgium, Greece, Ireland, Italy, Luxembourg, the Netherlands, Portugal, Spain, the United Kingdom, Austria, Finland, Sweden, and Germany*, 18, 19

Expectancy theory *The strength of a tendency to act in a certain way depends on the strength of an expectation that the act will be followed by a given outcome and on the attractiveness of that outcome to the individual*, 57-59, 72-73

Expertise, change as threat to, 260

Expert power *Influence based on special skills or knowledge*, 157

Explanations of behavior, 5

Extrinsic rewards, 233-34

Extroversion, 35

Exxon, 9, 35

Falbe, C.M., 156

Fear of the unknown, 259

Federal Bureau of Investigation (FBI), 241

Federal Express, 35, 64, 109, 126

Feedback, 125, 134-35, 211, 228-29

Femininity *A national culture attribute that emphasizes relationships and concern for others*, 27-28

Fiedler, F.E., 144-47, 153

Fiedler leadership model *A theory which proposes that effective groups depend upon a proper match between a leader's style of interacting with subordinates and the degree to which the situation gives control and influence to the leader*, 144-47, 153

Filtering *A sender's manipulation of information so that it will be seen more favorably by the receiver*, 131

Firestone Tire, 73

First Chicago Corp., 215

Flexible manufacturing systems *Integration of computer-aided design, engineering, and manufacturing to produce low-volume products at mass-production costs*, 207-08

Flexibility, 10-11

Florida Power & Light, 109

Ford, H., 185, 241

Ford, H., II, 247

Ford Motor Co., 9, 18, 70, 113, 120, 185, 200, 204, 206, 241, 247, 263

Formal groups, 91-92

Formalization *The degree to which jobs within the organization are standardized*, 191-92, 240

Fox Television, 10

Framing negotiations, 180

French, J.R.P., Jr., 156-58

Friendship groups, 93

Fullers restaurant, 248

Functional conflict, 170-71, 175-76

Functional departmentalization, 187, 193-95

Gainsharing *An incentive plan where improvements in group productivity determine the total amount of money that is allocated*, 72

Gender
    communication style and, 132
    leadership style and, 150-51

General Electric, 6, 35, 66, 70, 109, 112, 113, 193, 197, 253

General Foods, 109

General Motors, 9, 10, 70, 87, 112, 113, 120, 175, 216

General Tire, 18

Geographic departmentalization, 188

Gillette, 18

Gimbel's, 10

Global context of OB, (*see also* National culture(s))

Globalization, responding to, 9

Global village, 17-18

Goal-setting theory *The theory that specific and difficult goals lead to higher performance*, 54-55, 59-60, 61, 63, 117

Gore, W.L., & Associates, 222

Grant, W.T., 10

Grapevine, 130-31, 137

Graphic rating scales *An appraisal method where the evaluator rates performance factors on an incremental scale*, 223

Greiner, L.E., 142

Group(s) *Two or more individuals, interacting and interdependent, who come to together to achieve particular objectives*, 91-107

cohesiveness, 97-98, 106
decision making, 101-05, 107
inertia, 260
order ranking, 224
Groupshift *A change in decision risk between the group's decision and the individual decision that members within the group would make; can be either toward conservatism or greater risk,* 103-04
Groupthink *Phenomenon in which the norm for consensus overrides the realistic appraisal of alternative courses of action,* 102-03
Growth-need strength, 211-12
G.S.I. Transcomm Data Systems, Inc., 213

Habit, 259
Hackman, J.R., 210, 211, 214
Hallmark, 206
Halo effect *Drawing a general impression about an individual based on a single characteristic,* 42
Halo error *Tendency for an evaluator to let the assessment of an individual on one trait influence his or her appraisal of that person on other traits,* 225
Hammer, M., 205-06
Hawthorne studies, 94-96
Hell's Angels, 140
Herzberg, F., 50-52
Heuristics *Judgmental shortcuts in decision making,* 83
Hewlett-Packard, 8, 70, 109, 112, 197, 241
Hierarchy of needs theory *There is a hierarchy of five needs—physiological, safety, social, esteem, and self-actualization—and as each need is sequentially satisfied, the next need becomes dominant,* 48, 49, 74
Higher-order needs, 48
High-performance teams, 114-19, 122
Hill, A., 160
Hofstede, G., 25-28
Holland, J.L., 37-39
Honda Motors, 18, 35, 113
Honeywell, 112, 222
Hooker Chemical, 73
Hoover, J.E., 241
House, R.J., 147
Hughes Aircraft, 254
Human relations view of conflict, 170
Hygiene factors *Those factors—such as company policy and administration, supervision, and salary—that, when adequate in a job, placate workers. When these factors are adequate, people will not be dissatisfied,* 51
Hyundi, 241

IBM, 16, 70, 113, 191, 193, 196, 199, 204, 241-42, 249, 263
Imitation strategy, 199
Impression management *The process by which individuals attempt to control the impression others form of them,* 164-66
Incentives (*see* Motivation)
Individual behavior, model of, 43-44
Individual decision making
alternative development, 82
bounded rationality in, 80-81
choices in, 83-84
constraints on, 87-88
creativity in, 78-79
cultural influences on, 88-89
ethics in, 86-87
heuristics, 83
implications for managers, 89-90
individual differences in, 84-87
intuition in, 81
problem identification, 82
rational, 77-78
styles, 84-86
Individualism *A national culture attribute describing a loosely knit social framework in which people emphasize only the care of themselves and their immediate family,* 26-28
Individual ranking evaluations, 224
Individual resistance to change, 258-59
Industrial revolution, 204, 216
Influence (*see* Power)
Informal groups, 92
Information, availability of, 189
Information processing, selective, 259
Initiating structure *The extent to which a leader is likely to define and structure his or her role and those of subordinates in the search for goal attainment,* 141
Innovation, stimulating, 10, 270-71
Innovation strategy, 199
Integrative bargaining *Negotiation that seeks one or more settlements that can create a win-win solution,* 179
Intel Corp., 216
Interactionist view of conflict, 170
Interest groups, 93
Intergroup development *OD efforts to change the attitudes, stereotypes, and perceptions that groups have of each other,* 268
Intrinsic rewards, 233
Intuition, 2, 81, 89
Intuitive decision making *An unconscious process created out of distilled experience,* 81
Involvement, employee (*see* Employee involvement)

Jackson, J., 151
Jago, A.G., 149
Jargon, 135
Job characteristics model *Identifies five job characteristics and their relationship to personal and work outcomes,* 210-12
Job design (*see* Work Design)

Job enlargement *The horizontal expansion of jobs,* 213-14
Job enrichment *The vertical expansion of jobs,* 214-16
Job obsolescence, 216-17
Job redesign, 264
Job rotation *The periodic shifting of a worker from one task to another,* 213
Jobs, matching people to, 37-39
Job satisfaction *An individual's general attitude toward his or her job,* 2, 31-32, 44, 50-52, 237-38
Job specialization (*see* Work specialization)
Johnson & Johnson, 185
Joint partnerships, 198
Jordan, M., 158

Kearns, D.T., 243
Kennedy, J.F., 139
Khrunichev Enterprise, 113
Kinesics, 128
King, M.L., Jr., 139, 143
Kluckhohn-Strodtbeck Framework, 23-25
Knight-Ridder Information, 249
Kohlberg, L., 86
Koresh, D., 239
KPMG Peat Marwick, 206
Krupp-Hoesch, 11

Lampreia restaurant, 248
Language, 132-33, 135
Law of effect *Behavior is a function of its consequences,* 43, 55
Lawrence, P.R., 209
Leader-member relations *The degree of confidence, trust, and respect subordinates have in their leader,* 144
Leader-participation model *A leadership theory that provides a set of rules to determine the form and amount of participative decision making in different situations,* 149-50, 153
Leadership *The ability to influence a group toward the achievement of goals,* 138-53
    behavioral theories, 140-43
    charismatic, 151-52
    contingency theories, 143-51
    of effective teams, 117
    integration of theories, 152-53
    leader-participation model, 149-50, 153
    Managerial Grid, 142-43
    Michigan studies, 141
    Ohio State studies, 140-41
    participative, 147
    path-goal model, 147-49, 153
    power vs., 155
    substitutes for, 152
    task-people approaches, 153
    team, 117
    trait theories of, 139-40, 151-52

Learning *Any relatively permanent change in behavior that occurs as a result of experience,* 42, 45
Least preferred co-worker (LPC) questionnaire *An instrument that purports to measure whether a person is task- or relationship-oriented,* 144-46
Legitimate power *The power a person receives as a result of his or her position in the formal hierarchy of an organization,* 157
Leniency error, 225
Levi Strauss, 222
Lewicki, R.J., 177
Lewin, K., 256, 272
Lickona, T., 86
Ling, G., 212
Listening, active, 135-36
Litterer, J.A., 177
Lockheed-Martin, 113, 121, 254
Locus of control *A personality attribute that measures the degree to which people believe they are masters of their own fate,* 36, 163
Lower-order needs, 48
Loyalty, employee, declining, 11, 12
L-S Electrogalvanizing Co., 112
Luthans, F., 65

M&M/Mars, 112
MacArthur, D., 151
McCann, D., 115
McClelland, D.C., 52-54
McColough, C.P., 243
McDonald's, 9, 186
McDonnell-Douglas, 113, 254
McGrath, M.R., 85
McGregor, D., 48-50
Machiavellianism *A personality attribute that measures the degree to which an individual is pragmatic, maintains emotional distance, and believes that ends can justify means,* 37
Malcolm Baldrige National Quality Award, 112, 126
Management, organizational culture and, 243
Management by objectives (MBO) *A program that encompasses specific goals, participatively set, for an explicit time period, with feedback on goal progress,* 61-64
Managerial Grid *A nine-by-nine matrix outlining eighty-one different leadership styles,* 142-43
Mandela, N., 139
Manipulation *Covert influence attempts,* 261
Mary Kay Cosmetics, 239, 248
Maculinity *A national culture attribute describing the extent to which societal values are characterized by assertiveness and materialism,* 27-28
Margerison, D., 115
Marks & Spencer, 93
Maslow, A., 48-49
Material symbols, 248

Matrix structure *A structure that creates dual lines of authority; combines functional and product departmentalization,* 193-95

Matsushita, 193

Mayo, E., 95

Mazda, 9

Mead Paper, 73

Mechanistic model *A structure characterized by extensive departmentalization, high formalization, a limited information network, and centralization,* 198-99

Melting pot assumptions, 8

Mercedes-Benz, 11

Merck & Co., 71

Michigan leadership studies, 141

Microsoft, 35, 216, 239

Moberg, D., 167

Mobil Corp., 18, 196

Modeling, 42, 43

Money and motivation, 60

Moral development, level of, 86-87

Moskal, B.S., 12

Mother Teresa, 151

Motivation *The willingness to do something, conditioned by this action's ability to satisfy some need for the individual,* 47
    of bi-modal work force, 12
    culture, effect on, 59-60
    hierarchy of needs theory, 48, 49
    implications for managers, 60, 75
    by job design, 210-12
    money and, 60
    performance appraisal and, 220
    process, 47
    rewards, 230, 231
    theories of, 47–59

Motivation-hygiene theory *Intrinsic factors are related to job satisfaction, while extrinsic factors are associated with dissatisfaction,* 50-52

Motorola, 18, 70, 109, 113, 120, 197, 206, 253

Mouton, J.S., 142-43

Multinational corporations *Companies that maintain significant operations in two or more countries simultaneously,* 18

Multiperson comparisons, 223-24

Multiple evaluation criteria, 226

Multiple evaluators, 227

Myers-Briggs Type Indicator (MBTI) *A personality test that taps four characteristics and classifies people into one of 16 personality types,* 35

Nader, R., 143

NAFTA, 19

National Bicycle Industrial Co., 207-08

National culture(s)
    communication across, 133-34
    conflict across, 174-75
    confronting parochialism and, 20, 21
    constraint on OB, 29
    decision making, effect on, 88-89
    differences among, 22-28
    globalization and different, 9
    homogeneity of, 21-22
    implications for managers, 29
    motivation theories across, 59-60
    negotiations, differences in style, 181-82
    organizational culture vs., 249
    performance appraisal across, 230

National Mutliple Sclerosis Society, 34

National Semiconductor, Israel, 16-17

National Steel Corp., 196

Nature of people, cultural dimension, 24

NEC Corp., 198

Need *A physiological or psychological deficiency that makes certain outcomes appear attractive,* 47, 48, 52-54

Negotiation *A process in which two or more parties exchange goods or services and attempt to agree on the exchange rate for them,* 177-82, 183, 261

Networks, communication, 129-30

Nike, 196

Nominal group technique *A group decision-making method in which individual members meet face-to-face to pool their judgments in a systematic but independent fashion,* 105

Nonverbal communication, 128-29, 133, 137

Nordstrom, 247

Norms *Acceptable standards of behavior within a group that are shared by the group's members,* 94-97, 106

North Amercian Free Trade Agreement (NAFTA) *An agreement that phases out tariffs on most goods traded among the U.S., Canada, and Mexico,* 19

Nucor Steel, 71

OB (*see* Organizational behavior OB)

OB Mod *A program where managers identify performance-related employee behaviors and then implement an intervention strategy to strengthen desirable performance behaviors and weaken undesirable behaviors,* 64-66

Obsolescence (*see* Job obsolescence *and* Worker obsolescence)

OD (*see* Organizational development)

Ohio State leadership studies, 140-41

Oldham, G.R., 210

Olivetti, 249

Openness to experience, 36

Organic model *A structure that is flat, uses cross-hierarchical and cross-functional teams, has low formalization, possesses a comprehensive information network, and relies on participative decision making,* 198-99

Organization *A formal structure of planned coordination,*

involving two or more people, in order to achieve a common goal, 2

Organizational behavior (OB) *The systematic study of the actions and atitudes that people exhibit within organizations,* 2
  challenges and opportunities for, 6-14
  contributing disciplines to, 3-5
  goals, 2, 5-6
  model, 14-15

Organizational change (*see* Change *and* Organizational development (OD))

Organizational culture *A system of shared meaning held by members that distinguish the organization from other organizations,* 236-37
  characteristics of, 237
  creation of, 241-42
  formalization vs., 240
  functions of, 240-41
  influence on behavior, 250
  innovation and, 270-71
  vs. job satisfaction, 237-38
  language and, 249
  learning, 246-49
  as liability, 241
  managing change in, 250-51, 263-64
  material symbols, 248
  national culture vs., 249
  paradox of diversity and, 250
  political behavior and, 163-64
  rituals, 247-48
  stories, 247
  strength of, 239
  subcultures, 239
  sustaining, 242-46
  uniformity of, 239

Organizational development (OD) *A collection of planned-change interventions, built on humanistic-democratic values, that seek to improve organizational effectiveness and employee well-being,* 262-68

Organizational politics (*see* Political behavior)

Organizational resistance to change, 259-60

Organization structure *How job tasks are formally divided, grouped, and coordinated,* 185
  computer's effect on, 196
  as conflict source, 172
  contingency views of, 198-201
  determinants of, 198-201
  effect on behavior, 201-02
  implications for managers, 202
  structural inertia, 260
  structural OD interventions, 262-64
  structural variables in innovation, 270
  types of, 192-98

Packard, D., 241

Paired comparison evaluations, 224

Paradox of diversity, 250

Parochialism *A narrow view of the world; an inability to recognize differences between people,* 20, 21

Participation, 9-10, 67, 261 (*see also* Employee involvement)

Participative leadership, 147

Participative management *A process where subordinates share a signficant degree of decision-making power with their immediate superiors,* 67

Path-goal theory *The theory that a leader's behavior is acceptable to subordinates insofar as they view it as a source of either immediate or future satisfaction,* 147-49, 153

Pay-for-performance (*see* Variable-pay programs)

Peer evaluations, 221-22

Penney, J.C., 191

People, nature of, 24

People dimension of leadership, 153

People Express, 258

People-focused OD interventions, 265-68

People skills, 1, 8

PepsiCo, 112

Perception *A process by which individuals organize and interpret their sensory impressions in order to give meaning to their environment,* 39-43, 45, 131-32, 169, 173

Performance, rewards and, 58, 231

Performance appraisal
  criteria, 220-21
  effect on behavior, 218-19, 235
  evaluators, 221-22, 227
  feedback on, 228-29
  in global context, 230
  improving, 226-28
  methods, 222-24
  motivation and, 220
  problems in, 224-26
  purposes of, 219-20
  self-evaluations, 222
  team, 118

Personality *The sum total of psychological traits that define how an individual reacts and interacts with others,* 34-38, 45, 181

Peters, T., 258

Physiological needs, 48

Piece-rate pay plans *Workers are paid a fixed sum for each unit of production completed,* 71-72

Pillsbury, 18, 254

Planned change *Change activities that are intentional and goal-oriented,* 255

Planned Parenthood, 192

Playboy Enterprises, 140

Polaroid, 70, 73

Political behavior *Those activities that are not required*

as part of one's formal role in the organization, but that influence, or attempt to influence, the distribution of advantages and disadvantages within the organization, 162-67

Political science *The study of the behavior of individuals and groups within a political environment*, 5

Politics, world, 253, 254

Position power *The degree of influence a leader has over power variables such as hiring, firing, discipline, promotions, and salary increases*, 145

Power *A capacity that A has to influence the behavior of B, so that B does something he or she would not otherwise do*, 154-62

    bases of, 156-58
    change as threat to established, 260
    coalitions, 159-60
    dependency, 155, 158-59
    group, 159-60
    leadership and, 155
    managing, 167
    need for, 52-54
    sexual harassment and, 160-62

Power distance *A national culture attribute describing the extent to which a society accepts that power in institutions and organizations is distributed unequally*, 26-28

Power need *The desire to make others behave in a way that they would not otherwise have behaved in*, 52-54

Predictions of behavior, 5

Price Club, 35

Problem identification, 82

Problem-solving teams *Groups of 5 to 12 employees from the same department who meet for a few hours each week to discuss ways of improving quality, efficiency, and the work environment*, 111

Process consultation *An outside consultant assists a client, usually a manager, to perceive, understand, and act on process events with which he or she must deal*, 266-67

Process departmentalization, 188

Procter & Gamble, 70, 159, 242

Product departmentalization, 187

Production-oriented leaders, 141

Productivity, 2

Profit-sharing plans *Organization-wide programs that distribute compensation based on some established formula designed around a company's profitability*, 72

Psychology *The science that seeks to measure, explain, and sometimes change the behavior of humans and other animals*, 3

Purpose, common, 116-17

Quality, 6-8 (*see also* Total quality management)

Quality circle *A work group of eight to ten employees and supervisors who meet regularly to discuss their quality*

problems, investigate causes, recommend solutions, and take corrective actions, 68-69, 111

Quality of work life *A process by which an organization responds to employee needs by developing mechanisms to allow them to share fully in making the decisions that design their lives at work*, 265

Rational *Choices that are consistent and value-maximizing within specified constraints*, 77

Raven, B., 156-58

Raytheon, 113

Reader's Digest, 199

Reality vs. perception, 39, 45

Reebok, 196

Reengineering *Reconsiders how work would be done and the organization structured if they were being created from scratch*, 7, 205-07, 208

Referent power *Influence based on possession by an individual of desirable resources or personal traits*, 158

Regional cooperative arrangements, 18-20

Reinforcement theory *Reinforcement conditions behavior*, 55, 66, 74

Relationship to the environment, cultural dimension, 23

Representative heuristic *The tendency for people to judge probabilities of future outcomes by trying to match it with a preexisting category*, 83

Representative participation *Workers participate in organizational decision making through a small group of representative employees*, 68

Requisite task attributes theory, 209-10

Resource allocations, threat to, 260

Responsibility, focus of, cultural dimension, 24

Reward(s),
    change and, 263
    determinants of, 231-33
    effect on behavior, 230, 235
    extrinsic, 233-34
    implications for managers, 235
    intrinsic, 233-34
    performance and, 57-59
    team, 118, 121
    types of, 233-34

Reward power *Compliance achieved based on the ability to distribute rewards that others view as valuable*, 157

Reynolds Metals Co., 10, 188

Ringelmann effect, 99

Risk propensity *A personality attribute that measures an individual's willingness to take chances*, 37, 103-04

Rituals *Repetitive sequences of activities that express and reinforce the key values of the organization, what goals are most important, which people are important and which are expendable*, 247-48

Riverso, R., 191

RJR Nabisco, 249

Roles *A set of expected behavior patterns that are attributed to occupying a given position in a social unit,* 93-94, 106, 114-16
Roosevelt, F.D., 151
Routineness of technology, 200
Rowe, A.J., 85
Royal Dutch Shell, 193
Rumors, 130-31

Saab, 109
Safety needs, 48
San Diego Zoo, 109
Satisfaction, job (*see* Job satisfaction)
Satisficing model of decision making, 80-81, 82
Saturn Corp., 120, 186
Scarcity-dependency relationship, 159
Schein, E.H., 245
Scientific-Atlanta, 113
Scott Paper Co., 72, 263
Sears, Roebuck, 10, 175, 191, 216, 231, 259
Security, 259
Security Pacific National Bank, 231
Selection, employee, 121, 242-43
Selective appraisal, 227-28
Selective information processing, 259
Selective perception *People selectively interpret what they see based on their interests, background, experience, and attitudes,* 41, 131-32
Self-actualization need, 48
Self-confidence, 151
Self-managed work teams *Groups of 10 to 15 people who take on responsibilities of their former supervisors,* 111, 112-13
Self monitoring *A personality attribute that measures an individual's ability to adjust his or her behavior to external, situational factors,* 37
Semco SA, 213
Seniority, as reward criterion, 232
Sensitivity training *Training groups that seek to change behavior through unstructured group interaction,* 265-66
Sexual harassment *Unwelcome advances, requests for sexual favors, and other verbal or physical conduct, whether overt or subtle, of a sexual nature,* 160-62
Shaping behavior, 42, 43
Shell Oil Company, 140
Shenandoah Life Insurance Co., 109
Shiseido, 109
Siemens, 11, 206
Similarity error, 225
Simple structure *A structure characterized by a low degree of departmentalization, wide spans of control, authority centralized in a single person, and little formalization,* 192
Six-personality-types model, 37-39
Size and group behavior, 98-99, 114

Size, structure and, 200
Skill-based pay *Pay levels are based on how many skills employees have or how many jobs they can do,* 73-75
Skills
    active listening, 135-36
    feedback, 134-35
    job enrichment, 214-15
    negotiating, 183
    people, 1
    as reward criterion, 232
Skill variety, 210
Social information-processing (SIP) model *Employees adopt attitudes and behaviors in response to the social cues provided by others with whom they have contact,* 212-13
Socialization *The process that adapts employees to the organization's culture,* 243-46
Social loafing *The tendency for individuals to expend less effort when working collectively than when working individually,* 99, 106, 117
Social needs, 48
Social psychology *An area within psychology that focuses on the influence of people on one another,* 3
Social trends, 253, 254
Sociology *A discipline that studies people in relation to their fellow human beings,* 3
Sociotechnical systems, 264-65
Sony, 35, 239
Space, conception of, cultural dimension, 25
Span of control *The number of subordinates a manger can efficiently and effectively direct,* 189-90, 201-02
Specialization (*see* Work specialization)
Sprint, 222
Status *A prestige grading, position, or rank within a group,* 100-01, 106-07
Stereotyping *Judging someone on the basis of one's perception of the group to which that person belongs,* 42
Strategic alliances, 198
Strategy-structure thesis, 199
Stress *A dynamic condition in which an individual is confronted with an opportunity, constraint, or demand related to what he or she desires and for which the outcome is perceived to be both uncertain and important,* 268-70
Strong culture *A culture where the core values are intensely held and widely shared,* 239
Structural OD interventions, 262-64
Structure (*see* Organization structure)
Subcultures, 239
Subordinate, sexual harassment by, 161-62
Sun Petroleum Products, 187
Supervisor, sexual harassment by, 161
Supportive leader, 147
Survey feedback, 266
Suttle, J.L., 211, 214

Systematic study, 2

Task characteristics theories, 209-13
Task dimensions of leadership, 153
Task force
    vs. cross-functional team, 113
    structure, 145
Task groups, 92
Task identity, 210
Task significance, 210
Task structure *The degree to which job assignments are structured or unstructured,* 145
Task-technology OD interventions, 264-65
Taylor, E., 158
Team building *High interaction among team members to increase trust and openness,* 267-68
Team players, creating, 120-21
Team structure *The use of teams as the central device to coordinate work activities,* 195-96
Teams (*see also* Work team)
    cross-functional, 111, 113
    high–performance, 114–119, 122
    leadership of, 117
    performance evaluations of, 229-30
    problem-solving, 111
    rewarding, 118, 121
    roles on, 115-16
    self-managed, 111, 112-13
Technology *How an organization transfers its inputs into outputs,* 200, 203-08, 253
Temporariness, 10-11
Texas Instruments, 70, 112
Theory X *The assuumption that employees dislike work, are lazy, dislike responsibility, and must be coerced to perform,* 48-50, 70
Theory Y *The assumption that employees like work, are creative, seek responsibility, and can exercise self-direction,* 48-50, 70
Thermos Corp., 117
Thomas, C., 161
360-degree evaluations, 222
3M Co., 35, 199, 270, 271
Three-needs theory, 52-54
Time orientation, cultural dimension, 23-24
Top management, organizational culture and, 243
Total quality management (TQM) *A philosophy of management that is driven by the constant attainment of customer satisfaction through the continuous improvement of all organizational processes,* 6-8, 204-05, 206, 208, 259
Toyota Motor Co., 9, 109, 113
Traditional view of conflict, 169-70
Training team players, 121
Training of performance appraisers, 228
Trait approach

to performance evaluation, 221, 226-27
to leadership, 139-40
to personality, 34-36
Transactional leaders, 151
Transformational leaders, 151
Trust *A characteristic of high performance teams where members believe in the integrity, character, and ability of each other,* 118-19
Turner, A., 209
Turner, T., 139, 151
Turnover, 2

Uncertainty avoidance *A national culture attribute describing the extent to which a society feels threatend by uncertain and ambiguous situations and tries to avoid them,* 26-28
Uncertainty, environmental, 200-01
United Airlines, 70
United Parcel Service, 222
USAA Insurance, 66
U.S. Marines, 243
U.S. Postal Service, 204
U.S. Shoe Co., 214
U.S. Steel, 216
Unity of command principle *A person should have one and only one superior to whom he or she is directly responsible,* 189, 193

Vagelos, P.R., 71
Valasquez, M., 167
Van Maanen, J., 245
Variable-pay programs *A portion of an employee's pay is based on some individual and/or organizational measure of performance,* 71-73
Virtual organization *A small, core organization that outsources major business functions,* 196-97
Vision, 151
Vocational Preference Inventory, 38
Volkswagen, 193
Volvo, 109
Vroom, V.H., 149-50

Wal-Mart, 199, 241-42
Walton, S., 241-42
Watson, R.A., 72
Watson, T., 241-42
Weirton Steel, 70
Welch, J., 197
Western Electric Co., 95
Westinghouse, 10, 70, 72
Weyerhauser, 66
White-water rapids simile, 257
Whole Food Market, 112
Whyte, W.F., 100-01
Wilson, J.C., 243

Winner's curse, 180
Women
    communication style of, 132
    leadership style, 150-51
    in work force, 8
Work design, 209-17, 264
Worker obsolescence, 208-09
Work force, motivating bi-modal, 11-13
Work force diversity *Organizations have become more heterogeneous in terms of gender, race, and ethnicity,* 8-9, 114-16, 250
Work group *A group who interact primarily to share information and to make decisions to help each other perform within his or her area of responsibility,* 110-11
Work redesign, 213-16
Work specialization *The degree to which tasks in the organization are subdivided into separate jobs,* 185-86, 201
Work team *A group whose individual efforts result in a level of performance that is greater than the sum of those individual inputs,* 110-11
Works councils *Groups of nominated or elected employees who must be consulted when management makes decisions involving personnel,* 68
World politics, 253, 254

Xerox Corp., 66, 70, 112, 206, 243, 263

Yetton, P.W., 149
Yukl, G., 156
Yung, ChungJu, 241